ENGINEERS, MANAGERS AND POLITICIANS

ENGINEERS, MANAGERS AND POLITICIANS

The First Fifteen Years of Nationalised Electricity Supply in Britain

Leslie Hannah

Research by
Margaret Ackrill, Frances Bostock, Rachel Lawrence,
Judy Slinn and Stephanie Zarach

First published 1982 by
THE MACMILLAN PRESS LTD
London and Basingstoke
Companies and representatives
throughout the world

ISBN 0 333 22087 0

Typeset in Great Britain by
Tradespools Ltd, Frome,
and printed in Great Britain by
Pitman Press, Bath

CONTENTS

LIST OF FIGURES AND TABLES

FIGURES

TABLES

PREFACE

Many books have been written on the subject of Britain's public enterprises, and many of these have concerned the electricity supply industry, Britain's biggest capital spender in the 1950s and 1960s. The present work differs from them all in being based not only on published material but on free access to the surviving, but not publicly available documentary evidence in the industry and government, and to the people involved in the decision-making. As far as I know, such an exercise in business history has not yet been attempted for other nationalised industrial enterprises, though there is no lack of prescriptive comment on these industries from economists, political scientists, administrators and politicians. The temptation for the author explicitly to join in their debates on the objectives, control and performance of public enterprise was considerable. I have none the less felt it best rather to present a narrative account of the historical experience of the industry which at least approaches Ranke's simple definition of the historian's task as telling history as it really was. Of course, my own prejudices intrude in the selection of evidence and in the interpretation, but the reader will not find here a set of explicit policy prescriptions to lead him, according to his taste, to the salvation or damnation of the principle or practice of public enterprise. Even so, I would be disappointed to encounter a reader who was not led by the book to reflect critically on the models of economic behaviour, and of the policy process, which typically lie behind much of the discussion of the public sector currently produced by the academic and political debating machines. In particular, if politicians can read these pages without blushing at the sins committed by their kind (whether Conservative or Labour), one's faith in the possibility of constructive self-analysis would receive a large dent.

The genesis of this book should be made clear. It is a sponsored history, commissioned by the Electricity Council on behalf of the Central Electricity Generating Board, the Area Boards in England and Wales and the two Scottish Electricity Boards. None the less, the views expressed are those of the author and not those of the Council or of the Boards. The author's independence was guaranteed by

provisions for free access to documents in the industry's possession
dating from 1973 or earlier, and for arbitration in the event of any
disagreement on the interpretation of the first fifteen years of
nationalisation. (The Council reserved the right to review material
from the period after 1963 covered in the brief Epilogue.) The
Council have honoured that agreement. The only changes requested
were minor modifications to several sentences for legal reasons and
on agreed matters of fact, so that recourse to arbitration was not
necessary.

This is not to say that those who worked in the industry and have
experienced the events described do not have strong views on the
subject matter. I was fortunate to be able to draw on the memories of
more than a hundred of the staff of the industry as well as of the
politicians and civil servants who agreed to be interviewed. I am also
indebted to those who read the whole of the draft manuscript and
commented on it: Lewis Allan, Robert Brown, Sir Stanley Brown,
Philip Chantler, Lord Citrine, Philip Colinese, Fred Colmer, David
Fenton, Richard Hancock, Lord Hinton, Duncan McGrouther, Cecil
Melling, Ronald Richardson, Richard Savinson, Paul Schiller, Alan
Wheatley and E. J. Wigmore. It was a particular sadness to me that
Brian Murphy, one of the original movers of the project, did not live
to read and comment on more than the early chapters. All of these
commentators, while unstinting in their suggestions for additions or
amendments, and sometimes spirited in their disagreement, were
scrupulous in insisting that the final judgement should rest with me.
Many other individuals within the industry have given assistance on
specific points and I am grateful to them all. Mr Hancock and his staff
in the Intelligence Section of the Electricity Council, in particular,
have been an unfailing source of advice and enlightenment; and the
secretarial, records and library staff in the Council and the Boards
have responded to the myriad enquiries with unfailing courtesy and
helpfulness. The staff of the British Library of Political and Economic
Science, Churchill College Archives, the Institution of Electrical
Engineers, the Public Record Office and the Scottish Record Office
also gave invaluable assistance.

This book is not part of the official Whitehall civil histories, but the
Department of Energy and the Scottish Economic Planning Department were kind enough to provide access to their official files, still
closed under the thirty-year rule. Without this assistance, it would
have been significantly harder to do justice to the complexities of the
relations between the industry and government. This access was

subject to the Official Secrets Act, but no requests for alterations to the submitted manuscript were made by the Departments.

I have also benefited from discussions on the nationalised industries in general (and the electricity industry in particular) from the advice of academic colleagues: notably Charles Baden-Fuller, Theo Barker, Michael Beesley, Duncan Burn, Ian Byatt, Sir Norman Chester, Donald Coleman, Tony Corley, Malcolm Falkus, James Foreman-Peck, Howard Gospel, Margaret Gowing, Thomas P. Hughes, Geoffrey Jones, John Kay, Sir Arthur Knight, Jonathan Liebenau, Peter Mathias, Richard Pryke, W. J. Reader, John Smith, Barry Supple, John Turner, Philip Williams, Sir Alan Wilson, and Graham Wilson. In the days before the word-processor, the skilful conversion of a difficult manuscript to a readable typescript by Marjorie Huntley and Lynda Prosser was particularly appreciated.

My major debt, to the researchers, is recorded on the title-page. Without their assistance, it would have been impossible to penetrate even that small percentage of the total archival material available which we selected for research. Margaret Ackrill was primarily responsible for research on the Department of Energy and the Area Boards, Frances Bostock for commercial policy and the CEGB, Rachel Lawrence for generation and the Central Authority, Judy Slinn for industrial relations, and Stephanie Zarach for nuclear power and Scotland. Only the author should be held accountable for the judgements which appear in the book.

London School of Economics LESLIE HANNAH
December 1981

ABBREVIATIONS AND GLOSSARY

AC   alternating current. An electric current which alternately reverses its direction of flow. Now almost universal in Britain. Cf. DC.

amp   ampère. A measure of the quantity of electricity flowing in a circuit. The standard domestic ring-main circuit in Britain delivers up to 13 amps.

AGR   Advanced Gas-Cooled Reactor. The standard British design of reactor ordered from 1965 onwards; a development of the earlier gas-cooled Magnox reactors.

BEA   British Electricity Authority. The national electricity authority for England, Wales and South Scotland between 1948 and 1955. The Authority was also sometimes referred to as the 'Central Authority' to distinguish it from its Area Board associates. See also CEA.

CEA   Central Electricity Authority. The national electricity authority for England and Wales between the hiving-off of the South of Scotland Electricity Board in 1955 and reorganisation into a separate CEGB (qv) and Electricity Council at the beginning of 1958.

CEB   Central Electricity Board. The public corporation responsible for the National Grid transmission system prior to nationalisation in 1948.

CEGB   Central Electricity Generating Board. The national authority responsible for generation and main transmission in England and Wales from 1958 to the present.

d.   old penny. There were twelve old pennies in a shilling and 240 in a pound (£), prior to the adoption of decimal currency. Changes in the price of electricity in real terms are shown in the Statistical Appendix, Table A.4 (p.295, below).

DC   direct current. An electric current flowing in one direction. On nationalisation a large minority of consumers still received DC supplies, but they were gradually converted to AC, qv.

EPEA   Electrical Power Engineers' Association. The trade union for employees with advanced engineering training.

°F   degrees Fahrenheit. The conventional measure of steam temperatures prior to metrication in the UK electricity supply industry. (°F = 32 + $\frac{9}{5}$°C.)

GWh   Gigawatt-hour. One million kWh, qv.

kV   kilovolt. One thousand volts. Typical local distribution voltages in Britain were 11kV, 33kV and 66kV; longer-distance Grid transmission was at 132kV initially, rising to 275kV and 400kV in the later Supergrid.

kW   kilowatt, or one thousand watts. The work done when current is caused to flow in an electrical circuit, approximately equal to 1.34 British horsepower. A one-bar electric fire is typically rated at 1kW.

kWh   kilowatt-hour. Sometimes referred to in British English as a (Board of Trade) 'unit' of electricity: the basic unit for measuring the consumption of electricity. A 1kW electric fire will in one hour consume one kilowatt-hour of electricity.

MW   Megawatt. One thousand kW, qv.

NJAC   National Joint Advisory Council. The consultative body for all grades of workers within the industry.

NJIC   National Joint Industrial Council. The negotiating body for manual workers' pay and conditions in the electricity supply industry.

psi   pounds per square inch. The conventional measure of steam pressure prior to metrication in the UK electricity supply industry. (1 psi = 0.703 kg/cm^2).

V   volt. A measure of the force which causes an electric current to flow in a circuit. For domestic purposes British electricity supply is normally at 240V.

1

INTRODUCTION

ELECTRICITY BEFORE

NATIONALISATION

No one with any intimate knowledge of the electricity supply industry can maintain that changes are not overdue and would be brought about by any Government in power, Labour, Conservative or Liberal.

> Letter from A. J. Fippard, chairman, Electricity Supply Corporation, *Electrical Times*, 21 November 1946, p. 684.

The Labour Party's victory in the election of 1945 made it inevitable that the public supply of electricity in Britain would be nationalised.[1] Clement Attlee, the Prime Minister, and Herbert Morrison, who took charge of the nationalisation programme, had in their earlier political careers served on municipal electricity committees, and had long been personally committed to extending public ownership in the industry. The programme to nationalise electricity, though not an immediate priority like coal, was an essential part of Labour's strategy, in their first term with a parliamentary majority, of fundamentally changing the balance of capital ownership by an extensive programme of nationalisation. When their intention to nationalise electricity supply was confirmed in 1946, therefore, it was in this light that it was presented, particularly to the Party faithful.

In reality, the movement to public ownership in the industry had already gone a long way, and, until then, had been at least as much the work of Conservatives as of Labour. In the closing decade of the nineteenth century, before the Labour Party had even been formed, many municipalities, particularly in the large provincial cities, had entered the business of distributing electricity; and these local authorities soon accounted for two-thirds of electricity sales. The remaining one-third of sales – mainly in London and in the less prosperous rural districts and market towns – were in the hands of private sector companies. However, most of their franchises were due to expire, and only the War had prevented those local authorities who wished to do so from exercising their purchase rights. Private enterprise had a future only in power generation and bulk supply, where companies typically had longer franchises, and had raised their share of British electricity production to half, the rest being generated by the municipalities themselves. Even in bulk supply, the Central Electricity Board, a public corporation established by the Conservative Government in 1927, had controlled the operation of power stations since the completion of the initial National Grid transmission network in 1933. A body of Electricity Commissioners also supervised matters such as cooperation between the undertakings. While rather more than a third of the capital in the industry was still under private control in 1945, public ownership already dominated, and there was a wide degree of public supervision.

Moreover, Labour's commitment to extending public control was, as Morrison liked to point out, not only part of a political programme, but was also fortified by a good deal of expert and non-political opinion, both inside and outside the industry. Although the private sector trade associations had told the Government that they opposed nationalisation, several senior managers in the best companies had said privately that they favoured it. In 1936 a government committee, chaired by a leading private industrialist, Lord McGowan of ICI, had recognised the need for the rationalisation of distribution into larger units. A wartime all-party cabinet committee had endorsed the view that rationalisation was needed, and only two Conservative members dissented from full nationalisation, proposing instead compulsory mergers of the 600 municipal and private undertakings into 30 mixed ownership organisations. During the War, a step towards nationalisation had been taken with the establishment of the publicly-owned North of Scotland Hydro-Electric Board, to prepare plans for developing this previously neglected area, using the water power of the Highlands.

Nationalisation was, then, somewhat less of a radical departure for the industry than Labour (and Conservative) speakers sometimes claimed. It was, however, undoubtedly the archetypal 'commanding height' of the future. The centralised organisation which was to take over the industry in April 1948 would inherit assets of £831 millions, and planned new investment of at least £650 millions.[2] It was the largest electric utility unified under common ownership in the western world, whether measured by assets, employment or number of consumers; and was by any standards an industrial giant.[3] In the first half of the century its growth had been the most rapid of any major industry in Britain, with sales rising from an average of only 3kWh per head of population in 1900 to almost 800kWh per head annually on the eve of nationalisation. There was no apparent reason why this growth should not continue in the future. Indeed, in the first fifteen years of nationalised management, with which this book is primarily concerned, more than 8 per cent of UK capital formation was to be devoted to the industry's expansion,[4] rather more than in earlier periods.[5]

Electricity's powerful and expanding position in Britain's energy economy rested on its record of increasing efficiency. The British economy was still essentially coal-based, and advances in the thermal efficiency of electric power production had been one of the means by which the spectre of energy shortage had been avoided. By 1939 a ton of coal produced more than three times as much electricity as had been possible in power stations in the first decade of the century. There had also been significant efficiency gains from economies of scale as the electricity industry expanded. By the 1930s a typical coal-fired power station cost only half as much in real terms to build as even the best stations before the First World War. Wholesale electricity prices had fallen by two-thirds in the interwar years, and with technical change and productivity improvements in distribution, retail prices had fallen by almost as much. Most homes in Britain were connected to a public electricity supply during the 1930s, though on the outbreak of War nearly a third of homes still lacked a supply. During the War, expansion plans were shelved and the building of new power station capacity virtually stopped for all except military and industrial purposes. There was thus a substantial backlog of investment to make up.

As the industry's engineers and managers prepared for this task of postwar reconstruction, they viewed the prospect of nationalisation with mixed, but generally neutral or favourable feelings. Labour's commitment to extending the benefits of electricity service struck a responsive chord in an industry which already had a service-inspired tradition and rather weakly-developed profit motivation. For some time, moreover, senior people in the Central Electricity Board, and in the larger private and municipal undertakings, had favoured some form of reorganisation. The division of the country into around 600

separate distribution areas was widely regarded as inhibiting economies of scale and the efficient layout of local distribution mains.
Engineers, in particular, formed a self-conscious professional community, with their own technocratic ideals, and were not always at
one with those local councillors or private capitalists who opposed
moves to larger groupings. At the Central Electricity Board, already
a public corporation, the engineers regretted that their control over
power station planning, finance and operation was only partial; and
they felt that further improvements would require more central
control, involving outright ownership and management of the municipal and company stations.

There was, then, an emerging consensus on the desirability of
reorganisation, but there was none the less considerable concern
within the industry about the form it would take. The rhetoric of
workers' control, which accompanied Labour's nationalisation
pledges, was unwelcome to managers and engineers who saw no
problem in their existing, generally peaceful labour relations regime.
The increasing stress of Labour on planning boards – even at one
time a 'National Fuel and Power Board' – also raised eyebrows in the
industry. The industry's own planning techniques were probably
more advanced than was typical elsewhere at the time; but some half-
baked, political versions of 'fuel planning' seemed to be little better
than a gas industry plot to stop electricity's competitive development.
There was also, of course, understandable personal concern about
the inevitable upheaval of reorganisation, and the potentially painful
choices involved in the allocation of senior jobs in the new organisation. Much of the debate on the public corporation had centred on
the need to leave decisions to a professional, technocratic élite, and
this model had worked well in institutions like the Central Electricity
Board, which had been generally free of day-to-day government
control. There was, however, a long tradition in the industry of
distrust of political intervention in its affairs from politicians of all
colours. Doubts as to whether, when they owned the whole industry,
the Government would be inclined to leave them to pursue their
objectives of expansion and rationalisation were fortified by recent
events. The civil service now seemed to have greater confidence in
intervention derived from their experience of wartime controls and
the backing of an explicitly socialist cabinet. The senior men in the
industry thus awaited the elaboration of Labour's plans with ap-
prehension, as well as with interest.

Part I

NATIONALISATION:
THE PROBLEMS OF TRANSITION
(1947–9)

2

CITRINE'S WAY

I felt I would be able to do something creative, something in which I believed. Public ownership had for many years seemed to me an essential step ...

Lord Citrine, *Two Careers* (1967) p. 262.

Within a few months of Labour's election victory, Herbert Morrison, who had overall charge of Labour's nationalisation programme, confirmed the Government's intention of nationalising electricity and other fuel industries. Emmanuel Shinwell, the Minister of Fuel and Power, started on the legislation for nationalising coal, and electricity nationalisation was relegated to the 1946/7 session of Parliament.[1] The Electricity Bill then introduced followed in broad outline the plans foreshadowed by wartime working parties on the future of the industry, and, to the relief of the industry, confirmed that it would remain independent of coal and gas, and not be part of a National Fuel and Power Board. The 200 companies and 369 local authority undertakings, together with the Central Electricity Board and the nearly 300 power stations owned and operated by these organisations, were to be transferred to a new public body, the British Electricity Authority. (The industry unsuccessfully requested that 'Supply' should be included in the title to avoid confusion with the other 'BEA', British European Airways.) Within the BEA, a Central Authority would be responsible for running the power stations and the Grid transmission system, but the distribution and sales functions to the eleven million consumers were to be decentralised to fourteen Area Electricity Boards, each with their own local board appointed by the Minister. This assuaged some of the fears expressed by managers and engineers in the existing supply undertakings about possible over-centralisation of power in a nationalised undertaking. Even so the proposed reorganisation did, of course, represent a

7

substantial concentration of power into fewer decision-making organisations.

The Government had initially aimed at a 1 January 1948 vesting day for the new Central Authority and Area Boards to take over, though eventually a date three months later was agreed. Emmanuel Shinwell was helped in piloting the Bill through Parliament by his able young Parliamentary Secretary, Hugh Gaitskell. Shinwell, always a better politician than administrator, was widely felt to be doing a poor job in this crucial economic ministry. Thus, shortly after the Electricity Act received the royal assent, in September 1947, Attlee appointed Gaitskell as Minister in his place, and it therefore fell to him to carry through the Government's work of nationalisation by completing the appointments to the Boards and the working out of the new relationship of Ministry and BEA.

Some years later both Shinwell[2] and Reuben Kelf-Cohen[3] (the civil servant who then headed the Electricity and Gas Division in the Ministry of Fuel and Power) suggested that the Labour Government's nationalisation plans had generally been ill-prepared, but in retrospect their complaints of the absence of nationalisation 'blueprints' seem wide of the mark, at least in the case of electricity. For more than a decade there had been detailed debate in the industry on the best form of securing greater coordination of distribution. Several wartime reconstruction working parties in the Ministry had outlined plans for reorganisation very similar to those adopted by the Labour Government.[4] Moreover the whole point of the form of the public corporation favoured by moderate opinion in all parties (and represented in the Labour Party by the Morrisonian conception) was that it was up to the management (and not the politicians or civil servants) to develop the details of policy and organisation within only very broad guidelines. Indeed, Lord Plowden (who was at the time a civil servant engaged in economic planning and subsequently the chairman of a public corporation) has recently suggested that the blueprint laid down in the Act was arguably too detailed, and that questions such as the division of powers between the centre and Area Boards could rationally be placed within the purview of nationalised industry management rather than of Parliament.[5]

Be that as it may, the major work of planning for the change to public ownership was certainly delegated to the men the Labour Government intended to appoint to the Central Authority. Lord Citrine, the chairman-designate, began work in the offices of the Ministry of Fuel and Power early in 1947,[6] and, after the Bill had passed its second reading in the Lords in May 1947, he was assisted by an Organising Committee. Five members of this Committee joined the Central Authority under Citrine's chairmanship when the Bill received the royal assent in September of the same year.[7] At the regional level, there were delays in the appointment of Area Board members. The Ministers had as many as 140 appointments to make to the Area Boards and Central Authority (43 of them full-time). All the chairmen were appointed by November 1947, and all Boards were functioning by the beginning of 1948. Most of the recruits to the senior positions were from within the industry and in the months up to the planned vesting day – 1 April 1948 – most retained their old jobs in the pre-vesting undertakings as well as carrying out their new responsibilities of planning for the change.

The two major exceptions to appointment from among existing managers were the chairman, Lord Citrine (a trade unionist), and his deputy, Sir Henry Self (a civil servant). Both of these appointments caused some discontent among the senior men of the industry, who resented the appointment of outsiders. Harold Hobson, the chairman of the Central Electricity Board (who had expected the top job in the new organisation himself), pointedly refused to work as Citrine's deputy and resigned from the CEB prematurely. Several senior men on the private company side were fundamentally opposed to nationalisation, and preferred to seek a career elsewhere in the private sector.[8] There were inevitably accusations of political jobbery[9] – four of the twelve members of the Central Authority had distinct left-wing sympathies – but both Shinwell and Gaitskell (though determined not to appoint anyone bent on making nationalisation a failure) were open to suggestions for appointing qualified candidates of any political persuasion. Thus, although W. R. T. Skinner of the Yorkshire Electric Power Company was tarred with the company's extreme anti-union reputation (and not wanted by Citrine or the new Yorkshire Board) the chairman-designate of the South Eastern Area Board was able to persuade Gaitskell to make him his deputy chairman, a position in which Skinner served loyally and efficiently for more than a decade, before himself succeeding to the chairmanship of that Board.

A potentially more serious problem in attracting staff was the level of salaries in the nationalised industries. Many of the leaders of the industry were already earning salaries of £4000–£6000 per annum and in the larger companies they could earn more. Yet Ministers only received £5000 and Permanent Secretaries in the civil service £3500, and the Treasury were naturally concerned that public sector industries should not get too far out of line. In competition with lucrative private sector offers, however, the Treasury's approach had to give way to pragmatic concessions to attract able men. The resulting salaries were still rather below market rates for top managers and engineers. The chairman of the Central Authority was paid £8500, his deputy chairmen £5000 and other full-time members £3500, while Area Board chairmen were offered salaries of £4000.[10] These in effect became ceilings for the whole pyramid of staff salaries so that those senior men below board level also found their salaries constrained. Some engineers and managers, especially those coming from municipal employment, found the new salaries they were offered higher than their pre-vesting salaries, but others found that they were expected to take a cut. In the case of a number of key senior men appointed by the Minister and the Central Authority, 'personal allowances' to make up some or all of the difference were thus necessary to attract them.[11]

Despite these problems of appointments and salaries, the great majority of the senior managers and engineers did join the new nationalised organisations. The major exceptions were managers from the south with directorships or financial expertise, who could readily find more lucrative (and to many of them more satisfying) employment in the private sector. None the less the electricity industry was fortunate compared with, for example, the coal industry, where politics had long bedevilled management relations with both government and workers, and nationalisation led to the departure of senior managers in larger numbers.

While the Labour Government were anxious to preserve an image of political fairness and reasonable salary flexibility in order to attract the technocratic skills that they recognised were essential for success, they were none the less clear that the public corporations should not simply be the old gang operating 'business as usual'. Nationalisation had to have a clear socialist stamp on it. The rhetoric of participation was to achieve its concrete expression principally through the appointment of Lord Citrine as chairman. Citrine was a powerful symbol of the elevation of workers to a new role in the industry. He had started work at the age of twelve as an apprentice electrician, wiring the houses of the rich in Liverpool before the First World War. (He still had traces of his Liverpool accent.) In 1914 he had become a full-time trade union official rising to the general secretaryship of the Trades Union Congress in the 1920s. He had advocated electricity nationalisation in the 1930s, and during the War (as the TUC were drawn increasingly into the government consultative machine) had distinguished himself as an administrator and committee-man of high repute with members of all political parties. A gradualist in his socialism, he was now convinced that the trade union movement had 'passed from the era of propaganda to one of responsibility'.[12] When the industry's senior engineers and managers met him, he appeared to them as a strong-willed, humourless, puritanical idealist, but he was sane, reasonable and had a strong sense of the practical realities of power. The early steps in their relationship were not easy, and a few in the industry were never reconciled to his leadership, though all recognised that he was acquiring a strong sense of identity with the industry's interests. In his autobiography, Citrine himself was to look back on this second career, taken up at the age of sixty, as the happiest time of his life,[13] when his creativity and other faculties were exercised to the full.

The power exercised by Citrine and his colleagues was daunting. The 1947 Electricity Act laid down in some detail procedures for matters such as capital authorisations from the Ministry and the relative spheres of interest of Central Authority and Area Boards, but on the major questions of business policy the industry had a relatively free hand, subject only to a requirement to consult the Minister on matters of broad policy. It is true that the legislation was liberally loaded with declaratory phrases enjoining them to provide an 'efficient, coordinated and economical' supply of electricity, to extend supplies 'so far as practicable', and to make 'proper' financial provisions. Such phrases were a fashion of the time and sufficiently vague to be meaningless as a guide on any serious policy matter. Sceptics might feel that they betrayed a lack of informed thought on the issue of objectives; and certainly a good deal of the time of the economic planners, the Treasury, the Ministry and the industry over the following decades was to be devoted to the search for more meaningful objectives and standards of performance to supplement these minimal statutory requirements. At the time, however, they were accepted (indeed assiduously pored over and frequently quoted by Citrine and others) as embodying two widely-approved aspirations: firstly, a general desire to spread the benefits of cheap electricity widely (with the 'public interest' implicitly seen as overriding the tyranny of the profit-and-loss account); and secondly (but not entirely consistently) the view that these economic objectives should be pursued not through political or civil service channels but by the 'business' board of a public corporation with some genuine independence.

Citrine himself was fully committed to both slogans and saw no conflict between the two. Trained in the hard school of the Labour movement to win legitimacy for their political aspirations toward higher living standards and greater popular participation, he also had a realistic appreciation of the benefits of the economic organisation already achieved by capitalism. He had grown to admire the broader-minded industrial statesmen with whom he had had contacts in his trade union career: men like Lord Melchett and Lord McGowan of ICI or Lord Hirst of GEC, who had created large-scale industrial organisations and represented a progressive capitalism with which the Labour movement could work. He relished the thought of showing that he could create a viable large-scale industrial organisation in the public sector, as they had in private industry. His mission was to show that socialism was not only politically possible but could work well in practice, a natural extension and not (as it was sometimes portrayed by the left) a betrayal of his previous commitment.

As a politician and a realist, Citrine recognised that his plans needed the support of his new colleagues, and consequently that he would have to make tactical concessions and choose carefully the issues on which to fight. When Shinwell discussed the men from the industry to be appointed to the senior positions, he had at first wanted two deputy chairmen, one to look after generation and the other to oversee distribution and the Area Boards, but Citrine proposed an alternative division between operations and administration, feeling that it was 'essential to have someone familiar with the operation of large-scale organisations'.[14] Citrine was thus delighted when, after several men from the industry had refused to serve under him, he persuaded Sir Henry Self to join him as his deputy chairman in charge of administration. Self was a career civil servant who, after a wartime spell in Washington, had returned as Permanent Secretary of the Ministry of Civil Aviation. A toweringly tall man, he echoed Citrine's sparse, puritanical personality and they shared common ideals of public service. Both men were later to look back on their partnership with great affection, and their views on organisation (culled from the trade union and civil service worlds) coincided remarkably.

John Hacking, the second deputy chairman, in charge of operations, brought engineering expertise to the senior triumvirate. (He received a knighthood shortly after his appointment.) He had been chief engineer to the Central Electricity Board, and would have preferred the division of duties to have left the control of generation and transmission to the ex-CEB engineers and himself. He was never equal to Self in Citrine's esteem, and he remained jealous of intervention by Self in matters of engineering and the development of policy on the generation side, for which his background and experience made him the natural senior voice among other engineers and managers. Ernest Bussey was the fourth full-time member of the Central Authority, taking charge of labour relations and welfare. He was formerly the general secretary of the Electrical Trades Union, though (like Citrine) he had had to resign his union post on taking up the new managerial appointment.[15] Outside the industrial relations field, he played only a minor role.

The other eight members of the Central Authority were part-time. Four were Area Board chairmen, serving in rotation. Initially they were Josiah ('Jack') Eccles, formerly head of the Liverpool Corporation electricity undertaking; Alderman Lewis, a trade unionist and local Labour politician from the Midlands; John Pickles, ex-county electrical engineer of Dumfries and an expert in rural electrification; and Harry Randall, who had been chairman of the London Supply Companies Association. The most helpful among the other members was E. H. E. Woodward, who had been general manager of one of the best private sector companies, the North-Eastern Electric Supply Co. He had given some of the more frank and open-minded advice on the future of the industry before nationalisation,[16] and his critical and constructive approach and blend of engineering and commercial experience were to be a valuable input to Central Authority discussions. Sir William Walker was an ageing Conservative ex-Lord Mayor of Manchester, engineer, and member of the CEB, who had been the architect of the employers' side of the industry's labour relations machinery prior to nationalisation. Dame Caroline Haslett was a remarkable woman who had trained as an engineer and was founder-director of the Electrical Association for Women.[17] She voted usually with the 'top table' of Citrine, Self and Hacking. Finally, Tom Johnston, a former Labour minister (who had set up the North of Scotland Hydro-Electric Board and was now its chairman), had little interest in matters south of the border, and attended only intermittently.

Although these members of the Authority were formally responsible for determining general policy, there were obvious weaknesses. Earlier plans to have a full-time member with financial expertise or to take charge of relations with Area Boards had been abandoned.[18] On the other hand as many as five out of twelve members had industrial relations expertise. This was hardly a rational allocation of talent for an industry which, above all others, was capital-intensive, but had an unrivalled record of good labour relations. Inevitably, much of the real policy making was done in committees of the more active, full-time members working together with their senior officers. The BEA relied a lot in recruiting its chief officers on the main central executive body of the pre-vesting industry, the CEB, taking both D. W. Coates, their chief accountant, and E. R. Wilkinson, their commercial manager, into similar positions under Self in the new Central Authority, and V. A. Pask, in the crucial post under Hacking, that of chief engineer. All three remained wedded to the ways of the CEB even in the new organisation. There were also newcomers among the chief officers, including the secretary, H. F. Carpenter, who had been manager of the West Midlands Joint Electricity Authority.

The full Authority met monthly. In practice much of the initiation and review of management policy fell to the four full-time members acting with the chief officers. Citrine insisted that the departmental chief officers met with his full-time colleagues on the Authority weekly, encouraging the officers to comment on general policy matters rather than confining their comments to their own special-isms: a method he had found worked well at the TUC. Although the Central Authority formally made decisions, and decisions at this weekly meeting were subject to their ratification, the full-time members and chief officers had substantial *de facto* authority. Committees of the Central Authority – permanent committees on General Purposes and Finance, Staff and Organisation, Labour Relations, Estates and Real Property, Technical Development and Contracts, Tariffs and Operations, and *ad hoc* ones on an ever-changing range of topics – also had policy-making and decision-making functions, subject to report or approval by the full Authority. Again appropriate chief officers played a part on many of these.

Great strain was placed on top management by the process of centralisation, implied by nationalisation, and by the luxuriant growth of committees to develop new policies. This was particularly so in the early months before and after vesting day, and the concentrated pattern of working which was then established proved very resistant to change in later years. It was not unknown for one man to chair a dozen committees and even to attend more than thirty committee meetings in one week, though the average load was, of course, much less than these extremes. The senior people – particularly Self – had an extraordinarily wide span of responsibilities, and were involved in multiple capacities in committee work. Already stretched by their individual remits, they had to spend time, much of it unproductive, in preparing papers and attending meetings. Self and Citrine frequently had to sit through the same item of business as it made its way through three, or in extreme cases five, formal meetings of different bodies before being finally approved. Moreover, the level of detail was frequently too great to be effectively dealt with by the committes, many members of which were non-specialists. Once policy had been hammered out – and sometimes before it had – there were also a whole series of committees with representatives from the regions who needed to be consulted and informed on the views of headquarters.

To many in the industry, unused to this degree of central policy making and coordination, the luxuriant growth of committees seemed to represent an unholy conspiracy of bureaucracy rather than real organisational requirements. Even within head office, the level of unnecessary detail with which headquarters committees were burdened attracted criticisms. But Citrine and Self defended their policy against critics, whom they felt were ignoring the new and differing requirements of larger organisations. In reviewing the early management structure in 1951, Citrine said firmly:

> I challenge the view that any large scale organisation can be effectively administered without recourse to committee and conference methods. Further, I affirm that the bigger the organisation the more essential do these methods become. One often hears charges of bureaucracy levelled against large public undertakings. But the method of consultation is itself a very healthy antidote to bureaucratic tendencies. The purpose of a conference is primarily to explain and exchange ideas, so that those who are eventually required to make decisions do so in the full knowledge of the view of those who have to operate them.[19]

He recognised that the criticism to which he was replying had its root in fundamental differences between the culture of management in the pre-nationalisation industry and what he was trying to create. Discussing frustration with the new organisation at a gathering of managers and other staff in 1949, he admitted:

He did not know how widespread this difficulty was, but that it did exist was certain. Perhaps some individuals felt they were not getting the opportunity in the new organisation to which they were entitled. But it was difficult to deal with intangible things and, as had been said, this was an emotional condition rather than one that could be reasoned with.... If it meant that in the change some had been treated unfairly, according to them, that must be looked into and, if possible, put right. But it would have to be done by collective bargaining.[20]

Collective decision making, the sharing of responsibility, and solidarity in a common task had been Citrine's way of life in the Labour movement; and the new organisation should, he felt, be formed in that image. The interpretation of his objective through committees, in which he could win over doubters, was to him a central part of the chairman's task. Such concepts of group loyalty and common purpose were, moreover, not entirely unfamiliar to the business world he had entered: many of the pre-vesting undertakings had developed a strong group identity among staff. More generally, a Japanese businessman would probably find them more intelligible and appealing than the liberal individualist doctrines which outwardly were claimed as the cornerstone of British management ideology. The internalisation of values based on a commonality of experience and reinforced by collective committee decision making is certainly, in principle, capable of producing formidable business success.

Yet Citrine was working within a specific, more individualist business culture and, though change could only come slowly, collective discussion remained the only antidote to bureaucracy that he ever really understood. Managers and engineers could not help but admire the assiduity and skill with which he could wear down his opponents in discussion, but for many of them this approach conflicted with other managerial values. It discounted their felt need for individual responsibility and their desire to be entrusted with tasks over which they alone had control. The frustration was perhaps greatest among the senior men who had come from the company sector, but municipal engineers also could find the professional, full-time and expert Central Authority control daunting in comparison with the earlier part-time, politically-appointed municipal electricity committees which had been easier to manipulate. Some centralisation and bureaucracy was, of course, inevitable, but Citrine's way probably accentuated it. He was well aware of the depth of the chasm which separated the past from the future he hoped to create, and he was above all a realist, but inevitably the fusing of nearly 600 formerly independent undertakings into a new corporate identity was not painless.

Citrine and Self were the architects of the central administrative system established on nationalisation, and the other deputy chairman, Hacking, was also keen on centralisation. There were, however, limits placed on their centralising tendencies by the Electricity Act itself, which specified the decentralisation of the distribution and retail functions to the fourteen Area Electricity Boards. The wartime discussions on the future of the industry had envisaged entirely independent Area Boards, but after 1945 new pressures for centralisation were evident. Herbert Morrison was an advocate of tighter centralised control, and the Permanent Secretary of the Ministry of Fuel and Power, Sir Donald Fergusson (who believed nationalisation would only work if the public corporations were genuinely independent) felt that independence was more likely to be achieved with a larger corporation which was more able to resist direct government intervention.[21] Shinwell, however, helped tilt the balance in favour of maintaining some regional independence, and he told the House of Commons that:

> each area board, within limits assigned to it, should have freedom to carry on its detailed work without reference to the Central Authority. It is far from my desire that problems which can be settled locally shall be taken to London. . . . I am very anxious that there should not develop any possibility of divergence of outlook between the Central Authority and the area boards . . . I regard them (area boards) as autonomous bodies . . .[22]

The fact that the men on the Area Boards were appointed directly by the Minister (and not by the Central Authority – though the Organising Committee and later the Central Authority were consulted) meant that the Boards were something rather more than subsidiaries of the larger entity. Yet under the Act the Central Authority had clear responsibility for coordination and financial policy, and to enforce its powers it had, in the last resort, powers of direction, though only the Minister had powers of dismissal. The Authority also had specific powers over the retail tariffs and labour relations machinery of the Area Boards.

The fourteen Area Board chairmen were men of some seniority and experience. Five of the initial appointees were from supply companies, five from public electricity authorities, while one was from the engineering industry, two from the trade unions and one from the civil service. The ones who served on the Organising Committee and the embryo Central Authority, and the remainder who joined them on appointment later in 1947, were quite clear that they would not give up their statutorily entrenched independence to Citrine and Self. Because of the delays in appointments to the Area Boards, much of the initial planning work on organisation had to be done centrally, but the chairmen were soon stoutly defending their autonomy. In December 1947, for example, when they had agreed a memorandum on Area Board organisation, Randall, the London Board chairman, insisted that it should be a purely advisory document not binding on the areas; and some degree of variation in local organisation did in fact emerge.

The resistance of Area Board chairmen to the encroachment of the centre on their powers was persistent, and Citrine, conscious of the strength of the chairmen's position, gave way. Speaking of the Boards, he said:

Our policy is a policy of decentralisation, and so far as we can operate that policy consistently with the purposes that Parliament has devised for us, we shall do it. There will be errors, there will be occasions when we shall find that one particular Board is dealing with its problems in quite a different way from another Board. . . . I ask you to understand at the beginning that this is inseparable from a policy of decentralisation. You cannot have autonomy devolving upon Area Boards . . . if it is exercised, as distinct from existing in theory, without differences showing themselves. And I know that as soon as a practice in one Area is shown to be superior to a practice in another Area we shall have a clamour to generalise and standardise the better practice. I invite your attention to that point in the months that are to come.[23]

At his first formal meeting with the chairmen after all had been appointed, he outlined how he might achieve the generalisation and standardisation of 'better practice':

the Central Authority . . . had overriding responsibility for co-ordination. The one factor essential for close cooperation was adequate information and, speaking broadly, he was satisfied that it would be mutually advantageous for a maximum exchange of information ... Coordination and cooperation between the Central Authority and the Area Boards would obviously be beneficial to all and might be ensured by, for instance, a series of conferences similar to the present and by meetings between officials. ... As a start there were four Area Board Chairmen serving in rotation on the Central Authority for a period of three years. [This was initially envisaged, but the normal period became two years.] To keep the remaining ten Area Boards informed of the thoughts and intentions of the Central Authority, either the four Area Board Chairmen could meet the remaining Chairmen and interpret to them what the Central Authority were thinking and doing or periodical meetings between the central Authority and all the Area Board Chairmen, and possibly their deputies could be arranged – he inclined to the latter suggestion.

The latter suggestion was indeed taken up and the Area Board chairmen met monthly with Citrine, Self and Hacking to work out a common policy. The chief officers of the Area Boards – engineers, commercial officers, secretaries and accountants – also had regular meetings with their opposite numbers at the Central Authority. Citrine's policy was the standard one: to hammer out a consensus by discussion. He and Self devoted infinite pains to making this democratic centralism work. The Area Board men, worn down and frustrated by committees and discussions, sometimes resented the method. But the Central Authority always preferred persuasion, keeping their powers of direction in reserve.

In principle the Central Authority could also delegate some of the functions reserved for it in the Electricity Act. Some Area Board chairmen pressed for increased devolution to them on matters such as labour relations or generation. This Citrine resisted. On labour relations he was, understandably, quite clear that his own central direction was required.[24] On generation, there had been a long-standing debate within the industry, and Citrine felt it was best to avoid any further uncertainty by being firm on the issue. Prior to nationalisation many of the larger undertakings had been vertically integrated, both generating power and distributing and selling it. Although the generation and distribution functions had become increasingly specialised as the industry developed, there were still many who felt that 'power boards' – fully integrated undertakings –

had significant advantages. If the Central Authority had delegated its powers of generation to the area distribution boards, they would, in effect, have become integrated power boards. Despite Citrine's attempt to settle this issue by firmly rejecting the proposal, this organisational option still had many advocates within the industry whose views were to surface in later years.

Although the power board option was initially ruled out, the Central Authority (which inherited nearly 300 power stations previously operated by 130 separate generating authorities) clearly required some kind of regional devolution of management, though they were not, on this side of the industry, constrained by any statutory provisions for regional organisation. The CEB had previously exercised coordinating functions over generation, and it was thus natural that John Hacking and his other ex-CEB colleagues should play a large part in determining policy in this field. Hacking was much liked by the professional engineers and managers in the industry and faced less initial distrust than his colleagues Citrine and Self, though he was no less committed to a policy of centralisation. Most of the CEB men, Hacking included, saw as one of the great prizes of nationalisation the possibility of escaping from the voluntarism which had characterised their former relations with the undertakings. They advocated central technical control, ideally by the six Grid control regions which the CEB had operated. Many other members of the Organising Committee felt, however, that the devolution of power in generation should be to the smaller areas covered by the fourteen Area Boards. Those advocating power boards found this argument especially persuasive, since it opened up the possibility of continued cooperation between the two sides of the industry at regional level, and of the continued joint use of common services. There was also a genuine fear that open conflict between the two sides of the industry must be avoided (a fear which was shown to be not entirely illusory in a subsequent reorganisation, see pp. 194–5 below). The issue was not resolved by the Organising Committee, but eventually Hacking retreated from the CEB view and accepted the arguments for fourteen generation areas coterminous with the distribution boards. He also felt that the burden of duties on the divisional controllers who would head the area organisations for generation was sufficiently great to justify more, but smaller areas. A further advantage was that this provided more top posts for senior and experienced men from the undertakings.

The Central Authority thus created fourteen generation divisions for the construction, management and operation of power stations. They recruited as divisional controllers six former CEB managers, six municipal engineers, and two engineers from the power companies. These jobs on the generation side of the industry had a larger engineering content than the Area Board jobs in distribution, and, in terms of assets and capital expenditure, were a weightier responsibility. Yet the salaries were typically below those of Area Board chairmen, and the prestige of these posts was arguably compromised from the beginning by the salary and status differentials. The divisional controllers also lacked the independence conferred by ministerial appointment on Area Board chairmen, and were more constrained when they were called regularly to London head office conferences. The centralised technical control, exercised by the chief engineer's department at headquarters, meant that the men who had accepted these posts were to find their room for independent and creative action significantly more constrained than was the case for their colleagues in the Area Boards. The extent to which management powers over generation were devolved depended on the central triumvirate of Citrine, Self and Hacking, and not on a statutorily entrenched position. It is a measure of the fundamental instincts of Citrine and his colleagues that, where they had the greater power to centralise, it was centralisation, and not devolved responsibility, which was their watchword.

As vesting day, 1 April 1948, approached, the shape of the organisations which were to take over the industry, and the men who were going to lead them at national and regional level were known. During the preparations for the switch from control by company boards and municipal electricity committees to control by the new national and regional authorities, there was both excitement and concern about the future in the industry. For most workers and consumers, the change was noticeable only in the gradual change in letterheads, titles and nameplates: the familiar paraphernalia of institutional changes. For most managers, too, the local interim managerial arrangements for transfer – under which an executive officer, usually already in post, was appointed to supervise arrangements – were relatively painless. Mergers are usually disturbing to employees and managers alike, and a merger of nearly 600 undertakings might have been expected to create more pain than most. Problems there certainly were: the disentangling of assets with multiple uses (for example, some offices had been used for gas billing as well as for electricity) inevitably caused some headaches. However, the absence of any major disruption suggests that the careful preparation of the transition to the new organisation had paid off. As midnight struck on vesting day, Lord Citrine, after more than a year of planning, was waiting up excitedly with Sir Henry Self in the flat above their new London headquarters in a converted block of flats in Great Portland Street. John Hacking stayed the night at home in bed. This partnership – a trade unionist, a civil servant, and an engineer – now had a large slice of Britain's economic future in their hands.

3

MEETING THE CAPACITY CRISIS

You can't fight a war and scrape right down to the bottom of the barrel, throwing in everything you've got, and then start up again as if nothing had happened.

> Clement Attlee, quoted in Francis Williams, *A Prime Minister Remembers* (1961) p. 94.

In the whole history of engineering did anyone dream up anything more like the Mad Hatter's Tea Party?

> Lord Hinton of Bankside, *Heavy Current Electricity in the United Kingdom* (1979) p. 69.

The most serious problem faced by the British Electricity Authority in 1948 was the chronic disequilibrium of supply and demand.[1] For some years after the War there had been severe power cuts in winter, when demand reached its peak, because of shortages of both power station capacity and coal to burn in the plant that was available. In the fuel crisis of February 1947, an already overstretched system had been brought to breaking point: electricity supplies to many users had been periodically interrupted for weeks on end and other supplies had been restricted, in the severest winter for more than a hundred years. The situation had then improved, thanks partly to higher priorities for allocations of coal, steel and men to the electricity supply undertakings and partly to the milder weather in the winter of 1947/8. Even so, the industry had to cut off between 10 and 20 per cent of peak loads in these winters, despite attempts to reduce the peak demand by less drastic means. The latter included exhortations to consumers to switch off appliances, reductions in supply voltages by 5 per cent (which was considered the maximum tolerable limit), and encouragement to industrialists voluntarily to stagger their factory hours away from peak times.

This situation was primarily the consequence of wartime cutbacks in investment in new generating plant and the difficulties of transition back to the peacetime construction programme. At a time when the growth of electricity sales showed no signs of slackening, the four years lead-time for the installation of new power station plant meant that there was little chance of any of the new postwar orders released by government planners for manufacture providing much relief until 1949 or later. There had been some plants under construction for wartime-approved purposes, but in 1945 itself only 170MW of new plant had been completed, and in 1946 this could only be increased to 288MW and in 1947 to 340MW. This was well below the levels which had been necessary to meet the annual growth of demand before the War (712MW had been completed in 1938), and also well below the level of around 1000MW a year which the CEB now considered necessary. It was fully recognised by the Government, moreover, that it would take some years for normal conditions to be restored. At the first meeting of the Central Authority, Shinwell had told Citrine and his colleagues that a reasonable aim would be to meet full demand by 1951 'if that was at all possible' in the light of other national investment demands. The Government's economic planners knew full well that, with shortages of essential materials such as steel, even that was an optimistic target.

The planners had in fact already taken out of the hands of the industry a good deal of the coordinating responsibility for making up the plant backlog, recognising electricity supply as a crucial sector in their overall economic planning and taking steps to intervene directly where they were dissatisfied with the progress made by the pre-vesting electricity undertakings. In key respects the views of Whitehall coincided with those of the Central Electricity Board, which had for long felt that its own, indirect control of power station construction was inadequate. In particular, CEB engineers considered that stations designed and ordered by the separate municipalities and companies led to a proliferation of designs and a failure to gain the advantages of replication. The manufacturers, flooded with a backlog of orders far in excess of their capacity, also felt that they would be able to do a better job if designs could be standardised, and had pressed the Government for action in 1947. The Ministry of Supply's Directorate of Power Station Equipment was already engaged, with some assistance from the CEB, in piecemeal standardisation initiatives and attempts to allocate materials and orders between manufacturers more rationally.[2] In November 1947 they had issued a statutory order (which was to remain in force until July 1950) limiting all new orders for turbo-alternators for the home market to sets of 30MW capacity (with prewar standard steam conditions of 600psi and 850°F) and 60MW sets (with more advanced steam conditions of 900psi and 900°F).[3] This was later to be criticised as imposing an unnecessary conservatism on design (pp. 104–10, below), but at that time (with shortages of skilled draughtsmen and engineers, and the overriding priority of speeding up the installation of safe and reliable sets) it was widely supported by the manufacturers and the CEB as well as in Whitehall. The turbo-alternator manufacturers reckoned that it would enable them to cut between six and nine months off delivery dates, and the boiler-makers reckoned the standardisation of boilers to supply steam to the standard units would also speed up construction. However, given the long lead-times in manufacture and construction, it was recognised that the standardisation could only have an effect in the forward programmes for 1950 onwards.

When the British Electricity Authority and its divisions took over responsibility for generation design in April 1948, the engineers from the CEB, particularly Hacking, and Pask, his chief engineer, looked forward to strengthening the role of the centre in the design function, but that too could only have an impact in the longer run. To meet the immediate problems, the vital priorities were the proper progressing of the manufacture of designs for nearly 6000MW of plant planned or under construction by the former undertakings, and the acceleration of work in progress on sites. At the Organising Committee, the retiring CEB chairman had confidently suggested that the old CEB organisation could continue to handle matters in this field and there would be little need for change: 'The CEB in conjunction with a strong committee on which the Ministry of Supply were represented were working hard on the generating plant extensions and it would not be necessary for the Organising Committee to worry over-much about the details of this programme in the meantime.' Citrine and Self were preoccupied with the administrative problems of vesting, organisational initiatives, and Area Board relations; and their new cramped headquarters in Great Portland Street could not absorb the CEB organisation. Many of the staff continued to look on Hacking and his staff at Trafalgar Buildings (the old CEB headquarters) as a continuation of the CEB. His engineers were glad to continue with the central job they had been engaged on before: the attempt to speed up power station completion rates in undertakings they now controlled more directly. Hacking had an additional office in Great

Portland Street headquarters, so that he could liaise with Citrine, Self and the administrators, but his organisation at Trafalgar Buildings remained basically that of the CEB.

In the postwar economy, still beset by shortages of materials, and particularly of steel, the BEA, like the pre-nationalisation industry, had to fight a continuing battle for resources with Sir Edwin Plowden's Central Economic Planning Staff and ultimately with the Cabinet. The civil servant on Plowden's team in charge of the power station construction programme was F. W. ('Bomber') Smith, who had made his name in the War by successfully stepping up aircraft production in Beaverbrook's celebrated Ministry. In August 1948, Gaitskell specifically asked that he be transferred to the Ministry of Fuel and Power to coordinate the power station construction programme. Like the old CEB, the new Central Authority bombarded Smith and the Cabinet's Investment Programmes Committee with a barrage of complaints against cuts in their forward programmes, but Smith seriously doubted whether they had the capacity to implement the large programmes implied by new requests for men and materials. They had had high priority since the fuel crisis of February 1947, but boilers and site work had in many cases been delayed (mainly because of steel shortages) so that 300–400MW of plant completed by the turbo-alternator manufacturers had had to be put in store for a year or more. Smith therefore felt that the manufacturers' allocations should be cut back to a more realistic level than the BEA's plant-ordering programme, while he allocated more steel for the foundation and building work on power station sites which was the bottleneck. He telephoned Hacking in September 1948 to offer an extra 50000 tons of site steel immediately and a further 180000 tons for 1949.

As the engineers within the BEA began to take over direct responsibility for the power station sites during 1948, the prospect of strengthening the organisation improved. The faulty programming of work in a situation in which everyone was trying to beat the planners, and having variable success, but not producing whole working power stations, was clearly ludicrous. Within the chief engineer's department the main responsibility for sorting things out fell on Group-Captain C. E. H. ('Charles') Verity, who came from one of the best pre-vesting undertakings (the London Power Company), after a wartime spell of directing the bombing of German power stations, to be the headquarters Generation Construction Engineer. Verity found that as many as ten government committees were responsible for coordinating the work of all the former undertakings, manufacturers, construction firms and consultants, and that, in addition to the planners, four Ministries – Fuel and Power, Labour, Supply (responsible for manufacturers) and Works (responsible for construction sites) – were involved. The tangled web of committees seemed to him likely to retard rather than accelerate development, and he hoped that clearer BEA responsibility would, as their headquarters staff were built up, lead to quicker progress. By November 1948, it was agreed that they could take over the responsibility for progressing work on the manufacture of plant and on-site construction from the Ministries of Supply and Works, and the following year they did so.

Although liaison work with the Ministries and the planners was still necessary, Verity, a natural conciliator, created a progressing organisation which was more streamlined and probably as effective as possible in the prevailing conditions of materials shortages.[4] Carefully logging the state of progress on all manufacturing and site work, they were able to determine priorities which were likely *overall* to increase the rate of commissioning of working stations rather than partial completions. The work was not easy – manufacturers, for example, sometimes had to be asked to ease off on an item of plant in a fairly advanced state of completion (but for which the site was not yet prepared or the boiler installation delayed) to press on with others at an earlier stage of manufacture which could be installed earlier. In Whitehall, Smith was pleased with the progressing organisation built up by Verity, but in 1949 it became clearer that the bottlenecks were not only on site steel but in the inadequate response of the pipework and boiler manufacturers. Hacking and the BEA engineers were, Smith felt, reluctant to press hard to get additional boiler manufacturing capacity. At the end of September 1949, therefore, Smith was himself seconded to the BEA to work on sorting out this problem, and he was in fact to stay, in a sustained attempt to work out a better contracts system, thus further strengthening the BEA's management of the construction programme.

The joint efforts of Smith and Verity also introduced more realism into BEA planning. In April 1948 they had inherited work in hand from five CEB annual programmes with nearly 6000MW due for completion by 1950. This was far more than could be justified in the straitened circumstances of the time (and indeed it would have produced a large margin of spare capacity on the actual early 1950s peak demand). It was more a CEB attempt to point out their difficulties than a serious construction programme. By the end of

1948 Smith had worked out more plausible commissioning targets rising from around 562MW in the current year to 1107MW in 1949, 1155MW in 1950 and 1600MW in 1951. Even targets of this order implied an ability to commission a boiler every six days and a turbo-alternator every twelve days for several years: well above the levels ever achieved before in Britain. There were subsequent cuts in allocations to the BEA because of the devaluation crisis of 1949 and the Korean War crisis of the early 1950s, and the difficulties of construction and boiler manufacture remained persistent. Thus even these reduced targets were not met: actual commissioning levels were 37 per cent below target in 1949, 19 per cent below in 1950 and 42 per cent below in 1951, with the programmed stations for these years being rolled over into 1952 and 1953. This shortfall arose partly because, even when difficulties could be foreseen, it was sensible to aim high and maintain manufacturers' confidence in a sustained market growth, though, as we shall see, it also reflects a persistently poor record for the British power station construction industry on completion times. Power cuts were thus to remain a fact of life at winter peak times in Britain into the early 1950s. Although the widespread disruption of the earlier 1949 crisis was avoided, the load which had to be shed in the severe winter of 1951 (2109MW) was in absolute terms the highest ever, and still amounted to 17 per cent of the load on the system.

4

HALF-PRICE ELECTRICITY?

... we had to urge consumers, not only to go easy at peak times but at other times also. I became so economy minded that when I walked into a restaurant or a hotel it made me indignant to find all the lights blazing away in broad daylight. A fine state of affairs for a Chairman whose job was to sell electricity!

Lord Citrine, *Two Careers* (1967) p. 275.

The impact of power cuts in an advanced industrial society is inevitably serious. In the circumstances of the 1940s, it was felt most by the large industrial users, who could be contacted quickly to switch off demand 'voluntarily' to avoid the collapse of the supply system which would follow if the load were too great and the frequency were allowed to drop below the safe minimum. Voltages were also cut, producing an annoying slowness in the cooking of breakfasts and a reduction in the output of heating appliances, but again there were practical limits to the relief of the peak load by this means. All consumers were urged to 'switch off at the peak' and in periods of severe difficulties moral suasion was backed up by statutory controls, though for small consumers these were practically impossible to enforce, so that voluntary restriction remained the more important. The cooperation of consumers enabled the disruption of production to be minimised; and the industry's expertise in avoiding the more serious problems developed with experience and with the higher priorities they were granted for scarce coal supplies after the disastrous crisis of February 1947. The widespread power cuts to factories which had then been necessary had caused nearly 15 per cent of the UK workforce to be laid off and were estimated to have cost some £200 millions of vital production.[1] By the early 1950s, however, the cuts, though more severe in terms of the number of megawatts cut off, were less sustained, widespread and damaging. In the winter of 1950/1, for example, government estimates were that

29

consequential industrial production losses had been £8–10 millions. There were also financial losses to the British Electricity Authority from having to operate old and inefficient plant for more extended periods than they would have chosen in normal times: in the early 1950s the extra cost of burning scarce coal inefficiently was reckoned at £3½ millions a year at the low official coal prices of the time, though the real resource cost was somewhat higher than this.[2]

Given the difficulties of making up the capacity backlog in the short term, attention inevitably focussed on the other side of the equation: the growth in demand and the possibility of restricting it. Industry was not here the culprit. With the restrictions firms accepted, industrial sales grew very slowly and, after falling in the later years of the War, did not again reach the 1943 level until 1949. A committee at the Ministry of Labour had also worked out with industrialists methods of shifting the hours of work to avoid the winter peak times, and this load spreading helped a lot to contain industrial peak demand at these crucial times. The restlessness of industrialists at being expected to take the brunt of sacrifices had led to commercial consumers (shops, offices, hotels, etc.) also being brought into the load spreading arrangements in 1948.

The demand on the system none the less continued inexorably to grow. Sales by 1948 were almost double those of ten years earlier, though the installed capacity of power stations had been increased by less than half of this. All categories of sales had shown an increase in the decade, but the really spectacular growth, especially after 1943, had been in sales to domestic consumers. By the later 1940s, domestic sales were approaching nearly three times the prewar level. While moral suasion had been favoured in the War (in preference to rationing) as a means of restricting domestic demand, and had for a time been partially successful, as peace returned it lost much of its impact. The British public, after years of sacrifice, were less and less inclined to tolerate prolonged austerity; and, though in other fields the Labour Government was extremely successful in diverting resources away from consumption and towards investment and exports (at considerable cost to its own political popularity), there were limits to the extent that this could be achieved in electricity. Electricity, indeed, now became a major loophole in the rationing system by which common sacrifices were imposed on all. This was particularly evident in space heating: coal had been the normal method of heating for British householders, but with a low coal ration now applied in order to conserve coal for industry, they still had the option of switching on electric fires. Understandably, these fires – which at thirty shillings were cheap to buy and easy to install – were widely sold in their millions in the postwar years. By the time the Government tried to close up this loophole, by restricting steel allocations for electric fire manufacture, it was too late. When the industry was nationalised, three-quarters of domestic consumers had fires, compared with only a quarter before the War. The growth of domestic demand was also boosted by the connection of many new consumers: the Boards naturally gave priority to the new estates and 'pre-fabs' of the postwar housing drive which urgently needed to have electricity connected. The controllers of the National Grid could see the shift in domestic demand directly reflected in the pattern of load on their power stations. Whereas before the War, the peak had come with lighting demand in the late winter afternoons, it was, for some years after the War, between 8 and 9 a.m. when the domestic space heating demand was at its height.

Inevitably the industry came under some pressure from the Government to control this burgeoning demand from domestic consumers, without which the capacity crisis would have been a good deal less serious. The first years of nationalisation were thus regularly punctuated by government demands for consideration of rationing by price or by direct load limitation. The prices being charged by the industry after the War were undoubtedly excessively low, and this in itself had artificially stimulated consumer demand. In the decade prior to nationalisation, electricity tariffs had hardly increased at all in money terms, and the average domestic price of electricity had fallen faster than in any other decade in history, both in real terms and relative to the price of its major competitors, gas and coal. By 1948, although living standards in general were no higher than a decade previously, the average domestic consumer was using twice as much electricity as then, but paying only half as much for it per kWh in real terms.[3]

Such a record might appear to be an occasion for delight in consumers and pride in the industry, but it did not in fact arise from efficiency increases (indeed physical indices of efficiency showed a decline because of inadequate investment in new plant). Rather it arose from a fortuitous combination of circumstances which bore little relation to the long-run economic costs of producing and distributing electricity. During wartime and the postwar era of government price control, electricity undertakings had in many cases been prevented from raising domestic tariffs to meet increased costs, and had drawn instead on their reserves and on the automatic increases paid by larger (mainly industrial) consumers under the coalcost increase clause of their special tariffs. Moreover, many domestic consumers were on tariffs in which extra kWhs purchased were cheaper than the initial units. This had in part been justified by cost conditions – a larger domestic consumer was cheaper per kWh to supply than a small one – though in the conditions of shortage which prevailed it was arguably foolish to maintain such a strong incentive to increased usage. There were some undertakings still charging only ½d. (or even, in a few cases, ⅓d.) per additional kWh to domestic users after the War, and ½d. was not even enough to pay for the coal needed to generate that amount of electricity in the majority of the power stations they were then using, far less to pay the other costs of supply. As nationalisation approached, moreover, the independent undertakings were in no mood to increase prices. Indeed, for the local authorities (many of whom were angry that the Government were treating nationalisation merely as a book-keeping transaction within the public sector and thus paying them little compensation for the takeover), the maintenance of uneconomically low prices was one way of getting their own back for the local ratepayers (who were also usually electricity consumers). The Central Authority were extremely worried about the transfer of lump sums to municipal coffers, or rebates paid to consumers, and tried to persuade the Government to act to prevent such abuses pending nationalisation. Eventually, however, they concluded that the best the Ministry could do was to prohibit a reduction of charges, though this limited only the most flagrant abuses.[4]

The result of these various pressures was that, when they were taken over, some 150 undertakings were heading for an aggregate deficit of £7 millions (more than 3 per cent of total BEA revenue) over the year.[5] Within a month of nationalisation, the Authority's commercial manager had identified the more serious black spots in which tariffs for additional domestic kWh were below ¾d. – which he reckoned to be the level required to cover costs – and in the next few months prices were generally raised to this level as a 'first aid' measure, pending the development of a proper pricing policy. In order to put this over sympathetically to consumers, the Central Authority issued a directive enforcing it on Area Boards: thus underlining the absolute necessity for this increase. There were also some presentational reductions in prices in some isolated, small-scale undertakings, where domestic consumers using electricity for very little more than lighting had been charged very high flat rates per kWh. (The maximum price was reduced to 6d.) Sensible and necessary price increases none the less attracted a predictably irresponsible press reaction, with Conservative newspapers bearing anti-nationalisation headlines such as 'You own the electricity industry – AND UP GO THE PRICES'.[6]

These price increases restored the industry's income to levels sufficient to cover book costs, but prices still remained low relative to the higher costs the industry was having to incur to meet the new demand. This was realised by some in the industry, but there was little agreement on whether it was proper to take account of those long-run costs immediately. In retrospect, we can see that there were strong economic reasons to do so, certainly by the canons of modern public sector pricing theory which suggests that prices should be set at the (long-run) marginal costs of supply.[7] However, the costs appearing in the books of the newly nationalised industry were considerably below these, largely because, while capital charges normally formed a large proportion of the total costs of electricity supply, the industry had in recent years been prevented from investing heavily and most of its inherited equipment stood in the books at prewar values. This was particularly serious because of its impact on relative prices in the energy sector. The coal and gas industries, which were significantly more labour-intensive, had seen their current costs escalate more rapidly, and lacked the cushion of historically low capital charges. This change in relative prices would have been rational if it had reflected any real improvement in the competitive power of electricity (and there had been a continuing shift in favour of electricity for the whole century), but now the shift was artificially exaggerated by historic cost accounting in a period of inflation, and by temporarily depressed investment levels.[8] The demand for electricity was thus being artificially boosted: the price was known to be sufficient only to meet the historic average costs of supply, not the costs which in future would have to be paid if the demand were met.

These price and cost interrelations were not well and explicitly understood at the time, and it is perhaps anachronistic to criticise the industry for not adopting them. Indeed the major criticism is properly addressed to the advocates of nationalisation, who had given far too little attention to the general question of pricing and investment rules by which the public sector should operate. The contemporary academic debate among economists had become bogged down in a rather arid byway of marginal costing and subsidies, and provided little useful guidance on the substantive issues of the day.[9] Labour politicians, even those with a training in economics, were muddled about the issues,[10] and generally seemed to favour the historic average cost principles, which also seemed to many at the time [11] to be enshrined in the wording of the Act, which merely required the industry to break even 'taking one year with another'.[12] The political pressures reinforcing this attitude were powerful, and Shinwell, with his eye on the working class cost of living, told the Central Authority at its first meeting that they should not charge prices higher than costs (without, however, specifying how this was to be interpreted). If higher prices had been used to ration demand, the industry would, of course, have made large book profits, and this would probably have been politically unacceptable to a government which remembered election promises that nationalisation would mean cheap electricity. *The Economist* sensibly saw an electricity tax as a way of resolving this problem,[13] but, with the Conservative opposition ready to taunt the Government with unfairly raising prices, the prospects of a rational price policy were not good.

Some civil servants did see the need for higher prices. Some planners, for example, saw that their economic planning might be more effective if they used the price mechanism to work with them rather than against them, and Philip Chantler, the economic adviser brought into the Ministry of Fuel and Power in 1947, consistently advocated a move to higher prices. These were largely voices in the wilderness: the politicians, administrative civil servants and managers in the industry simply lacked an understanding of the common language of economic discourse which was essential to a rational analysis of energy prices. (It was more than a decade before Chantler's ideas were fully accepted even within the Ministry.) Any hope that the new Ministry of Fuel and Power could rationally 'coordinate' a national policy on energy inevitably went out of the window with this absence of an acceptable common vocabulary with which to discuss the issues.

Within the industry, the consequences of a rudderless Whitehall were welcomed at the commercial grass roots level. Managers were delighted at the price advantage which they had gained over their gas competitors and the question of whether it was artificial did not seriously concern them. Other senior men in the industry, equally, were not averse, either in principle or practice, to the low price of electricity. Municipal men had traditionally operated in a service-inspired environment and were strongly committed to the spread of electricity use, especially to domestic consumers. Men from the company sector might find the jargon of competitive market solutions more appealing, but most recognised they were now entering a new milieu. Citrine was happy to tell them, in the traditional (if somewhat imprecise) formula, that the industry was now to be operated in the national interest and not for private gain. While a good case can, in retrospect, be made for the national interest being served by higher prices, there were few at the time who argued against the interpretation of Citrine and Self that there was a long-run obligation to sell as much electricity as possible at as low a price as possible.

This objective of growth could not, of course, in the early stages, be pursued without restraint, for the capacity crisis prevented the industry from meeting all demands. Against the protests of many of their salesmen, then, the Central Authority and Area Boards gave in to government pressure to restrict promotional advertising and hire purchase schemes in order to curtail the over-rapid growth of demand. Publicity was directed to persuading people to switch off at peak times, and some Boards, notably the Eastern, banned sales of space heaters at their showrooms. The commercial men resented thus having to create a negative image of their product, but this was the least the industry could do to allay government criticism that they were expanding more rapidly than resources allowed. The Boards' own impression, strengthened by many consumer complaints about power cuts, was that people wanted faster expansion. Inevitably, then, their major strategy for meeting demand became the long-term one of building enough new capacity to meet the demand placed on the system at the low price levels which enabled them to increase sales while just balancing the books. Yet, until that capacity could be built, it seemed, power cuts in winter would remain a fact of life.

The one Minister with the political courage and economic sense to attempt to alleviate this situation by using the price mechanism selectively was Hugh Gaitskell. He and Shinwell had told the Central Authority at their first meeting in September 1947 that, while general price rises could be ruled out, they were prepared to look at the possibility of controlling demand at peak times by differentially higher prices for peak use or by mechanical load-restricting devices. In February 1948, under increasing pressure from industrialists to control the growth of non-industrial demand at the peak, Gaitskell established a committee, under the chairmanship of Sir Andrew Clow, a former governor of Assam. Edgar Wilkinson, the BEA's Commercial Manager and Ronald Edwards, an LSE economist, played a leading part in the deliberations of the committee, which heard some powerful evidence of the damage done at the peak, particularly by the space heating load, and of the need for restriction by an increased winter price or other means. Despite Wilkinson's attempts to moderate criticism of the Area Board's policies, and a trade unionist member's introduction of some woolliness in the text to accommodate his dislike of any rationing by the purse, the committee's report, submitted to Gaitskell in June, did make some strong proposals.[14] In addition to some longer-run experiments with 'off-peak' supplies, time-of-day metering and load limiting devices, the committee recommended that the main practicable way of meeting the short-term objective of cutting peak demand was to impose a surcharge on winter purchases of electricity.[15]

Gaitskell was convinced that this proposal was right, and gained the agreement of his cabinet colleagues and, eventually, of Citrine. When Citrine revealed the proposal to the Area Board chairmen, however, they reacted angrily. The Clow Committee had recognised there would be practical problems: the quarterly cycle of meter reading would make it difficult to concentrate the higher charge on the crucial months of December, January and February when demand was highest; in really cold weather or if coal remained in short supply it would have only limited deterrent effect; and off-peak demand might be adversely affected. But they reckoned without the mood of the chairmen, who saw the committee's proposal as an intolerable and misguided interference in the detail of their management policy. Only a few months after vesting day, they were still wrestling with the enormous problems of reorganisation and the standardisation of the many different electricity tariffs they had inherited: this additional burden seemed to them too much. They were, moreover, quite convinced that the Clow differential would cause greater problems than the committee realised. When Gaitskell met the chairmen on 22 July 1948, however, he mercilessly exposed many of their arguments as the specious reasoning of bigoted men. Their professed need for a load valley in summer to permit overhaul could not be reconciled with the common observation that their capacity problems were not at their worst then; it could not both be true that the differential charge would have no effect and that it would have so large an effect in cutting consumption the Boards would make losses. As Gaitskell recalled in his diary:

The meeting with the Area Board chairmen was an uproar. After I had spoken they got up and one after another opposed. I did not mind the opposition but the unbelievably stupid and muddled arguments which they put forward. I was really horrified that so many men, earning so much money, should be so silly. The trouble, of course, is that they are all madly keen to sell electricity and just cannot get used to the idea that at the moment they should stop people from buying it. When I left there was deadlock ...[16]

Citrine's trade union negotiating skills now came into their own. After initially agreeing with Gaitskell, he had won the confidence of the chairmen by putting their case loyally and firmly, excusing his outburst later to Gaitskell as a necessary way of bringing the chairmen round to compromise. The compromise which Citrine was able to cobble together was, however, in the worst tradition of the proverbial camel: a horse designed by committee. Gaitskell, Citrine, Self and Wilkinson had all seen earlier that, to be effective, the differential charge would have to be large: perhaps 1¼d. per kWh in winter as against ½d. in summer, which might cut peak consumption by around 10 per cent. Eventually, after much arguing, the Area Board chairmen agreed to 1.1d. in winter and 0.65d. in summer. To protect themselves, they were to be permitted to say that this differential was being implemented 'at the Minister's request'. The experiment was, as might have been predicted from the chairmen's opposition, a failure. The differential was too small to have a big impact, and, when it was publicised at all, was accompanied by assurances that the cost would be cancelled out by the lower summer charge. Many consumers did not even know of the charge until after the winter of 1948/9 when it was imposed; because of cyclic meter reading, many received their winter bills only as the charge was lowered; and some were never surcharged at all. By the spring of 1949, the Boards were triumphantly arguing that they had been proved right in that the differential charge had had no effect on consumption and merely provoked public discontent. Although Gaitskell at first stood his ground, it was obvious that, in the face of obstruction from the industry, he could not make a sensible price policy stick, and in July he announced the abandonment of the Clow surcharge.[17]

The memory of this episode had an impact on government–industry relations and on the future development of pricing policy. For years, the Clow surcharge was misleadingly referred to by electrical enthusiasts as proof that demand for electricity at peak times was completely inelastic within the relevant price ranges. Gaitskell's initiative, powerful and well-intentioned though it was, was counter-productive, reinforcing rather than dissolving the prejudices within the industry which stood in the way of a more rational pricing policy. The industry's cause was not a particularly noble one, but their victory was an important step in establishing a degree of independence from government, and it is in this that its major significance lies. Gaitskell was probably the brightest and most administratively experienced Minister the industry has ever had to deal with. He had been defeated, and he knew it. As Citrine had earlier told his colleagues, a tactical retreat of accepting the Minister's suggestion and then showing it to be ineffective would enable them better to assert their independence in future. Gaitskell now knew that there were practical limits to the extent to which the Government could exert control over the industry. He mused for a time over alternative means of strengthening control, even on the possibility of a Minister replacing Citrine as chairman, but in the end he accepted the logic of the independent Morrisonian public corporation on which Labour's nationalisation had ostensibly been based. The tragedy of the industry was that they had won the battle only by turning their back on the price mechanism: a procedure for resource allocation which, arguably, is the best medium for the decentralisation of decision making to firms in the modern economy. As events were to show, the underlying problems of resource allocation remained; and the failure to solve them was insidiously to add to the pressures gnawing away the industry's independence. In winning the battle, as we shall see, they had sown the seeds of losing the war.

Part II

RECOVERY AND DEVELOPMENT
(1948–57)

5

MINISTERS AND MANDARINS

'Perhaps, Lord Privy Seal, you might care to have a personal word
with Walter Citrine?'
''Im,' replied Bevin, 'I'd rather negotiate with Molotov.'

> Douglas Jay, *Change and Fortune: A Political
> Record* (1980) p. 100

I

The Clow episode showed how much the Whitehall view of the
permissible level of intervention in the affairs of public corporations
had changed since before the War. The relationship between
Ministers and the new Electricity Boards, though laid down by
statute, was not rigidly specified, but large powers of fuel policy
coordination, and of oversight of finance and general policy, were
given to the Minister. He could use these to intervene on virtually any
aspect of policy, though, in practice, as we have seen, his prospect of
imposing a policy against the united opposition of the Boards was
slim, and there was a widespread commitment to at least the principle
of independent management for public corporations. None the less,
this was a significant change from the days of the old CEB, which
(though hedged about by precise legal requirements on matters such
as pricing) had not been subject to government limits on finance
(choosing to raise its fixed-interest capital without government
guarantee) and had ignored ministerial requests when it felt they
were unjustified (being protected against the sanction acquired by the
Minister in 1947: the power of dismissal). The rule of law in the 1926
Act had, in a real sense, been replaced in 1947 by the rule of the
Minister. The examples given in Parliament [1] of areas where the
Minister would feel free to intervene – the military implications of
power station siting, research policy and the development of rural
supplies – were to be only a small part of ministerial initiatives in the
evolving relationship between the alternative centres of decision-

making power enshrined in the Act.

Citrine was, of course, the ideal person for the top job which this created, for his skills were essentially in politics and public relations, not in management. He knew the corridors of power from the angle of the politicians, and he was determined to use that knowledge to maintain as much independence for the industry as possible. He aimed, where he could, to take the industry out of party politics, but was willing to conform to the national interest where that was clearly defined by a Minister who had obvious Cabinet support. Citrine became the doyen of the nationalised industry chairmen, sometimes leaving chairmen in other industries aghast at the audacity of his refusal to agree to ministerial requests, notably on matters such as wage policy (see pp. 132–3, below). He symbolically refused to sign the first *Annual Report* to the Minister with the traditional 'Your obedient servant', preferring the more neutral 'Yours faithfully'.[2] His image as a tough negotiator in his new job, as in his old one, soon became the common talk of the corridors of Whitehall and Westminster, and his reputation for firmness in the exercise of power became legendary.[3] He traced its origin to his former position in the trade union movement (hinting that he had an agreement to go back to the TUC where he could make more trouble for any government if they pressed him hard).

The reality of Citrine's position was somewhat less dramatic than was sometimes imagined by contemporaries. It is true that he knew the Prime Ministers of the later 1940s and early 1950s, Attlee and Churchill, personally, and he was not averse to breaking protocol by raising policy matters with them behind the back of their Minister of Fuel and Power on a few occasions.[4] These occasions bore no fruit, however, and the effectiveness of his power really depended more on the skilled team he had behind him – with Sir Henry Self coordinating their relations with Whitehall from his own intimate knowledge as an ex-mandarin – and on the strength of the pressure of argument which they maintained. Citrine – sometimes with Self and Area Board chairmen, sometimes with other nationalised industries' chairmen and sometimes alone – had irregular unminuted meetings with the Minister of Fuel and Power (and sometimes with other senior Ministers) at which they hammered out compromises on the more difficult policy questions. Yet months could go by without such a meeting, and they were less regular than those of, for example, the National Coal Board chairman.[5] This infrequency was in part at Citrine's choice: he could maintain it partly because the industry's problems were less serious than those of coal. (Success, if skilfully presented, did bring greater independence.) Citrine recognised, moreover, that his own highly visible profile could sometimes be counterproductive. To Gaitskell, the defeats he had to accept from Citrine and the Area Board chairmen clearly rankled. The Conservatives also were to find it difficult to forget that he was not from their side, but a Labour appointee with clear and continuing sympathies for the trade unions. Citrine's interventions largely succeeded because they were in general well-timed; on issues on which he was utterly sure of the rightness of his cause; and on ground which had been well prepared in advance by correspondence between officials at the BEA and the Ministry, so that the Minister's brief could be effectively exploited in the discussion.

Nationalised industries usually have an advantage against their 'sponsoring' ministry in that their management is more continuous than that of ministers and mandarins, but this was not the case for Citrine. It is true that there were six different Ministers of Fuel and Power while he was chairman: Shinwell when the Central Authority was constituted, Gaitskell between 1947 and 1950, then Philip Noel-Baker until Labour's defeat in 1951, and, under the Conservatives, Geoffrey Lloyd until 1955, then Aubrey Jones for just over a year, followed by Lord Mills. In fact, Gaitskell dominated policy throughout Labour's period – first as Shinwell's deputy, then as the Minister proper, and finally in senior Cabinet economic posts for the period when Noel-Baker (who had no Cabinet seat) was formally in charge. Under the Conservatives, Lloyd's four-year stint also provided unusual continuity. Among the mandarins, at Permanent Secretary level, Sir John Maud (who succeeded Fergusson in 1952) was to outlast Citrine, and his smoothing magisterial presence was an important influence in questions such as board appointments (reserved for the Minister's private office) and fuel industry coordination (which brought together the various Ministry divisions 'sponsoring' each energy industry). Much of the routine work of correspondence with the BEA, and the practical implementation of statutory ministerial duties, fell to the Electricity Division, where again there was remarkable continuity: M.P. ('Pat') Murray headed the division between 1947 and 1959.

The initial pathway of the developing relationship between Whitehall and the BEA was not entirely smooth. Both sides were in a new situation and anxious to set precedents which would entrench their position. The Ministry, though in general it had a weak set of personnel by Whitehall standards,[6] was imbued with the common cultural attitudes of the mandarinate. It left the BEA in no doubt that it represented the 'public interest', and did not wish the BEA to forget its responsible, national status. For their part, the BEA were anxious to prevent detailed intervention, and tried (though not always successfully) to insist on the protocol of official exchange through their secretary, rather than permitting Murray and the other civil servants direct access to specialist BEA personnel for information on particular policy issues. Senior engineers and managers in the industry were often contemptuous of the amateurishness and lack of detailed knowledge of the civil service. They sometimes excelled in the art of misleading Whitehall with what at best were plausible half-truths, and expressed astonishment at the mixture of the trivial and the monumental which the political origins of some queries forced on civil servants. They soon learned that an internally consistent paper with logical relationships to what had gone before stood a better chance of acceptance than something which was right but new: civil servants after all knew little about the industry and had little basis on which to judge proposals except consistency with what had gone before. But gradually a mutual respect, based on agreed boundaries for each other's territory and mutual usefulness, built up.

At Citrine's suggestion Murray attended the majority of the meetings between the Central Authority and the Area Board chairmen, and he was able to convey government thinking to them informally, while sometimes receiving information 'off the record' and relaying signals back to Whitehall. As usually happens, the 'sponsorship role' of the Electricity Division led to Murray becoming not so much a controller of the industry as an honest broker between the BEA and the Whitehall machine in general. Being closer to the industry's own thinking, for example, the Electricity Division was soon pressing within Whitehall for higher capital investment allocations for electricity both against the other fuel divisions in the Ministry and against the Treasury. Murray and other civil servants were clear that they were being bamboozled on issues like the Clow differential (p. 37 above) but accepted much of the industry's case. They still (like Citrine himself) lacked the threshold level of knowledge necessary to make serious contributions to the more technical decisions, but they soon acquired the expertise to translate known needs into appropriate Whitehall language, according to the changing fashions dictated by public opinion or cabinet preoccupations. In that, they became a valuable ally of the BEA, enjoying in return an increasing influence over the latter on matters where presentational concessions could smooth the industry's political path. The BEA and the Area Boards reciprocated by, in general, not 'padding' their capital applications with bogus figures to anticipate cuts, though the BEA did, on occasion, deliberately withhold information which they felt would prejudice their case within the Ministry.

As the relationship developed, the rhetoric staking claims to differentiated skills and functions remained, but each side moved culturally closer to the other. Officials in the Ministry wrote to the BEA for the 'facts for next year's campaign' against the Treasury, and were thought by the BEA officials 'quite genuinely to be trying to fight our battle'. Despite the Permanent Secretary's disapproval in principle, several senior civil servants from the Ministry[7] were later to join the industry's management. The commercial and business orientation which the public corporation (as distinct from Ministry) form of management was designed to preserve, was inevitably diluted by this process, though it remained an important part of the self-image of those working in the industry. While they became more like civil servants, and adopted some civil service ways, the primary loyalty of many of them remained to the business and commercial ethic of suppliers of an electricity service.

II

The central issue to be determined in this evolving process of acculturation and of bargaining was the proportion of the nation's investment resources to be devoted to electricity supply. In the early years, the crucial controls on investment (for private industry no less than nationalised boards) were the physical allocations of resources such as steel. The steel control remained in force (apart from a brief interval from June 1950 to February 1951 when shortages none the less remained) until May 1953; building controls lasted into 1954. The Cabinet, advised by the economic planners under Sir Edwin Plowden, decided year-by-year allocations of the vital materials, and the Ministry used this as a basis for their discussions on financial investment limits with the BEA. (Under the Act, the Central Authority had to discuss their forward programmes and gain approval for their specific annual investment needs from the Minister.) Inevitably this procedure, in the early years, worked less than smoothly, with budgets drawn up hurriedly under the pressure of reorganisation, and the Ministry being quite glad on occasion if they were exceeded, since this simply meant that the industry had achieved more than expected with limited physical resources. As a Ministry minute of March 1951 noted:

> It is essential that the industry should be allowed to do the best it can with the industrial capacity at its disposal. If this results in more installation of plant than was expected, we should rejoice and take that as a new starting point.

The financial constraints were initially rather phantom-like (in the first year, for example, there was prolonged and somewhat inconclusive discussion with the Ministry about the budget and it was not finally authorised until the financial year was over!), but the physical constraints were none the less effective in limiting the industry's expenditure. With the September 1949 devaluation of the pound (requiring redirection of resources to exports) and the Korean War in the early 1950s (requiring the diversion of investment to defence industries), the physical constraints became distinctly painful. Gaitskell (now dominating Labour's economic policy and still smarting from the defeat over Clow) cut the allocations to electricity more than to the other fuel industries (which the planners felt could meet energy demand at less capital cost). Investment in power stations, to overcome the capacity backlog, was cut relatively little, but the Area Boards' budgets for 1950 and 1951 were severely pruned, particularly for the building of what were considered frills: new offices, showrooms or service centres.

The chairmen were, of course, willing to make some cuts where the national interest required it, but Gaitskell pushed them too far, making what seemed to them impossible demands. While they were being asked to trim investment, the Government's own policies were creating additional needs for investment in electricity distribution: airfields and other new defence installations for the Korean mobilisation, for example, required new electricity mains, as did the new housing estates which were a vital part of Labour's drive for electoral popularity. Between February 1950 (when the electorate returned the Labour Government with a barely adequate majority) and October 1951 (when Labour went to the polls again and were defeated), the confidence and authority of Gaitskell, as of his Government, withered. He had failed to control the growth in demand by the Clow experiment. In follow-up discussions in December 1950 the BEA agreed to further limitations on promotional advertising and a series of somewhat inconclusive committees and working parties on alternative mechanical methods of load limitation, but these had no perceptible effect on sales. With demand still growing rapidly, it was obvious that the lower levels of investment in electricity imposed by Gaitskell (however necessary they might seem from his broader viewpoint) were inadequate. By 1951 the Area Board chairmen had a burgeoning portfolio of examples of demand outstripping supply: tens of thousands of new houses would have to be left without electricity if their investment allocations were not increased.

The Boards' main weapon in a situation like this was public opinion, and, with elections pending, it was a particularly effective one. Citrine, who, despite his wrangles with Gaitskell, was keen that Labour should win, warned in the summer of 1951 that he could no longer hold back the Area Board chairmen from politically damaging attacks on the Government if the investment controls were not relaxed. Some of the extreme cases (such as the Yorkshire miners who would strike unless electricity were connected to their village) did reach the public eye, and it became clear that Citrine was not fooling when he said there were many equally damaging examples for which the chairmen would insist on pinning the blame where it belonged – on government. Under this threat, Gaitskell allowed them to increase the investment allocation for supplying industry and new housing estates, though there were some cuts in the rural electrification programme.

In return for such concessions, the Labour Government generally won the silence of the chairmen on politically-sensitive issues. It was agreed, for example, that the post-devaluation cuts and the later cuts in rural electrification should not be subject to public announcement. It suited both parties for their accommodations to be by 'gentleman's agreement'. The public were a 'voice offstage' to be used by each side in their threats, but only in the last resort was public debate considered to have a useful role in decision making. Within the BEA, the need for collusion with Whitehall on matters of this kind immeasurably strengthened the instincts of centralisation and secrecy with which the top management were imbued. The hostile Conservative press environment into which the nationalised organisations were born, and the unusually vituperative and irresponsible anti-nationalisation tone of Churchill's parliamentary opposition, also strengthened their preferences for keeping a low profile politically. All the chairmen made an effort to reply to inaccurate or unverifiable press criticism, and to stress their Boards' positive work in maintaining supplies in difficult conditions of great austerity, but experience proved truth to be of only limited effectiveness against prejudice.

The 'orgy of slander'[8] against the Labour Government and all its works had already had severe direct impact on the chairmen. In 1949, for example, it emerged before the Lynskey Tribunal that George Gibson, the chairman of the North Western Board, had somewhat unwisely accepted a gift of clothing from the flamboyant contact man, Sidney Stanley.[9] Gaitskell and Citrine were clear that Gibson was innocent of the whiff of corruption surrounding the allegations, to which he had no opportunity to reply (and Churchill in this case expressed his sympathy for Gibson), but his resignation had, inevitably, to be accepted. Some years later, the chairman of the Yorkshire Board, W. M. Lapper, was tried on a charge of breaching the building control regulations. The leaders of the industry were shocked when Lord Chief Justice Goddard sentenced him to six months imprisonment. Lapper had certainly been guilty of conceit (a wrought iron gate had been ordered with senior managers' initials worked into it), but the sentence was interpreted as a politically motivated attack on wastrel public corporations, and was widely felt to be unjust. Several other chairmen wanted a concerted public admission that they too had inadvertently breached the regulations (and it was indeed difficult to avoid technical breaches of the detailed regulations), but the choice was made rather to maintain a prudential low profile. Yet, when any mistake or misjudgement could not only be pounced upon by the press and magnified as an indication of bureaucratic muddle or high-handedness, but also lead in extreme cases to job loss or imprisonment, the instinct for self-preservation by secrecy and tight central control was understandably strengthened.

The preference of ministers and mandarins – none of whom had a desire to be exposed to public criticism – for the 'gentleman's agreement' rather than the public discussion of serious policy issues was equally understandable. When ministers uttered phrases such as the need for 'public accountability' – a suitably imprecise but popular slogan – they usually meant accountability to themselves, rather than to Parliament or the public. Such a conception was, moreover, implicit in the ideal of the independent public corporation, not subject (like the civil service) to parliamentary scrutiny of the details of its policy. Labour Ministers consistently refused to answer questions in Parliament on the day-to-day administration of the industry, though the Board chairmen themselves courteously replied to direct queries from MPs. The Labour Government also refused to countenance a select committee on nationalised industries.[10] Debates in the Commons on the industry were thus inevitably general, trivial and partisan,[11] but Ministers often preferred this situation to detached scrutiny by a more expert parliamentary committee. In opposition the Conservatives had, it is true, pressed for a select committee, but when they returned to power the Commons committee they established was quite ineffective. Conservative Ministers in office (like their Labour predecessors) remained uncooperative, and the select committee on nationalised industries was immersed in procedural wrangles over its terms of reference until the late 1950s and transacted no serious business.

III

The Conservative election victory of 1951 also brought little immediate change in the control of the level of investment by the supply industry. Physical controls on capital spending remained, but, as under Labour, with the gradual restoration of the weakened economic base more resources could progressively be made available. The level of investment by the BEA rose from only £92 millions in the financial year 1948/9 to £125 millions in 1950/1 and £196 millions in 1954/5 (only about two-fifths of this overall rise being accounted for by the fall in the real value of the pound[12]). In the election campaign, the Conservatives had made much of 'setting the people free' of the planners, and of making the nationalised industries more 'businesslike' and 'commercial', but the reality of controls remained for some years, as indeed was inevitable given the physical limits of a national cake whose size was fixed in the short term. In the first meeting with the Area Board chairmen in February 1952, the new Conservative Minister of Fuel and Power, Geoffrey Lloyd, stressed the need for economy as forcefully as Gaitskell, and capital allocations were still as carefully scrutinised. The higher interest rates and credit squeeze control used by the Conservatives did, however, slow down growth in the economy overall. Electricity demand responded (rising only 3.7 per cent in 1952/3 compared with 8.4 per cent in the previous year and 12.4 per cent in the year before that), thus providing some respite in the BEA's struggle to keep up. Moreover, with a politically more secure government and fewer power cuts (the benefits of new investment were gradually coming through), the threat of public exposure could not be as effectively used by the Boards against Whitehall, though the mandarins remained for a time concerned that Citrine was aiming at such an anti-government campaign. However, with the Treasury less hostile towards electricity than under Gaitskell, and from 1953, the general economic situation improving considerably, the BEA were able to raise investment to a relatively high level. The spirit of cooperation with Whitehall at official level thus survived the change of government intact.

As soon as the Conservatives came into office, there had been some signals to the nationalised industries that financial disciplines were likely to displace physical controls on investment. From 1952 onwards rising interest rates were another outward indication of this. Within the BEA, the majority of the top management initially seemed relatively happy with the old regime of physical controls,[13] though Ernest Long (who took over as BEA secretary in 1951) was more flexible than most, seeing that financial disciplines were, at least potentially, the medium for achieving greater independence from Whitehall. Within the Ministry, however, there was increasing discontent with the existing controls. Chantler, their economic adviser, told the new Minister frankly that the Conservatives had over-estimated the reality of controls, and most of his colleagues shared his view that any new system of control could scarcely be worse than the one they were attempting to use. Chantler noted, however, in 1952, that 'the current investment review has been even more fantastic than its predecessors if that were possible', and it was not until 1953 that the Treasury had worked out a new system of investment control. This led to the partial abandonment of physical controls and a move towards financial disciplines for the nationalised industries. Ernest Long summarised the change snappily in his note to the Authority's accountant when they were working out the implications in 1954: 'instead of being messed about by the long-haired boys at the Treasury we are now dealt with by the Finance boys – and we much prefer it that way'.

The subjection of the industry to 'financial disciplines' was inevitably at first a slogan rather than a policy. Its precise effect on the allocation of investment resources would depend on the detailed working out of the disciplines, and the Treasury certainly took no chances on a complete return to the free market in investment capital. Annual budgets still had to be checked by the Ministry and Treasury, and continued to be pruned. As before there were considerations of restricting overall investment to physical avail-ability of materials, and of maintaining leverage over the nationalised industries as part of Keynesian demand management in the economy (allowing greater expenditure when a slump threatened and reining it in when the economy appeared to be overheating). R. A. Butler, the new Chancellor, was, moreover, unwilling to take chances on market forces in areas which were vital for his economic strategy, such as the export drive. He thus insisted that quantitative limits on the capacity of generating plant the BEA were permitted to order should remain, so that home manufacturers would have sufficient spare capacity for export markets. Much paper passed between the BEA and the Ministry, with the BEA agreeing to these limits for presentational purposes. Yet in reality neither they nor the manufacturers took the limits seriously, and Central Authority engineers deliberately ignored the agreed commissioning limits. The result – a rather higher rate of completion of power stations and higher spending four or five years later in the mid-1950s – was welcomed by the Electricity Division, but it annoyed the Treasury and caused political embarrassment for the Government (which had been promising restraint in the public sector). The desire of politicians to control annual outcomes in this way was unrealistic when applied to a policy in which the industry's own long-term objectives (in this case overcoming the capacity backlog) were in conflict.

Physical limits after 1953 were progressively less effective (and in most other areas not even formally retained), but the Government hoped that the new financial disciplines would have some effect in curbing the industry's investment demand. For this hope to be fulfilled, however, there would have to be fundamental changes in BEA attitudes and decision-making procedures. These were slow to develop, and the realisation of this made it difficult (even had they wished to do so) for Ministers to treat them like private sector companies, subject largely to control by fiscal and monetary policies rather than detailed intervention on capital spending. Under the old regime, the Central Authority had treated their financial policy as a quite separate exercise having no relationship to their investment policy. Their aim in borrowing money to finance new investment (either short-term from the banks or longer-term through their public issues of fixed-interest capital) had simply been to minimise the interest rate paid, an objective Citrine and Self pursued avidly.[14] The signals that such interest rates might normally be expected to give initially had very little impact on investment policy, whether in determining the quantity or the type of capital projects undertaken. Indeed some years later (when examined by the Radcliffe Committee on the working of the monetary system) Sir Henry Self was to show that his basic attitudes to this question remained fundamentally unchanged: interest rates, he said, affected their costs, not their investment behaviour. For many years the response of the Central Authority remained the traditional one of the physical planner: new investment, irrespective of any rate of return required, was determined by predictions of demand made in physical terms with no allowance for the effect of price increases. To them, it was axiomatic that prices and interest rates should be kept down to further their objective of cheap electricity. These non-market attitudes were slow to give way, and their persistence helps to explain the Government's reluctance to abandon quantitative controls over programmes of investment.

There were none the less growing pressures on the BEA to discipline their own requests for capital through the achievement of a higher rate of return on capital, and higher rates of self-financing, both of which conformed to the Conservative Government's image of efficient private enterprise industry and 'commercial' disciplines. The Treasury and the Ministry were involved in continuous discussions with the Authority's officials to establish the point from the early 1950s onwards, whenever capital programmes, borrowing limits (which required ministerial and parliamentary authorisation), or depreciation policy came up for discussion.

The Boards were, of course, also subject to the macroeconomic signals of the shift to a more market-orientated economy, particularly the trend rise in interest rates. Labour's traditional view had been that interest rates should be kept down and investment restricted to feasible levels, not by monetary policy, but by quantitative credit controls and physical materials controls.[15] Although this could, as Labour-inclined economists increasingly accepted,[16] lead to the misallocation of resources (through the underpricing of capital relative to other inputs), lower interest rates were still being trumpeted by Labour spokesmen as a great advantage for nationalised industries well into the 1950s.[17] The Conservatives relied more on monetary policy, and, with R. A. Butler as Chancellor of the Exchequer, interest rates fluctuated around a rising trend, and gradually forced up the BEA's borrowing costs. For new short-term borrowings (which on several occasions rose above £100 millions) the BEA were charged bank rate (or only slightly more): this rose from 2 per cent under Labour to 4 per cent in March 1952, falling slightly in the following years, but rising again and, from February 1955 never falling below the 4 per cent level. On most of the nationalisation stock (paid to compensate former owners) and earlier long-term borrowings they inherited at nationalisation (much of it raised at the low interest rates of the 1930s) they paid only 3 per cent. On the six new long-term capital issues they made between 1948 and 1955 to finance expansion – each for £100–200 millions – they paid a rate which rose from a little over 3 per cent initially to just over $4\frac{1}{2}$ per cent by 1955. These rates were somewhat better than those obtained by blue-chip industrial companies, being attractive to fixed-interest investors because of the cast-iron British Treasury guarantees behind them.

In the later years, however, these issues were pitched at optimistically low interest rates: the last BEA issue, of £200 millions in August 1955 (among the largest seen by the London market), was left largely in government hands. The nationalised industries' borrowing as a whole had, in fact, become part of the public sector borrowing requirement and, in order to tighten up the monetary control, all new capital for the electricity industry (and other public sector industries) from 1956 was raised directly by the Treasury, and then lent by them to the industry. These loans continued to reflect the progressively higher interest rates, which enhanced inflationary expectations were leading the market to demand on Government issues. The interest rate paid on the first tranche of capital direct from the Treasury, at $5\frac{1}{4}$ per cent, was the highest they had ever paid. Citrine and Self hoped that the rise was temporary and would be reversed (wedded, as always, to a philosophy of cheap capital and low prices, and the world as they hoped it would be again), but high interest rates continued to reflect the buoyant competing demands for capital and mild inflationary tendencies in the UK economy.

IV

The large demands which the BEA made on the capital market – at first directly in their own capital issues and then indirectly through the Treasury borrowing requirement – attracted criticism that electricity was 'crowding out' more desirable investment projects with potentially higher rates of return in the private sector.[18] Certainly the industry's borrowings amounted to a significant portion of the new capital raised on the London market, and the profitability of its investment was below that typically earned by private industry. The traditional Conservative cry against the nationalised industries thus had some plausibility for anyone concerned with a correct allocation of investment resources in the economy: though it should be remembered that the electricity boards were (unlike private industry) *not* in general free to invest as much as they wished at low rates of return, but were subject to annual quantitative limits agreed with the Minister. There were, moreover, good reasons why a rapidly-growing industry such as electricity should raise a large proportion of its capital on the market rather than financing itself through higher earnings, as some of the critics suggested. Geoffrey Lloyd (who had ministerial experience of the oil industry) pointed out that, despite similar economic characteristics, the oil companies were able to achieve a higher degree of self-financing. Too great a reliance on self-financing would, however, require prices which were well above long-run costs (or as it was differently but conventionally expressed in the contemporary discussion by officials, would burden present-day consumers with an unfair proportion of the costs of supplying electricity in the future). On this argument higher rates of self-financing would lead to the artificial depression of sales and to *under*-investment in electricity, precisely the opposite of 'crowding out'.

In fact, Ministers were rarely happy to contemplate the rise in prices which would be necessary to raise the industry's earnings and its capacity to finance itself, though limited pressure was exerted. This was principally directed toward the gradual adoption of more realistic depreciation provisions. We have already seen (on pp. 33–4, above) that in 1948 the conventions of historic-cost, straight-line depreciation of capital led (if the Boards broke-even on book costs) to artificially low prices. There was some allowance made for this indirectly by assuming rather conservative lives for the inherited assets, and by the early 1950s, more of the higher postwar investment costs were also entering into the historic cost depreciation charges. The conservative bias in estimating lives was maintained for new investment, and other highly conservative accounting practices generally had an effect similar to replacement cost depreciation.[19] Prices were gradually raised to meet these higher costs. By the mid-1950s, moreover, with technical progress and economies of scale expected to reduce the capital cost of future generating plant below typical early 1950s levels (see pp. 111–22, below), a respectable case could be made that eventually historic average costs would come into line with replacement costs. Within the Ministry, there had been some pressure for the explicit adoption of replacement cost depreciation conventions. The Boards' lines of defence against this – replacement costs were hypothetical and difficult to estimate, tax complications might follow – read like a weary defence of the status quo, but the Ministry did in the end accept that their creation of special *ad hoc* depreciation reserves did go some way to meeting the point.

The Electricity Boards were generally reluctant to go further and show large surpluses in their accounts, for fear of criticism both from consumers and from workers in the industry, though some Boards went further than others in this direction. The chairman of the London Board, Harry Randall, for example, was convinced of the need for Boards to earn a more 'commercial' rate of return, and his Board consistently had bigger surpluses and a higher level of self-financing than the others. For most chairmen, however, Citrine's view that they should move only slowly in this direction, doing little more than break even (but conceding part of the case for higher depreciation), seemed quite consistent with the philosophy of nationalisation. It was also acceptable to a Conservative Government which, despite its rhetoric, had no desire to see politically unpopular price rises laid at its own door. In March 1956, for example, the Prime Minister appealed to nationalised industry leaders for price stability. Citrine and the chairmen agreed to freeze their prices, despite rising costs and a less than enthusiastic approach to this Cabinet policy from the new Minister of Fuel and Power directly responsible, Aubrey Jones. By early the following year some Boards were, as Jones had foreseen, going into deficit, and this inevitably compromised the industry's ability to meet the higher self-financing targets they had previously agreed with the Ministry. The upshot of these pressures for self-financing was that in the first ten years some 36 per cent of the industry's investment was internally financed: £488 millions from depreciation allowances and £98 millions from surplus after interest payments. Almost all of the remaining capital required to make up the £1551 millions invested came from borrowing. The self-financing ratio was no higher in the later years of the period than at the beginning, though, without the pressure from the Ministry, it would no doubt have declined.[20] The ratio was slightly lower than that achieved by the industry before nationalisation, but it was not markedly out of line with other countries.[21]

As the postwar economic recovery progressed, the cost of borrowing increased, but physical supplies of investment goods became less scarce. Thus the BEA (though still constrained by annual capital budgets agreed with the Ministry) found its own task in meeting the satisfactorily buoyant demand for electricity less constrained by physical shortages. The Conservatives had clearly let the economy overheat for electoral advantage in 1955, but as soon as the election was over, clamped down with a credit squeeze and requests to trim expenditure below the agreed levels. Citrine, now more aware of the new world they lived in, was more willing to contemplate price increases to finance investment, but conflicting signals came from Whitehall about both the merit and the practicability of such a change. At times it seemed that price increases would be favoured as a means of raising self-financing and reducing pressure on the capital market; at others that rises would be deprecated as contributing to inflation. The dilemma was to persist, with no clear and consistent signal coming to the industry. Meanwhile, both on power station sites and on distribution works, with physical controls over materials gone, Central Authority exhortations to spending units to curtail expenditure were less effective. In 1955/6 budgets were generally overspent and by a larger margin than in earlier years. It was known that the financial controls within the industry left a good deal to be desired, but when the new Minister of Fuel and Power, Aubrey Jones, tried to tighten up in 1956 (even beginning the publication of annual investment targets in a bid to increase the Boards' commitment to them), he found it was not easy to impose such discipline when his target was fixed unreasonably low, as the Boards assured him it was. With the rest of the economy still showing healthy expansion, the Boards were soon faced with the option of disobeying Whitehall or failing in their statutory duty to supply new consumers, and they chose the former, with one Board bluntly saying they were ignoring the Government's financial allocation (which was then increased for the industry generally). Conservative Ministers were, then, no more able than Gaitskell to hold back the rising tide of demand for electricity, which, if the system were not to break down and new connections to be refused, the Boards had to follow up with new investment.

As their experience built up, the Treasury became less and less convinced that the role that had been envisaged for the nationalised industries in overall demand management was a desirable one. The public corporations – and especially the capital-intensive Electricity Boards – had, it is true, underpinned the sustained high level of both private and public investment spending in postwar years which was one option in a Keynesian strategy for the avoidance of slump and the maintenance of full employment.[22] In the 'fine tuning' required in year-to-year economic management, however, the record was less impressive. In most years, the Boards had spent more than their budget, and neither Whitehall's control of the Central Authority, nor the Central Authority's control over Area Boards and other spending units, was capable of accuracy within margins as large as five per cent (a margin by no means unusual in the private sector also). Over-spending sometimes exceeded this level even after such window-dressing as was feasible.[23] Even if the Treasury had been *able* to use electricity investment for 'fine tuning', however, the wisdom of doing so was now widely doubted. When the economy was overheating and the Government wished to cut investment demand, the over-expansion in sectors such as industry and housing usually placed demands on the electricity supply system which required increased rather than decreased investment. In such circumstances, cuts in one sector over which the Government happened to have direct control could merely create an imbalance and shortages. Short-term con-tracyclical changes in electricity investment were, moreover, ex-tremely difficult for the Boards to accommodate, given the long lead-times of their investment projects. Power station projects took four or five years, and major distribution schemes eighteen months. Large adjustments downwards required the costly cancellation of contracts (which the Boards understandably resisted), and sheer logistic and managerial problems also limited their capacity quickly to accelerate their planned programmes. Macroeconomic policy makers could, it seems, use general fiscal and monetary tools, more effectively than revisions of nationalised industry investment programmes, for short-term adjustments.

V

What was the upshot for resource allocation of the wrangles between the Electricity Boards and Whitehall in the first ten years of nationalisation? The share of the electricity supply industry in UK domestic capital formation rose from 7 per cent in 1948 (about the same as in the 1930s) to above 8 per cent in the mid-1950s.[24] This was, in the view of many contemporary economists,[25] whose conclusions have subsequently been accepted by economic historians,[26] too high. There were strong a priori arguments for this view, based on the industry's low achieved rate of return compared with potentially more profitable projects in the private sector. If free-market con-ditions had generally prevailed, and if the BEA had got all the investment resources it required at low interest rates, this conclusion would be unassailable. Yet these conditions patently did not apply. The resolution of the question thus depends on the extent to which the *actual* mix of physical controls, slowly improving financial disciplines and quantitative annual investment limitations were effective in limiting the very real possibility of over-expansion by the industry. That they were at least in part effective was clearly the case. Investment programmes were consistently cut back and the BEA remained short of power station capacity at peak times throughout their first ten years.

To say more precisely whether these cuts produced something like the optimal solution to the level of investment (though with the inconvenience of power cuts at the peak), is problematic in an economy which (even in the 1950s) was subject to considerable disequilibrium in prices and inherited production patterns. There are, however, a number of considerations which suggest that the economists who criticised the industry exaggerated their case. Firstly, the proportion of British investment resources devoted to electricity was, if anything, low by international standards,[27] so that, other things being equal,[28] Britain at least would appear to have suffered no greater investment 'distortion' than elsewhere.[29] Secondly, economists may have over-estimated the elasticity of demand for electricity, and thus exaggerated the distortions caused by prices that were too low. In some areas, such as domestic (especially space heating) sales (as we shall see in Chapter 7), the economists' criticism that the demand could have been more efficiently met by other fuels was generally convincing, but they greatly exaggerated the extent to which electricity investment was dominated by the need to meet this demand.[30] Moreover, while it is perhaps plausible that, because of such factors, there was *some* over-investment in electricity, the potential economic penalties of this misallocation were probably rather small.[31] There is certainly no reason to believe that the electricity industry *generally* wasted investment resources in the manner of, for example, the nationalised railway industry in the same period, which (far from making even the minimal return required by the public sector) incurred mounting annual losses, yet persisted in uneconomic investment programmes.

We have focussed attention in this chapter on the Government's control of aggregate investment levels, but government influence on the details of investment was, in some areas, no less strong. The supposed division between 'general policy' as a matter for the Minister, and 'detailed execution' as a matter for the Boards – which was implicit in much earlier discussion of the public corporation – proved in practice to be meaningless. As we shall see in subsequent chapters, a wide range of managerial decision making was subject to ministerial intervention, while over substantial areas of 'general' policy ministerial views made no significant impact. The whole bias of the leading engineers and managers in the industry was, of course, to maintain their independence both in the development of policy and in its execution. In pursuing this object, they had the formidable weapons of their superior knowledge and direct executive control. Whitehall recognised the wastefulness of attempting to duplicate their expertise,[32] though the Ministry of Fuel and Power had appointed expert advisers on both economics and science, perceiving the need for at least some expert technical knowledge if they were to exercise their overseeing role.

The long, arduous and structured process of conflict over the annual budgets gave the mandarins a chance to probe detailed questions of rural electrification, delays in connecting particular consumers, hire purchase finance, and other relatively minor areas. Their overall fuel policy role was also to give them influence over more central aspects of BEA decision making on the choice of fuel for power stations, particularly when oil and nuclear power began to look like attractive options to add to the industry's coal-fired base. The leading engineers and managers who were involved in these consultations often retained strong negative stereotypes of the civil service.[33] While they generally accepted the legitimacy of Whitehall interventions as 'bankers' to the industry in the annual investment review, when it came to discussion of other policies they were more likely to complain about the time that Whitehall committees and correspondence pre-empted, and to show impatience with civil service style. In some areas – notably labour relations policy – Citrine was able successfully to keep the mandarins and ministers at bay, but he lacked the independent powers of the old CEB to say a straight 'no' in the last resort on a point on which the Minister had strong feelings.

6

SYSTEM EXPANSION: THE AREA BOARDS

I think you might get these people [the Area Board chairmen] in the frame of mind that they are acting as Father Christmas rather than acting as commercial men running a business.

Professor Ronald Edwards, on the Committee of Inquiry into the industry, in discussion with Sir John Maud, Permanent Secretary of the Ministry, 12 July 1955.

Although the Central Authority initially resisted the more direct encroachment of Whitehall on the Area Boards (successfully insisting that communication should normally be through the Authority), the semi-political process which determined the Whitehall allocation of resources to electricity was mirrored within the British Electricity Authority. The division of power and cash between the Authority itself (responsible for generation) and the Area Boards (responsible for distribution) was subject to a complex process of bargaining not only with the Ministry but also internally, with discussion there directed as much to political, consensual ends as to traditional commercial disciplines. This was pre-eminently the case where the Area Boards were united in opposing the Central Authority or the Government (as on the Clow differential), though Citrine was more willing to give in to such pressure on matters where he respected the Board Chairmen's views, such as tariffs, than on matters where he was determined to impose his own, as in labour relations. However, the statutorily-entrenched power of the area chairmen meant that they were more successful than any other group within the Authority in forcing reconsideration of headquarters' views.

This consensual bargaining process also played a significant part in determining the allocation of resources between individual Area

Boards on matters on which their interests differed. The chairmen, jealous of their independence, would have been happy to see less uniformity in practice, but as the requirements of justifying the industry's policies to Whitehall became more apparent, they accepted (albeit often reluctantly) the Central Authority's point that consistency between Boards was easier to defend than were individual policies which each Board considered right. Attacks on the Area Boards from the press and the Conservatives also strengthened the instinct to develop a defence of their position through consistency. The Central Authority's ambition to standardise was also based on the role accorded to it by statute '. . . to co-ordinate the distribution of electricity by Area Boards and to exercise a general control over the policy of those Boards'.[1] Citrine sometimes threatened a directive as his ultimate bargaining counter, but Area Board chairmen could call his bluff and he usually preferred to search for collective agreement.

In some areas, the Central Authority's status, despite its statutory powers, was weak because of its own lack of experience and knowledge. The chairmen could not help but note, for example, that on tariff policy the headquarters staff were less expert than the former regulatory body, the Electricity Commissioners. The commercial department of the Central Authority was staffed at the top by three ex-CEB men who had been experts in the complex bulk tariff rules laid down in 1926 to secure equity between independent undertakings: a job which no longer existed. None of them had direct experience of retail tariff-making and they were to find most of their initiatives on tariffs blocked by the Area Board chairmen.

While some of the less experienced chairmen welcomed guidance from the Central Authority, the majority were more rugged in their resistance to headquarters encroachment on their commercial responsibilities. Harry Randall of the London Board was vociferous in opposition to headquarters, and made the running in the questioning at Area Board chairmen's meetings. For many years there were political overtones in this opposition, with Citrine seeing Randall as the representative of a capitalist rump in the industry which must be controlled. However, contrasts in personal style between chairmen inhibited concerted action on some matters and helped Citrine. Randall, for example, had a rather starchy personality, while Alderman Lewis, the ex-trade unionist chairman of the Midlands was rough and loquacious: they had no personal rapport. Dissident chairmen were, however, frequently able to gain the support of other chairmen on specific issues of Area Board independence, and it was these issues that became the substantive ones between the central regime and the Boards.

Some chairmen expressed their discontent with Citrine's centralising tendencies, for example, by asking to be released from their turn at occupying one of the four Central Authority seats reserved for them, or by sending deputies to headquarters meetings. This annoyed Citrine and he had formal resolutions passed requesting the presence of the chairmen, but these also were sometimes ignored. The chairmen met Citrine and his colleagues formally once a month, prior to the meeting of the Central Authority, and (again in the face of Citrine's active discouragement) sometimes co-ordinated their views by meeting in advance. Citrine was always reluctant to withdraw from a Central Authority position, but the more effective chairmen soon learned that careful preparation on committees beforehand and advance lobbying of Citrine and Self were a surer way of winning their point than the abrasive technique of frontal opposition. The sometimes strident expressions of independence at Area Board chairmen's meetings were often just theatrical reminders to Citrine and his headquarters colleagues that limits to consensus existed beyond which they would be unwise to step.

Once a consensus had been reached, it had no legal standing, but Citrine expected the chairmen to go back to their own Boards and secure acceptance of the common policy. Chairmen did not always agree with this interpretation, though they were aware that the Central Authority could in the last resort compel compliance by issuing a directive. This option was, however, never used without the agreement of the chairmen, and then only on those rare occasions when they felt it would help secure acceptance of unpopular measures by their colleagues and the broader public. More commonly, Citrine and Self took infinite pains to secure voluntary acceptance of central guidance, and were successful. In the early months after nationalisation, for example, the ex-trade unionist chairman of the North Western Board, George Gibson, initially opposed the much needed price rises (with the backing of his Board) but Citrine was able to talk them round.

The most potentially explosive area of contact between headquarters and the Boards was in financial control. In the early years, when physical investment allocations were more important, and no adequate financial procedures had been established, the Boards were keen to establish their independence in this area. The position of the

Central Authority was strong: they were responsible for the Boards as a whole breaking-even over a period of years; their approval was required for capital and current expenditure; and they raised the capital and controlled the reserves and bank-balances of the Boards. The Boards accepted the general financial oversight, and also the cuts imposed on their early capital budgets, at government behest, on some of the less essential items such as Board offices and shops, rural electrification and hire purchase finance. However, when the Central Authority's engineers and accountants suggested that they would require technical details of proposed capital schemes before authorising the expenditure, the area chairmen rebelled. The critics attacked the 'detailed time-wasting and expensive procedure involved in the proposals', and deplored the second-guessing of the decisions of responsible Boards which they implied. Faced with a determined revolt, the Central Authority settled for the submission of capital programmes with less detail. In the following years discussions continued between the officers at the Boards and at headquarters in an attempt to sort out a practical level of detail which preserved the Authority's control over general policy and coordination, while reserving clearly local matters to the Area Boards. The Authority had, however, conceded the central point that responsibility for technical efficiency and financial viability of individual schemes lay with the Area Boards.

This might be taken to imply that each Board should be financially self-supporting. Under the legislation this was not in fact required (only the Boards *as a whole* were required to break even 'taking one year with another'), but Citrine and his senior colleagues believed that it was a desirable principle that *each* Board should break even, and within a few years of nationalisation this was also tacitly accepted by the Boards. Some chairmen, notably Randall of the London Board, created considerable surpluses and reserves, and his Board was the only one never to make a loss. Others, such as the South Western, North Western and Midlands Boards, were less keen to raise tariffs to meet rising costs, and had to be given financial aid occasionally by the Central Authority from its reserves. The Authority spent a good deal of time trying to persuade such Boards to avoid deficits by raising tariffs to remunerative levels, but commercial disciplines were inevitably weakened by such dual responsibility and *ad hoc* decisions. This was also the case when external or internal politics, rather than commercial performance, seemed to be becoming a yardstick in financial allocations between Boards. In 1951, for example, the Boards had been asked by the Minister to cut their spending on rural electrification, and most did so; the South Western Board, by contrast, pressed on and a few years later were praised by the same Minister for pursuing this uneconomic development. They also received a grant of £250000 from the Central Authority to cover losses. Cecil Melling, the chairman of the Eastern Board, drew the inevitable lesson, and in a subsequent year overspent his budget by as much as 12 per cent. When the Central Authority carpeted him for this, he stated that he had done it both to meet statutory obligations and to make faster progress on rural electrification than agreed. He pointed out that, unlike the South Western Board, he was not asking for any subsidy. Self was 'reluctant to criticise a Board for showing enterprise' and no action was taken.

Such deliberate flouting of the financial control of the centre was rare, though overspending was, as we have seen, common, and financial controls were generally weak. Moreover, the cases that did occur (and the Central Authority's reluctant acquiescence in them) pointed up the importance of internal politics as well as commercial disciplines in determining both the Boards' behaviour and internal resource allocation. Some of the former private enterprise managers (notably E. H. E. Woodward on the Central Authority and Harry Randall at the London Board) had seen from the beginning that proper decentralisation required that the Boards relate capital expenditure to revenue-earning potential in order to retain direct control of their financial viability; and outside commentators were sometimes surprised that the Boards' decisions on capital expenditure to meet statutory obligations were made quite separately from the revenue estimates which determined their profitability. Yet this was in part a reflection of the special conditions they faced. Much of their investment was pre-determined by their statutory obligation to supply (which was restored in 1953 as general supply shortages disappeared), and their revenue could (given their quasi-monopoly position) be fixed (within broad limits) by the level of tariffs which they chose. Some schemes were, moreover, undertaken, even though it was known that they would make a loss, because of the statutory duty to supply. Inevitably, then, the logic of the more normal commercial practice of decentralisation to independent profit centres was compromised, irrespective of Central Authority preferences.

Citrine and Self also felt a duty to ensure some fairness between Boards in cases where resources or needs differed, or where temporary financial difficulties were encountered. There were, however, considerable practical problems for the Central Authority in disciplining this instinct by devising measures of performance alternative to the profit yardstick.[2] The Area Board barons liked to keep the Central Authority distant from their own fiefs, but they did come to court to bargain on the issues which had to be resolved between them; and when they did this personal and political factors could be as important as commercial or economic ones. Some of the Area Board chairmen could not help noticing that their colleagues who shouted loudest could sometimes induce appeasement, Citrine and Self seeming to show more regard for consensus than for the merits of the case. Of course, all human institutions must rely heavily on consensus, and it is proper that they should, but in the British Electricity Authority, partly because of the predilection of the chairmen and partly because of the difficulty of defining yardsticks, internal politics were to dominate commercial allocative mechanisms more than in most businesses.

While they were subject to important central pressures, the Area Chairmen and their Boards had considerable authority and status at the local level, which they sought to develop by rooting their Boards firmly in the local community. Municipalities had, prior to nationalisation, often controlled local electricity sales and distribution, and the 1947 Act required the Minister to establish Consultative Councils of consumers, to expand this tradition of consulting those who used the monopoly electricity service. Many former elected municipal electricity committee members were initially appointed to the Councils, but there were also other local personalities and representatives of local interest groups, notably farming, industry and the trade unions. On one issue which centrally concerned the Consultative Councils – electricity prices – their attitudes were predictable and damaging: the Councils generally added to the pressure for uneconomically low prices, though members who adopted an aggressively consumerist line were unlikely to find themselves reappointed by the Minister. The members who got most out of it, and were most appreciated by the Boards, were those who saw their role as a symbiotic mixture of representing consumer complaints to managers and presenting a favourable public relations image for the Board. This 'give-and-take' role was encouraged by the requirement that the chairman of the Consumer Consultative Council be appointed as a member of the Board, thus giving him direct access to the decision makers, but also creating a reciprocal responsibility. Within a few years, most Boards felt that the Consultative Councils helped to

Areas of the Boards, and of the corresponding
Generation Divisions of the Authority

1 London
2 South Eastern
3 Southern
4 South Western
5 Eastern
6 East Midlands
7 Midlands
8 South Wales
9 Merseyside
   and North Wales
10 Yorkshire
11 North Eastern
12 North Western
13 South-East Scotland
14 South-West Scotland

x South Western
   and South Wales
   Divisions extend
   to broken lines o
   their respective
   sides of Severn
   estuary

——— County boundaries
▬▬▬ Division and Area Board boundaries

0 10 20 40   60   80 100
          miles

Source: BEA, *Report and Accounts 1951/2*, p. ix.

Fig. 6.1 *British Electricity Authority and the Area Boards*

defuse individual complaints and to present a favourable image to the
public, and were willing to defer to them on some matters of general

policy of an essentially political or presentational nature, such as priorities in rural electrification or aspects of domestic charging. While the Conservative Political Centre later referred to the Councils as 'wet and windy', and consumerists felt they were inadequate, the Boards saw their work as a solidly realistic achievement.[3]

Within the Boards, policy formulation in practice lay largely in the hands of the chairman and his deputy (one of whom was usually an engineer) and their senior officers (usually four: an engineer, commercial officer, accountant, and secretary). Although the Boards had somewhat uninspiring regional names, most of them tried to present a more appealing local public face by using acronyms or logos such as 'MANWEB' for the Merseyside and North Wales Electricity Board, and 'Seeboard' for the South Eastern Board. Their areas varied considerably in size and in composition (see Figure 6.1). The smallest, the South-East Scotland Board, sold much less electricity than Birmingham Corporation (the largest pre-nationalisation under-taking). The most rural – and also small – South Western Board had no city larger than Bristol and a large rural hinterland. The London Board, by contrast, was heavily urbanised and had a dominant domestic load; whereas Boards in South Wales and the North had a preponderant industrial load.

The fourteen Area Boards themselves had to devolve some functions further and they initially set up about 500 local districts (slightly fewer than the number of pre-nationalisation undertakings). A district typically had 20–25000 consumers and covered 130 square miles, and initially they were grouped into an intermediate level of control, the 'sub-area'; with an average of five sub-areas in each Board. There was some variety in this local organisation. In some Boards devolution of management to the districts was restricted; other Boards were more adventurous. In some, districts were headed jointly by an engineer and a commercial manager (on the argument that there were essentially two different functions: system engineer-ing, and sales and contracting); in others each district had only one manager (usually an engineer). Some Boards tried to preserve a sense of identity, basing districts on pre-nationalisation undertakings (encouraging rivalry between them), while others aimed to blur old loyalties in merged districts, and encouraged increased cooperation between them. In all Boards, however, there was an increasing tendency to merge districts; and in a few, to eliminate the sub-area tier of management completely, decentralising management directly to enlarged districts. London, with its highly compact districts, took the lead in this, and moved to a two-tier rather than three-tier organisation. They ignored pressure from the Central Authority to await common agreement on a matter they were surely right in considering as one best left to the judgement of each area according to local conditions.

The advocates of reorganisation and nationalisation in the 1930s and 1940s had claimed there were potentially large gains in efficiency in distribution,[4] and, while their forecasts were probably exaggerated, the new Area Boards were able to reap some of these advantages of larger-scale distribution and more centralised management. Functions such as stores and meter testing and repair were centralised, and costs reduced. More specialist managers and salesmen were employed; and supplies of engineering and office equipment were standardised and thus cheapened. In the South Western Board, for example, it was decided to centralise accounting functions, reducing billing costs by more than a quarter in the first eighteen months, and there were further economies subsequently through mechanisation and centralisation on their Plymouth accounting office.[5] The biggest and most general gains, however, were in system engineering, as the Boards modified inherited plans for the reinforcement and extension of the distribution networks. The large wartime backlog of investment left considerable scope for economies in new investment, as in the first ten years the length of distribution mains in service were extended by nearly a third. Many older mains also required reinforcement to raise their capacity to match increased demand. For several years, however, with investment restricted, Boards had in parts of their areas to postpone such work. Here they attempted to persuade consumers not to install additional appliances which would overload the mains: where they failed in this, breakdowns inevitably followed.

The engineering works to extend and reinforce the system absorbed the bulk of the Area Boards' capital budgets, but could now be more efficiently planned. Whereas, before nationalisation, the planning of bulk supply points from the National Grid had been constrained by complex legal and financial negotiations between the CEB and the undertakings, engineers were now able to plan the cheapest effective layout, resulting in more supply points and increased usage of the high-voltage 132kV system for energy transfer and thus reduced transmission losses. An agreement with the Central Authority that the National Grid and local distribution systems would be planned to minimise joint costs (without regard to the incidence of expenditure on the Authority or the Boards) largely overcame the earlier inefficiencies of divided ownership. The local distribution systems, usually based on lines of 66kV, 33kV and 11kV, were also now more rationally planned, with the aim of minimising all local distribution costs without regard to the former local undertaking boundaries which had often borne no relation to the electrical load characteristics of an area. The long-run gains were greatest in areas such as London, where an illogical patchwork-quilt of undertakings had persisted before nationalisation, and jealousies between municipalities and companies had limited cooperation in rational distribution development. London began with one of the most expensive distribution systems and developed one cheaper than some other Boards. Moreover, the new Area Board planning not only reduced the costs of developing the system, but also significantly improved the security of supply, with most towns served by several alternative sources on the new integrated distribution networks designed by the Area Boards.

These benefits were not, of course, costless, and there were aspects of the reorganisation which some managers felt were decreasing their efficiency. The centralisation introduced an extra tier of administration at the Area Board headquarters, and in one Board, the North Eastern, this extra tier was somewhat unnecessarily introduced into an area which prior to nationalisation had had a rather efficient, centralised company undertaking, in order to conform to the organising committee's purely advisory organisational blueprint for Boards. In all Boards there was certainly an increase in red tape and committee work, and perhaps a loss of initiative and an unwillingness to take responsibility among managers and engineers, and, in a very few cases, simple unchecked extravagance. Yet, the dangers of centralisation certainly seem to have been avoided in the main spending area, that of system engineering. Subsequent criticism of inadequate standardisation suggests indeed that there was some sensitivity to the benefits of using the remaining economic life of non-standard systems and older equipment within Boards. The independent philosophies of system design in the Merseyside & North Wales and London Boards and the fast movement to a two-tier rather than three-tier management devolution in the latter Board also suggest that the drive to standardise did not significantly constrain local initiative where local conditions were thought to require a less orthodox approach.[6]

Whatever the balance of gains and losses, the nationalised Area

Boards were certainly more frugal than their predecessors had expected to be in their capital expenditure. In the War, distribution expenditure had been running at only a fifth of the prewar level, and the plans prepared by the undertakings for the Electricity Commissioners show they expected to continue to spend more than half of all their capital on developing distribution, as they had in the 1930s. In the first ten years of nationalisation the proportion in fact declined to around a third. This was partly because of government restrictions on capital spending on distribution to below what engineers in the industry considered desirable. In some cases, for example, to keep within trimmed budgets, Boards had to install mains of too low a capacity to accommodate reasonable expectations of future load growth (causing greater expense later on); they also retained old vehicles and offices with excessively high running costs to save on capital expenditure. The Central Authority also felt that Whitehall pruned the Area Boards' budgets, which could be relatively easily adjusted to meet short-term government policy, more severely than their own budget for generation.[7] Yet the substantial reduction in the planned expenditure on distribution suggests that the gains from reorganisation did outweigh the losses, and enabled the Boards to expand the system on a more economical basis than their predecessors would have found possible.

The pruning of distribution budgets by government also restricted the Area Boards in an aspect of standardisation which many were anxious to pursue: that of converting non-standard AC consumers, and those who still had DC supplies, to the British standard 240V AC domestic supply. There was an extraordinary range of voltages: the London Board, for example, (where the fragmentation of undertakings had been extreme) inherited 17 different DC and 20 different AC voltages. In earlier decades it had been generally agreed that there would be benefits from standardisation, but with the benefits accruing variously to consumers, undertakings generally and appliance manufacturers, while the costs fell on the non-standard undertakings alone, there had been a failure to agree on finance for a common scheme. Meanwhile the estimated costs of standardisation were increasing as consumers purchased more non-standard appliances. There were nearly three million non-standard consumers (nearly a third of the total) on nationalisation, and this number increased as resources were simply not available to convert local networks when new houses required a supply. However, as materials supplies improved in the mid-1950s, the Boards increased their expenditure on standardisation. They usually started on the DC networks, where the benefits from both reinforcement and standardisation (which were usually tackled together) were greatest. With a statutory duty to promote standardisation, the nationalised Boards were willing to go ahead with these schemes, paying for the conversion of consumers' apparatus as well as of their own mains, even where the returns to themselves were not adequate. There were, of course substantial external benefits – through greater consumer convenience when moving house and cheaper standard equipment and appliances – and such a policy was, arguably, economically justified. There would, indeed, have been a good economic case for some sharing of the burdens between Boards, since all benefited from standardisation though some incurred larger costs than others. However, Randall (with more concern for principled commercial independence than for the economic logic of external benefits) refused to ask for such a subvention from central reserve funds for his London Board (which carried the greatest burden of standardisation expenditure).

In all Boards, the highest priority was accorded to the connection of new consumers who would otherwise be without a supply. On nationalisation around a quarter of households in Britain still lacked a supply of electricity, most of them in urban slums (which had been uneconomic to connect either because of their short expected life or the inability of the occupants or unwillingness of their landlords to pay for internal wiring). The proportion without electricity was to be reduced to less than one in ten in the first decade of nationalisation.[8] The principal beneficiaries were those who moved to the new houses built in the postwar housing drives, which (with a few exceptions in remote rural areas) all had electricity as a basic service. More than 2.7 million new houses were built in the first ten years of nationalisation, and 1954, the peak year of Macmillan's housing drive, saw 354000 completed.[9] In Britain as a whole the number of domestic electricity consumers rose from 9.7 millions on nationalisation to 14.3 millions ten years later, reflecting the increase in the number of households as well as a sharp reduction in the proportion without electricity. For many of the poor, the novelty of electricity was a symbol of access to a new postwar affluence, though consumption by such consumers typically remained small, and the Boards reckoned that many of these connections would be economic only in the longer run. The capital charges typically incurred by the Boards on new domestic connections were as much as £1 per quarter,[10] while many consumers (especially new ones) paid little more than this (and thus insufficient to cover the additional costs of supplying current) in the early years. Although the real cost of electricity had fallen dramatically, the quarterly electricity bill for small consumers used to budgeting weekly could still present a financial challenge. Over a quarter of households prior to nationalisation had opted for a coin pre-payment meter to ease the burden, though some Boards now discouraged this (because of the high cost of installation and adjustment, and the risk of theft). Quarterly bills were thus more widely used by the mid-1950s, even for the relatively poor consumers.

The Boards usually carried out the work of laying distribution mains themselves, though sometimes they used independent contractors. They were also in the business of wiring installations for consumers (in houses, factories, schools, offices, shops) beyond the mains terminals, and this brought them into direct competition with the 7500, usually small, independent electrical contractors. They agreed with the Electrical Contractors' Association at an early stage that they would operate on 'fair and unsubsidised' commercial lines. A few Boards, seeing this as an essential part of their electricity service, expanded their contracting activities enthusiastically, while others left the business largely to private contractors. The London Board, which inherited a particularly efficient contracting subsidiary from a company undertaking, expanded it further (even being allowed for special contracts to compete in the area of other Boards) and it became the most profitable part of their operation. Inevitably, however, the Electrical Contractors' Association were annoyed if their members were undercut by nationalised Boards. There was thus some political pressure from Conservative Ministers to ensure that Boards allocated overheads to their contracting activities properly and secured an economic profit, but the contractors' association director was so politically inept in following this up that Citrine had no difficulty in exposing him to Whitehall as a biased anti-nationaliser who was unwilling to accept a reasonable accommodation. Most Boards were, however, able to reach agreement with local contractors on acceptable principles of fair competition, to which they formally agreed to adhere. The Boards were far from innocent, however, and when they later developed a proper accounting system to allocate overheads fairly it was found that there had indeed been some unfair cross-subsidisation to their contracting accounts. As we shall see in the next chapter, their commercial urge to expand was not adequately disciplined by proper costing, though in this particular case the distortions caused were quite small.

The most difficult part of the Boards' programme of expanding the distribution system was in rural areas. The method of distribution by overhead lines on wooden poles (rather than underground cables) was cheaper per mile, and usually tolerated in the countryside (especially when the Boards pointed out that it was a pre-condition of receiving the benefit of electricity supplies), but even so distribution to scattered rural premises was more expensive per consumer than in compact urban areas. Most of the larger villages which could economically be connected already had electricity supplies on nationalisation, but rural pressure groups had been successful in gaining an opposition amendment to the 1947 Electricity Act safeguarding further development by enjoining the Boards to 'secure, so far as practicable, the development, extension to rural areas and cheapening of supplies of electricity'.[11] Prior to nationalisation rural areas had been served either by companies (which charged prices which reflected the higher costs of rural supplies), or by nearby local authority undertakings extending beyond their municipal boundaries. In the latter case, rural consumers were also typically charged higher prices, since the pressure from the local voters and ratepayers in the town was usually effective in curbing any idea of subsidy to the rural areas to meet the higher costs of supply.

On nationalisation, this local democratic pressure was removed, and most Boards took the statute as meaning they should do their best to extend supplies to rural areas even if they incurred losses in doing so which had to be made up from surpluses elsewhere. It was agreed at an early stage (principally at Citrine's insistence) that sales in urban and rural areas should be at common prices, so that many rural dwellers already having a supply had prices reduced, though new consumers distant from the mains still had to pay a one-off contribution or line rental (which varied according to the Board) to meet part of the cost of connection. The Boards preferred the wholesale development of rural districts (rather than piecemeal individual connections) since this reduced their costs, and they were generally able to use public meetings and written publicity to bring collective pressure on all potential consumers in a village to sign up for a supply, thus making comprehensive zoned development possible. In the early years, the reluctance of some Boards to incur losses, the physical shortages of essential supplies like the wooden poles, and government cuts in their capital budgets, all delayed their rural programmes. None the less, the proportion of farms connected rose from 32 per cent in 1948 to 47 per cent in 1953.

Most of this rural development was unremunerative, and the South Western Board, with one of the largest rural populations and an accumulating deficit, determined to resolve its problems by political lobbying. Stanley Steward, its first chairman – who had been an electrical manufacturer in the private sector – mobilised considerable pressure from the 'county' set on his consumer Consultative Council, and lobbied both the Government and the Central Authority for a subvention. The Minister refused a direct subsidy, but brought pressure on the Central Authority to do something. They felt that a good deal of the South Western Board's troubles were brought on by excessive expenditure and inadequate tariffs, and Steward found little sympathy from the other Boards, since some of them had equally serious system extension, reinforcement and standardisation problems, and were financing them by adequate tariffs. By 1953, however, with Conservative rural constituencies pressing their MPs for a rural electrification subsidy, and the Minister looking more favourably on capital expenditure for this purpose, the Area Board chairmen hammered out a national plan for rural electrification, which was finally agreed at an extended and controversial meeting at a country hotel in Moretonhampstead in 1953. It was reckoned that, within ten years, 85 per cent of farms could be connected (enough to satisfy the Minister and ease political pressure), though the overall programme would cost £130 millions and result in annual losses of the order of £4 millions. Some Boards were not keen to bear these substantial losses. The South Eastern Board, for example, generally refused to subsidise rural connections (charging the full cost to new rural consumers), and other Boards tried to minimise their commitment. Still more Boards disliked the idea of subsidising other areas. None the less, the South Western Board was clearly in financial difficulties, and in 1954 the Central Authority did make a subvention of £250000 from central reserves, with the possibility of further help five years later, hoping that the Board would now make reasonable charges to its consumers to cover expenditure. Randall for the London Board did not fail to point out the contrast between this and his own refusal of central funds for standardisation (for which there was in fact a far sounder economic case). Some feared that the concession would weaken the financial discipline on the Boards, though in fact the conditions imposed by the Central Authority raised the South Western Board's financial targets and they were soon in healthy surplus.

The agreed national rural electrification programme proceeded faster than planned, and by 1958 72 per cent of farms were already connected. Compared with earlier, politically-inspired rural schemes in countries such as France (with a larger rural vote), British rural electricity development was efficiently executed with, generally, lines of adequate capacity, planned zoned development, and the revenue–cost gap eased by a higher consumption than was common overseas. If it offended against purist commercial canons, then it could fairly be pointed out that the alternative might easily (like overseas systems) have offended more. The price to urban consumers of bearing the losses incurred (probably of the order of 2 per cent of their bills) would have been considered by many to be an acceptable concession to the aspirations of country dwellers, and perhaps few would have endorsed the complaint by a contemporary free-market economist that 'a slum dweller has to contribute to the cost of providing electricity for a country mansion'.[12]

Yet it was undeniable that the Conservative political pressure to extend rural electrification had led to a diversion of scarce capital resources into investments which were known to be unremunerative and in fact turned out to be so. There were, moreover, rather more poor urban dwellers still lacking electricity supply than there were rural dwellers, and investment in the reinforcement, standardisation and extension of urban supplies (some of which the Boards considered would be remunerative) was being cut back while this uneconomic development of rural areas was pressed forward. When the pressures of the market and of urban local democracy (which had earlier restricted rural development) were replaced by ministerial investment control and rural pressure group activity at the national level, the consequences for efficiency and equality were not always those which the rival contemporary slogans of left and right might lead one to expect from them. Such pressures would, however, probably have materialised in the postwar political climate, whether the industry had been nationalised or not. For some chairmen, moreover, the prospect of playing Father Christmas (which their rural electrification largesse offered them) provided a not entirely unwelcome opportunity to affirm their commitment to the local community, and the voices of discontent raised against the policy were few.

7

COMMERCIAL DEVELOPMENT:
PRICING FOR GROWTH

The electricity industry has completely failed to set up a pricing system which will enable it to produce amounts of electricity which are in the national interest. It is interested only in selling as much as possible, consistent with covering total costs, and not in the least in selling the right amounts.

> I. M. D. Little, *The Price of Fuel* (Oxford, 1953) p. 151.

the technical leaders of the industry are inspired by few ideas except the value of expansion

> Memo, Sir Andrew Clow to Hugh Gaitskell, 20 May 1948, in file POWE 14/365 (Public Record Office).

The objective of the Area Board chairmen in the 1950s is perhaps best interpreted as maximising the rate of growth of electricity sales consistent with covering book costs overall. In the early years, they were constrained severely by the shortage of generating capacity and, in many areas, by the low capacity of inherited distribution mains; though the backlog of investment in both was, by the mid-1950s, being overcome. Even in the earlier period, however, it was difficult to hold back the commercial urges of line managers, though some marketing effort was initially canalised into the job of discouraging the sale of electric fires or persuading people to go carefully in the use of electricity at peak times. When accused of promoting sales at a time when they were incapable of supplying the electricity, the Board chairmen were robustly defensive. They were doing their best to restrict peak growth, but neither the Central Authority nor the

Government, they argued, should attempt, for short-term reasons, to blunt the commercial edge of the industry. They were anxious to build up their Board's commercial skills and saw this as an essential part of gaining the advantages of larger-scale management after nationalisation.

Earlier, the large undertakings had been able to appoint specialised commercial officers to deal with the special selling requirements in markets such as that for industrial power. Many pre-nationalisation undertakings had also entered the retail market for electrical appliances, with shops or 'showrooms' where consumers could pay their electricity bills and get advice on electrical products. In many cases, however, the new Boards felt that their predecessors had not gone far enough. The smaller undertakings generally had possessed only weakly-developed sales functions, and they had sometimes had to call on outside expertise. This had occasionally been available from the Central Electricity Board, whose own commercial staff negotiated some large industrial sales contracts for undertakings. More generally, the cooperatively financed Electrical Development Association (EDA) ran joint industry advertising campaigns and provided advice from specialists in particular areas such as commercial or industrial sales. Citrine, with his instinct for seeking stability and continuity, wanted to preserve the EDA intact on nationalisation, but the area chairmen felt the Boards should take over its work. After a year of arguments, Citrine finally relented and the EDA's local work was taken on and expanded by the Area Boards, though its London headquarters, with a staff of 67, survived as a formally separate organisation but with its £150000 annual budget financed principally by the industry. (It was not finally to be absorbed as the industry's central marketing department until 1968.) Many of the chairmen were also anxious to strengthen their presence in the retailing of electrical goods by extending the number of shops and releasing the commercial drive of managers. Earlier some engineers had derided this side of the business as mere 'ironmongery', and there had also been political constraints on development. The opening of shops, for example, had been restricted in some municipal undertakings by pressure from Conservative town councils dominated by local shopkeepers who feared the competition. In some such areas the shops the Boards inherited were known as 'showrooms' and were precisely that: places where electrical appliances could be shown, but not sold. Many in the industry hoped that such political restrictions would now end.

None the less, sales promotion was, in the early years of shortages, pursued in a restrained way. Advertising was directed to restricting peak sales, and capital spending on the building of new shops was limited by the shortages of building materials. The goods they had previously concentrated on selling, like cookers, were difficult to move when power cuts were a regular winter occurrence; and many appliances were only available in small quantities. Staff training stressed service and advice rather than aggressive selling, and people found the Board shops (or 'service centres' as they were rather coyly called before the 1960s) helpful on matters such as fixing plugs, and advice on safety, reliability, running costs and brand choice. More aggressive marketing was carried out by door-to-door canvassers in some Boards, and promotional advertising also increased as the supply situation got easier. The first big postwar EDA campaign was in 1954: the 'Four Foundations of Modern Living' advertisements promoted electric cookers, water heaters, refrigerators and washing machines, and were heavily supplemented by the Area Boards' own campaigns. The Boards also aimed to expand sales through the provision of hire and credit facilities. They had inherited a large number of hire schemes, and sometimes (particularly for cookers in working class areas) found it economic to continue these.[1] In the mid-1950s nearly half of all cookers used by consumers were still on hire. In general, however, they found that consumers took better care of appliances on hire purchase and that servicing costs were lower. They thus increasingly promoted this alternative means of easing the financial burden of appliance ownership. From the beginning of 1956, pleased with the success of hire purchase, they abandoned hire schemes for cookers, after securing agreement from the gas industry, their major rival, to do the same.[2] They did, however, continue to offer exceptionally generous hire purchase terms on cookers: one Board, for example, offered repayments over ten years and a free parts and replacement service over that period. On other appliances, terms were less generous and usually subject, like those of other retailers, to government credit restrictions.

In the 1950s, the Boards found the Conservative Government increasingly concerned about their shops' competition with the private sector of electrical retailing. Ministers and MPs complained about their allegedly 'luxurious' service centres or excessive advertising in one breath, while berating the nationalised industries in the next breath for being insufficiently 'commercial'. Despite some pressure from sales staff to be allowed a more adventurous policy of price cutting and quantity marketing, the Boards agreed to maintain manufacturers' list prices in order not to offend competing retailers, though there was some disguised price-cutting in their favourable hire purchase terms, especially for cookers. As with their installation and contracting accounts (p. 72, above), later investigation showed that there was some inadequate accounting for overheads on retailing. It also provided some justification for Conservative Government pressure, showing that their intervention was not simply politically-motivated protectionism of their own supporters in private retailing. The Conservatives' attempts to deal with it were hardly fair to the Boards, however. In the mid-1950s, when the private sector finance houses were increasing their facilities for private retailers, the Government withheld some of the funds the Boards requested for developing their own hire purchase schemes, thus further hobbling them against the competition. Rather more reasonably, the Government also insisted that they raise the interest charge in hire purchase schemes to market rates (rather than the privileged rates at which the Boards borrowed capital from the Treasury). Even so, a rise in the proportion of appliance sales on hire purchase from only a tenth on nationalisation to nearly a half ten years later enabled them to retain their share in the growing retail market for electrical goods at about the 25 per cent level which they inherited on nationalisation.[3] By then they were selling more than half a million major appliances annually.

The industry's own appliance selling effort was not dictated purely by its retailing interests, but was biased towards winning that part of the domestic electricity load which most helped them to increase electricity sales while minimising costs overall. An important aspect of the industry's own cost structure (which shaped their strategy) was the high cost of servicing a small account, and of cabling and metering a house which used little electricity. In many homes, apart from the essential lighting load, there were only infrequently used appliances such as electric irons or low-consumption ones such as radios. The charge to such consumers did, of course, reflect some of the higher cost of supplying small quantities of electricity. Nearly one-third of domestic consumers in 1948 were on very high flat-rate tariffs designed for small users, but these were gradually induced by Area Boards to shift to 'two-part' or 'block' tariffs which had been adopted by most of the larger, progressive undertakings before nationalisation. These encouraged greater electricity use and more accurately reflected the underlying decreasing cost structure of domestic supply. Under a two-part tariff there was a basic standing charge (aiming to cover costs of servicing the account, connecting supply and providing generating capacity) and a low charge per kWh of electricity purchased. Under a block tariff, the initial kWh purchased carried a high price, but if consumption increased the extra blocks of kWh were charged at a significantly lower rate. The effect of both tariffs was the same: the more electricity the consumer used, the less he would on average pay per kWh. The Boards directed their marketing policy to the same expansionary end as their electricity tariffs: trying to sell those appliances – particularly cookers and water heaters – which used additional large quantities of electricity. Whereas a consumer using electricity only for lighting, an iron, a radio and a vacuum cleaner might use under 300kWh a year, the addition of one heavy current-using appliance like an immersion water heater or a cooker would more than quadruple that basic demand.

In connecting new houses, the Boards made generous allowances for such future load growth in distribution cables, though, in the early years especially, the shortage of materials inhibited the adoption of an expansionary sales and investment policy. Another initially important barrier to the spread of appliance use was the limited capacity on the consumers' side of the terminals. Many homes, especially the older ones, were wired for lighting only or had only one or two, low-powered socket outlets.[4] The Boards' own contracting services and the customer canvassing activities of their salesmen played a part in remedying this situation; and in most new houses 'ring' mains, with a range of socket outlets and the new standard 13 amp fused plugs, became the norm. There was a temporary setback to this trend in Macmillan's housing drive, when housing standards were cut to increase construction speeds. The expense of twelve lighting points and six socket outlets (as high as £30 in the mid-1950s when this was being promoted as a desirable minimum) also deterred some builders. None the less by the mid-1950s some 58 per cent of consumers had power sockets of about five amps rating, with an average of 3.4 sockets each, and many new houses had nine or more.

In the 1950s only a quarter of the growth in sales of electricity to domestic consumers came from newly-connected homes and another quarter from the extended use of existing appliances, but as much as half came from newly-purchased appliances. Irons and radios had been the only appliances owned by the majority of consumers before the War and they were joined by electric fires at the end of it. By the mid-1950s only two other appliances had reached majority ownership: vacuum cleaners (which had already been well-established in the 1930s) and televisions (which, though new, proved the most rapid growth area, approaching 50 per cent ownership levels among consumers by 1957). On most appliances (except cookers which were exempt) the high postwar level of purchase tax (varying between 50 per cent and 100 per cent for much of this period), government restriction of credit facilities, and the limited adoption of modern design and mass production techniques severely limited the market size. Refrigerators were especially expensive and only one in ten consumers had them by 1957, while washing machines (few of which were automatic) had reached only one home in five. In the first ten years of nationalisation, the 'age of affluence' was, for most people, still on the horizon, though the taste for consumer durables was visibly spreading.

It was the thermal load – cooking, water heating and electric fires – which created the greatest challenge for the industry's domestic sales strategy. Their success in winning this load (which formed the bulk of domestic sales) explains why domestic consumers accounted for almost a third of the Area Boards' sales in the first ten years, rather more than was typical in other industrialised countries. The spearhead of their sales drive was cooking and water heating, in which their major competitors were the gas boards. Gas cookers were cheaper to buy and operate than electric cookers, and the Electricity Boards discussed the possible production of a cheap standard cooker to boost sales. They failed to agree on a design, but the 'modern' image of electric cooking, particularly among young housewives, led to a gradual expansion of cooker sales. The improved design of hotplates (and faster electric kettles for boiling water) also enhanced the image of electric cooking. The Boards were conscious that cooking was generally an off-peak load (and thus cheap to supply), and, to reflect this advantage to themselves and meet gas competition, they generally accepted lower retail mark-ups on cookers than was usual on other appliances. The consequence of this policy (already well established in many areas before nationalisation) was that they had a virtual monopoly of electric cooker sales, other retailers finding the trade unattractive. Although the gas industry retained the larger market share for cooking overall, more than a quarter of consumers had electric cookers by 1958 and electricity for cooking continued to account for a fifth of domestic electricity sales.

There was also competition with gas (and with oil and coal) in the more rapidly growing market for water heating. At the end of the

War, around a half of British households still lacked a fixed bath with hot, running water, but electricity played a part in changing this (whether as the only heat source or as summer immersion heating to complement water heating by the more common coal-fired back boilers). By 1958 more than a quarter of consumers had electric water heating (compared with an eighth on nationalisation) and water heaters accounted for about a quarter of all domestic electricity sales. Electricity was still more expensive than gas on a 'heat-only' basis, but its cleanliness, relative cheapness of installation, and convenience were powerful selling factors, and the rapidly rising trend of gas prices was gradually narrowing the gap between them.

Competition with gas was non-existent in many rural areas which lacked gas supplies but was at its most fierce in new urban housing estates. Most electricity men were convinced that, just as in lighting they had outmatched gas completely, it was only a matter of time before they did the same in other uses. To many it seemed that for new houses to be carcassed for gas as well as electricity involved an unnecessary duplication of expense. Their patronising public attitude to their old and stagnant gas competitor[5] was complemented locally by fierce competition to win the new housing market. Each Board devised its own policy, sometimes offering developers incentives like free connection of a new housing estate if they installed electric cooking or water heating or an agreed minimum of sockets. The gas industry legitimately complained that this competition was sometimes far from fair: the Electricity Boards were using the leverage provided by the necessity of electric lighting to try to exclude gas and deprive consumers of a free choice. The Electricity Boards' defence (that the offers reflected their costs because small consumers were expensive to supply) was plausible in principle, but in a few Boards collapsed under more careful probing, and allegations of unfair competition continued to flow both ways between the industries. There is, of course, always a danger that, in industries with some monopoly power, an element of competition, far from being beneficial, will induce uneconomic cross-subsidisation to win business, and this certainly happened in some areas. However, the controls over local management in this respect were tightened up from the mid-1950s onwards. It is, moreover, debateable whether the dynamic, competitive stimulus of the rivalry between the two industries also had good effects in sharpening the commercial edge of both of them. Certainly that was the view of many of the senior managers who welcomed this exposure to the tests of the market-place as an important discipline and validation of the 'business' status of the nationalised Boards.

The Achilles' heel of their competition with gas, and, more particularly, with coal (which still remained the mainstay of domestic heating in Britain) was the sale of electric fires. We have seen (pp. 30–1, above) that the vast expansion in the number of such fires in the postwar years had provided consumers with a way of avoiding the consequences of coal rationing, but the effects on the electricity supply system were devastating. Although in public statements the Boards tended to minimise this effect, their own load experts reckoned that space heating accounted for a significant proportion of the load at peak times. (It was, of course, the load at peak times which imposed the highest costs on the system, partly because it was then that the least efficient power stations were used for generating, but principally because, since electricity could not be stored, it was the peak load which determined expenditure on new capacity.) Appliances like cookers and water heaters tended to be used at off-peak times, but the use of electric fires was concentrated on the colder times in winter which coincided with system peak demand. In the extreme case, a consumer who bought a one-bar electric fire for thirty shillings and paid less than a penny per hour for the electricity at peak time, imposed costs on the Electricity Boards of at least £60 for the kW of power station capacity needed to meet the demand. In practice, not all fires were used at the peak, but even at the higher real prewar price levels, research had shown that only about a third of the costs imposed by the peak space heating demand were being recovered in contemporary domestic tariffs. It is hardly surprising that marketing efforts in the 1930s had typically concentrated on other appliances.[6]

The attitude of the nationalised Boards to the accelerating growth of the postwar space heating load was ambivalent. They generally did not promote the sale of fires through showrooms or canvassers, and in the Eastern Board even banned their sale for several years until the peak capacity shortage eased. Yet, of course, electric heating remained attractive to consumers (most of whom by then had fires or, if the Boards refused to sell them, could obtain them from other shops). The view that keeping warm was socially undesirable was not a convincing argument for most consumers, whatever appeals to their spirit of cooperation on peak use were made. The common misery imposed by coal rationing could be avoided by the simple expedient of plugging in and switching on, and in the later 1940s about two-fifths of domestic electricity sales were for space heating. There were, moreover, many commercial men within the Boards who felt that in the long run it would be desirable and economic to win the space heating load. All but a few households in Britain relied for heating on solid fuel fires in the principal room, and few considered it necessary to heat bedrooms or bathrooms continuously, even in winter. Many electric fires were thus used as intermittent bedroom heating at night, or to heat the main room on cooler spring or autumn evenings when the coal fire had not been needed during the day. In British conditions, electric heating seemed a natural complementary heating source at a time when central heating with individual room control was virtually unknown. Many in the industry felt it was worth while taking risks on the peak space heating load, by keeping prices sufficiently low to attract in addition such off-peak evening or spring and autumn space heating loads, as well as the cooking and water heating sales. Others (who were more justly accused of commercial megalomania or electrical messianism by critics) felt that the 'all-electric' future was near at hand, and that it was only a matter of time before all heating – continuous or intermittent – would be by electricity.

The crux of the debate was whether this was the most cost-effective way of meeting the demand for heating in Britain,[7] and the Boards were under considerable pressure from the Government to justify their commercial policy, which seemed to be attracting peak loads at uneconomic prices. We have seen the deep resentment of the chairmen at Gaitskell's imposition of the Clow differential, which was an attempt to create a pricing structure which reflected the higher winter peak costs (pp. 36–8, above). Although the Government had then retired hurt, the Clow Committee's more general criticisms of the industry's slowness in responding to the need to limit the peak by experimentation with load limiters or time-of-day tariffs remained, both within government and from bodies like the Federation of British Industries. The Central Authority were, however, able to continue to deflect this criticism. A government committee, investigating fuel and power policy under Viscount Ridley in 1952, suggested tighter control of pricing policies to ensure fair competition between the fuel industries. This, the committee felt, was important if (as they recommended, and the fuel industries readily agreed) a system of price competition with free consumer choice was maintained, as the best way of ensuring efficiency in the allocation of resources in the energy sector.[8] The Minister's response was to set up a coordinating committee of the nationalised fuel industry chairmen.

They were, however, able successfully to fob him off with various working parties, with joint industry–civil service membership, to look at detailed questions such as the principles of pricing and the possibility of load limiters. Predictably the committees and working parties achieved little. They spent small amounts of money on load limitation experiments, but decided to do nothing. On pricing, the conclusions which could be generally agreed were so flabby and meaningless that they might have made even the most brazen practitioner of newspeak blush. It was sensibly decided not to publish the draft White Paper they prepared. It is perhaps reassuring that they at least recognised utter nonsense when they wrote it, if disappointing that this was essentially a confession of failure by a Ministry whose central function had been to coordinate energy policy. It was accepted within the Ministry that the fuel industry chairmen's coordinating committee (which rarely met) existed solely in order to provide an illusion of activity and allay parliamentary criticism.

The industry thus managed to maintain its freedom on this central aspect of commercial policy making, but its competence in living up to this challenge left much to be desired. In the abstract, it is true, the principles they professed were exemplary. The official Central Authority view was that their prices should fully reflect costs and that the 'all-electric' home was not a practicable proposition, since solid fuel would be more economical for continuous space heating. However, they felt it important that consumers should retain the freedom of choice so that those who found the extra cost of electrical 'refined heat' worthwhile because of its cleanliness and convenience were free to pay for it. They also stressed the importance of maintaining a price structure which continued to attract off-peak loads, such as cooking, water heating and non-winter space heating, and which would enable them to increase the consumption of small consumers to more economic levels. In justifying their policies, however, they sometimes stooped to making public statements that were palpable nonsense: denying that space heating was a peak load, and devoting efforts commensurate with those of the ostrich to shift discussion to more defensible territory.[9] The stridency of their assertions tended to grow in inverse proportion to the extent of their knowledge on costs. Outside critics, of which the most devastating was the Oxford economist Ian Little, had no difficulty in showing that their arguments 'fail to wriggle out of the obvious',[10] which was that much of the domestic thermal load was being sold below cost and was thereby winning heating markets which could be more efficiently supplied by alternative fuels at lower overall national cost.

This controversy could in principle have been resolved if the Electricity Boards had had effective knowledge of their own costs in meeting specific loads, but they conspicuously failed to develop and use the research necessary to establish this. Their main source of information was meter reading, which, of course, told them nothing about what purposes domestic electricity was used for, and, more importantly for their costs, about what times of day it was used. Some of the defenders of the domestic load, such as Dennis Bellamy (chairman of the Yorkshire Board), occasionally quoted cost and load data to justify their views, but these were based on such a biased sample of observations that it was difficult for any serious enquirer to accept them at face value.[11] In most Boards, commercial officers were preoccupied with the immense task of standardising the mass of different consumer tariffs inherited from the separate undertakings on nationalisation, avoiding rapid change which would upset consumers, but producing a coherent, standard charge which would be defensible.[12] Faced with these immediate problems, few of them had time to reflect that such an exercise might logically be based on proper cost research.

A basis for such costing investigations had existed in a team at the Electrical Research Association, jointly supported by the more forward-looking pre-nationalisation undertakings. On nationalisation this small research staff, under a refugee from Nazi Germany, Paul Schiller, had been taken over by the BEA's commercial department. They continued their research, but their reports were no longer published (as they had been up to 1948); and, at a time when cost research was more clearly needed than ever before, Schiller's team was starved of funds and talent. Many Area Board chairmen were also dilatory in providing the researchers with information, and opposed the expenditure of resources on this research (preferring to concentrate commercial research on appliance development). Most chairmen remained implacably opposed to any rethinking of their basic commercial philosophy as a result of the limited investigations which were possible, and Schiller's results were deliberately and systematically suppressed, since they showed the outside critics to be right on the space heating load. Schiller had demonstrated the danger of space heating sales before nationalisation and he continued to dissent on that issue within the BEA headquarters, backed by a genuine concern to advance scientific knowledge in this area.

Unfortunately, the manner of his presentations and his attitude to criticism tended to alienate support for his case further, though his views were balanced and based on careful research. (They did, for example, show that the external critics, who claimed that the cooking and water heating loads were fully on-peak and failed to cover costs, were mistaken.) Horrified by the obstructionism of his superiors and unable to make progress, Schiller leaked information to the press[13] and helped fortify the outside criticism, though his superiors decided not to discipline him for this.

With political pressure (following the Ridley Committee) mounting for the industry to develop proper costing, Schiller's position improved slightly and he worked to change views within the industry. He was able partly to overcome continuing obstructionism by using techniques of regression analysis to estimate load characteristics. His first major costing exercise suggested that domestic consumers not only failed to meet costs on peak loads but, in all except one Area Board (where the data may have been biased), failed even to cover the average costs of supplying them. This conclusion was, of course, extremely uncomfortable for the chairmen, since, if correct, it exposed as baseless their assurances to the Ministry on pricing policy. There were genuine reasons for doubting its accuracy – the issues of joint cost allocation were (and remain) problematical – but the senior management response to it (they insisted it be withdrawn even from internal circulation) betrayed a greater devotion to the cause of suppressing criticism than it did to that of searching for the truth. Schiller none the less continued his research and provoked controversy by his estimate that, by the mid-1950s, though space heating sales had fallen to only a fifth of domestic sales, they still accounted for some three-fifths of the peak: significantly more than the BEA had ever publicly admitted. The price of additional kWh in the domestic tariffs remained far below the costs incurred in supplying this demand (even on generous assumptions about margins of error in the calculations), and Schiller pressed the undesirability of adding to peak demand through further space heating sales. His warnings were private to the industry and went largely unheeded. It was only some years later, when the over-expansion he had forecast had materialised, and some of the more obscurantist leaders of the industry had been replaced by new men, that the industry came to terms with the problem (see pp. 212–17, below).

The critics of Schiller's cost research argued that electricity tariff policy could not be 'handed over to a set of calculating machines', and claimed instead to base their prices on 'judgement and wisdom'.[14] Inevitably, this meant something between 'charging what the traffic would bear' and subjective cost assessment or extrapolation of past practice. The Central Authority itself had to fix its own tariff for the bulk supply of electricity to the Boards and initially did well in reflecting costs by resisting pressure for 'postalisation' or charging a common national price. They sensibly retained a regional fuel cost differential to reflect differing local coal costs, and their two-part bulk supply tariff, based on both a capacity charge per kW of peak demand and a running charge per kWh also sensibly reflected costs. Attempts to make this cost reflection more sophisticated at a later date were, however, jeopardised by internal BEA politics, which reduced initiatives to the lowest common denominator acceptable to the Area Boards. There were minor improvements: capacity charges to Boards whose peaks were on Sunday and did not coincide with system peaks were reduced a little in 1950 and further in 1954; an allowance was made for lower-cost regional energy imports in 1957. But further proposals for the better reflection of system costs were rejected.[15]

Cecil Melling (the chairman of the Eastern Board, who had supported Schiller's work since before nationalisation and took costing more seriously than his fellow chairmen) for a time gained the support of the Central Authority's commercial department for the better reflection of off-peak costs in the bulk tariff, but the other Area Board chairmen strongly opposed the initiative. Fearing criticism if their bulk supply costs were better known (unsustainable assertions on off-peak generating costs had been made to the Ministry), they felt that the less guidance they got in tariff making from the Authority's bulk supply tariff the better. Tariffs, they considered, were a matter for their own judgement at local level, and the existing simple bulk supply tariff, together with their own knowledge of the industry, were argued to be a sufficient incentive to develop off-peak sales. Inevitably, the requirements both of compromise and of secrecy meant that Citrine and his colleagues at the top backed the obscurantism of the majority of the chairmen against Melling.

In his own Board, Melling was none the less able to pursue an off-peak pricing policy, despite criticism from the other chairmen that he was breaking the common front against Ministry interference on pricing. He introduced an optional tariff in which all night units were cheaper, and persuaded manufacturers to produce night storage heaters, though this night tariff was not widely promoted and was used by shops and offices rather than by domestic consumers initially. All other Boards preferred to develop special separately-wired circuits for off-peak electricity, and, in the two southern Scottish Boards, this load was sold with enthusiasm. In most other Boards, however, the off-peak rate was pitched high and the selling effort was minimal, off-peak supplies being offered in some Boards only from 1955, under pressure from both the Central Authority and the Ministry. Most chairmen continued to believe, as they had told the Ministry in July 1953, that 'the role of tariff policy, taken by itself, in improving the load factor of the system is not capable of much further advance.'

It is difficult to view this obscurantism of the chairmen with sympathy. Their policies were riddled with the logical absurdities on pricing of which Gaitskell had earlier been so critical. Yet they did face a genuine dilemma, which the simple formulas offered by critics could not resolve. Demand was not always as price-elastic as the critics suggested, and the contrast between the views of managers within an industry (that price elasticity is low) and that of economists (that it is high) is a familiar one from other industries. It is not always the case that the economists' bias is right. It was conceivable that, as the area chairmen feared, higher prices in domestic tariffs would not only have discouraged undesirable loads such as peak space heating, but also the ones such as water heating and cooking which helped them in their overall commercial strategy and were largely off-peak. If demand were more elastic in these uses than in peak space heating, higher prices could have damaged their cost-reducing strategy, and might even have worsened the load factor. They had done virtually no research on the elasticity of demand, relying as usual on their intuition and experience, but in this case intuition may not have played them entirely false. Most subsequent studies have shown the difficulty of measuring the price response of demand. There are wide variations in different uses, and substantial effects from income, complementary appliance ownership, other fuel prices, and other factors largely beyond the control of the Electricity Boards irrespective of the pricing policy they adopted.[16] The policy of developing a diverse range of domestic uses by a moderate price policy and vigorous but selective appliance sales promotion might in these conditions have been a reasonable one.

Yet it was accepted privately within the industry that their 'promotional' pricing could be below cost in order to compete with gas (precisely the kind of uneconomic cross-subsidy of which critics accused them). Many chairmen were content to adopt a 'swings and roundabouts' approach to this, provided they broke even on sales overall. In the less cautious Boards, they were even prepared to let their more bullish exponents of domestic electrification pursue all domestic sales without regard to costs, with growth as the sole objective. For a time, however, this policy seemed to be achieving expansion without the problems predicted by their critics. As they had hoped, when domestic coal supplies became more plentiful in the mid-1950s, the share of electricity sold for space heating did indeed decline sharply. By contrast, off-peak sales developed faster than peak sales overall, so that the underlying load factor (conventionally measured as the actual sales over the year compared with the sales that would have resulted if peak demand had been supplied throughout the year) rose satisfactorily from around 43 per cent on nationalisation to around 47 per cent ten years later.[17] Many chairmen took this faster expansion of off-peak than on-peak sales as evidence that their domestic sales strategies were justified, but Schiller later developed estimates which suggested that the true significance of domestic sales were masked by this experience. By his calculations, domestic sales (about a third of total sales) accounted for as much as half of the peak load (most of it space heating) in severe weather, and thus imposed rather higher system costs than industrial and commercial sales. It was, however, to be some years before the broad outlines of his findings were accepted. After all, what were a theorist's research results worth compared with a lifetime of experience in electricity supply?

In the meantime, electricity prices were gradually raised to nearer long-run costs. The bulk supply capacity charges to Area Boards rose 64 per cent in the first ten years of nationalisation, as the higher postwar investment costs were reflected in the Central Authority's books; and running charges were raised by 45 per cent, reflecting the rising cost of coal supplied by the National Coal Board. These increases were significantly more rapid than the general rate of inflation but, as we have argued (pp. 31–4, above) they were entirely desirable. Yet, not all this increase in bulk costs was passed on to the consumers in retail tariffs. Each household's peak demand was not measured directly. Instead most Boards adopted a standard proxy measure such as the number of rooms or the floor area of the domestic premises concerned, and based their standing charges or the charge for the first 'block' on this. Even in 1948, this was already a poor proxy for peak demand,[18] but ten years later, when the peak demand of a typical domestic consumer was significantly higher, no adjustment other than increases proportionate to the increased bulk capacity charges had been made. Since incremental kWh charges were also increased only in step with the bulk running charge, the Boards were in effect making no charge for any additional capacity necessary to meet the increased domestic sales over that ten-year period. There was thus still a substantial subsidy, reducing prices below costs on domestic sales, at the end of the period as at the beginning, and the Boards showed no signs of facing up to this. Indeed, they boasted proudly that retail electricity prices had risen more slowly than the retail price index in general: although their own tariffs had risen faster, average consumption had gone up and the extra kWh had been sold at the lower incremental charges of two-part or block tariffs, thus bringing the average domestic price in their first ten years down by a fifth in real terms. Their boast was in some respects justified, for some of the fall in the real price of electricity was indeed a result of their successful promotion of domestic loads: reducing supply costs by increasing the average consumption per consumer. Yet, while many chairmen persisted in denying it, the probability is that domestic prices remained inadequate to meet the overall costs of supplying domestic consumers, as they had been on nationalisation, though now for a new set of reasons, which betrayed a continuing inadequate degree of attention to proper costing exercises.

The contemporary debate on energy policy and the sales effort of the Boards concentrated on the domestic sector, though two-thirds of electricity sales were in fact to other consumers; industry, commerce, transport and farms. The industry's preoccupation with domestic sales derived not only from political pressure, but also from the fact that a large proportion of their resources (both capital and man-power) was necessarily devoted to servicing the generally small and thus more expensive-to-supply domestic consumers. Yet nearly two-thirds of the Boards' revenue came from the generally larger industrial and commercial consumers. Sales to these consumers (which had been more effectively restrained in the difficult 1940s) rose more rapidly than those to domestic consumers in the first ten years of nationalisation.

Citrine liberally laced his public speeches advocating electrical expansion with references to the need to emulate the Americans in improving industrial productivity by increasing the amount of electric power per worker. The nationalised Boards, being larger than their predecessors, could, moreover, now afford to employ more specialist sales staff to cater for these markets (though they found that their pay scales made it difficult to recruit and keep good industrial salesmen in competition with the electrical manufacturing concerns).

The problem of pricing was somewhat easier in the case of larger consumers than of small domestic ones. The rising cost of coal was automatically reflected in their contracts, so that, on nationalisation, there was less of a backlog to make up in price increases and consequently less ill will from necessary increases. With large consumers, moreover, the cost of more complex metering was justified, and most were placed on a tariff based on their measured maximum demand as well as a cost-based running charge.[19] Some industrial consumers regretted that the Boards' attitudes to tariffs were much more rigid than that of their predecessors (who had been more willing to negotiate special rates). Boards differed in their attitudes, the best being willing to modify standard tariffs where variations in costs justified it. There were, for example, special agreements for the waiving of demand charges for off-peak supplies, and special terms for standby supplies for industrialists generating their own electricity, though these fell far short of what some industrialists, perhaps ingenuously, demanded. In so far as the historic cost pricing rules applied, the large consumers were subsidised like others initially, but, by the mid-1950s, their prices probably reflected long-run costs fairly accurately (though they correctly, if somewhat ineffectively, complained about the continuing subsidy to the domestic consumer, which they suspected but could not prove).[20]

The average price paid by industrial and commercial consumers declined only slightly if at all in real terms over the first ten years of nationalisation, but electricity usage in industry was probably less price-elastic than in most uses, and other factors were the main stimuli to sales growth. Sales grew fastest, for example, in the rapidly-expanding, electricity-intensive chemical industry, and in the more prosperous areas of the South and Midlands. They grew slowly in transport, where trams and trolley buses were being replaced by diesel buses, and where the British Transport Commission's railway electrification proposals were slow to mature. Overall, industrial electricity sales grew twice as fast as industrial output. Electricity continued to replace steam-powered mechanical drives, and the subdivision of power which it made possible remained a fundamentally attractive characteristic. New industrial methods based on assembly lines and continuous processes were typically more dependent on electricity than the ones they replaced. By contrast, electricity for the production of heat was less successful against its competitors, though in special situations where off-peak supplies could be negotiated or, as in the pottery industry, where cleanliness, lack of flame and ease of control were at a premium, new supply contracts were won. In areas where manufacturers or users were unwilling to pioneer applications, moreover, the Electricity Boards were able to finance demonstration projects, with some success in areas such as off-peak concrete-embedded electric floor heating for new factory, office and housing projects, and novel industrial processes of small scale.

Before the War, many large consumers had generated their own electricity (45 per cent of industrial electricity came from self-generation in 1938), and some of the larger firms, such as ICI and Ford, had been pioneers in generation technology. As the benefits of large-scale integrated operation of power stations on the National Grid increased, however, the threat of such competition receded; and the share of self-generation, already down to 31 per cent on nationalisation, had been further reduced to 22 per cent ten years later. Private generation remained economic where a firm had complementary process steam requirements (and could use back-pressure sets to produce both steam and electricity), where waste heat from another process could be used, or where investment incentives (not available to nationalised industries) or local property taxation (for which the Electricity Boards were more highly rated) gave an artificial subsidy to private firms. Industrialists sometimes argued that they would generate even more electricity privately if the Boards did not make excessive charges for standby supplies,[21] and this view derived some plausibility from the fact that the share of private generation was lower in Britain than in other European countries.[22] At least part of the explanation of this was, however, the efficiency of the National Grid's integrated programme of power station planning and operation, with which smaller private generating stations were less and less able to compete economically as the 1950s progressed.

8

GENERATION: CENTRALISATION AND CONSERVATISM (1948–53)

After the years when nothing ever lived up to delivery date, it was necessary to tie things down to something practical, something that would be achieved, but they rested content with that.

Pat Murray, head of the Ministry's Electricity Division, to the Committee of Inquiry on the Industry, 6 May 1955.

Responsibility within the BEA for the design, construction and operation of power stations lay principally with Sir John Hacking, the deputy chairman with engineering expertise, and with the senior of the officers, V. A. Pask, the chief engineer, who like Hacking came from the CEB. The urgent problems of accelerating the construction programmes inherited in 1948 were being tackled, as we have seen, under Verity and Smith (pp. 23–8, above). The headquarters engineering department found, however, that for new stations it had to take on many more staff, both to develop its limited expertise in generation design, and to fulfil its function of coordinating the work of the fourteen divisions to which generation operations and construction had been decentralised. Most of the supply industry's generating expertise had previously been in the larger power companies and municipalities (which had been in the forefront of developing the more advanced power stations), but the first power company engineer they recruited as head of generation design fell ill shortly afterwards and died. With many of the other leading generation engineers having taken positions as divisional controllers, he was difficult to replace, and responsibility as Pask's deputy for generation thus fell to J. D. Peattie, an ex-CEB operations engineer, with little experience of the power station design side, and to other ex-CEB staff who had previously liaised with the undertakings on power station design. Lower down the organisation, recruitment was no easier. There was a considerable shortage of skilled designers and draughtsmen, and, despite several years of efforts, and assurances by Hacking that headquarters would build up their design expertise, recruitment problems remained. When a delegation of US engineers in 1953 criticised power station design and construction, the engineers pointed to the inadequacy of their staffing levels for the unusually wide headquarters responsibility. None the less the chief engineer's department had expanded considerably since CEB days (when they numbered 65); the technical and engineering staff at headquarters grew from 173 in 1948 to 330 by 1952.

The chief engineer's department remained in the old CEB headquarters, and Hacking and Pask were looked upon by the divisions as the engineering heads of the industry, but the division of responsibilities at the top of the BEA, as we have seen, envisaged a role also for Self, as the deputy chairman in charge of administration (pp. 12–13, above). While Hacking had accepted joint responsibility for this organisational blueprint, his own instincts were to preserve the independence of the chief engineer's department from Self's administrative control as much as possible. Pask more determinedly attempted to block Self's attempts to assert control, which he saw as unnecessary complications at a time when their efforts should be directed single-mindedly to overcoming the serious generating plant backlog. The most conspicuous battleground in this prolonged conflict over the locus of control was the procedure for placing contracts. Pask's initial strategy was simply not to reply (and to discourage his other senior engineers from replying) to communications from Self and the secretarial and accounting departments. Thus Verity, the generation construction engineer, replied to an enquiry in September 1949 as to why the engineers had not reacted to a draft contracts procedure sent to them six months ago:

> ... the difficult problem of inducing by every means and ingenuity in one's power, the utterly elusive and reticent megawatt to come forward and show itself whilst at the same time fighting with equal energy the ceaseless and unwelcome flood of paper has kept me so fully occupied that I have just not had a moment to get at the memorandum.

While Self knew that the pressures were great, and respected the engineers' need to retain control of technical aspects of contracts and tender assessments, he also knew that the engineers were deliberately fending him off and impeding the agreement on procedures which he felt was essential for Central Authority financial control. 'Bomber' Smith (who joined the Authority's staff from the Ministry in September 1949) had his own doubts about the engineers, feeling that their desire for a good technical liaison with the manufacturers, and particularly the boiler-makers, tended to paralyse the BEA's capacity to exercise commercial pressure on them. He wanted a more determined effort to speed up deliveries and to force an expansion of manufacturing capacity to meet the BEA's greatly enlarged needs. With backing from Citrine and Self, Smith tried to exercise such leverage, and (when he failed to persuade the existing boiler manufacturers to respond) proposed to attract new firms to the industry by the promise of orders to keep them in business. This determination to prevent the manufacturers exploiting a sellers' market induced Self to ask Smith to stay on and establish a Contracts Department as a step towards firmer financial control over the engineers. The engineers strongly opposed this, but Citrine gave his backing to Self at a Central Authority meeting in March 1950 (when Pask was absent abroad). The meeting was one of the most acrimonious they had experienced, but Citrine firmly overruled the engineers;

> Gentlemen. We are here to decide whether to establish a Contracts Department. I have decided there will be one. Now we must go to lunch.

Self's victory was bitterly resented by the engineers and, on his return, Pask tried (unsuccessfully) to overturn it. For some months the engineers tried to obstruct and by-pass Smith, until Hacking told them firmly that there must be a considerable change of heart by all concerned to work together. Contracts thereafter became a joint responsibility, and the commercial edge of BEA pressure on manufacturers did improve, though financial controls remained weak.

Although Self was accused by the headquarters engineers of bureaucratic interference, his own doubts about the policies being pursued by the chief engineer's department crystallized into a conviction that they were guilty of unnecessarily over-centralised procedures, a view shared by many engineers in the divisions, though not by Hacking. There were delays of months while specifications and tenders for new power stations were cleared by the headquarters engineers, but Hacking insisted that there must be close technical control of design from the centre, claiming variously that the limited technical skills of divisions or the requirements of standardisation made centralisation necessary, or (quite implausibly) that anything else was illegal under the 1947 Act. Self, by contrast, felt that the creativity of the divisions could be unlocked if central controls over both design and expenditure were relaxed somewhat. From 1951 divisions were allowed a slightly greater say in designing power station layouts and in the placing of small contracts, but Hacking and Pask opposed any further decentralisation. Self and Ernest Long, the secretary, devoted a good deal of thought to methods of budgetary control which would make decentralisation possible, but the head-quarters engineers, still deeply distrustful of anything from Self, had little conception of the financial and management principles of decentralisation. They reiterated the old CEB faith in the imperatives of central technical control, and brushed aside potential gains from decentralisation, but themselves maintained a very weak financial control over the divisions. Attempts by Long and Self to fix annual financial budgets for the divisions were initially opposed by the headquarters engineers. 'I think I should react more favourably to an attitude of confidence and trust ... than to an attitude of suspicion that I am inherently extravagant and require continual supervision,' wrote one in 1952, showing his misunderstanding of the decentralising potential of financial controls. Even when a budgetary procedure was first reluctantly accepted in 1953 (under extreme pressure from Self), the engineers continued to see their task in technical not financial terms, and the financial controls remained rudimentary in the extreme. Self, worn down by the struggle, seems eventually to have been convinced that the measurement of divisional performance by budgetary control and other yardsticks was not possible. This militated against any substantial devolution of managerial power and initiatives to the divisions. Meanwhile the controllers and their senior staff fulminated against excessive interference from both engineers and administrators at headquarters, who, in their view, lacked the experience of power station design, construction, and operation which the divisions themselves had inherited from the local undertak-ings. The feeling that the centre only wanted financial and technical control to check every detail of their action, rather than to stimulate responsible management decentralisation, inevitably increased.

The policy confusion at the top did not preclude efficient manage-ment lower down. The operational side of the BEA's generation responsibilities were perhaps least compromised. On nationalisation, the divisions had acquired around 300 power stations, initially grouping them for management at an intermediate level. Gradually, as the smaller, obsolete stations were closed and the skills and authority of remaining power station superintendents increased, the divisions decentralised responsibility directly to them and intermediate 'group' offices were abandoned. The day-to-day operation of power stations remained under the control of the six National Grid Control Centres, which (now they were freed from the financial provisions which had governed their relationship to the independent undertakings) were able to run them in a more efficient merit order, reducing the cost of generation. This completed the process begun in the early 1930s of concentrating generation on the most efficient stations, and using the least efficient only during the winter peaks.[1] The BEA were also able to make savings of about 1 per cent of generation costs by centralising the purchase of coal and rationalising its transport, eliminating cross-hauling and sharing facilities such as sea-going colliers. A system of operational efficiency comparison was also evolved by the mid-1950s, which allowed for the development of rivalry and emulation between power stations and contributed to the development of cost-consciousness.

On the generation design and construction side, the picture was a good deal less inspiring, though improvements were made and some of the inherited handicaps were overcome. The transmission design and construction function (which was in the hands of a centralised headquarters group inherited from the CEB) was a model of efficiency, but the power station side posed more serious problems. The task the divisions faced on the generation construction side was unique in British industry. No other organisation needed to meet such a rapidly expanding demand for a single product that they had, in effect, to build one new factory every two months, as the BEA did during their first ten years. This power station construction programme absorbed the greater part of their capital budgets, as well as a good deal of management time both at headquarters and in the divisions. The capacity of the fourteen divisions to shoulder this responsibility, and the load placed on each division both varied enormously. The largest division had more than ten times the construction workload of the smallest (which had quite inadequate technical staff). Many of the projects taken over on nationalisation were, moreover, either wholly or partly in the hands of civil and electrical engineering consultants, whom the BEA assured of continuing support for the forseeable future.

Although both 'Bomber' Smith and the engineers hoped that in time they would be able to bring construction times down nearer to three years (from the beginning of work on site to the commissioning of the first sets), the time actually taken was typically five or more years. The BEA planning and design procedures, far from cutting this back, sometimes seemed designed merely to codify delays. The divisions were given the go-ahead for construction five years in advance of the anticipated need for capacity, but during the previous three years there had been detailed consultations between headquarters and the divisions, about the power requirements, about the site, and about the design and layout of the proposed plant. There were also regular conferences at headquarters for divisional controllers and further coordinating meetings for other divisional officers, with whom their headquarters functional equivalents liked to maintain direct contact. The divisional controllers themselves complained that this compromised their own line of authority within the division, and they generally harboured a strong feeling that headquarters interfered too much in the design of new stations. The controllers' own awareness of local conditions and operational requirements (not to speak of their pre-nationalisation experience in design and construction) could, they thought, have been more fully harnessed to the task. When headquarters control extended to such mundane questions as whether a chemical or flushing toilet should be installed and whether surrounds should be grassed over or concreted, it is easy to understand the frustration of the engineers in the divisions. The 'strong technical control' which had been seen by the CEB men at the centre as essential for efficiency was seen by many in the divisions as an unnecessary drag on initiative and responsibility. The invariable response of headquarters was, however, to reiterate their ideas on the desirability of centralised technical control and to ignore its cumbersome, deadening effect.

Some improvements were, however, possible as a result of centralisation. The work of Smith and Verity in this field, for example, represented a real gain for central coordination which was not always fairly appreciated by the controllers, who had a narrower local viewpoint. For some years after nationalisation, the overall materials supply situation remained bleak. There were still serious steel shortages, and materials were diverted to fulfil Macmillan's 'housing crusade' targets in the early 1950s. Then, under pressure from the Chancellor, Whitehall insisted on the manufacturers diverting turbines and other equipment to export markets rather than to the BEA. Yet the bottlenecks in the industry's own programme were identified, one by one, and their control over the manufacturers was gradually increased. Smith allocated orders to bring in new manufacturers where the existing ones proved excessively unreliable in breaking delivery promises or refusing to build new capacity. The BEA also looked carefully at the possibility of importing plant and materials, but (with steel prices significantly higher in the USA and Europe and considerable difficulties in obtaining foreign exchange) they confined themselves to importing only a few specialist components which were causing serious delays in the programme. For example, after British manufacturers had failed to provide adequate supplies of boiler tubes, they decided to import some from Italy in the early 1950s. As with the Area Boards, the materials supply situation eased considerably after 1953, and they were able to negotiate tighter contracts with better delivery dates for the mid-1950s and after.

Whether because of the easing of the general supply situation, or because of the improved coordination, the delays in completing power stations were progressively reduced in the 1950s, with completion on average nearly eleven months behind pessimistic schedules in the early 1950s but down to eight months by the mid-1950s. This still meant that they were taking more than five years on average, a rather miserable performance when compared either with American or with some continental European power stations.[2] In the mid-1950s only a few of the simpler, standard power stations were beginning commissioning three to three-and-a-half years after the start of work on site, but the BEA failed to get their average performance near to that of their best or up to the similar three-year timings achieved by the Atomic Energy Authority[3] in developing their smaller (but more challenging) demonstration nuclear power plants. The problems encountered on these large power station construction projects were variously blamed on restrictive practices by site labour, inadequate resources at the design stage, insufficient materials priorities for the industry, and ineffective project management combined with over-centralisation of detail.[4] Whatever the causes of construction delays, they were to remain a persistent and seemingly insoluble problem, not only for the electricity supply industry but for a wide range of other British industries embarking on such large capital projects for decades thereafter.[5]

Despite these problems, the BEA were able, in the first ten years of nationalisation, to double the capacity of National Grid power stations. Commissioning levels were well below target initially, but, with the roll-over of previously uncompleted programmes, they began comfortably to exceed annual targets from 1952 onwards (when the annual commissioning rates averaged double the prewar level). As a result, by 1956/7, although there remained a cumulative backlog of nearly 1800MW of uncompleted power station capacity, the system was capable of meeting the demands placed on it in a mild winter, and power cuts had by then become a rare occurrence. The margin of safety was, however, still less than they considered desirable, and was inadequate to meet the space heating peak in a severe winter.

This reduction in the gap between supply and demand had been achieved despite a consistent forward under-estimation of the peak demand in every year and a consequential under-ordering of plant. In determining the level of planned capacity five years ahead, separate estimates had been made by the BEA commercial department (taking into account national economic trends), the engineers (using simple arithmetical extrapolation of past growth), and the Area Boards (using their local knowledge). Their forecasts had one thing in common: they all under-estimated the growth (the commercial department's forecasts being least, and the Area Boards' most, accurate). By the mid-1950s, the actual level of demand being experienced averaged 8 per cent more than the compromise estimate which had been adopted in determining the forward programmes. Nevertheless, the high reliability of most of the new postwar plant, together with the policy of keeping very old plant in service virtually until it dropped apart (there were few plant retirements in this period)[6] was sufficient for the National Grid Control to maintain a supply, albeit with immense efforts from the operating staff during the winter peaks, when virtually all available plant had to be maintained in readiness.

The high reliability of the new postwar plant may, however, have been purchased at too high a cost. Certainly there were those, both in the divisions and outside, who felt that the BEA headquarters design policy, in its search for reliability and speed of construction above all else, had imposed an unnecessary conservatism on development. Long-term planning took a back seat in the deliberations of the senior engineers whose efforts were principally devoted to overcoming short-term problems. Forward planning (matching load forecasts and planned capacity, thinking about the future regional spread of power stations), was, of course, necessary, but was in practice merely a part-time function of the ex-CEB engineers in charge of system operation.

The CEB had, in fact, been quite sophisticated in its long-term planning, and their interwar prognostications had proved remarkably accurate. The old CEB's pooling of national demands and its integrated operating philosophy had also been quite uniquely effective in reducing the level of standby plant required in Britain, and in planning national needs for capacity extensions in the most economical way. The CEB also had an enviable record both in practical technical research preparatory to new Grid developments and in meeting Grid construction targets.[7] By 1948, however, the CEB engineers had become unusually conservative, and this appeared both in their views on future load growth (which they greatly underestimated) and in their unwillingness to develop beyond the inherited 132kV National Grid to meet the demands of the decades ahead. In the early months of the BEA, these conservative attitudes remained strong (though experimental work on higher voltage transmission was continued), and many CEB men felt it would be best to break the Grid up into three to meet the future demands they were expecting, rather than to raise the voltages and maintain a national system. This seemed to one leading outside consultant unnecessarily restrictive.[8] A higher-voltage superimposed Grid would, the consultant argued (in a report prepared on his own initiative and published in the leading electrical engineering journal), extend the benefits of pooling demands nationally to gain economies of scale, a smaller spare plant margin, and increased reliability, as had the original Grid. There was also, he felt, a good economic case with the higher voltage for transporting energy from coal mines to the load centres in the form of electricity cheaply via the Grid rather than in expensive coal trains by rail.

There was still considerable doubt among the ex-CEB men about the merits of this thesis, but Hacking and Pask, annoyed at being upstaged by an outside critic, pressed for a reconsideration of the issue, while D. P. Sayers, a new non-CEB recruit as head transmission engineer, catalysed the headquarters engineers into a new approach. The precise costing of the alternatives was difficult (particularly since the nationalised rail and coal industries both refused to give guidance on their future prices which were a crucial element in the analysis), but by 1950 a working party chaired by Sayers concluded that, on balance, a higher-voltage superimposed network – Citrine insisted it be more elegantly referred to as the 'Supergrid'[9] – would be worthwhile. In July of that year the Central

Authority accepted a proposal to invest £52 millions over ten years in 1150 miles of 275kV Supergrid lines. The new lines, with more than six times the transmission capacity of the old 132kV Grid lines, would greatly strengthen the north–south interconnections which had been weak in the original Grid design (see Figure 8.1). Sections of the Grid which were expected to carry increasingly heavy loads (such as those between the coalfield power stations in the East Midlands and load centres in London) were to be constructed with wide clearances so as to be suitable for conversion to even higher voltages later should the need arise.

Source: CEGB.

FIG. 8.1   *Schematic outline of the 275kV Supergrid, 1950*

This decision was criticised at the time as unnecessarily ambitious, both by visiting American engineers (who were unused to Britain's highly integrated planning approach) and by the press,[10] but the BEA's experience was to prove the critics wrong. Demand on the system grew faster than expected (thus building up the economic usage of the Supergrid rapidly and increasing the efficiency gains). There were considerable savings both on the capital cost of power stations and on their operating costs. In retrospect, indeed, the only criticism was to be that the whole Supergrid had not been designed for conversion to even higher voltages. The system had to be extended considerably beyond the 1950 plans at both 132kV and 275kV in order to meet the greatly increased demands of the late 1950s. From 1950 onwards, the BEA in their annual development plans also increasingly relied on the Supergrid to overcome the constraints on power station siting. Many of the sites they inherited in 1948 were near the towns and cities which were the main load centres, but such sites seemed less likely to gain planning permission in the 1950s. The BEA thus increasingly looked for sites more distant from the load centres, locating them instead on the coast (where cooling water supplies were cheap and plentiful) or on the coalfields (where coal would be the cheapest).[11] The Supergrid gave them more freedom to optimise their siting by these criteria. They failed to obtain any long-term understanding on future regional coal price differentials from the National Coal Board, but their discussions did seem to indicate that there would be advantages to shifting away from the high-cost coalfields of Kent, South Wales and Scotland, and towards the cheaper coal of the East Midlands and Yorkshire. As the 1950s progressed, therefore, new power station investment was increasingly concentrated on the latter areas. Their forward planning guesses on coal fortunately proved correct, and substantially lower coal costs developed in those areas in the 20–30-year lifetime of the stations.

In the field of power station design, the conservatism of the headquarters engineers was more persistent than in the case of the Supergrid. While in the 1930s the CEB men had been leaders in advocating larger-scale power generation, with the undertakings sometimes dragging their feet, by the time of nationalisation they pinned their faith more on the benefits of standardising on 30MW and 60MW sets as a means of both cutting costs and overcoming the capacity shortage (see pp. 24–5, above). The 30MW sets were extremely conservative (the first set with the standard conditions had been commissioned as long ago as 1929), but Pask, the chief engineer, resisted pressure to reduce the number of such sets in the early years and concentrate more on the 60MW design. This was cheaper per MW and had more advanced steam conditions and higher thermal efficiency. It was as large a set as had been developed earlier for general use, except for the London area (where a few larger sets had been installed in the 1930s and some larger sets of somewhat antiquated design were also completed by the BEA in its early years). There were, however, doubts about the flexibility in start-up and shut-down times for the new 60MW and other new designs, and *a fortiori* about more advanced designs. CEB engineers feared that an over-commitment to the 60MW and other new designs would compromise operating flexibility. Some 86 per cent of the plants built in the early years of the BEA were therefore the 30 and 60MW sets with standard steam conditions.

This conservatism was arguably excessive, given the subsequent relatively trouble-free experience of most of the innovations in power station design which might realistically have been on the agenda at this time. These were generally recognised to involve no large changes in technology, but there was considerable potential from a series of small innovations, which reduced both the capital and operating costs of generating equipment. Historically, the movement towards larger sizes (which reduced capital costs) and more advanced steam temperatures and pressures (which increased the amount of useful energy extracted from the fuel used) had gone together. This was because the higher pressures and temperatures required more advanced materials engineering, which was often only worthwhile if there were also economies of scale (the 200MW sets with advanced steam conditions built later, for example, used less than half as much steel per MW as the simple 30MW sets the BEA were installing). It was not until 1950 (three years after a similar set had been commissioned in America) that the BEA decided to go for some of these gains from larger scale by ordering an advanced 100MW set for 1955. They and the manufacturers then successfully persuaded the Government to withdraw the order standardising turbo-alternators in the 30 and 60MW sizes. A more serious constraint earlier had been the weight of components which had to be transported by road, but the adoption of hydrogen-cooling of the rotor (pioneered in America before the War) now made it possible to reduce the size of components in the larger sets. The first 100MW set at Castle Donington (Leicestershire) was not in fact commissioned until 1956. The next advance in scale, a 120MW set, was ordered in March 1952 for Blyth (Northumberland) but not completed until nearly seven years later. The 120MW sets (and some of the later 60MW and 100MW sets) also incorporated a considerable advance in steam conditions, with pressures of 1500psi (compared with 900psi in standard 60MW sets) and temperatures of 1000–1050°F (compared with 900°F). In such conditions some of the turbine blades would glow at a dull red heat, and this represented the practical limit for ferritic steel: higher temperatures could only be attained with the use of special (austenitic) steels, which were in short supply in Britain at the time. Yet this modest advance in steam conditions was approached late and with circumspection: the sets on order for the whole of the 1950s commissioning programmes remained mainly the 30MW and 60MW sizes, and only a third of the sets adopted the more advanced steam conditions.

Other innovations were also approached with circumspection by the BEA headquarters design engineers, even though significant experience of them had been gained both in this country and abroad. The technique of introducing a steam re-heat cycle (in which steam is extracted from the turbine at an intermediate stage, raised to a higher temperature and reintroduced into the lower pressure stage) had been pioneered in Britain by consultants and widely adopted in America. Yet, despite inheriting a successful re-heat design under construction at Dunston (Tyne and Wear) on nationalisation, the CEB engineers doubted the operational flexibility of the re-heat sets in meeting the more variable load on the British Grid. Only when they had gained experience of the re-heat sets at Dunston (in 1952) did they concede its flexibility, and re-heat became standard in their new stations from then onwards. Dunston and other non-standard stations also pioneered 'unit' boilers in Britain. British engineers in the 1930s had preferred to have several boilers per turbine and a station spare, though this involved expensive interconnecting pipework and American experience showed that 'unit' boilers (one per turbine) could be reliable. The BEA engineers, in consultation with the boiler-makers, initially concentrated on alternative options for improving boiler reliability, and they had serious doubts about the manufacturers' capacity to make reliable unit boilers with the higher postwar steam conditions, though gradually these were adopted after 1952.

The conservatism of Pask, the chief engineer, seems to have derived from pressure from his ex-CEB colleagues in operations, who stressed the need for absolute reliability in new machines. In the conditions of capacity shortage which they faced, short-term considerations favoured priority attention to reliability rather than optimising long-term efficiency. The headquarters generation design engineer, Freddie Shakeshaft, also a CEB man, had a 'seat of the pants' approach to engineering, stressing practical experience rather than theoretical extrapolations of design parameters. (Like many British design engineers at the time – and unlike Continental or American ones – he had no university training and had come up through the usual apprenticeship route with evening and part-time study.) He took Pask's conservative philosophy even further by stressing that even in less strained times Britain should not pioneer technology, but should let America develop experience and then copy the designs. He and his colleagues were well aware of the more rapid progress in America, and there were regular transatlantic visits by headquarters engineers, but only when they were quite sure of new techniques and had discussed them thoroughly with the British manufacturers were they prepared to make a move.

There were some engineers who wanted more experimentation and more rapid adoption of larger sizes or re-heat, arguing that, while Britain had at last caught up with American levels of thermal efficiency in 1938, she was now again falling behind. Given Shakeshaft's conservatism, and the BEA's long power station construction times, relative backwardness was indeed inevitable, since it effectively placed eleven years between the trial of new technology in America and its first adoption in Britain. It is hard to believe that a more adventurous policy would not have been justified (even had it led to more mistakes and power cuts at the winter peak). None the less, given the pressures on the BEA at the time, it is perhaps understandable that in the early years speed (which proved elusive) and reliability (which they achieved) were given priority over efficiency and economy.

By 1952, however, impatience with the conservatism of Pask and Shakeshaft was growing within the BEA. Although Self and Citrine lacked the confidence and knowledge to pressure the engineers on technical questions, both Hacking and Woodward on the Central Authority began asking increasingly awkward questions about whether they were unnecessarily foregoing the potential benefits of more advanced sets. Pask stonewalled, claiming variously that he had no staff to answer questions, that only one boiler-maker in Britain was capable of making unit boilers for large sets, that they would encounter operational difficulties, that there would be economies to replication of smaller sets, that larger sets were more expensive than small ones, and that station layouts would not accommodate them. There was something in several of these points, but they ignored the obvious, and when proper figures were forced out of Pask, it was evident that substantial potential economies were being bypassed. The experimental 100MW sets were expected to burn 9 per cent less fuel per unit of electricity generated than the standard 60MW sets and 20 per cent less than the 30MW sets; their capital costs were 6 per cent lower than 60MW sets and 23 per cent lower than 30MW sets. The decision-making procedures within the BEA were, however, slow and, even when a decision to advance design had been taken, some headquarters engineers argued that there should be no change in station designs even in the two years before its sets were ordered (typically seven years before planned commissioning and eight years before actual commissioning). This was undoubtedly overdoing the advantages of forward planning, and unnecessarily froze their rate of technical advance (particularly since some manufacturers were known to hold BEA orders in abeyance for several years after receipt).

The manufacturers were generally happy with the BEA's conservatism, which suited their export concentration on low technology markets, and gave them a relatively easy and highly profitable life (though as the 1950s advanced more of them were to become worried that they were missing out on new technical developments as their world market share slipped).[12] As with the Supergrid, the leading electrical engineering consultants were generally more adventurous and expressed surprise at the conservatism of the BEA, though, in order to keep their power station consultancy contracts, they went along with headquarters' design policy.[13] Price signals also failed to provide significant pressures on the BEA. Initially, indeed, the generating programme was not subject to Central Authority financial appraisal of costs, and, even when alternative technologies were later evaluated properly, the prices used (interest rates, steel and coal prices) were those fixed by the Government at below market levels. This blunted the edge of their potential impact, though the steady rise in factor prices to nearer market levels in later years did help propel the BEA into more adventurous policies to achieve capital economies and improved fuel efficiencies. Pressures from the consumer market to go for cheaper and more efficient plant (which earlier, when there had been competition from generation by private industry, was a major spur to efficiency for CEB planners and the undertakings) was now less effective. Firms like ICI or Ford might, as in earlier years, have been able to build larger or more technically advanced sets for their own electricity supplies, but faced with the same shortages of steel and skilled men as the supply industry, they were now less inclined to branch out in this way, particularly as the BEA were selling electricity to them at prices based on historic costs, even though the new power stations were costing more. (By the time this artificial advantage had evaporated, moreover, the supply industry, as we shall see, had moved to larger, more technically advanced sets, and few large private firms had sufficiently big demands to justify the ordering of sets of a competitive size.)

With pressure from the market, the consultants and the manufacturers all weakened, then, any change in BEA policy would have to come from a change of heart at central headquarters. Hacking, though he favoured a more adventurous policy, was indecisive about making the personnel changes required, and preferred a low-key campaign of persuasion. Peattie and some others were converted to the view that they should build more 120MW sets in 1952, but Shakeshaft and Pask remained attached to a conservative mix of 30MW and 60MW units, with only a cautious experimentation with larger sets. The result was that, as late as 1953, 30MW sets were still being ordered, no decisive commitment to the larger sets with more advanced steam conditions had been made, and effectively the majority of the sets planned for the whole of the 1950s were of conservative design. The price paid was a more expensive supply system than was strictly necessary.

This is not to say there were no gains from the policy. The costs of some less rewarding false trails in technical advance (for example, cyclone boilers, cross-compound turbo-alternator layouts, supercritical steam conditions) were avoided by the conservatism of the early 1950s. The sets that were built showed another advantage of conservatism in that, despite some initial trouble with 60MW sets, they settled down to be more reliable than the engineers counted on. This enabled the Electricity Boards to meet demand in the late 1950s despite under-forecasting of loads and overrun construction times (see p. 213, below). Moreover, despite the conservatism in design, the capital cost per MW of generating stations did decline in real terms, by more than a quarter in the period affected by the BEA's decisions in its first five years,[14] a decline almost as rapid as that achieved later. Some of these gains were from replication of standard designs, though these were reckoned to be small, presumably because the large number of separate manufacturers and divisions involved in the work greatly reduced the potential cost reduction through learning effects. Most of the reduction came from the limited move away from the smaller sets towards the more advanced 60MW and 100MW designs which was possible within the conservative framework. If the move had been even faster, then the capital costs would no doubt have declined more, and less coal would have been used in more thermally efficient stations. The contrasting experience of France (which like Britain had a relatively integrated national supply system) is illuminating. French engineers, facing similar difficulties of a wartime investment backlog (but, significantly, steel prices which reflected real shortages), based more of their immediate postwar programme on sets of 100MW and above, and soon standardised on 125MW sets (the first of which, with re-heat, was commissioned in 1955, three years before the BEA's first 120MW re-heat set). The average thermal efficiency of French steam power stations, which had been well below that in Britain initially, was to overtake it in the later 1950s, as the more advanced French sets were commissioned; and France caught up with American levels of thermal efficiency, while Britain remained behind.[15]

9

GENERATION: THE BROWN
REVOLUTION (1954–7)

... in general, abrupt changes to the policy of an industry ... [are]
inherently undesirable. This is not to say ... impossible ...

Stanley Brown, in engineering department
memorandum, December 1956.

When Sir John Hacking decided to retire from the deputy chairmanship at the end of 1953, the old CEB promotional ladder would have
indicated Pask as his successor, but Central Authority members
opposed this and the Minister (who made the appointment) decided
to bring in new blood from outside the BEA headquarters. The
appointment went to Josiah Eccles, then chairman of the Merseyside
and North Wales Board. He had a first in engineering from Queen's
University, Belfast, and before nationalisation had served as the head
successively of the Edinburgh and the Liverpool Corporation electricity undertakings, gaining more experience of generation design
and construction than his ex-CEB predecessor and colleagues. The
CEB group which still dominated the chief engineer's department
found Eccles a more difficult taskmaster and sometimes resented his
presence, but he was to prove a breath of fresh air, giving top level
support to those within the department who were seeking changes
over a wide range of policies. The time was, moreover, now ripe for
considerable rethinking: the more serious capacity problems had
been overcome and steel and other materials were more freely
available, as the economy generally seemed to be achieving a full
postwar recovery.

Peattie, an older but less conservative engineer who was Pask's
deputy on the generation side, was now given more of a hearing.
Under Eccles he was increasingly able to overrule the conservatives
on generation design, as both he and Hacking had been cautiously

attempting to do since 1952. Crucial in this was the appointment, within six months of Eccles' coming to the headquarters, of F. H. S. (Stanley) Brown to replace Shakeshaft as the generation design engineer. Shakeshaft, who had held this post as Brown's boss, was pensioned off with a nominal 'consultancy'. Brown was only forty-two at the time, but he had had a distinguished career since graduating from Birmingham University with a first in engineering in 1932. Before nationalisation, Eccles had appointed him as an assistant on design and construction work in the Liverpool Corporation undertaking. After three years as the construction engineer with the Merseyside division of the BEA, Brown had been moved up to London as deputy to a reluctant Shakeshaft. He had concentrated on new set development policy, and by the time Eccles came to the BEA his ideas had crystallized into a proposal to install a 200MW set in the new High Marnham (Nottinghamshire) power station in the 1959 forward programme. Encouraged by Eccles and Peattie to pursue this, he ascertained from the leading manufacturers that the more advanced steam conditions he had in mind (2350psi, and 1050°F with reheat to 1000°F) were feasible, given recent advances in metallurgy and welding techniques. This adventurous proposal (bigger than anything being contemplated in European countries, and with higher steam conditions than the few sets of this size already operating in America) was accepted as BEA policy. Brown replaced Shakeshaft shortly afterwards in July 1954. Early the following year, he showed his willingness to extrapolate from design work, before they had gained any operational experience on sets larger than 60MW, by proposing further 200MW sets as the major element in the forward programmes for 1960–62.

Eccles and the Central Authority accepted this. Their new willingness to extrapolate from design experience on smaller 60MW prototypes (on which, for example, advanced cooling systems were tested), and generally to take greater risks, was also shown by their insistence that the proportion of the larger sets in earlier programmes should be increased. They as yet had no experience of operating either the 100MW or the 120MW sets, and Pask had wanted to continue with 60MW sets as the mainstay of the programme. By 1955, however, design work seemed to show that the larger sets would be sufficiently flexible. Rising coal prices made their higher thermal efficiency more attractive and higher steel prices and interest rates increased the potential economies in capital costs. Eccles therefore insisted that 26 of the 60MW sets planned for power stations in the 1960 programme and beyond be replaced by thirteen 120MW sets (producing an estimated saving of over £7 millions in capital costs and £1 million each year in operating costs). Except for one 60MW set (to complete a station which could take nothing larger), the smallest sets installed thereafter were to be 100MW and 120MW. The construction programmes were now clearly less rigid, and the policy had changed to one of eliminating small sets and accepting a calculated degree of risk to promote technical advance.

For several years, Brown and Eccles consolidated this policy, but by the end of 1956 Brown thought that the 1962 forward programme could accommodate a further advance.[1] Some outside opinion favoured 'supercritical' sets (with very high pressures at which water reaching boiling point passes immediately into steam without change of volume) but this was sensibly shelved while further experimental work was undertaken. Neither coal quality nor the high cost of the special steel required seemed to justify any significant increase in steam conditions above those of the 200MW sets, but there would, Brown felt, be economies of about 4 per cent in capital cost by increasing the size to 275MW.[2] Developments in cooling techniques now enabled the components for such sets to be transported by road, but larger components were still not transportable. It was, however, possible to arrange the components of two 275MW sets with the turbines and alternators in two lines, as was common in America. Eccles and Brown proposed that a 550MW 'cross-compound' set of this type (reducing capital costs by a further 2 per cent) should also be included in the 1962 programme. However, their colleagues felt, with some justice, that this was pushing development too rapidly, though by the end of 1957 they were sufficiently reassured to order such a 550MW cross-compound set as well as another straight 275MW set and a prototype 300MW set in the forward programme for 1963.

As Figure 9.1 shows, the Brown revolution represented a substantial advance in the technological frontier for Britain's electricity supply industry. The 275MW set (bottom) was no bigger in profile than the now antiquated slow-speed designs of London's largest prewar sets (top). The standard 30MW sets and 60MW sets (all with relatively undemanding steam conditions and correspondingly low thermal efficiencies) had, after a brief flirtation with 100MW sets, from 1954–5 been replaced in forward programmes by 120MW sets with re-heat and moderate steam conditions, and 200MW sets with re-heat and very advanced steam conditions. By 1956, the forward programmes also included a 275MW set, and serious thought was

	Size and steam conditions	First installed	Station cost per kW installed (1957 prices)	Average annual thermal efficiency (1957 estimates)
	105MW 600 psi 850°	1935	n.a.	27.5%†
	30MW 600 psi 850°F	1929 (first post-war 1948)	£75.5	25.5%
	60MW 900 psi 900°F	1950	£61.9	28.0%*
	100MW 1500 psi 1050°F	1956	£57.9	30.5%
	120MW Re-heat 1500 psi 1000°F/1000°F	1958	£54.7	31.0%
	200MW Re-heat 2350 psi 1050°/1000°F	1959	£54.2	32.0%
	275MW Re-heat 2300 psi 1050°F/1050°F	1962	£50.0	33.5%

0 10 20 30 40 50 60 70 80 90 100
feet

Source: *Proceedings of the British Electrical Power Convention 1957*, pp. 50, 109.

* Some of the later, non-standard 60MW sets, incorporating more advanced steam conditions and re-heat, achieved higher thermal efficiencies around 30 per cent.
† Estimated.
n.a. Not available.

FIG. 9.1   *Major Developments of British Turbo-Alternators 1935–62*

being given to supercritical pressures, 550MW cross-compound sets and other sets of larger size. No one, of course, could tell at the time whether this more adventurous policy would be justified, but events were to prove that at least some of the risks they knew they were taking would pay off. The 100MW and 120MW sets, like the 60MW sets, had teething troubles, but they were minor and completion delays were also not exceptional. The 200MW and larger sets encountered more severe problems (mainly due to poor design work by the manufacturers), though after a few years of difficulty these were to be largely ironed out. High Marnham's first 200MW set was, moreover, the first 'development' set to be commissioned on time in October 1959, and was then the largest in Europe. The lead (lost for a short time in 1961 to France) was to be regained in 1962 with the commissioning of the first 275MW set and in 1963 with the first 550MW cross-compound set (though the inherited relatively small and inefficient sets ordered earlier prevented the Grid system's *average* set sizes and efficiencies equalling France's).

There was more to this than the winning of technical medals. The performance of the sets generally came up to promises: the 200MW sets were, as predicted, flexible in use and consumed 5 per cent less fuel per unit of output than 120MW sets, and 20 per cent less than the standard 60MW sets. Greater problems were encountered with the few larger sets. The 275MW sets unexpectedly had lower thermal efficiencies than 200MW sets, and one 550MW set failed to reach designed output. Despite such problems, the concentration of the programmes for 1959 and the early 1960s on the better of the larger sets (i.e. 120MW and 200MW designs) accelerated the rate of decline in real capital costs to the fastest achieved in postwar Britain. Station capital costs per kW of output (at constant 1958 prices) fell from levels of above £60 in the mid-1950s to around £54.5 when the 120MW sets began to bulk large in the programmes and £43.7 when the 200MW sets joined them and 60MW sets were abandoned.[3] The main criticism to be levelled against the programme in retrospect was that it took too many bites at the cherry of technical advance. In America (with a much larger market, and only two major manufacturers) variety in design did not require engineers to forgo benefits of replication. Britain might have been better advised to emulate France's well-judged, stepped standardisation, initially on the 125MW sets (commissioned from 1955 onwards) and then on 250MW sets (commissioned from 1961 onwards). However, with around forty 120MW sets and nine 200MW sets ordered in these years and only a few sets in the more experimental higher size ranges, British engineers were able to gain some of the advantages of replication whose potential they well knew from their 60MW experience. At the same time they were cautiously exploring new potential advances as the technological frontier receded. All in all, then, the Brown revolution must be accounted an economic and technical success.

This is not to say that it did not create difficulties, both for the manufacturers and for the BEA's own ways of doing things. For the manufacturers, in particular, the increase in the size and technical demands of the new orders was to have a profound influence, and it came at a time when the BEA were able to exercise increasing commercial pressure on them. Indeed comparison of the out-turn costs with the (higher) costs which the BEA anticipated when they embarked on the large set programme suggests that the manufacturers' margins were squeezed considerably and that this factor, as well as economies of scale, explains the acceleration of cost reductions which followed Brown's policy changes.[4] The manufacturers were gradually losing their export market share as foreign competitors recovered from the War, and the BEA were more successful in forcing prices down as supply conditions improved after 1953. Hacking and Pask had agreed in principle to introduce the policy of competitive tendering which Sir Henry Self advocated, but in practice orders had usually been allocated to manufacturers to accelerate work and increase confidence. In the early years the BEA had, indeed, been glad to get any order accepted. In 1954, however, it was agreed that all future orders would normally be put out to competitive tender, though the demanding technical requirements of the larger set developments led them to confine initial discussions to the leading firms.

With the increase in size of sets (and of the related unit boilers, which were now universal), the largest orders in the mid-1950s were nine times as big as in the postwar ordering boom. It was thus evident that the existing number of turbo-alternator manufacturers and boiler-makers was too great to maintain a steady annual flow of orders for each firm. Some engineers wanted to resolve the issue by excluding technically weaker makers completely from the advanced technology sets, but Eccles, conscious of possible public criticism, insisted that they be allowed to tender at least for the later large sets. Although the BEA were not obliged to accept the lowest tender, they in practice sometimes did so when a weak maker, faced with bankruptcy as the alternative, quoted an attractive but uneconomic price to stay in business. (In order to overcome their doubts on such firms' technical and managerial competence, the BEA engineers sometimes had to put their own men in the manufacturers' works to oversee operations. It was not an ideal solution and merely perpetuated a fragmentation of the industry which weakened it commercially and technically in the years ahead.) The fashion of the time was, however, to believe that competitive market forces should be allowed to take their course, however unrealistic this was in a highly organised, semi-monopolistic market such as this, with price-fixing rings on the manufacturers' side and only one major buyer.[5]

Citrine, guided by his socialist inheritance, never liked the competitive market option,[6] but his attempts to get the manufacturers to agree to cost and profit disclosure as a preliminary to agreement on prices was unsuccessful. It foundered partly on the manufacturers' reluctance in the early 1950s to disclose the degree to which they were exploiting the sellers' market and, later, on the change in government policy favouring free market solutions. Citrine's discussions with the manufacturers were finally broken off in February 1957 when a long-running Monopolies Commission enquiry finally condemned the turbo-alternator manufacturers' ring,[7] and the Restrictive Trade Practices Act of the previous year also seemed to make further price discussions illegal. The move towards freer competition did produce reductions in contract prices for the BEA. Among the boiler-makers (who had refused to expand capacity to meet BEA requirements, thus forcing the BEA to bring in new firms) competition was particularly fierce. The turbo-alternator manufacturers' ring, by contrast, (though severely constrained in the early 1950s by the defection of the most efficient firm, Parsons) gained new strength in the mid-1950s despite the change in government monopoly policy. The Central Authority's engineers, who had some fellow feeling for their colleagues in the manufacturing firms, had never been keen to pressure them by importing equipment, but by 1956, against Citrine's protests, the Central Authority also agreed in principle to force ring prices down by importing. Despite earlier suspicions that they would not be permitted to do so, government clearance was given, but the Central Authority remained reluctant to employ this weapon seriously.

The ring system had the effect of sustaining the weaker manufacturers and discouraging rationalisation. The Central Authority engineers increasingly felt that (provided some competition could be maintained, as in America) the proliferation in numbers of competitors was unnecessary. Some would have been happy if the technical leaders were to be the only survivors of the competitive tendering process. In turbo-alternator manufacture, where there were seven competitors, they expected English Electric, Parsons and AEI to do best in the years of high technology, whereas in boiler manufacture, with ten competitors, the leading firms were more clearly Babcock & Wilcox, International Combustion, and Foster Wheeler. Most of these firms had access to American technology through US associates, and the remainder, who were either independent or (like Richardson Westgarth) linked to continental makers, were not considered likely to be capable of meeting the more demanding requirements for the larger-scale, high-technology contracts which by the mid-1950s had begun to dominate forward construction programmes.

The structural adjustment of the electrical manufacturing industry was, however, to be left to market forces and the commercial judgement of the manufacturers, and a *dirigiste* role was, for the time being, abjured both by the BEA and by the Government. The BEA's experience of the new buyers' market, after years in which the manufacturers had been giving them low priority service and late delivery dates in a sellers' market, made some Central Authority engineers feel, moreover, that the new era of competition might be no bad thing. They were to discover, however, that the commercial and political reality of structural adjustment to technical innovation and larger scale was to be more complex than the facile simplifications of the competitive model; and readjustments were to take longer than they had hoped.

It was an essential part of Brown's philosophy (as it had been of Shakeshaft's) that the manufacturers rather than the BEA should shoulder the main burden of research and development in generation technology. The BEA had inherited and expanded the excellent CEB research department at Leatherhead, and this made an invaluable contribution to the Supergrid and transmission development, where the BEA rather than the manufacturers settled the fundamental parameters of design.[8] On turbines and boilers the BEA's engineers did carry out some semi-technical on-the-job research (sometimes jointly with manufacturers) aimed at problems such as improving gas pollution control and boiler performance or preventing corrosion. They also modified small sets to test out proposed manufacturing advances to be incorporated in larger sets, in order to give themselves and the manufacturers a reasonable basis for design extrapolations. The BEA also supported outside research by universities and the Electrical Research Association, but, like most electric utilities abroad, they did not see research as one of their primary functions. There had been a deputy to the chief engineer in charge of research until 1952 (when he left to become a divisional controller), but Pask,

Peattie and Brown all agreed that they did not wish to appoint a deputy to succeed him in this function. Their own research budget was typically substantially underspent and in the mid-1950s Brown and the Central Authority turned down proposals from the head of the Leatherhead laboratory for substantial expansion of research into new areas. The BEA were thus committed to reliance on the manufacturers for the quality of the technical developments on which they had embarked, and to the survival of a competent and integrated research and design function in manufacturing firms subject to increasing competitive pressures. They were, however, to experience a decade of disappointments and disillusion on this score, in the course of which it became increasingly obvious that the manufacturers did not have the financial and technical resources to meet the more demanding requirements of the changes they had launched.

By the mid-1950s, with the development of a buyers' market, the manufacturers were no longer the bottleneck in power station construction. It was the contractors' sitework, supervised by the divisions and their consultants, which was now the major determinant of construction times. Eccles still expressed the hope that they could achieve the original three-year construction target, and this was achieved on a few exceptional stations in the easier years of the mid-1950s, but the average construction time remained at five or more years. The consequences for the policy of innovation were serious. British manufacturers could now usually meet their delivery dates even on advanced sets (and indeed exported large sets to America to fulfil some advanced technology orders there), but while BEA sets were sometimes equal to (or even in advance of) American designs at the time of order, by the time of commission (five to six years later in Britain, three to four in America) they had been overtaken.

The trend towards large sets, moreover, was likely to place just as great a strain on the organisation of the fourteen divisions as on the manufacturers, since it implied that only four stations would be commissioned each year and more would be concentrated on sites such as the Midlands, leaving some divisional construction teams without work in some years, while others would be overloaded. At first the Central Authority had been reluctant to merge the divisions, since the view that they should retain common boundaries with the fourteen Area Boards remained strong, and Citrine disliked any threat of redundancy for the staff. In February 1954, however, they cautiously agreed to an experimental amalgamation (with full protection for staff) of the Merseyside and North Wales division with the North West division. This proceeded smoothly and it was understood that other amalgamations would eventually follow, but the headquarters engineers remained reluctant to devolve significantly greater responsibilities to the larger division, and criticisms of over-centralisation remained.

At the headquarters, moreover, it seemed to Eccles and Verity by 1955 that divisional amalgamation was possibly not enough to cater for the technical changes they were facing. It was not just a question of the larger sets requiring fewer project teams, but also new developments in oil-fired generation and nuclear power (in which the divisions possessed no inherited expertise) would require more centralised guidance. They discussed the idea of setting up three project groups to take over construction, leaving only operational responsibilities to the divisions, but such proposals for organisational change, as usual within the BEA, encountered a profound lack of enthusiasm. The initiatives were shelved, and Verity left for a post in the private sector at the end of 1955.

In some respects, then, the Central Authority remained highly conservative, though they did take the least painful step available to reduce the threatened over-capacity among construction teams. Since nationalisation they had formally guaranteed power station contracts to the three leading electrical engineering consultants, Merz & McClellan, Kennedy & Donkin and Ewbank & Partners. However, in the programme of larger stations there would not be sufficient work to go round, so in 1956 letters were written to all three firms cancelling the arrangement. Future stations were to be controlled almost exclusively by the industry's own teams (though they continued to employ *civil engineering* consultants). The chief engineer's department view (never entirely accepted as fair either inside or outside the BEA) was that the consultants' fees were not justified by lower costs (the industry's own teams were reckoned to construct power stations marginally more cheaply). The truth probably is that the headquarters engineers' insistence on central technical control, just as great for consultants as for their own divisions, effectively barred them from getting the benefits either of 'turnkey' contracts (being offered by some consultants in the early years of nationalisation) or of related modes of contracting permitting more devolved responsibility. Centralised technical control was no less a tenet of the Eccles–Brown faith than it had been of their predecessors. The abandonment of the consultants thus represented a logically consistent (and to them painless) response to the reduced requirements for construction project teams which they now faced.

As Eccles and Brown developed their new policies at headquarters, an internal showdown with the traditional ex-CEB establishment who had previously dominated policy became inevitable. The conflict finally came into the open over the issue of planning, which, as a part-time function of the operations department, had been dominated by ex-CEB men. The rigidity of the planners, both in discouraging experimentation which might compromise operational flexibility and in freezing the design of sets as much as seven years ahead, had been a traditional discontent of the more adventurous generation designers like Brown. By the mid-1950s, moreover, though he had established control of set design in forward programmes, he was increasingly dissatisfied with the control of the planners over questions such as station siting. Brown considered that the development of economies in generation he was proposing should have more weight in siting decisions than the transmission considerations which seemed to dominate the minds of the ex-CEB men. (He felt, for example, that his policy should marginally reduce the amount of capacity being built in the Midlands, since cheaper stations using less coal and requiring less transmission capacity could be more economic away from coalfield sites.) Eccles and Brown were also more in tune with the increasing stress on economic appraisal which governmental financial pressures and the end of physical planning controls were bringing.

At the beginning of 1956, Pask resigned at the age of sixty, conscious that his conservative views were being overruled, and encouraged by his seniors on the Authority to retire early. After a year's interregnum under the older Peattie (who had proved to be the CEB man most sympathetic to new ideas), Eccles persuaded his colleagues to promote Stanley Brown to the chief engineer's post, with men sympathetic to a more central role for generation considerations in future policy as his deputies. At forty-five, Brown had leap-frogged over the senior CEB engineers of the same generation. Within a year, three of his senior rivals had resigned to take jobs outside the electricity supply industry. The revolution was complete; but like most executive revolutions it left blood on the office floor, and the promotion of young and able men was only achieved with the sacrifice of others. The ex-CEB men had not made a great success of the headquarters engineering function in the first five years when they unequivocally dominated it. It remained to be seen whether the problems could be more effectively tackled by a team in which generation design experience was not only more central but also significantly stronger.

10

LABOUR MANAGEMENT UNDER PUBLIC OWNERSHIP

... we start off from the knowledge, that at all events, the projection of ideas comes from the top; from a person who has given a lifetime of service to the workers in industry in general.

> Secretary of the manual workers' trade union side,
> addressing regional conference on Joint
> Consultation at York, 19 November 1954.

... most of us would like to see a greater degree of 'workers' control'; and there will be general agreement on the desirability of creating a greater sense of partnership and participation. But the very hesitations and doubts which assail the Labour movement on 'workers' control' at the moment show how much more complicated the issue of 'power' is than at first sight appears.

> Hugh Gaitskell, *Socialism and Nationalisation*,
> Fabian Tract no. 300, 1956, p. 11.

The electricity supply industry was pre-eminently capital- rather than labour-intensive: it accounted for 8 per cent of UK investment but employed well under 1 per cent of the national workforce. Many engineers and managers naturally devoted their primary energies to the technical and financial policies which were the major touchstones of the industry's performance. Yet the importance of good industrial relations had also traditionally been recognised, since it was vital (not only to the industry but to the British economy generally) that the plant they operated be maintained in continuous operation free of strikes. On nationalisation, the industry also became an important test case for the Labour Party's somewhat imprecise commitment to the control of industry by 'the workers by hand and by brain'. Citrine, though he insisted on participation in the engineering and financial

123

areas in which his deputy chairmen had responsibility for developing policy, devoted his own energies most firmly and consistently to the improvements he considered necessary in the area of labour management. It was evident to his colleagues from the beginning that he would insist on a high priority for labour questions, and that on some central issues on which he felt strongly he would brook no opposition. His moral authority as an unchallenged trustee of the Labour movement's commitment to greater consultation of workers and less authoritarian management was never in doubt. Formally, labour relations were the responsibility of Ernest Bussey (the ex-general secretary of the Electrical Trades Union, now a member of the Central Authority), but he was never more than a trusted lieutenant implementing Citrine's views, and after an illness in 1950 became little more than Citrine's shadow.

For the 70 per cent of the industry's 155 000 employees at the time of nationalisation who were manual workers, collective bargaining machinery – the National Joint Industrial Council (NJIC) – already existed, though adherence to its recommendations had varied throughout the country according to the views of managements and local union strength. The power station engineers (who were, unusually, more highly unionised than the manual workers, under the auspices of the Electrical Power Engineers' Association (EPEA)), also had national collective bargaining machinery, the National Joint Board (NJB). Citrine made it quite clear from the beginning to both managers and unions that the decisions of these bodies would in future be binding throughout the industry. He also insisted that new collective bargaining machinery would be required for all other grades except the chief officers and similar very senior people whose salaries, he agreed, could be the subject of individual bargaining within agreed headquarters guidelines. Two new bodies were set up. The National Joint Council (NJC) negotiated with the unions for clerical and administrative workers, whose salaries and conditions had previously largely followed local government practice (though company undertakings had tended to pay less). It took several more years to gain agreement from the 1300 senior managers and their associations, but eventually, under strong pressure from Citrine, an agreement was drawn up for their representation in separate collective bargaining machinery: the National Joint (Managerial and Higher Executive Grades) Committee. These four collective bargaining bodies determined wages, salaries and conditions for almost all the employees in the industry. Only 150 individuals, mainly the top men earning over £2000 a year, were excluded.

For Citrine, however, the extension and enforcement of collective bargaining was only one step on the way towards 'industrial democracy'. Citrine had never as a trade unionist considered some of the more chimerical proposals for 'workers' control' practical; but he was quite certain that there should be more consultation of workers, less petty tyranny by weak management, and greater participation in areas of policy making where a real impact from the workers would improve decision making. He recognised that conflict would persist over wages and salaries, but felt that the more productive work of consultation could be developed in the nationalised industry through a National Joint Advisory Council (NJAC) on which unions representing all grades of employees were represented. By January 1949, against the pressure of union leaders (who resented the fact that the NJAC was only consultative rather than executive) and managers (who feared that nevertheless it would encroach on their prerogatives), Citrine had forced acceptance of such a body. To the unions he explained that, while constitutionally the NJAC was purely consultative, he would personally ensure that the Central Authority would be morally committed to implement its decisions, and this indeed proved to be the case. The trade unions had half the seats on the NJAC and management the other half, but Citrine usually barred the management side from concerting policy initiatives beforehand. On most aspects, except wages and salary questions, which belonged to the four separate negotiating bodies, decisions on personnel policy emanated genuinely from the NJAC with 50 per cent worker representation. In the case of the Central Authority and its generation divisions NJAC policy was automatically accepted on all occasions (save one when a technicality was invoked to protect an individual). In the Area Boards the majority of NJAC recommendations were accepted in whole or in part, though some of the less sympathetic chairmen from time to time insisted on spiking Citrine's guns and retaining managerial autonomy on specific matters (which were constitutionally their right) by refusing to follow a recommendation.

To keep up the pressure on the divisions and Area Boards, not only on consultative matters, but on collective bargaining (where the Central Authority had powers to enforce national wage and salary agreements on Area Boards), Citrine appointed local officers reporting directly to the headquarters labour relations department, many of them ex-trade union officials. These men – seen by many managers as

Citrine's 'fifth column' – were sometimes resented. Their activities and the new power of the national machinery which they represented did threaten a real loss of autonomy for local management. At the top, also, many senior managers felt that Citrine was spending far too much time and money in this area. Harry Randall, chairman of the London Board, raised this point within six months of nationalisation at the Area Board chairmen's conference and gained some support. Citrine, however, attacked all such comments as being contrary to the intention of nationalisation. Even the two trade unionists who had become Area Board chairmen resented Citrine's central intervention in their Boards, but Citrine stood his ground, insisting in 1948, for example, that a country hotel in Buxton bought by one Board as a staff training centre should be turned over to the Central Authority for general use. The message rang loud and clear: initiatives in this field must be in accord with Citrine's central policy. His energy in hammering out that policy left others behind. Both Board chairmen and union leaders complained at the heavy workload on committees which Citrine's labour policies required of them, but Citrine reduced the pressure only slightly, and that after some managers and union representatives had made clear their discontent by pointedly failing to attend meetings. Anyone who did not accept the importance of labour relations bore a black mark for Citrine thereafter: the initiatives on consultation and negotiations were, for him, central to the purpose of the 1947 Act.

At first the NJAC and its related district and local committees ranged freely over a wide range of issues.[1] Citrine insisted, despite managerial disquiet, that there should be no formal limit to their consultative remit, and he welcomed the flood of local welfare proposals on matters like sports and social clubs, baths, and works canteens which followed from headquarters enquiries and local discussion. Central policy was perhaps most effective in the area of education, where Citrine tried to implement traditional Labour aspirations for equality of opportunity. He insisted on positive discrimination in favour of manual workers on matters such as the award of university or HNC scholarships (in the face of EPEA pressure to exclude manual workers entirely). He energetically promoted general, rather than purely vocational, programmes of education; ranging from elementary physics for stokers to general electrical industry topics at the summer schools which he started and insisted be open to all grades of staff. The consultative machinery also developed policies in areas such as safety, but Citrine's hopes that it would become a vehicle for discussions on efficiency improvements were largely dashed. The shop stewards who usually dominated the local committees (of which there were already 400 by the end of 1948, with a further 100 to follow) preferred to maintain their separate and direct communication with management on pay and conditions. The committees did, however, help the more receptive local managers to develop a local community spirit, loyalty and stability. In that sense, in the hands of good local management, they were a valuable adjunct to the more intangible human relationships which helped reconcile workers to the authority structure required in the industry, and they made that structure more effective.

The expectations of some workers of the benefits of nationalisation had been more ambitious, and, if they were disappointed, this was perhaps more a reflection of the lack of definition and realism in their hopes than of a BEA failure to meet them. Even Citrine, a realist *par excellence*, had occasionally speculated that he might be founding 'a great new economic system, a system which is built on resiliency, flexibility and industrial democracy'.[2] The nationalised Boards were, of course, doing nothing of the kind. Most workers were unaffected by the consultative machinery, and 'participation' was for them merely an irrelevant political slogan. Yet, if success is to be measured by a more modestly realistic yardstick, then, as one later commentator reflected, this was 'one of the most consistent and successful attempts yet made in Britain to bridge the great divide in industry between management and workers'.[3] It did not transform class and authority relationships, and it did not win the wholehearted support of all managers, which was no less central than that of workers to its success. To managers, as to the union leaders, the nitty-gritty of the wage and salary negotiations bulked as a larger consideration than the dream (or nightmare) of consultation and participation. In salary and wage matters, the decisions taken in the negotiating bodies were binding on all Boards, and the unions were probably reflecting their members' wishes when they devoted their energies principally to this end, rather than to the more nebulous pursuit of consultation on wider matters.

The white collar employees, whose salaries were determined by the NJB, NJC and the new higher management negotiating body, initially saw a considerable readjustment of relativities as nationalisation created new jobs and new standards. The general impact was to improve the salaries of a substantial portion of those on lower incomes, and to improve job security. There were some worries, particularly among the engineers in the EPEA, about the erosion of their managerial authority, and later in the 1950s, among the clerks, about the introduction of mechanised accounting, but they were generally resolved to the satisfaction of both parties. Although the white collar staff had more secure conditions than the manual employees, their salary settlements generally followed the movements of manual workers' wages upwards in the early years. By the mid-1950s, however, there was a marked tendency to fall behind. The staff unions, with the EPEA in the vanguard, then increased pressure on the Central Authority, taking them to arbitration, which found in the unions' favour. Staff salaries generally were thereafter restored to their traditional relationship to those of manual workers.[4] There were also substantially higher rises for the more senior staff, thus to some extent restoring differentials *within* the staff grades. In all these negotiations the Government was generally kept at bay, though on the question of equal pay for women, government guidance was accepted and the inequitable differential (women clerks were typically paid only 80 per cent of the men's rate for the same job) was gradually reduced from 1956 onwards in electricity supply, as in the rest of the public sector.

The issues of recruitment and promotion and of management development offered the trade unions an important opportunity to turn back the tide of influence and heredity which they had long felt were regarded as more important than merit in capitalist industry.[5] For Citrine this was a central moral issue. He was scrupulous to the point of unfairness in his determination to turn his back on the nepotism of the capitalist class. When his own son (who had been trained as a lawyer) successfully applied for a job in the legal department, Citrine indignantly vetoed the appointment as soon as he heard of it. He would not have believed any capitalist boss who claimed his son had been appointed on merit, and he did not expect any worker to believe him. Citrine's convictions also coloured corporate policy. He successfully sued for libel when he was accused of favouritism in the appointment of a divisional controller and went to great pains at the NJAC to stress the fairness and openness of the system to the trade unions. Outside critics sometimes said that favouritism had been replaced by 'Buggins' Turn': that the BEA positively discriminated against excellence in favour of seniority. There were no doubt many individual cases of this, but the accusation is too sweeping. Examples such as Brown's promotion over the heads of older men on the generation side show a quite different approach;

and, of course, it was still the case that individual managers throughout the organisation were able to pick high flyers if they wished to. However, there was now perhaps a greater reluctance to single out young men for accelerated advancement at an early stage, and at the very top there was occasional discontent with inconsistent policies on promotion. In 1956, for example, one Area Board chairman wanted to promote his chief engineer to the Board, but the Minister insisted it must be an *outside* appointee; a year later, a different Minister to whom the same chairman made a proposal for a cross-posting said that he could not accept it on the grounds that the appointee should come from *inside* the Board. However, the civil servants did their best to discipline Ministers to greater consistency on matters of this kind. There was, moreover, some cachet to be gained from the political appointments procedure at the top, which conferred a greater sense of independence and status on members of Area Boards, and this for many of them made up for the occasional fickleness of the procedure.

Perhaps the most serious problem in management development was the level of salaries. Although, for many municipal men, nationalisation had brought salary increases, and for some company men there had been personal allowances to compensate for cuts (pp. 9–10, above), their salaries in the 1950s tended to lag behind those in the private sector, certainly for the best men. At the very top the Boards' members' own salaries still formed a ceiling (fixed by government and tending not to rise) which senior employees could not exceed (see pp. 184–5, below). Ungenerous pension rights, the absence of performance-related remuneration, and subjection to political intervention also reduced job satisfaction for senior men. For financial and other reasons, then, there was a rather larger flow of men at the top leaving the industry for private sector jobs than there was in the reverse direction.[6] The possibility which had existed before nationalisation of senior men bidding up salaries by approaching other supply companies was now less feasible, since there were common negotiated pay scales for senior managers throughout the industry and a gentleman's agreement between the Boards and the BEA to limit poaching of each other's staff. Many managers, particularly electrical engineers, felt locked into this industry by their training, though some left for the electrical manufacturers and consultants, who offered the most closely comparable outside employment and, by the mid-1950s, significantly higher salaries.

At the very time when this haemorrhage of ability and the salary differentials were greatest, the BEA's own intake of young graduates fell to below ten a year. Again salaries were partly the problem. The EPEA successfully opposed special salary grades and promotion paths for new graduate engineers, fearing unfair competition with their own older and less well-trained members. In an increasingly competitive market (with an inadequate supply of good graduates in Britain and a burgeoning industrial demand for them), the headquarters attitude was simply to hope the problem would go away. Self condemned the 'swollen heads' of graduate entrants, and insisted that 'touting' for them only made matters worse.[7] The leaders of the industry were slow to recognise their weak position in the job market. Yet their industry offered perhaps some of the brightest opportunities of growth and technical challenge, particularly on the generation side, and their need to recruit young managers and engineers to staff their expansion was self-evident. Their anaemic approach to wider recruitment and management development must, then, be accounted one of the weaker aspects of their personnel policy.

It was the NJIC negotiations of the manual workers which made most of the running on pay in these years. Their pay was the major determinant of the Electricity Boards' wage and salary bills, accounting initially for about a fifth of overall costs – four times as much as white collar salaries – but declining as the higher postwar capital charges dwarfed labour costs in the Boards' financial accounts. The Boards were faced by four major unions, the Electrical Trades Union (ETU) and Amalgamated Union of Engineering Workers (AUEW), representing the skilled men, and the Transport and General Workers (TGWU) and General and Municipal Workers (GMWU), for the unskilled men. While it would have been more convenient to face one union (and the management side regretted sometimes that the senior union negotiators were non-specialists, often lacking adequate knowledge of their members' jobs in electricity supply), the unions' attempts at merger (which were made periodically before and after nationalisation) failed.

Citrine and his colleagues concentrated their attention on supporting the official leaders of these four unions, and impressed on junior managers a commitment to unionisation which had typically existed before nationalisation only in Labour-controlled municipal undertakings. Only about 60 per cent of workers were unionised in 1948, and there was strong opposition from managers to a closed shop, but Citrine insisted on giving shop stewards generous facilities to see men during working time to persuade them to join. Under Citrine's guidance men who refused were also now called in by the local manager, who explained that it was official policy for men to join a union. A daunting set of interviews and discussions with local, district and national officials followed if the man persisted in refusing to join. It was a brave man who ran this gauntlet very far. Grievance procedures were also firmly based on the unions as the sole and legitimate representative of the workers. Understandably the level of unionisation increased considerably (and, by the time the closed shop was finally introduced, in 1969, approached 100 per cent). Management also acted firmly to avoid further union fragmentation, discouraging recruitment by and refusing recognition to the National Union of Public Employees (NUPE) and various supervisory unions. They also consistently refused the ETU's pressure for separate negotiating rights for its members engaged on electrical contracting work in the Boards, successfully fighting ETU strikes to force other unions out of that area by, for example, subsidising the legal costs of men opposing such an ETU monopoly. The maintenance of the status quo of vested union interest was their watchword throughout. This recipe had, of course, been well tried in the TUC's own inter-union disputes machinery (which Citrine knew so well), and in this context also the ETU eventually accepted it (formally withdrawing its claims to monopoly over contracting in 1959).

The quid pro quo of this support for the vested interests of unions was that Citrine expected the union officials to deal firmly with unofficial strikes as he instructed his own line managers themselves to do. In December 1949, for example, there was a strike led by the unofficial shop stewards' movement in London, where there was a long history of Communist influence. The strikers knocked out one fifth of the generating capacity in the capital and the Home Counties. The Labour Government, with Citrine's full backing, brought in the army to operate some stations (a not entirely successful initiative since they lacked experience and damaged equipment). More successfully, they relied at other stations on staff engineers and clerks to break the strike, and it was on this strategy that emergency plans for strike-breaking were thereafter based.[8] Meanwhile Citrine brought the official union leaders in, insisting that they disown their members on strike (which they did). The men were forced back, and Citrine increased the BEA's expenditure on welfare schemes in the stations where he felt local grievances were legitimate. In all cases of concessions, he gave as much credit as he could to the official union leaders, trying to win the union members' support away from the unofficial movements. In this he was largely successful. For the next ten years, the unofficials, though they sometimes appeared as a 'voice offstage' at the negotiating sessions, were relatively quiescent.

The official union side at the NJIC was chaired by Frank Foulkes, who had succeeded Bussey (when he moved to the BEA management side) at the head of the ETU. A Communist, Foulkes denounced Citrine and Bussey publicly as no better than their capitalist predecessors in being the 'representatives of monopoly finance',[9] but, aside from his colourful jargon, he operated within the norms of the British industrial relations tradition. He was accepted by the other unions (as the overall leader of the union side) and liked by managers (who respected him as a man who would keep to an agreement). On Citrine's insistence, Foulkes had disowned the London unofficials, and his cooperation was vital in sorting out the mass of different special allowances for workers inherited from the pre-nationalisation undertakings. The early years were largely taken up with this problem of standardising wages and conditions throughout the industry. As local bonuses for long-service and profit-sharing, and 'perks', like cheap electricity concessions, were gradually phased out, there was inevitably some discontent. Foulkes used all his bargaining power to win cash benefits for ending these anomalies, but unions and management did eventually agree on a more uniform wages structure.

Throughout all the negotiations, Citrine insisted that the Government should keep out of the arena. Both Labour and Conservative ministers asked for wage restraint at various stages, and Citrine would occasionally discuss the BEA position with them (while severely rebuking any of his colleagues who did so). He did, however, refuse point blank to consult Ministers before arriving at any settlement. This was, he felt, clearly the Central Authority's job, and in 1950 he told his colleagues why he had refused direct cooperation with the Government's incomes policy:

> ... I replied to the Minister informing him that his letter had left me under the impression that it was the desire of the Government to intervene in the actual progress of negotiations on wages and salaries and this policy appeared to me to raise very serious principles and to affect the freedom of negotiations between the Central Authority and the Trade Unions. I told the Minister that I could give no such assurance as he had asked for (on consultation

during wage negotiations) without an official request to do so from the Ministry and then only after referring the matter to the Central Authority ... No further correspondence has taken place.

Some of Citrine's colleagues were taken aback at his breathtaking nerve, but the Minister in fact recognised the force of Citrine's point that the Government must not try to exert pressure informally where they did not carry responsibility. Later Conservative Ministers were also concerned about wage settlements, but Citrine none the less managed to hold this line of independence. All the same the unions continually accused him of bowing to government policy, and he admitted to having national policy in mind in restricting potentially inflationary wage settlements.

The overall levels of manual workers' earnings in the industry were not on nationalisation very generous. From being near the top, the electricity supply workers had fallen to 59th (out of 95) in the earnings league by 1947. They were then on average earning 6 per cent less in real terms than they had before the War, a rather greater wartime sacrifice of living standards than had typically been suffered by other workers.[10] None the less, in the first ten years of nationalisation their negotiated pay settlements did nothing to make up this decline in their relative position, with settlements generally just keeping ahead of the inflation rate to produce a 15 per cent improvement in earnings in real terms. This was no more of an improvement in living standards than that which other workers could expect in these years of recovery, and electricity workers remained surprisingly low in the earnings league. The unions occasionally put pressure on the Electricity Boards by calling an overtime ban, or insisting on arbitration. Recourse to arbitration was required by the NJIC constitution in the event of disagreement, though Citrine greatly disliked it (seeing it as a confession of management failure). On the few occasions when they did resort to arbitration, however, the findings were usually for the unions. This, together with the maintenance of a depressed level in the earnings league, suggests that Board chairmen such as Randall were being intemperate when they criticised Citrine for giving away too much. (In 1956 Randall resigned and, to the delight of many Conservatives, attacked Citrine publicly in a letter to *The Times*.[11])

The industry's fringe benefits in this period, equally, cannot be said to have been excessive. The terms for sick pay and holidays had, it is true, been traditionally good in electricity supply, but there was no major improvement in these after nationalisation. For pensions, some 70 per cent of manual workers had (unusually for British industry) been covered in the schemes inherited on nationalisation, but this proportion actually declined in the early years, as no fresh schemes were started for new recruits. The unions explicitly ruled out a superannuation scheme initially (they believed the Government should pay for a national scheme), and the Ministry initially also discouraged it (feeling the unions might use it as a way round the voluntary pay restraint to which the TUC had agreed). Eventually, however, a new superannuation scheme was introduced in 1955 (with 5 per cent contributions from employees who wished to join matched by an equivalent amount from the employer) and the proportion of workers with adequate pensions thereafter gradually increased.

The contemporary criticisms of excessive overall levels of pay settlements were, then, misdirected, but that is not to say that the emerging pay structure for manual workers was ideal. Indeed, Citrine and Bussey were appalled to find that the differential for skilled men, which had fallen during the War, remained too small, as the union negotiators pressed for flat-rate rather than percentage increases. The management side successfully forced larger increases for skilled men in some years (feeling that this was needed to attract labour while the unskilled rate was quite adequate), but at other times they found the union side hostile. It seemed that Foulkes was deliberately overriding the interests of his own (largely skilled) ETU members in the interests of the unskilled unions, and in 1956 Citrine called him in to discuss the situation. Foulkes explained that the representatives of the unskilled men were in a majority on the NJIC, and that solidarity with this majority view prevented him acting in the way Citrine proposed, which he agreed was the right one. In other respects, moreover, the ETU had interests in the status quo: they insisted, for example, on a uniform skilled rate, whereas the management would have preferred to pay more for the greater skills of power station fitters (mainly AUEW men) than for the (largely ETU) service electricians. Management was thus prevented from rationalising the wage structure to encourage the acquisition of skills because of the balance of power on the union side. Labour market conditions alone would have favoured higher skill premiums.

More serious than this was the effect of nationalisation and the national wage structure on middle and lower management morale and on work disciplines. The setting of quite rigid national pay scales greatly limited the freedom of local management to determine the earnings of their workers. There was virtually no 'wage drift' beyond the level of national settlements in electricity supply, in contrast to many of the other industries like engineering in which the same unions had members. This strong central control was seen by some senior managers as a useful discipline on wage costs, but lower down there was increasing resentment that most questions of gradings, demarcation and pay had to be referred from the local officers up through the district machinery and, if significant precedents were involved (as they often were), even up to national level. On the shop floor, management powers were weakened. Real power over allocation of holidays or overtime, special work conditions allowances, and other items subject to local negotiation, sometimes lay with the shop stewards. Their power was considerably strengthened by the official support of union membership coming right from Citrine at the top, while the power of the lowest management tier, the foremen, declined. The manual workers insisted that foremen, who had previously often had privileged pay and conditions to match their management status, should be subject to the manual workers' negotiating machinery and not join separate supervisory unions. Citrine reluctantly conceded this in the early 1950s (in return for union agreement to superior pay and conditions for foremen), but many middle managers considered this a mistake, since it opened the possibility of foremen being disciplined by unions for carrying out management policy.

The effect on work intensity of these changes in the relative powers of management and stewards was soon noticeable. The industry already suffered from a number of restrictive practices, and these appear to have been strengthened, and even spread to areas (such as rural districts) where they had been virtually unknown before. An internal 1955 survey of all the Boards and divisions by Bussey showed a rich variety of sources of inefficiency through artificial demarcation barriers or other restrictive practices. Electricians would insist on plumbers doing simple work on water heaters; fitters and electricians would insist that any jobs which required the use of tools were for skilled men only. Meter testers would not repair meters. Electrical repair-men insisted on chauffeurs (or extra payment for driving themselves); by the same token, drivers refused to carry out simple repairs, or to load or maintain their vehicles. In some cable-jointing teams there was an absurdly low level of cooperation between the jointer, mate and labourer, and a correspondingly low rate of completion. In power stations, operational workers refused to do any other work such as painting or maintenance when the plant was shut down; and new large boilers or turbines with simpler control techniques requiring only one attendant were still manned by two.

The object of much of this make-work activity was to create overtime, which remained one of the few matters subject to local bargaining.[12] Local managers often colluded with the stewards, conscious that this was the only way to meet competition on pay in the local market, given the rigid national pay scale. They paid for overtime (above the 44-hour week which had become standard in Britain after the War) at time-and-a-half or at double time for Sundays. Significantly overtime working by electricity supply workers was highest in areas like the Midlands, where competition from other prosperous and expanding employers was greatest. Overtime thus became the industry's own alternative to wage drift: the only form available to local managers. Those who refused to make use of this device, such as the South Eastern Board, found they simply could not attract labour at the rates for the standard week which they were offering. They thus had to stop the expansion of their own contracting business, and contract out jobs like cable-laying to private firms who could pay higher wages.

It is not difficult to understand, then, why, in the industry generally, overtime grew from an average of under $2\frac{1}{2}$ hours weekly on nationalisation to nearly five hours ten years later. This increase came, moreover, despite a considerable increase in manpower, particularly in the years immediately after nationalisation. In each of the first two years, for example, the numbers employed increased by more than 10 ten per cent, much of this in order to meet the needs of the 44-hour, 5-day shift systems agreed shortly before nationalisation. The unions at local level insisted on the most inflexible interpretation of shift working, despite national agreements on flexibility. Inevitably this continued to boost the recruitment of new workers to the industry in subsequent years. The inexorable drive for overtime from both management and men was a clear attempt to get earnings up to more sensible levels than were allowed by the national pay structure. Certainly the make-work practices were not motivated in this expanding industry by fear of job losses. Indeed the industry committed itself to a no-redundancy policy on nationalisation, and later on divisional reorganisation. The only redundancies were in areas such as clerical jobs or in obsolete power stations closing down. Here unions and management were able to negotiate satisfactory transfers or voluntary redundancies.

The result of the reinforcement of restrictive practices was abysmally low productivity. Most of the gains made in the War (when restrictive practices had declined and work effort had been enormously increased) were lost. By the mid-1950s the value added per worker in the industry was still below the level achieved two decades earlier, despite substantially increased levels of capital investment per worker.[13] Although there are difficulties in international comparison, it is probable that the physical productivity of labour in the British electricity supply industry was not only below that in America but also below that of some European countries.[14] A few of the more imaginative senior managers in the Boards and divisions could see that they were trapped in this productivity stalemate because of the rigid application of national wage rates, but few could see the way out, and the will to change was generally weak. There were, after all, management gains from centralisation in avoiding wage drift, and for union leaders in enhancing their own prestige and bringing the bargaining power of their strongest members to bear to gain rises above market levels for their weaker members. Some local managers pressed for the right to introduce local wage incentives, and consultants employed by them recommended incentive schemes, but Citrine and his colleagues (rightly) feared that the unions might exploit these to create anomalies, which could only be rectified nationally by a general increase. On several occasions they persuaded Foulkes and the unions to make a general verbal commitment to flexible shifts or productivity discussions. The unions, however, gave nothing but words at the national level in return. At the local level they banned 'work study', which managers had to do under the guise of 'operational research' (a term then confusingly used in the supply industry to mean work measurement, despite the clearly different usage in the rest of the English-speaking world). Headquarters management effectively acquiesced in the general failure to follow up such studies as were possible, and little thought was given to how to break the stalemate. Neither stewards nor managers were offered tools which would enable them to cooperate without sacrificing pay levels, which not only the workers but also the managers (faced with tight local labour markets) wanted.

It was, of course, possible for local management to raise the issue of productivity through the consultative machinery rather than the pay negotiating bodies. Yet the NJAC and its local counterparts were not taken seriously by the unions on matters which they rightly felt could only be discussed in the context of NJIC pay negotiations. The former bodies were far too concerned with the activities of welfare and morale-boosting to be truly effective on the central issues of pay and productivity, with which management and men were concerned. At headquarters, the realisation of what was happening made some, like Self, recognise that they had given far too much attention to consultation and not enough to these issues. Neither Citrine nor Bussey were, however, able to suggest any solution to the problems posed by the machine which they had created, and indeed they resented criticisms in this area. When shortcomings in the practical application of a man's ideals are revealed, it is not easy to persuade him to do anything more than reiterate his faith in the ideals, and this was what Citrine in his later years did. The broadened understanding and 'great human change'[15] which Citrine had wanted from worker consultation had not resolved the fundamental problems of conflict. Indeed the machinery which he had created had strengthened the unions and weakened management, but, rather than an improvement in efficiency, the industry was beset by restrictive practices which compromised its efficiency. An industrial relations machinery had been designed by a trade union leader for trade unions to make their full contribution; yet the goods had not been delivered. The consultative machinery remained as an enduring legacy of Citrine's very personal statement on labour management in the early years of BEA personnel policy. Yet it is hard to believe that, for most workers, that compensated for the loss of leisure through increased overtime, or for the inadequate skilled pay scales. Union leaders and headquarters management had conspired together, albeit often for the best possible motives, to create a system which locked them into this stalemate. It was not until more hard-headed union leaders and more imaginative management had taken over that system in the 1960s that they realised the full potential of Citrine's tightly centralised national bargaining (p. 281, below).

11

RETROSPECT: CITRINE, SELF AND THE MANAGEMENT OF CHANGE

I had another kind of dream, which recurred on several occasions.
This was that while I remained Chairman of the BEA I no longer
possessed any authority. People with whom I conversed in my
dreams would smile at me indulgently and show general friendli-
ness. But they took no notice of any orders I gave.

Citrine, *Two Careers* (1967) p 255.

Lord Citrine, as chairman of the British Electricity Authority for
more than ten years, was, quite simply, the biggest British businessman. No other industrialist at any time in history has had control
of so large a share of national investment for so long a period. The
organisation which he headed was massive by any standards, and his
dream of losing authority within it (see quotation above) was not
unique to him. None of his successors have been able to ignore the
enormity of the challenge that faces them, nor failed to experience
doubts about their capacity to monitor and direct such a large
organisation. The burden on Citrine was, moreover, immeasurably
greater since he lacked experience as a businessman or engineer and
was faced with the more difficult initial task of welding together many
disparate pieces into one national organisation. Any achievements
and failures of the first ten years of nationalisation must, then, be
seen in the context of the almost superhuman task which its
organisers faced.

The chairmanship of such a huge organisation inevitably takes on a
representational, political role, indeed almost a symbolic regal one,
as on Citrine's frequent public appearances at power station opening
ceremonies. At these aspects of the job Citrine was undoubtedly a

success. To both workers and managers his complete commitment to the success of nationalisation was never in doubt, and they grew to admire his efforts on the industry's behalf in bargaining for the resources they required for expansion. His solidarity with the industry soon made as strong an impression on Ministers as his earlier solidarity with the trade union movement had. His full-blown commitment to the industry's interests seemed to many a good substitute for the engineering and management skills which he clearly lacked, but on which he was willing to take advice from his deputies. He publicly expressed his own role as excluding the questions of management efficiency, which he could confidently leave to Self and Hacking; and indeed (even had he possessed the time) he lacked the threshold level of knowledge necessary to participate fully in many of the management and engineering decisions resolved at deputy level. None the less he insisted on being consulted on all major issues and he felt it important that he should set the tone of the whole organisation.

For Citrine the essential part of the corporate ethos was human relations.[1] He was conscious that such a large organisation would inevitably be criticised for being too anonymous, over-centralised and bureaucratic, but he personally fought an unceasing battle to overcome this, which became almost an obsession. He insisted on his photograph being widely displayed (despite criticism from both management and unions of this personality cult), arguing that such symbols of individuality were a means of overcoming impersonality in organisations. When he received papers he encouraged the writers to identify individuals by their name rather than just their office; and he worked hard to memorise lists of names of those he was to meet, so that he could greet them as acquaintances rather than as subordinates. He kept shorthand notes of a myriad of conversations and visits so that, at the next meeting with a person he had already met, he could refer to the previous topic of conversation. This attracted genuine admiration from people at all levels, who saw it as an earnest of his intention to become the leader and representative of the industry from personal acquaintance with its people and its problems, and not simply as the standard bearer of the abstract political ideal of nationalisation.

This did not mean that he merely reflected the industry's views. On some subjects, notably labour relations, where his own views were clear and firm, he imposed his ideas despite all opposition. On others (such as the move away from coal-fired power stations to oil and nuclear power), he was to impose unpopular views on which he saw the Government would insist (see pp. 169–71, 177–8, below). He was able to preserve independence from government precisely because he had a better political sense than many managers and engineers of what the Government would or would not accept.

Within the industry, he seemed to many senior colleagues to be a demagogue and an autocrat, but he rarely failed to consult, and on many issues followed the guidance of his deputy chairmen. Once his mind was made up, there was never any doubt about the toughness with which he wielded authority. He never seemed to tire in debate and had a tremendous capacity for thinking on his feet, recalling previous arguments of his opponents and turning them to his own advantage. He knew when to show patience and kindness, or when to appear stern and angry. Individual colleagues were on several occasions reduced to tears in his office, sometimes as he rebuked them for dealing unfeelingly with subordinates. He was a good enough psychologist to use such tactics to create loyalty and respect, and he is remembered with awed affection even by those few who opposed him.

Much of the responsibility for developing major policies none the less fell on his two deputy chairmen, who were understandably restive in playing second fiddle to Citrine, who remained chairman for the (subsequently unequalled) period of ten years. The Ministry pondered the desirability of replacing him throughout the 1950s, and received some encouragement from his colleagues when they raised the question privately. When their first five-year terms were up, both Hacking and Self said they would not remain for long if Citrine were reappointed, but the Ministry decided to call their bluff (holding out the hope of subsequent change by only reappointing all three for three-year terms). Hacking accordingly left in 1953, but Self did not carry out his threat either then or in 1955, when the Ministry again successfully called his bluff after he threatened to resign if he were not appointed to Citrine's job. Despite Self's discomfiture in playing a secondary role, on which he spoke frankly to Citrine (though not revealing his attempts to replace him), the two had a deep and genuine affection for each other. They were both newcomers to the industry and were both, in a sense, self-taught. (Self had acquired a string of six science and arts part-time degrees since joining the civil service at the age of sixteen, culminating in 1951 with a Ph.D in philosophy for a thesis attempting to reconcile religion and science.)

Citrine and Self kept each other's counsel more than they shared it with the third member of the triumvirate (first Hacking, then Eccles). For many Area Board chairmen and engineers, this civil service and trade union cocktail seemed unappealing. There were, moreover, signs that the division of duties Citrine had proposed between Self as deputy chairman for administration and the other deputy chairman in charge of engineering was not working well. Self's attempts to impose administrative and financial controls over the engineers on the generation side, though they identified a real weakness, merely provoked opposition from the engineers and only reluctant and partial acceptance of the principle of control. No proper decentralised system of budgetary control and decentralised management emerged from this. Hacking, on the other hand, had not even made a serious attempt to extend his engineering control to the Area Board side as envisaged in Citrine's organisational plan. He participated in discussions and decision making on distribution in a formal sense, but showed little real interest. The formal division between one deputy's responsibility for administration and the other's for engineering and operations was, then, by the mid-1950s *de facto* suspended in many areas. Self, though retaining control of secretarial, legal, and financial affairs throughout the industry, concentrated more on Area Board affairs, while Eccles devoted most attention to the generation side (as indeed the early planners of nationalisation had envisaged). The overlapping of the responsibilities of what were effectively two joint chief executives under Citrine was recognised within the Ministry as potentially awkward, but they also recognised the emerging *de facto* division of responsibility. Citrine, who had argued for the original overlapping responsibility on the organising committee in 1947, was brought up against the difficulties it created when he had to make firm choices (such as supporting Self against the engineers in setting up the contracts department), but it was only under later government pressure that he was willing to take steps to reverse his earlier decision formally (see pp. 167, 186, below). For the time being the Ministry considered Self an 'essential foil' both to Citrine's centralising autocratic tendencies, and to the 'over-enthusiasm' of the electrical engineers.

Contemporary assessments of the success of the newly nationalised electricity supply industry depended more on the political views of the assessor than on objective ratings, but even Conservatives were forced to concede that in some respects the industry had done well. Its reputation was certainly superior to that of the other industries nationalised by Attlee's Government, though this was perhaps as much because of its inherently strong market position and rich technical and managerial inheritance as because of post-nationalisation developments. Some of its achievements were, none the less, a direct result of reorganisation and nationalisation. The acceptance of the burden of standardising consumer voltages, the improved Grid merit order of power station operation, the economies in capital expenditure on distribution and improvements in the reliability of integrated local networks, all came more rapidly than had been the case under the previous regime of divided ownership. The experiments in workers' participation and increases in welfare and education expenditure by the Boards also directly followed from nationalisation, or rather from Citrine's forceful interpretation of it. There was a fuzziness about what exactly the industry's 'national' (as opposed to 'profit-seeking') role ought to be, but Citrine and Self were strongly wedded to the overtones of public service implied by this role, and Ministers were in practice happy to see its definition remain fuzzy. On rural electrification, for example, the politicians were glad that the subsidy came from the industry rather than the Treasury, and the engineers and managers in the industry were glad to retain the freedom to carry out the programme in the way they felt was least uneconomical. Arguably their rural subsidies went no further than a prudent private enterprise firm would have gone in recognising clearly-felt social and political priorities in the community in which they operated, though some outside critics did feel that a clearer demarcation between the business and commercial function (to be determined by the Boards) and broader national interest issues (to be determined by the Minister) would be desirable.[2]

In the last resort, moreover, it is as business firms, responding commercially and technically to the needs of consumers, that the Electricity Boards must be judged. Their most tangible achievement was the more than doubling of power station capacity in the first ten years. By 1957, the rate of new capacity commissioning was two-and-a-half times the highest prewar level. By the winter of 1953/4, voltage reductions alone were sufficient to limit the peak load at most times and there was only one major power cut; by the winter of 1956/7 both voltage reductions and power cuts had largely disappeared. Difficulties in the management of construction projects persisted (with construction times remaining excessively long), and the move to new technologies was, until 1954, excessively hesitant, but real cost reductions were being achieved. By 1957 the cost of new power station capacity was still the same in money terms as ten years earlier, despite a 70 per cent increase in the cost of materials and wage rates over that period. The thermal efficiency of Grid power stations had increased by a fifth, and station siting had been shifted to cheaper coal areas following the Supergrid decision, both of these helping to offset the rise in coal prices. The Boards had had to increase their prices to consumers by only 34 per cent between 1948 and the end of 1957, compared with a rise of 60 per cent in the retail price index (though, as we have seen, this involved some undesirable underpricing). The number of consumers had been increased by more than a third, and perhaps only a tenth of homes still lacked a supply, with the majority of them confident that they would be connected soon, as the distribution investment backlog was gradually made up.

Perhaps their most impressive achievement, however, was in building a series of national, area and divisional organisations out of the close on six hundred separate entities which they had inherited. We have at times focussed on disagreements and overlapping between the various components, but it was arguably more surprising that the disruption caused by the 1948 reorganisation of the industry was not greater. Certainly the record of the private sector in multi-firm mergers of this kind had been sufficiently bad, in terms of personality disputes, organisational problems and reduced profitability, to discourage such large mergers from being undertaken at all,[3] while other nationalised industries with similarly gargantuan mergers to undertake (e.g. coal and transport) were subjected to earlier and stronger criticism on the organisational forms they adopted.[4] The BEA too were criticised for excessive centralisation and bureaucracy, though their initial centralising policy in fact paralleled that in the more successful large-scale private enterprise mergers such as ICI in matters such as establishing common control procedures, staffing practices and a sense of identity.[5] Post-merger conflicts of personality persist in most such large organisations, and the BEA was no exception, but the central figures in electricity, for all their disagreements, did build on the existing *esprit de corps* of the industry and were in many areas able to work efficiently together.

There were, however, real weaknesses in the organisation, which went beyond the overlapping responsibilities of the deputy chairmen, and in some areas these weaknesses were reflected in errors of policy with profoundly damaging consequences. Both critics and defenders of the nationalised industries have offered them the alibi that the transitional problems of organisation were so great that significant efficiency improvements could not be expected in the first ten years,[6] but for electricity this seems inappropriate. The grass roots organisation they inherited was sufficiently strong to carry them through, and the real weaknesses were caused by poor decision making at the top rather than by dislocation at the periphery. In labour relations, Citrine's strong measures to enforce national agreements deprived local managers of the control they felt they needed. This locked them into a very low level of labour productivity, and the industry learnt the hard way that appeals for cooperation between management and labour were insufficient. Yet no workable productivity procedures, based on the self-interest which dominated the value system of both workers and management, were devised. Citrine's appeals for cooperation on efficiency would have sounded quite familiar to a Japanese manager or worker (and to Citrine they at first seemed a reasonable corollary of the state take-over of industry), but they fell on the deaf ears of trade unions whose values were, for all their accompanying baggage of collectivist rhetoric, firmly within the liberal individualist tradition of the British trade union movement.[7]

Outside the field of labour relations, the Area Boards and divisions continued in many ways to follow the policies their personnel had developed before nationalisation, though in a number of crucial areas, headquarters' views became increasingly important. In the area of generation, as we have seen, the Brown revolution overcame some of the problems of inertia which earlier had afflicted policy making, though question marks remained on relations with the manufacturers and the best way of decentralising construction responsibilities. Financial controls, despite Self's attempts to improve them, were weak on both the generation and the distribution sides. The greatest weakness, however, was on costing and pricing. There was mounting pressure from government for proper costing of activities such as retailing and contracting, and from within the organisation for new thinking on domestic pricing. Yet the headquarters triumvirate and most of the chief officers and Area Board chairmen were simply unwilling to take the required initiatives in this field. The problem here was not so much poor organisation, as sheer conservatism at the top. It was frequently strengthened rather than modified by outside criticism as they reacted to critics with almost paranoid attempts at self-justification. Less public information was now available on the industry than before nationalisation,[8] and some of the outside criticism was (partly in consequence of this) wide of the mark. Yet there were few signs within the industry of facing up to the important strategic issues raised by critics (whose basic views, castigated at the time as 'irresponsible', the industry was later reluctantly to accept were right). Indeed the Area Board chairmen's conferences seemed sometimes designed to exemplify Sir Lewis Namier's dictum that an assembly around a table, whose objectives were dissimilar, would come to a collective decision which was worse than that which any of them would have arrived at individually. Compromise may promote harmony and the quiet life, but it is not necessarily conducive to rational decision making and economic efficiency. Many of the industry's leaders were implacably opposed to domestic price reform, while Self seemed by the mid-1950s to have lost his confidence and determination to impose effective budgetary control in the wake of persistent opposition from the engineers and others.

Organisational reform, meanwhile, was proceeding only slowly with the experimental merger of generating divisions. Citrine, Self, Hacking and Eccles all generally proved hostile to proposals for organisational change. Although they frequently used the word 'flexible' when discussing their organisation, they in fact were very reluctant to change it, usually appealing to the need to avoid further disruption and anxieties for employees after the already substantial change on nationalisation. They were none the less under some pressure from within to consider reforms. Some officers at headquarters resented the amount of committee work, and most divisions and Area Boards would have liked to see more responsibilities devolved to them. The complaint most frequently heard was that encapsulated in the words 'red tape'. The BEA bureaucracy certainly did sometimes show the classic symptoms of a trained incapacity to adjust, an inflexible and unresponsive official line, and an entrenched position which could only with great mental contortions be abandoned. All of this appeared more especially frustrating in an industry in which much of upper and middle management had not long before been used to greater independence. Citrine defended the committee structure (which was largely his and Self's creation) as being the only alternative to autocracy and essential to keep people informed, rejecting the idea that more individual responsibility was possible given the Authority's central responsibility. This distaste for delegation reinforced the inflexibility of the system. The top-level meetings which might have initiated change – the Central Authority itself, and the triumvirate's meetings with their headquarters officers, with Area Board chairmen, and with divisional controllers – failed to develop strategic policy initiatives in key areas. Managers frequently left these and similar lower-level meetings feeling, like Queen Victoria facing Gladstone, that they had been harangued as at a public meeting rather than that they had contributed usefully to policy formulation. Fortunately there were individuals who did enough work outside these sessions – notably Eccles in promoting the Brown revolution – for some sound strategic decisions to be taken in spite of the weaknesses of the decision making procedure.

When Citrine was taken to task for encouraging bureaucracy and committee-itis, he often pointed out that similar criticisms could, with equal justice, be levelled at large private sector organisations. Subsequent studies of the history of such large corporations tend to confirm this (though, it is now generally accepted that these could in part be overcome by improved management methods, and were shared weaknesses rather than shared strengths). Few private sector companies had come to terms with the complex strategic and organisational problems which rapid growth and technical change posed for them in the postwar years. ICI, for example, though it had adopted a decentralised multidivisional structure many years before, emerged from the War with many unclear boundaries between strategy formulation and execution, and their organisation, riddled with committees in the War, was still not fully decentralised to profit centres.[9] In many other large British firms modern managerial techniques of decentralisation and budgetary control were typically non-existent, or adopted in a form which severely limited their potential effectiveness.[10] The BEA's problems were, then, widely shared by British industrial firms.

The critics none the less had a point. At its worst the inadequacy of coordination and strategic planning in the BEA could border on the ridiculous. It was inconceivable, for example, that the government (rather than their own board) would *persistently* have to tell private industrialists to stop advertising a product which they could not produce, as happened to the Electricity Boards in the later 1940s and early 1950s. The split between sales and distribution in the Area Boards and generation under the Central Authority (and the absence of strategic coordination between them) was one of the serious weaknesses of the new larger-scale organisation, which the advocates of a more vertically-integrated 'power board' organisation had feared. While Citrine did his best to come to terms with the imbalance of supply and demand by political compromises, neither he nor the chairmen satisfactorily overcame the prejudice that the symptoms were exceptional and temporary, and they thus never resolved the fundamental strategic issues on costing and pricing. Their desire to spread electricity usage and maintain cheap electricity might have been excused as a political necessity (and Ministers were, it is true, typically two-faced when price rises were mentioned as a way of reducing the growth of consumption or increasing the rate of return). Yet, even when they were confronted by Ministers (like Hugh Gaitskell or Aubrey Jones) who showed signs of being willing to face up to the consequences of price rises, the Boards' uncooperative reaction revealed that it was essentially they rather than politicians who were the source of inertia. It was not until new men took over that this fundamental area of strategic choice was to be tackled as well as the Central Authority had handled the Brown revolution on the generation side.

12

THE NORTH OF SCOTLAND
HYDRO-ELECTRIC BOARD
(1943–60)

... if, as we hope and believe, the policy ... is to give the
Highlands ... a future as well as a past ... then we consider that a
few localised interferences with natural beauties would be an
insignificant price to pay for the solid benefits which would be
realised.

Scottish Office, *Report of the Committee
on Hydro-Electric Development in
Scotland*, Cmd. 6406, 1942, p. 34.

At the opposite end of the spectrum of scale, facing different
problems of strategic decision making (but ones which proved no less
challenging for all their smallness), was the North of Scotland Hydro-
Electric Board, the only British electricity undertaking which remained independent of the BEA after nationalisation. The North of
Scotland, with its sparse population, had always presented serious
problems for electrical development, and difficulties had been
encountered in exploiting its one potential natural advantage: the
availability of sources of hydro-electric power. Some hydro-electric
schemes had been developed earlier in the century, but the hydrolo-
gical conditions were much less favourable than in many countries.
These natural handicaps had, however, been artificially accentuated
in the 1930s by opposition from landed and sporting interests, who
wanted to preserve the Highland wilderness, and by coal-owners and
coal-miners, who resented the potential competition and lobbied
against the legislation required to establish hydro-electric schemes.
Six hydro-electric development bills had been rejected by Parliament
since 1929. There were a few earlier major hydro-electric schemes, by
industrial companies who generated for their own use (mainly for

aluminium production), and by the Grampian Company, which developed local electricity supplies as well as exporting its relatively cheap electricity to the National Grid. The CEB had accepted these bulk supplies from the north, but discouraged further proposals for hydro-electric development there, arguing that steam generation was generally more economic in Scottish conditions. They also decided not to develop the National Grid scheme to include Scotland north of Dundee, because of its poor market prospects.

Labour's wartime Secretary of State for Scotland, Tom Johnston, was determined to break this log jam, and in 1941 appointed a committee under Lord Cooper, the Lord Justice Clerk, to inquire into the possibility of further hydro-electric development. The following year, the committee reported in favour of establishing a new publicly-owned authority to develop hydro-electric generation in the areas of the north not already occupied by existing municipal or company undertakings.[1] There were, they thought, promising possibilities of more than doubling hydro-electricity output, thus enabling supplies to be made available to new industries and rural electrification schemes in the north. No precise costing of the schemes was presented, because every site had its unique geological characteristics, but, with interest rates low, and coal prices rising, the economic prospects for capital-intensive rather than fuel-intensive electricity production looked better than for some years. Those who feared the destruction of the beauties of the Highland scenery, of the crofters' traditional life style, or simply of their grouse shooting and salmon fishing, were not generally disposed to accept the committee's view that the amenity objections to dams, reservoirs and power lines could be overcome. There was, however, a determination among the engineers promoting the schemes (who were represented on and advised the committee) to get something done this time. This was complemented by a general political feeling that the kind of social transformation wrought by the publicly-owned Tennessee Valley Authority in the United States could also be achieved in the Highlands. Tom Johnston was determined to use this to wrest from the wartime coalition cabinet a socialist and Scottish Electricity Board for the north.

In 1943, he succeeded, and the publicly-owned North of Scotland Hydro-Electric Board was established. The new Board was charged with developing hydro-electric schemes in the Highlands and Islands outside the areas of the few existing undertakings, in order to generate the power for local supplies and for sale in bulk to private industry or the National Grid. In 1946 Johnston himself left politics and became the Board's part-time chairman. When nationalisation of the electricity undertakings throughout Britain was mooted shortly afterwards, the CEB engineers pressed hard for the new BEA to be allowed to take control, but Johnston was able to persuade his former Labour colleagues in the Cabinet that the Board should remain independent and continue to report to the Secretary of State for Scotland.[2] Johnston served as a member of the BEA, and the North Board shared in the national labour relations machinery, but the basic separation of the north of Scotland was continued in the 1947 Electricity Act. The North of Scotland Board then took over the Grampian Company, the Aberdeen and Dundee corporation electricity undertakings and 13 smaller undertakings in their northern area, thus consolidating under the control of their Edinburgh headquarters the electricity supplies for nearly three quarters of Scotland's area, and nearly a quarter of its population.

The ex-CEB engineers at the BEA initially tried to expand the vaguely-worded consultative status legally accorded to them on northern hydro-electric schemes, and to establish real technical and financial control of the North Board, but Johnston and his colleagues were firm in resisting this. They made no secret of their contempt for what they considered to be the over-centralised and bureaucratic regime further south. Citrine, worried at how infrequently Johnston was attending BEA meetings, fixed an Authority meeting in Edinburgh to encourage him to attend, but received an apology for absence from Johnston on the grounds that he was in London for the day in question! Even when he did attend, Johnston did not participate in voting. The message was clear, and after initial rebuffs the BEA also left its northern neighbour very much to its own devices under separate ministerial control.

Johnston had a flair for publicity and a Scottish patriotism which made him an ideal figurehead and political promoter of the Board's interests, but policy making within the Board was the preserve of more expert electrical engineers. The chief executives, first A. E. (later Sir Edward) MacColl, and then T. Lawrie and A. A. Fulton, had an important impact on the Board's schemes in the 1940s and 1950s. They gathered around them a team of young and enthusiastic Scots engineers attracted by the novelty of the task and its symbolism of Scottish economic revival.[3] They also made extensive use not only of civil, but also of electrical, engineering consultants, in contrast to the policy of their southern neighbours. MacColl, especially, felt that hydro-electric development had in the past been unreasonably held back. He had been the CEB's Central Scotland manager and had seen earlier proposals turned down by the CEB engineers at the London headquarters against his own advice. One of his first steps was to review and modify a scheme rejected by the CEB to generate electricity for export at the northern end of Loch Lomond, the water coming from the higher level Loch Sloy. In Scottish conditions (with low levels of water and limited river flows) substantial expenditure on dams, tunnels and aqueducts to expand the catchment area was necessary, but the Board and their consultants successfully designed a scheme which was reckoned to be economic. A new buttress dam – the highest in Scotland at 168 feet from base to spillway – was built to raise the waters of Loch Sloy, and the catchment area was extended from $6\frac{1}{2}$ to $32\frac{1}{2}$ square miles by a series of aqueducts. This collected sufficient water to drive the four 32.5MW turbines, operating at load factors of around 10 per cent, to meet the peak load in Glasgow, only 40 miles distant.

The second large scheme was an extension of the existing Tummel–Garry schemes of the Grampian Company. Further north, but with better catchment areas, the additions were designed for higher load factors than Sloy and produced a larger output, but were also principally for export southwards. Still further north, a proposal to flood Glen Affric, rejected earlier on amenity grounds, was redesigned to preserve the scenic features of the glen by using a loch in the neighbouring glen as a storage reservoir. In this – as indeed in most schemes – the propertied interests and environmentalists fought a rearguard action to preserve the Highland wilderness, but the Board fought the battles for public opinion and political approval, and, in most cases, won. Again an elaborate network of connecting aqueducts and tunnels was necessary at Affric to collect the water. The Board was usually obliged to make up the deficiencies of nature, which had not endowed Scotland with suitable 'run-of-river' sites, of the kind which made hydro-electric projects in other countries so economically attractive. Affric and other northern schemes – including similarly large developments at Shin, Conon Valley, and Garry Moriston – were generally to supply local consumers' requirements rather than for export; and there were a number of smaller schemes in both northern and central areas.

In the early years, concrete, steel and manpower were all in short supply (at first their labour force was composed very largely of prisoners-of-war), and little progress was made. None the less, their first small schemes were becoming operational by 1948, when they also took over 87MW of hydro-electric capacity from the Grampian Company. They continued to meet considerable opposition from local authorities, environmentalists, landowners and fishing interests, but Tom Johnston was, for their first ten years, able to keep political opposition at bay. By 1960 the Board were operating some 875MW of hydro-electric plant (ten times the amount they inherited) as well as 45MW of diesel plant (on the islands) and 133MW of steam plant (mainly inherited from Aberdeen and Dundee Corporations). At the same time they extended the 132kV Grid in the north from 200 to 2000 circuit miles by the end of 1960, interconnecting the main towns and the new hydro-electric stations, and closing down some of the less efficient steam and diesel stations they inherited. Despite the environmentalist fears of their opponents, many of the dams, aqueducts and reservoirs which were erected became tourist attractions. They were generally built with more concern for environmental amenity than some previous industrial schemes in the Highlands such as the aluminium hydro-electric plant at Kinlochleven. Paradoxically, they were, in the later nuclear age, to become a rallying cry as a symbol of 'clean power' from the environmentalist lobby whose predecessors had once opposed them.

The economic problems of hydro-electricity none the less remained. The economics of a hydro-electric scheme depended essentially on the level of interest rates (being highly capital-intensive, their main costs were capital costs) and coal prices (a major input of competitive steam generation). In the 1940s, with interest rates low, and coal prices rising, they looked especially attractive, though as interest rates began to rise again in the 1950s they looked progressively less so. It was not, however, until the later 1950s, when steam generation became more clearly competitive (with stabilising coal prices and improved technology), that the economic merits of the Scottish schemes were to be seriously questioned (see pp. 273–6, below).

In England, by contrast, the BEA engineers decided against a major scheme based on a Severn tidal barrage, which was perhaps the best prospect for hydro-electric power in the less mountainous south. Even with coal priced more realistically, such a scheme would have been economic only if its costs could be kept down to the level estimated. This was, however, a rather large assumption in the context of fears about silting and construction difficulties. The BEA's negative views have been confirmed by many successive enquiries, though the Severn barrage project has never lacked enthusiastic support. That BEA doubts about the cost estimates were not unreasonable is suggested also by the North Board's experience, for the schemes they built suffered from their inexperience in estimating and poor control by them and by their consultants or contractors. The schemes in fact cost more than twice the initial estimates.[4] By the later 1950s the North Board were making more realistic estimates,[5] but understandably the pace of development had slowed down, with great expense already incurred on the existing schemes and the better sites having been used. In retrospect, it is perhaps surprising that the capital-intensive schemes of the North Board were able to pre-empt such a large proportion of national resources devoted to electrical development. The Board typically absorbed 9 per cent of all the British supply industry's capital expenditure in the first ten years of nationalisation, though they were responsible for less than 2 per cent of final sales. Hydro-electricity (including that generated in the smaller schemes in Wales and Southern Scotland) consistently accounted for well under 3 per cent of electricity generated in Britain.[6] Understandably, the BEA several times complained to the Government that less rigorous standards of investment appraisal were being applied to their northern neighbour than to themselves.

The advocates of hydro-electricity had at first hoped that it would help to reverse the industrial decline of the Highlands, but these hopes proved false. The Board held discussions with a number of industrialists interested in the manufacture of electricity-intensive products such as carbide or phosphorous, but they could not offer the low electricity prices required to meet international competition from countries with far more attractive natural conditions for hydro-electricity. The North Board therefore concentrated instead on supplying electricity to light industries with local roots. Their industrial sales expanded only modestly, and were only half the levels achieved further south as a proportion of electricity sales overall. The failure to attract big new capital-intensive industrial projects was criticised at the time, but in retrospect it seems sensible. A few capital-intensive projects would have done little to help overall employment prospects in the Highlands, and the technologies being discussed were, as it shortly turned out, overtaken by new developments in manufacturing processes, so that the schemes would probably not have had a long life. The population of the Highlands continued to decline (in fact more rapidly than earlier), but this was due to economic factors beyond the Board's control.[7] They were probably right to confine their employment-creating schemes to their own direct and indirect impact in employing local firms and labour, which they deliberately favoured in their contracts policy.

The North Board had a clearer statutory duty than the BEA to take wider consideration of 'social and economic improvement'[8] into account in formulating their policy, and Tom Johnston and his colleagues made great play of this 'social clause'. In practice, however, they interpreted this not primarily as a duty to promote industrial development, but rather as a licence to use the profits of hydro-electric generation to subsidise new distribution schemes, to serve the farms and houses in the remoter rural areas which were quite uneconomic to supply. In order to pursue this strategy, they needed to sell their hydro-electricity in bulk at more than the cost of production. Since new electricity-intensive industries could not be attracted at such prices, they relied on sales to the BEA's National Grid as a major source of revenue. As we have seen, the North Board designed their more southerly schemes, such as Loch Sloy, explicitly with this in mind.

There remained the question of prices for the exports southwards. Prior to the 1948 takeover the CEB engineers seemed determined to extract a large share of the joint benefits for themselves, and had been unreasonably tough in bargaining with the North Board.[9] Johnston wanted to force the matter to arbitration by the Minister, but Citrine was able to persuade his BEA colleagues to come up with a significantly more generous offer on the price they would pay for bulk supplies from the north. Eventually, in 1951, they settled for a figure 4 per cent below the BEA's own bulk supply tariff. On whether this was economic, opinions legitimately differed,[10] but the North Board were glad that this gave them a gradually increasing export price in the early years, as the bulk supply tariff was raised to meet the higher postwar costs of new steam power stations and the coal used in them.

Unfortunately the costs of their hydro-electric schemes expanded faster than this export price, and the North Board found themselves less financially secure than they had initially hoped. They were also embarrassed by the late completion of the early schemes, which led to many power cuts in Glasgow in the later 1940s and early 1950s. Even when the basic capacity shortage was improving further south, the North Board continued to fall short on its export contracts, partly because of late completions and partly because of inadequate rainfall in some years. By the mid-1950s, there was a good deal of discontent in the rest of Scotland about both the poor load factor and the unreliability of supplies from the North Board, though they were then generally able to make up shortfalls by importing from England.

Despite these hitches, and the financial embarrassment that failure to supply caused to the North Board, the hydro-electric projects did produce a financial surplus which enabled them to promote the related rural electrification schemes in the north. Indeed, they were able to pursue rural schemes more rapidly than Boards further south. Though they abandoned initial plans to ask for few or no contributions from remote consumers towards the cost of connection, their connection charges remained relatively generous. By 1960 some 108 000 rural consumers had been connected at the high average cost to the Board of £250 each (rather more than many Highlanders earned in a year). The Board has also connected nearly 100 000 new urban consumers (at, of course, significantly lower cost). They also subsidised diesel generation on the islands, or (where electricity generation of any kind was grossly uneconomic) subsidised bottled gas supplies as part of their 'social' obligations. In 1948 some 44 per cent of potential consumers in the North of Scotland area had lacked electricity supplies. By 1960 only 9 per cent of homes and farms in the area still lacked supply, a proportion similar to the average in Boards further south, despite the significantly more difficult territory covered. This had been achieved by substantially higher levels of subsidy for uneconomic schemes in the north, paid for by the difference between hydro-electric generation costs and their revenue from electricity exports to the south. The Board reckoned that their rural schemes by themselves were by 1960 losing about £1¾ millions each year.

For the people who stayed behind in the Highlands, the North of Scotland Hydro-Board was undoubtedly a success. It brought electricity supplies (at prices no greater than those paid in the south) to many who had lacked supplies at the time of nationalisation. The long debates between landowners, industrialists and others about who, in effect, should appropriate the economic rent of potential hydro-electric sites, had essentially been resolved in favour of the people living there (to the extent that they were willing to take it in the form of subsidised electricity at home), and this had indeed been Johnston's intention. The Board's achievement in resolving this political question and bringing electricity to the people, gave it an especially warm place in the hearts of Highlanders, which was not paralleled by the local attachments which the Electricity Boards elsewhere were able to foster. It could be argued that this was not the best economic use of Scottish, or, more generally, of British resources, but Highlanders, who felt underprivileged, isolated and neglected by the south, understandably exploited what they saw as rightly theirs as far as their finances allowed, and indeed a little further. Despite a much stronger competitive position against gas and coal in the north, they pursued a policy of retail price restraint with the same blinkered vision as the southern Boards. Together with their substantial overspending on their major capital projects, this meant that they continued to show a cumulative deficit beyond 1958, by which time they had aimed to break even. The political roots of their achievement did, however, provide them with more insulation than the southern Boards against the increasing pressures for 'commercial' behaviour from the Conservatives. Indeed, it was to be on further moves towards independence for Scottish electricity that the Conservatives first based their attack on what they considered the over-centralised and bureaucratic organisation of the south.

Part III

THE CONSERVATIVE COUNTER-REVOLUTION (1954–7)

13

DEVOLVING POWER

I expect something better than purely negative criticisms.

Lord Citrine, addressing regional BEA conference
at York, 19 November 1954.

... the formal structure of the industry is not conducive to the
highest efficiency ...

Report of the [Herbert] Committee of Inquiry into
the Electricity Supply Industry, Cmd. 9672, 1956,
p. 138.

The Conservatives generally enjoyed the hot air of political rhetoric
against nationalisation, and when they returned to power in 1951,
some Ministers were willing to contemplate extensive de-nationalisation to reverse Labour's programme. In the case of electricity,
however, a return to pre-nationalisation organisation was widely
regarded as impractical, and many in the Cabinet felt that a full-
blooded commitment to de-nationalisation in areas like this would do
nothing to improve efficiency and provide no real political gains
either. Even so, it was not until two years after he came to power that
Churchill quelled speculation by announcing publicly that the supply
industry would remain under public control.[1] There remained
considerable discontent among Conservative back-bench diehards,
who felt the need to redeem some of their rhetorical opposition
pledges. In opposition they had attacked the Central Authority and
Labour Ministers for the industry's alleged inefficiency and bureaucratic over-centralisation. In the elections of 1950 and 1951 the
Conservatives had particularly stressed their intention to give more
independence to the Scottish and Welsh elements of the nationalised
industries, and (though in electricity the idea of an independent
Welsh board was dropped because of its expense) they returned to
power committed to hiving off Southern Scottish electricity from the

BEA. The Scottish Office were keen to take on responsibility for electricity throughout the whole of Scotland (rather than merely in the north), and this had already been seriously discussed by the Labour Government under pressure from Scottish politicians and civil servants. Although it was given a rather low priority in the new Conservative legislative programme, the new Minister, Geoffrey Lloyd, accepted in principle that he should cede control of Scottish electricity from his own Ministry of Fuel and Power to the Scottish Office. In June 1952, Citrine was finally told that all the BEA's Scottish assets (the two South West and South East Scotland Area Boards and the corresponding two generating divisions) would be hived off.

Citrine, backed by his engineers, spent the following months in an absurdly unconvincing attempt to persuade the Government that such a move would be disastrous, stopping only just short of the assertion that electrical civilisation as they knew it would collapse if the BEA's central technical control in the south of Scotland came to an end.[2] This cut no ice with the Minister. The decision had been taken on general political grounds and was quite irreversible. There followed some months of discussions between the Scottish Office, the Ministry, the Treasury, the BEA and the industry's leading men in Scotland. The initial Scottish Office proposals for various councils to coordinate the activities of independent Scottish units developed into an administratively tidier proposal for an integrated board to handle both generation and distribution in the whole of the South of Scotland. This was accepted as being the most efficient and neat solution to the political decision on hiving off. (No mention was made in the discussions of the potential advantages of integrated power boards, which, we have seen, were favoured by some of the Area Board chairmen.) The legislation went through in 1954,[3] with Citrine maintaining his formal opposition to the last, and ensuring that the Labour opposition in Parliament attacked it as a politically-motivated move.[4]

The new South of Scotland Electricity Board took over the 5 per cent share of the BEA's assets which lay within its designated area on 1 April 1955. Thereafter, to reflect its loss of Scottish responsibilities, the British Electricity Authority was known as the Central Electricity Authority (CEA). John Pickles, the chairman of the South West Scotland Board (who had first advanced the proposal for an integrated board in the discussions on Scottish reorganisation), became the first chairman of the new South Scotland Board. He had, paradoxically, been a good friend of Citrine and one of the chairmen least hostile to Central Authority power, though he now welcomed the new Scottish opportunity. Unlike the chairmen further south, he could look forward to a significant degree of independence, with responsibility directly to the Secretary of State for Scotland, rather than to Citrine's CEA and the Minister of Fuel and Power. Unlike other Area Boards, he also now gained direct control of Grid transmission and of power station operation and construction from the two generation divisions in his area. However, the National Grid interchange of power, voluntary cooperation with the CEA on matters such as the planning of generation and transmission, and London's statutory responsibility for industrial relations were all retained, and men on both sides of the new border were determined that relations between them would remain friendly and cooperative.

This experiment in devolution did not, however, satisfy Conservative back-bench critics of over-centralisation in the industry. These MPs were as self-indulgent in advocating over-simplified recipes for efficiency through decentralised organisation as some Labour MPs were in waving the wand of nationalisation. When Geoffrey Lloyd wanted to win parliamentary approval for increasing the industry's borrowing powers in July 1954, he made a concession to back-bench opinion by appointing a departmental committee 'to enquire into the organisation and efficiency of the electricity supply system in England and Wales in the light of its working under the Electricity Act of 1947, and to make recommendations'.[5] The committee was to be headed by Sir Edwin Herbert, a lawyer and businessman, very much the Lord Goodman of this day. His colleagues were Ronald Edwards (a veteran of the earlier Clow enquiry on the peak load and now Professor of Economics at LSE), F. C. Bagnall and A. Healey (both businessmen from the private sector), L. W. Robson (a well-known accountant), J. W. G. Church (an electrical engineer now retired from India) and Jack Tanner (recently retired as President of the Amalgamated Engineering Union).

The idea of holding periodical independent inquiries into nationalised industries had been mooted earlier by the Labour Government,[6] and it now seemed within the Ministry that the time had come to start on electricity. They knew of the problems of divided responsibility between the Central Authority's two deputy chairmen; and complaints from the Area Boards and divisions about Citrine's allegedly excessive centralisation had also reached them through both civil service and political channels. Lloyd had earlier asked Citrine to review the organisation, but possible initiatives by the Authority's internal committee established in 1951 to review organisation seemed to be bogged down. The Authority had in 1954 embarked on the experimental merger of two divisions in the North West, but Citrine seemed resistant to further organisational reform because of its possible impact on staff. He had also successfully side-stepped the implementation of many recommendations of earlier independent committees established by the Ministry on the peak-load, fuel policy and power station construction. Lloyd thus saw Citrine as a potential obstacle to change, but he needed the outside weight of an independent inquiry if he were to gain support for strong interventions to change the industry's management. Citrine himself recognised that it was his own power and competence which were under investigation by the Herbert Committee, and not just the organisation he headed. Knowing that Sir Edwin Herbert was the London Board's legal adviser and friend of Harry Randall (one of his leading critics among the Board chairmen), Citrine suspected that he was to be the victim of a politically-motivated attack.

The Herbert inquiry, though charged with producing something like a management consultancy report on the efficiency of the CEA's organisation, was thus in the difficult position of carrying out its work against the wishes of the senior man in charge of the organisation to be investigated. Citrine insisted, for example, that neither he nor his Central Authority colleagues could discuss with the committee any suggested modifications of the 1947 Electricity Act. This would, he argued, imply disrespect for the will of Parliament. The committee felt this was quaintly silly, but it gave them a first-hand view of Citrine's over-bearing belief in the power of debate (on which some of his colleagues complained to them). Citrine failed to persuade the Area Board chairmen to withhold criticism so that they could sort out their future by internal agreement. Several Boards expressed their satisfaction with the present structure, but most were uninhibited in their presentation to the committee of their discontents about the central organisation and management of the industry. Some divisional controllers were equally frank in describing their sense of frustration and delay at headquarters' conservatism and methods of control. One had members of the committee alternately appalled and convulsed with laughter at the ludicrous level of detail required by headquarters.

Any such inquiry runs the risk of bias emerging from its very nature, and the committee were perhaps insufficiently critical on some points where headquarters' staff were in advance of Area Board thinking (such as the underpricing of the domestic load). Equally they placed too much emphasis on past conservatism in generation design policy, giving little credit for the real advances which were being made at headquarters in the Brown revolution. However, that they acutely identified some real problems which Citrine and his colleagues had been unwilling to face is equally clear. Their report, presented to the Minister at the end of 1955, was clearly written, even breezy in style compared with most such official reports.[7] They diplomatically paid tribute to the zeal and devotion of staff at all levels in the industry, in the face of the postwar capacity shortage and political over-exposure from which they had suffered. However, they went on to make criticisms of inadequate budgetary control and decentralisation, of the over-staffed and excessively interfering headquarters, and of the lack of attention to productivity. The committee felt there was need for more selective posting and training of staff, for more research, and for increased knowledge of the industry's cost structure as a basis for tariffs. The heart of their report was their proposals for organisational change which, they argued, would contribute to overcoming some of these problems. They hoped to create a less centralised industry, with power devolved to the operating units and a more vigorous commercial outlook than the civil service style of Self and the trade union style of Citrine seemed to have imposed on the CEA.

Although Scotland itself was outside their terms of reference, they reviewed the possibility of establishing integrated power boards on the lines of the new South of Scotland Board, as was advocated by some Area Board chairmen. Their conclusions agreed here with the Central Authority's: the economies to be gained in such an arrangement were small and the existing split between generating divisions and Area Boards responsible for distribution was, they felt, a quite natural one, akin to that in the commercial world between wholesaling and retailing. Their proposals for decentralisation were thus that a new, separate generating board should be established with executive functions and a clearer commitment to decentralising much of the design and construction work to stronger divisional controllers. The Area Boards should also, they felt, be released from some headquarters controls and become individually self-supporting financially. A small Central Authority should, they suggested, none the less be retained to handle industrial relations nationally and, more importantly, to exercise a general supervisory role. This role could, they felt, be more effectively carried out if the executive functions were devolved to a new generating board and Area Boards. The idea which Citrine and his colleagues advanced to the committee, that since the Central Authority bore the final responsibility, they must control everything centrally, was firmly scotched.

Yet not all of the committee's ideas were unfamiliar to the Central Authority. Indeed Self was annoyed that the idea of a separate generating board (which he had put to the committee, recognising the problems of overlapping between himself and Eccles) was used by the committee without acknowledgement. Yet the official reaction of the Central Authority in their comments on the committee's report read like a weary defence of the status quo.[8] Citrine, in particular, was determined to oppose what he considered an unjustified and ill-informed attack on the organisation he had created. He had been disappointed that Labour had lost the 1955 election, and hoped he could delay or modify the implementation of the *Report*, until a Labour victory allowed him to scotch it. Neither he nor Self liked its overtones of commercialism, and they presented it to opposition spokesmen as a rejection of the public service principle and an unjustified attack on an efficient public enterprise.

Citrine had not yet, however, given up all hope of converting the Conservative Government. While it was obvious that the central themes of the *Report* (its espousal of commercial ideals and criticisms of over-centralisation) were music to the Government's ears, the committee had not just been an obedient ministerial poodle. Indeed some of their most telling criticisms (and arguably one of their more significant proposals in the long run) had related to the need for a clearer definition of the relative roles of the Ministry and the industry. Sir John Maud, the Ministry's Permanent Secretary, had told the committee firmly that in his view this relationship benefited from fuzziness, and that for the Ministry to issue clear directives when it desired to modify the Authority's preferred policies would be undesirable. Citrine knew well that on questions like rural electrification, Ministers preferred the present gentleman's agreements to any public recognition of government arm-twisting and explicit compensation for the losses incurred, of the kind the committee recommended. Other suggestions of the committee (such as that the boards should raise capital on the stock market rather than via the Treasury) were also known to be against current government policy. Government complicity in many of the areas criticised by the committee was obvious enough to Citrine and he felt he might exploit this and have the report thrown out.

During 1956, the discussions on the implementation of the report continued under a new Minister, Aubrey Jones, who had replaced Lloyd in the ministerial reshuffle when Eden succeeded Churchill as Prime Minister. Jones did not find the allocation of duties to the proposed new Central Authority at all to his liking, and in February he told Sir Edwin Herbert that he was considering an alternative scheme under which some of these duties would be carried out directly by the Ministry. Citrine, meanwhile, was trying to head off reorganisation by offering to implement, without legislation, those parts of the *Report* which the Authority accepted, for example by establishing a separate generating organisation under Eccles within the existing CEA structure. By August, however, Jones told Citrine firmly that he must accept new legislation in the near future which would impose substantial organisational change. As discussions advanced, however, government views on both the form of the new organisation and on the men they wanted to run it were increasingly coloured by the prospect of nuclear power, which seemed likely to dominate the future of the industry more than anyone had hitherto foreseen. It was to this new factor that attention was now turning.

14

COAL, OIL AND NUCLEAR ESCALATION

> The Authority, for the first time, will be in the fortunate position of having three fuels available to them, coal, oil and nuclear.
>
> Chief Engineer's Department memorandum on nuclear power, 17 October 1956.

The British economy had long been built on energy from coal, and even as late as the mid-1950s commentators were convinced that this would remain so for many years to come. The electricity supply industry at first shared this view and, as it happened, it was to prove a more accurate prognosis of its own future source of fuel than it was in other sectors, where the future potential of oil was generally under-estimated. There were, of course, postwar shortages and worries about future coal supplies. However, in the few harsh winters of the early 1950s when home coal production seemed likely to be insufficient to maintain electricity supplies, the National Coal Board had been able to provide small quantities of imported coal at a subsidised price. Even if world market prices had been charged for such marginal additions, they would still have been substantially cheaper than oil. The Ridley Committee (which reported on fuel and power resources in 1952) expected the Coal Board to be able to expand coal production in the medium-term to meet the greater part of increasing UK demand for energy at prices which would remain competitive with oil.[1] The major criticisms of this view at the time were that the committee had under-estimated the size of the future demand for coal, though experience was to show the contrary. Demand for coal was in fact to be well below their estimate, as oil made more rapid competitive advances in the fuel market than had been expected.

In the case of electricity supply, however, it was evident to the industry's engineers (even at the time the Ridley Committee had reported) that their own demand for coal by 1960 would substantially exceed the estimates of around 45 million tons which they had made at the beginning of the 1950s. Their introduction of more thermally efficient sets by the later 1950s was, it is true, expected to decrease the amount of coal required to produce a given output, but electricity sales were expanding more rapidly than they had initially expected, substantially increasing their anticipated coal requirements. In the early 1950s they decided to suppress this information, recognising the uncertainty of load forecasts and feeling that the Ministry would accept consistencies in forecasting but simply distrust them if they frequently changed these. By 1953, however, it was quite clear that their needs would be at least 50 million tons in 1960 and probably as much as 60 million tons by 1965. This was rather more than the Coal Board were planning to produce for them, and both the Coal Board and the Ministry were alerted. In the light of the estimated demands of other coal consumers, the supply industry's growing needs seemed likely to prolong the current coal shortage until well into the next decade. Thus prospects of physical shortages of coal in 1953 impelled both the Ministry and the BEA to examine more carefully the possible shift to alternative fuels, the front runners being oil and nuclear power.

The Minister, Geoffrey Lloyd (who had had charge of petroleum policy in the War), had been pressing the industry for some time to experiment with oil-fired power stations, but initially he had met a negative response. Only a few British power stations burnt oil, the major example being the new station at Bankside in London, where they had been forced by Attlee's Government to modify the design for oil-firing for amenity reasons. Their experience there confirmed that this option was more expensive than coal, and that air pollution problems remained as difficult with oil-fired stations as with coal-fired ones. As the future coal supply situation looked progressively more bleak, however, Lloyd was able in 1954 to get the support of his cabinet colleagues for increased pressure on the Central Authority to adopt dual-firing for coal and oil in some power stations. Eccles and the chief engineer's department firmly opposed this, preferring to meet any shortfall in coal supplies by importing coal, which at that time was still a cheaper option than oil. The Chancellor, R. A. Butler, seemed unwilling to agree to Lloyd going as far as issuing a directive to enforce a shift to oil-burning, but a cabinet clash on the issue was avoided by Citrine's willingness to impose his own views on the engineers. He responded to Lloyd's appeal to accept the cost of converting some stations under construction to oil burning on 'national interest' grounds. With Self's support, Citrine gained Central Authority acceptance of a policy which at the time they considered uneconomic. A contract was signed with Esso for cheap oil supplies from the new Fawley oil refinery to the nearby Marchwood (Hampshire) power station (then under construction). The relatively favourable terms of this deal reduced anticipated losses, but still, when the additional costs of conversion and of burning oil were taken into account, the experiment with oil firing was reckoned at current oil prices to be likely to result in a loss of £1.6 millions each year compared with burning imported coal at world market prices (and rather more relative to the subsidised price actually charged by the Coal Board). At the BEA the engineers argued, somewhat implausibly, that, since the future was unknowable, the relative prices of coal and oil should be assumed to remain the same as at present. There were, it is true, real difficulties in predicting the economics of operation over the fifteen or twenty years of a power station's intensive operating life, but the Ministry expected a fall in the price of oil relative to coal. On this question, experience over the relevant period was to prove the Ministry right and the industry wrong.

Shortly after these initial tentative steps towards oil-firing were agreed, the Coal Board for the first time officially informed the BEA that during the 1960s they would be unable to meet their increased requirements for coal. Some engineers and economists within the Authority felt that these fears were exaggerated, and proposed again that imported coal rather than imported oil should be used to fill in any gaps in supply. With remarkable foresight they suggested that eventually the Coal Board would be bringing political pressure to bear on them to accept larger quantities of poor quality coal as they lost their other traditional markets to oil. Within the Cabinet and Whitehall, however, pressures were mounting for an increased power station oil-burning programme. The industrial muscle of the National Union of Mineworkers (who were felt by Conservatives to have abused their strong bargaining powers in the coal shortage) could, it was felt, be tamed if an alternative energy base could be established. Apart from such political motives, the civil servants felt that their overall planning view (clearly dormant on the demand side ever since the concessions to the fuel chairmen on pricing) could play a strong positive role now on the supply side. Their projections showed increasing physical shortages of coal nationally, which had to be overcome somehow. Pressure on the CEA to adopt dual-firing in a large number of the stations being planned or just started therefore increased; and in 1955 Citrine again persuaded his colleagues to follow the Ministry line on this. They did so feeling that the cost both in extra equipment for dual-firing and in high oil prices would make it uneconomic, but by 1956 they were more optimistic. Conversion costs were minimised by allowing for oil-firing only in some stations; and in southern locations distant from the coalfields it now seemed more likely that oil prices (which were falling rapidly) would make the stations cheaper overall than the coal-fired stations they had originally planned there. For once, the engineers could be heard abashedly saying to each other that it seemed that the men from the Ministry had been right. Oil would, in fact, not only take them through the anticipated physical coal shortages of the early 1960s, but become their favoured fuel in the cheap energy decade of the 1960s.

Oil was not, however, the only available answer to the anticipated coal shortage. The alternative – nuclear power – had initially seemed more attractive to most engineers, for whom it had the undoubted technical appeal of the new. In the later 1940s and early 1950s, electricity supply industry personnel, from Citrine down to some of the more privileged engineers, had taken part in tentative discussions with nuclear scientists at Harwell on the potential for nuclear power.[2] The principle of using a controlled nuclear reaction as a source of heat for generating power had been known for some time, though it was not until 1952 that the first electricity was generated from a nuclear pile in the US, and in the same year the British nuclear programme (previously concentrated on the independent British atom bomb) began to devote substantial resources to developing civil nuclear power stations.[3] Earlier BEA statements had stressed the long-term nature of likely developments,[4] but in 1953 both they and the Ministry were told that power generated from nuclear electricity could become a reality in Britain in the relatively near future. The discussions were, however, shrouded in secrecy, since the civil power station project then being considered in Whitehall was also designed to produce weapons-grade plutonium, the raw material for the atomic bombs in Britain's expanding nuclear stockpile. At first the Central Authority had hoped to build and operate this dual-purpose station (and had earmarked a Devonshire site for it), but in the spring of 1953 they were disappointed to hear that the first station would be built at Calder Hall (Cumbria) by the nuclear engineers in the Ministry of Supply's industrial group. Although some electricity would be generated from Calder Hall (and sold for distribution via the Grid), the design would not be optimised for electricity output but for the production of plutonium which was its principal object. Later in the year, it was also announced that a new body – the UK Atomic Energy Authority – would be formed to take over the Ministry of Supply's responsibilities in the nuclear field. The BEA were again disappointed at this sign that their own potential role in nuclear power appeared to be pre-empted.

The security surrounding the early civil nuclear power decisions was tight, and it effectively cut off the BEA not only from participation in the Calder Hall decision but also from the subsequent decision to expand the programme to play a larger part in electricity generation. As with the oil-burning programme, Whitehall's commitment to nuclear power developed rapidly in 1954 with the emergence of forecasts of increasing coal shortages. A working party under a young Treasury Under Secretary, Burke Trend, considered whether there should be a civil nuclear power programme to complement that required by the military for plutonium production. The BEA were not represented, and such information as the committee had on their coal-fired generation costs and their future load estimates was inadequately filtered through the Whitehall machine. Although the working party completed its report in October 1954, Citrine did not learn of it until December nor receive a copy (with the details of military plutonium requirements excised) until the following January. The Atomic Energy Authority, it then appeared, were anxious to press ahead with a civil nuclear programme, and Whitehall (conscious of the fuel shortage and of rather loose talk about export potential and national prestige) seemed unusually keen to commit the required extra resources. The working party of civil servants and government nuclear engineers judged that enough was known from the initial work on the military reactors to justify the ordering of two more nuclear reactors, now optimised for electricity production, in 1957, a further two in 1959, and eight more in the early 1960s: some 1700MW of nuclear capacity in all by 1965, in addition to the Atomic Energy Authority's own programme optimised for plutonium production. The Treasury were worried that the civil nuclear stations (though they had substantially lower running costs) would be significantly more expensive in capital cost than conventional stations and, overall, nuclear electricity could prove more expensive than coal-fired generation. However, the Trend working party felt that the fuel shortage justified taking a calculated risk on starting a programme whose later stages might become economic, and which could in any case be considered flexible. In some respects, however, the committee were clearly over-optimistic. Not being in close touch with the recent thinking of Eccles and Brown, they were insufficiently aware of the technical advances being implemented which would substantially reduce the capital and running costs of conventional stations. Even more seriously, it was evident that for nuclear generation to be economic a substantial credit for the value of the plutonium by-product (reducing the basic cost of the electricity generated by a third) had been introduced into their calculations, on the assumption that the plutonium could be sold for use in bombs or as a fuel for a later design of reactor. The Atomic Energy Authority's nuclear engineers were not all convinced that this credit was a realistic estimate of future plutonium values (which were highly uncertain), but if the credit were reduced, nuclear electricity would initially be substantially more costly than conventional generation. These technical and economic risks in conditions of considerable uncertainty were frankly recognised, but the Trend working party considered 'that the time is now rapidly approaching when a modest initial investment would be justified by the expectation of a considerable return'.

Coming as it did when the Coal Board had formally announced that they would be unable to meet the BEA's fuel needs, it is perhaps not surprising that the Cabinet accepted the Trend programme. Although they were disappointed at not being consulted, the electrical men were pleased that Trend had recommended that they, and not the Atomic Energy Authority, should construct and operate the new stations, which would amount to a quarter of all new power station capacity from the early 1960s, and thus substantially modify their existing programmes. They were concerned at the greatly increased capital expenditure required for these capital-intensive stations, but in January 1955 agreed in principle to take on the responsibility for the programme, which the Government announced publicly in a White Paper the following month.[5] Geoffrey Lloyd, announcing the dawn of the civil nuclear age to the press, waxed eloquent. The announcement, he said, was

... the most momentous that any Minister of Fuel and Power has made since the office was created. . . . Here is new scope for our traditional genius . . . for mixing a small proportion of imported materials with a large proportion of skill, ingenuity and inventiveness. This was one of the secrets of our success in the industrial revolution which transformed the world in the nineteenth century. Our nuclear pioneers have now given us our second chance – to lead another industrial revolution in the second half of the twentieth century.[6]

In the post-coronation cliché of the time, Britain's nuclear pioneers were heralded in the press as guarantors of a cheap energy future in a 'new Elizabethan age' of British greatness.

The Central Authority were, however, ill-prepared for shouldering the new responsibilities of these dramatic developments. A nuclear power branch had been established within the BEA headquarters at the end of 1954 under J. C. Duckworth, a former nuclear scientist recruited from Ferranti's (where he had been working on the development of the successful Bloodhound missiles). Such was the secrecy surrounding the initial discussions, however, that little scientific and engineering experience was available to him, and it was several months before he discovered the size of the Trend programme which he was nominally responsible for implementing! During 1955 he and some of his colleagues attended courses at the Atomic Energy Authority and began discussions with the nuclear pioneers at Harwell and Risley, and with potential nuclear plant manufacturers, about the first orders planned for 1957.

The CEA also urgently initiated a search for nuclear power station sites. The existing planned sites for conventional power stations did not have the right characteristics. Heavier load-bearing capability and increased water supplies were required by nuclear stations. Like oil stations, nuclear stations could also often be more economically sited away from the coalfields. It was decided that the initial stations should be in the south of England. They looked for sites away from major population centres, recognising the possibility of public disquiet, though they were assured that a nuclear power plant was no more than a normal industrial risk. In fact there was no difficulty in finding sites – indeed the BEA and the Ministry were lobbied by local groups requesting one of the stations because of the employment prospects they would bring – and in October 1955 they were able to announce the sites for the first two stations on river estuaries at Berkeley (Gloucestershire) and Bradwell (Essex). These stations could be linked to the Supergrid by relatively short new sections of high-voltage Grid lines, thus fitting into the overall national development plan.

The men who worked in the nuclear branch – and there was no shortage of willing recruits among the engineers to this intellectually appealing new departure – did so behind a continuing veil of secrecy. In the early years they were heavily dependent on the Atomic Energy Authority's industrial branch at Risley, whom they found generally to be arrogant and unwilling to accept their advice, even on the more conventional electrical side of nuclear power station design. The outline agreement on cooperation with the Atomic Energy Authority left the basic questions of control of construction projects and prices to be paid for nuclear supplies and expertise unclear. It was not a commercial contract at all, but a statement of intent to work together on what politicians had approved, and sort out the details later.

In fact the Central Authority soon found that the basic details had already effectively been worked out for them, and they had little choice but to accept them. The Atomic Energy Authority and the Government had, for example, determined that the early stations should be of the gas-cooled type which had been chosen as the best practicable option for the military programme.[7] These used natural uranium as a fuel, graphite as a moderator, and carbon dioxide as a coolant (which extracted heat from the reactor core so that it could be used to generate electricity). These early reactors became known as 'Magnox' after the magnesium alloy cans in which the nuclear fuel was encased. There were many other possible reactor types, and Citrine, Brown and Duckworth on a trip to the United States in 1955 found the Americans were experimenting on a wider front. However, for the BEA, committed to an immediate programme based on existing British knowledge and resources, the Magnox design was the only practicable option for the early stations. It had, however, been agreed by the Trend working party that the later reactors in the programme might be of a different design, and the CEA kept an open mind on the size and nature of later stations, while accepting the Atomic Energy Authority's advice on the initial designs.

On the question of the organisation of manufacturing and construction, the BEA also found their initial decisions had been largely pre-empted. Recognising that the expanded civil nuclear power programme proposed by Trend would require more outside involvement, the Atomic Energy Authority had in 1954 encouraged four leading turbo-alternator manufacturers each to get together with one of the four leading boiler manufacturers to form consortia which could handle nuclear power station contracts. The enthusiasm of manufacturers to get in on the power of the future knew no bounds, and considerably exceeded their competence and knowledge in the field.[8] The CEA were unhappy about the proposal that they should offer turnkey contracts to these consortia (insisting that they retain central control of design and ordering), but by 1956 a compromise was agreed under which (unlike their practice for conventional stations) orders were to be placed for whole stations with a single consortium. Although the CEA would vet the design in detail (relying, like the consortia, on Atomic Energy Authority advice on the nuclear side), more design initiative would lie with the manufacturers than on conventional power station contracts.

In 1955 and 1956, as the discussions on design and ordering progressed, the CEA found themselves increasingly pressured by the Atomic Energy Authority and the consortia to accept an increase in the nuclear programme above the level of 1700MW by 1965 already agreed. CEA engineers accepted that they could start work on site earlier in 1957, and could increase the size of the first stations (as now seemed technically possible) in order to gain economies of scale relative to the smaller reactors already being built at Calder Hall. The Atomic Energy Authority made increasingly optimistic estimates of capital cost, and Lord Plowden (the former central planner who had become their chairman) was pressing hard within Whitehall for a doubling of the programme. His confidence and that of his nuclear colleagues was considerably increased in the summer of 1956 when their newly-completed reactor at Calder Hall underwent trials. It went critical in May, started producing power in July, and in October was officially opened by the Queen and started delivering power to the Grid. The 92MW reactor, completed on schedule, was the first with an output comparable to that of conventional power plant boilers, though this was essentially a by-product of a process optimised for the production of weapons-grade plutonium. (A further three reactors of similar design at Calder Hall and four at Chapelcross in Scotland were also being constructed primarily for military purposes.) The event was, however, heralded as the dawn of the civil nuclear power age, for it was on rather similar designs, though optimised for electricity production, that the CEA's own larger plants would be based. Confidence at both the Atomic Energy Authority and the consortia, as well as in the Government, was growing. The consortia, anxious that there should be enough orders to go round, had been pressing hard for an increase in the programme, to the extent, it was suspected, of inspiring press stories that Britain's nuclear effort was being unreasonably held back by

CEA officialdom.

The CEA were, indeed, somewhat alarmed at the speed of developments and at the pressure on them to order more of the still untried plants, of a substantially larger scale than Calder Hall, on the basis of conjectural AEA estimates, even before they had obtained firm tenders from the nuclear consortia. They knew that conventional generation costs (with both coal and oil) were falling faster than even the more conjectural Atomic Energy Authority estimates of nuclear costs. While Eccles thought it wise for them to acquire some nuclear experience, he felt that the existing commitment to a more-than-modest programme (rising to a quarter of all capacity ordered by the early 1960s) was sufficient for this, and that the nuclear enthusiasts might be over-optimistic about the potential economies of scale and the forecast operating characteristics and reliability of the nuclear stations. He therefore hesitated to order a third station as early as 1957, as the Atomic Energy Authority wished, and instead in the autumn of 1955 the latter by-passed the CEA and persuaded the newly-independent and inexperienced South of Scotland Board to order a nuclear station.

Most part-time members of the CEA initially supported Eccles in refusing the more extensive commitment to nuclear power for which the Atomic Energy Authority and the consortia were pressing. Some mandarins in the Treasury were also increasingly concerned at the likely expense, though the lower balance-of-payments costs of the uranium fuel (only about a quarter of the costs of oil for a given output) were considered an advantage. None the less Plowden's influence in Whitehall was considerable and in 1956 there was already tacit agreement to the proposed increase of the Trend programme. Citrine and Self, conscious of the consortia's press campaign and the political seduction of nuclear power, now placed themselves behind the nuclear expansion. Citrine (as in the case of oil) was aware that the Central Authority's best chance of surviving the Herbert inquiry and its consequences was to align themselves squarely behind emerging ministerial concepts of the 'national interest'. Increasingly, then, within the Central Authority itself there was pressure for accepting a doubling of the programme, and Citrine warned that (even if they refused on the evidence they had that nuclear power was likely to be uneconomic) they would be faced with a ministerial directive and have no choice. In October 1956 the Central Authority reluctantly agreed to support a nearly doubling of the Trend programme to around 3200MW over the following nine years, along the lines for which the Atomic Energy Authority were pressing. Citrine, it seemed, was no longer following the economic and technical advice of his engineers but decided to bow to the political pressures.

The political arena, in which Plowden had played skilfully for the Atomic Energy Authority in the first half of 1956, was transformed later in the year with the failure of the Anglo-French invasion of Suez, and all its implications for Middle Eastern oil supplies, on which the European economy was becoming so dependent. The actual impact of Suez on oil supplies was temporary and small,[9] but its psychological impact on British politicians was, as Hugh Thomas has remarked, 'comparable to the fear of castration'.[10] The mistakes and dishonesty of Suez broke Eden, who was succeeded as Prime Minister by Harold Macmillan. They also led to the partial collapse of rationality within Westminster, the Atomic Energy Authority and, to a lesser but still noticeable extent, within Whitehall. Throughout 1956, the supply industry's Minister, Aubrey Jones (who was not a member of the Cabinet), remained outside the inner Conservative policy-making circle. In December, however, seeing the political signs, he proposed that the nuclear power programme (whose tacit doubling had already been widely leaked to the press) should rather be tripled. The CEA argued that such pressure should be resisted until they had a better idea of the costs and reliability of nuclear stations, and the Treasury also counselled caution. In the Commons debate on 17 December, several days after the CEA awarded the first two nuclear contracts, no announcement of an increase was made, though it was clear that the programme would be stepped up.[11]

The shelving of Jones' proposal was, however, only temporary. Macmillan, the new Prime Minister, was now quite convinced that releasing Britain from dependence on imported oil should be a high priority and this increasingly dominated cabinet thinking on economic policy. In January 1957, he removed Jones to another post, making Sir Percy Mills the new Minister of Power, with a seat in the Cabinet and a peerage (with Reginald Maudling, the Paymaster-General, covering for him on energy policy in the Commons). Mills was a sixty-seven-year old industrialist who had helped Macmillan in the earlier housing 'crusade', which had established the latter's political reputation. Although this bluff, down-to-earth Midlander was outwardly very different from Macmillan (and perhaps because he posed no threat to him), he became Macmillan's most trusted confidant.[12] The Prime Minister had an exaggerated view of Mills' brilliance as an industrialist which perhaps reflected his own limited experience of industrial affairs. The new Government were more than ever determined to prosecute the expansion of the nuclear power programme with vigour, and in March Macmillan himself took on direct responsibility for the Atomic Energy Authority. The decisions in this area had by then already become a matter for the whole Cabinet, where, in the post-Suez panic, opinion had unstoppably shifted towards a greatly enlarged nuclear initiative. The senior Ministers were in no mood to brook obstruction of this objective by any Minister, civil servant or nationalised body.

A short time after taking office, Lord Mills received the report of a working party, chaired by Martin Flett, Maud's deputy secretary, recently recruited from the Treasury to strengthen the top management in the Ministry. This time, in addition to the relevant Whitehall departments and the Atomic Energy Authority, the CEA and the South of Scotland Board had been represented on the working party, which had reviewed the possibility of increasing the overall nuclear capacity target to substantially above the higher level which had already been tacitly agreed. The Atomic Energy Authority representatives, who in the summer of 1956 had said that British resources of materials and manpower would be insufficient to meet anything greater than 3400MW, were now willing to contemplate a maximum programme as large as 19 stations aggregating 5975MW. From the completion of these stations at the end of 1965, it was estimated, they would save 18 million tons of coal annually (around a quarter of all British power station fuel requirements and more than 5 per cent of total energy demand), thus considerably reducing Britain's dependence on imported oil. In contrast with oil, the required uranium imports not only imposed lower foreign exchange costs, but they were from friendly territories with settled governments such as Canada and South Africa. The tenders for the first stations showed that they would cost £174 per kW (including the initial nuclear fuel charge), three-and-a-half times the cost of conventional stations, but the Atomic Energy Authority representatives were confident that increases in scale and improvements in technique would reduce this excess capital cost to only two-and-a-half times that of conventional stations. The plutonium credit was now expected to be smaller, but the running cost of nuclear stations would be relatively low, so that there was, the nuclear enthusiasts felt, a sporting chance that the later stations would be economic overall. Within Whitehall, however, the strongest argument seemed to be the strategic one of limiting dependence on oil imports from the Middle East and meeting the forecast coal shortages of the 1960s, factors which increasingly dominated cabinet thinking.

The CEA engineers on the Flett working party, Eccles, Brown and Duckworth, were worried by the pressure on them to increase their commitment to a technology of which they had little experience to an extent which implied that more than two-thirds of the new capacity they would be building in the 1960s would be nuclear. Apart from their doubts about the operational flexibility, reliability and cost of the nuclear programme (on all of which they were less optimistic than the Atomic Energy Authority), two aspects of the proposed maximum programme seriously troubled them. A programme of that size implied that by 1970 nuclear stations would have to be sufficiently cheap and flexible to operate as two-shift, rather than continuously operating base-load stations. Alternatively the whole plant industry would in the mid-1960s have to be shifted back to the conventional technology as nuclear orders were cut back. However, the Atomic Energy Authority representatives felt that these fears were exaggerated: they were optimistic about two-shift operational flexibility and costs, and pointed out that, even if these expectations proved over-optimistic, nuclear plant exports would be able to take up any manufacturing slack in the later 1960s. The CEA were also concerned about the implications for the coal industry. They were already committed to increasing their oil burn to eight million tons of coal equivalent annually, and the cost of substantially reducing the oil burn by converting their new oil-only stations to coal would be high. On their own forecasts it seemed that there would be a surplus of small coal with the 6000MW nuclear programme, though they admitted that there were uncertainties in such forecasts. The working party could not resolve the differences between the Atomic Energy Authority and CEA on this and other matters. If the uncertain forecast of a possible coal surplus did materialise, it could, the Flett working party suggested, be solved by exporting coal or bringing 'pressure' on small consumers to burn it (*sic*). An exercise which had begun as an attempt to solve the expected coal shortage thus ended up producing a forecast coal surplus which was then seen merely as 'a challenge to be faced in securing the full potential benefits from an ambitious nuclear programme'. The means had, it seems, become the end.

The CEA engineers sensed that they had very little chance of holding the programme to 3400MW, as they recommended, but they were very disappointed to hear that even the middle programme was rejected by the Cabinet and the Atomic Energy Authority's maximum feasible target of up to 6000MW was chosen. None the less, the Central Authority, again conscious that a ministerial directive would be issued to enforce the Cabinet decision, chose voluntarily to accept the maximum programme. This programme (cautiously described as in the range of 5000–6000MW) was announced publicly by Mills, receiving an enthusiastic reception, in March 1957.[13] It seemed to the CEA to go beyond the bounds of common prudence, and they were appalled to find that the new Minister, Mills, seemed to have a quite inadequate appreciation of its far-reaching financial implications. Flett and the Treasury also were concerned lest the level of investment required would impose severe strains on the economy, particularly in the early 1960s when construction activity would be at its most intense. The capital expenditure on electricity supply was then estimated at £2580 millions over the ten years 1956/7 – 1965/6 for conventional technology, but on Flett's projections the maximum nuclear programme would increase it to £3350 millions concentrated in the first half of the 1960s. This implied a rise in electricity's share of domestic capital investment from 8 per cent at the time to nearly 12 per cent in the early 1960s,[14] though, as we have seen, the Conservatives were politically committed to the objective of containing public sector investment. This extra expansion would, moreover, according to CEA calculations, have a negative rate of return (the nuclear stations being more expensive overall than conventional ones) and also reduce the return on current investment (notably the Supergrid which had been designed for a set of national energy flows quite different than was implied by nuclear-dominated system expansion).

The CEA men could not help but be grateful that a substantial commitment in principle to expansion in a new field was being made, seemingly without financial strings, but it all seemed too much too soon. As 1957 progressed the doubts they expressed at the time of the decision were fortified. Their capital programmes (inflated now by a third nuclear power station at Hinkley Point (Somerset) to be ordered immediately) were clearly higher than the Ministry wished. In the summer it also became clearer that their tentative forecasts of a possible coal surplus were now more than fully confirmed by new Coal Board estimates showing an even larger surplus. The decision to build nineteen nuclear stations aggregating up to 6000MW was, however, a political one, a technological lifebelt offering protection

from the consequences of Suez, which would respond only slowly to
carefully applied doses of rationality. For the time being the CEA
had to live with it. The escalation of the nuclear power programme
was, moreover, having a significant and immediate effect on them, as
it began to dominate ministerial thinking on the still-to-be-deter-
mined post-Herbert reorganisation which bulked large in the minds
of the industry's leaders.

15

THE NEW MEN

'Circumstances compel you!' said the forceful Mr James Horton in
A. G. Street's novel. 'If you're a man, you'll go out and compel
your circumstances.'

> The first chairman of the new generating
> board, criticising by analogy the
> performance of parts of the industry.[1]

As the nuclear power programme was expanding behind the scenes,
the post-Herbert legislative process of reorganising the industry was
unfolding in Parliament, following the confirmation of the Government's intention to change the structure of the industry in November
1956. Aubrey Jones had initially met some resistance in Cabinet to
the proposal to decentralise power, but he had been able to show
strong back-bench support. As the nuclear programme clearly
interested the Cabinet, he placed the establishment of a separate
generating board (which he presented as vital to facilitate nuclear
development) at the centre of his argument for change. Guided by
the precedent of the gas boards, Jones and his civil servants also
agreed to take the Herbert proposal to give more autonomy to the
Area Boards even further, and to cut down the powers of the
proposed Central Authority. The bill he introduced thus made the
new Central Electricity Generating Board and the twelve existing
Area Boards in England and Wales responsible directly to the
Minister. The proposed new Central Authority was reduced to an
Electricity Council on which each of the twelve area chairmen and
three representatives of the Generating Board would sit together
with a chairman and other independent central members. This
Council would be empowered to oversee labour relations, raise
capital on behalf of the Boards, and provide common services and
coordinate matters of common interest such as research. It would
not, however, issue directives to any of the Boards (save in the

unlikely event of their defaulting on borrowings), though it would be free to express an opinion on the Boards' programmes to the Minister, with whom ultimate control lay. The Generating Board would be responsible for the generation, Grid transmission, and wholesaling of electricity, and the Area Boards for electricity distribution and retailing. The Electricity Council, it seemed, would largely be a forum for collective thought about electricity and advising the Minister. The new Electricity Act became law in July 1957, with the new organisations scheduled to take over from the CEA on 1 January 1958.

This reorganisation was a testimony to a deeply-felt desire, which had percolated from the Area Boards and elsewhere within the BEA to the Ministry (both directly and through the Herbert Committee), to be free of the central control of Citrine and Self. Jones was also quite clear that the Electricity Council should not have power where it did not carry responsibility, and that the functions at the centre should be exercised directly by the Ministry. Several members of the Herbert Committee feared that this would lead to more government interference of the kind they explicitly intended to discourage in setting up a central authority to act as a buffer between the Ministry and the Boards. They had tried vigorously, 'down to the last brandy', to get Jones to change his mind, but without success.

It was clear that Citrine, who was now nearing seventy, would have to go. Geoffrey Lloyd had resisted pressure from back-benchers earlier in the 1950s to get rid of Citrine as a Labour sympathiser, and had also resisted Self's attempts to displace him. Both Lloyd and Aubrey Jones had also appreciated Citrine's efforts to impose their oil and nuclear power policies on his unwilling engineers. In 1955, in view of the impending Herbert *Report*, Citrine's appointment had only been renewed to the end of 1957 (i.e. just beyond his seventieth birthday), but he had insisted that this should not be taken to mean that he would retire by then. However, members of the Herbert Committee had confirmed privately what Jones already believed, that Citrine seemed to be too wedded to the over-centralised regime at the CEA, and that a new start should be made with new men appointed to lead the industry. By 1957, Citrine recognised that his role as leader of the industry was at an end, and he accepted graciously the retirement peace-offering of part-time membership of both the new Electricity Council and of the Atomic Energy Authority.

The problem of recruiting new talent to head the industry was, however, one which the Ministry knew from experience was not easy to solve. Over and above the disincentive of repeated and publicised political interventions in management decisions, the salaries of nationalised industry chairmen were not attractive. The industrialists they considered from the private sector were earning substantially more than Electricity Board salaries, which remained at the level fixed in 1947: at £8500 for the Central Authority chairman, £5000 for his two deputies and £4000 for Area Board chairmen. The Central Authority, the chairmen and the Ministry had all been lobbying for increases, but the Treasury resisted on the grounds that it would have an adverse effect on other wage claims. The chairmen ruefully remarked that the same argument did not, curiously, apply to Whitehall Permanent Secretaries, with the result that the latter were now paid 20–50 per cent more than a CEA deputy chairman or Area Board chairmen whereas in 1948 it had been considered essential to offer a 30 per cent differential in the opposite direction to attract industrial talent. Politicians were also chronically reluctant to make a change which would be politically unpopular. The result was that salaries had dropped by more than a third in real terms in the ten years since they were fixed. Eventually, however, in the summer of 1957 the cabinet steeled themselves to accept increases. To reflect the imminent downgrading of the top post the rise to £10000 for the Central Authority chairman was rather less than the rate of inflation over the ten years, but the intention to devolve power was reflected by larger increases (more than enough to compensate for inflation) to £7000 for his two deputy chairmen and £6000 for the Area Board chairmen. (Not until 1964, when they had been eroded by a further 15 per cent, were salaries again increased.) The Ministry remained pessimistic about their chances of attracting leading private industrialists, though Sir John Maud was convinced that no one within the industry was good enough to hold its top post.

Increasingly that top post was seen by Ministers and civil servants not as the chairmanship of the new Electricity Council but rather of the Generating Board. The long process of reorganisation that had been launched when Geoffrey Lloyd appointed the Herbert inquiry, was carried on by Aubrey Jones introducing the legislation, and was completed by a third new Minister, Lord Mills, who thought little of the new structure devised by his predecessor. The Council, he felt would be a 'boneless wonder', and the Generating Board (initially controlling two-thirds of the industry's capital expenditure though less than a third of its employment) would inevitably dominate the industry. However, Mills saw no reason why, with the right people, the new Generating Board could not, within this structure, carry the nuclear programme through effectively. Eccles, then approaching fifty-nine, was the leading internal candidate for the Generating Board chairmanship. Citrine and Self had, indeed, offered to set up a separate generating board under Eccles within the existing CEA structure (thus recognising his *de facto* responsibilities) as a means of heading-off new legislation, though the Ministry made it clear that this was not acceptable. Citrine had then strongly pressed for Eccles to be made the chairman of the Ministry's new Generating Board, but this too was unacceptable. Eccles was considered to be too deeply implicated in the centralising policies of the old regime to be willing significantly to decentralise generation, and was known as an advocate of the less ambitious nuclear programme. His achievements in promoting the Brown revolution were insufficiently appreciated and he lacked that superficial 'presence' or charisma which attracts politicians. Whatever the thoughts of those in the industry, then, Eccles was simply a non-starter for Mills (though he received the consolation prize of a knighthood).

The Ministry were, however, clear that they wanted a strong man, probably an engineer. One candidate, who seemed both to civil servants and to Aubrey Jones right for setting the industry on a new path of vigorous promotion of nuclear power, was Sir Christopher Hinton. Then fifty-five, Hinton was a member of the Atomic Energy Authority and (as managing director of their industrial group at Risley) had been responsible for building the initial atomic energy factories. The strain of supervising much of Britain's nuclear effort had brought on severe nervous exhaustion, and he had spent six months on leave, but now seemed to be fully recovered. The chairman of the AEA, Plowden, was considering organisational changes which would move him from Risley (where his heart really inclined), and lobbied within Whitehall for Hinton's appointment to the Generating Board. Unlike the possible private sector candidates, he was willing to accept the public sector range of salaries. Hinton did, indeed, sit uneasily with the aura of increased commercialism with which the reorganisation was presented to Conservative back-benchers. No less than Citrine and Self, he was deeply imbued with the public service ethos, and had a considerable distaste for the commercial world, having turned down private sector posts at considerably higher rates of pay. He also had a reputation of being a difficult person to get on with (an Atomic Energy Authority sobriquet was 'Sir Christ'), though since leaving Cambridge with a first in engineering, he had an inspiring record of success, first as an ICI engineer, then in the wartime Ministry of Supply factories, and latterly as a leading figure behind Britain's successful manufacture of atomic bombs and the construction of Calder Hall. At a lunch arranged with Plowden at the Savoy in April 1957, moreover, Mills found that he liked Hinton, and the powerful symbolism of Britain's successful nuclear knight taking over the industry whose nuclear dawn had now arrived overrode all other possible doubts about offering him the post.

Hinton was, however, unsure. For personal reasons, he did not relish the thought of a move to London, and his experience of the electricity supply industry (when trying to get urgent new power lines for his various electricity-intensive nuclear projects) had not led him to form an enthusiastic opinion of them. He was, moreover, doubtful about taking the job as Generating Board chairman if he would be subject to Electricity Council control. This posed a problem within the Ministry since, in some respects, it was clear that the legislation implied supervision by the Council, but Mills (who thought little of his senior officials) was able to override their caution about negating the moral authority of the Council. To symbolise independence, the salary offered to Hinton was raised from the £7000 initially envisaged for the post to £10000 (equivalent to that envisaged for the Council chairman). The civil servants also accepted that it would be bad tactics to remind Hinton too strongly of the new Council's powers. A verbal formula was agreed between Hinton and Mills, which satisfied the former that he would have virtual independence as chairman of the generating side of the industry. On these conditions (which he was to quote freely in future against the Council) he felt bound to accept.

The appointment of an outsider above the head of Eccles was not welcomed within the industry. Eccles himself refused to serve as Hinton's deputy, as did two Area Board chairmen. When told of this opposition, Hinton offered to stand down, but Mills insisted on his staying. Eventually Robertson King, a former power company man who had been chairman of the East Midlands Board since nationalisation, agreed to become his deputy; and other less senior people, including the chief engineer, Brown, from within the industry, as well as some outsiders, were also persuaded to join the new Generating Board. The new Board in September 1957 finally began to prepare for the proposed take-over of responsibility in January of the following year.

The appointments to the new Electricity Council took a back seat during these negotiations with Hinton. Mills, though he thought little of the Council, did none the less feel that it, too, needed new blood, and he proposed as chairman Ronald Edwards, Professor of Industrial Organisation at the London School of Economics. Edwards had served on both the Clow and Herbert committees and was thus seen as a leading critic of the industry, particularly on its pricing policy and its financial performance. Having reached his academic eminence the hard way (he had left school at fifteen and practised as an accountant before becoming an academic accountant and economist), he had retained a strong practical streak and a profitable sideline in industrial consultancy. His seminars on industrial organisation at LSE attracted a large number of businessmen, including, on one recent occasion, Mills himself. He was developing the ideas of the Herbert Committee on the appropriate relationship between ministers and nationalised industries in a book whose draft chapters seemed attractive to Mills.[2] As a man of forty-seven, moreover, he could bring a freshness to an industry which had suffered from the absence of new blood at the top. Mills' Permanent Secretary, Sir John Maud, was, however, doubtful about appointing Edwards to the chairmanship, partly because it would sap industry morale if another outsider were given a top job, and partly because he disliked the principle of a member of a committee of inquiry benefiting from his own recommendations. For his part, Edwards was not keen to accept the alternative of a full-time deputy chairmanship if it meant giving up his academic position and consultancy earnings. It was, therefore, agreed that he would become a part-time deputy chairman to get to know the industry, and could within a few years be the natural candidate for succession to the chairmanship. Sir Henry Self, already sixty-seven, was made the caretaker chairman while Edwards was being groomed for the job. Eccles, the favoured civil service candidate, had annoyed Mills by refusing to serve as Hinton's deputy. He forfeited the chairmanship but was made full-time deputy chairman. It was made quite clear that Edwards not Eccles was the heir-apparent.[3]

The personnel of the Area Boards were less directly affected by the Conservative counter-revolution. Most of the chairmen were annoyed at the new appointments of outsiders, and Edwards (who was identified in their minds with the Clow differential and the Herbert criticisms) was particularly unwelcome. Cecil Melling, who had been among the more positive chairmen at the Eastern Board on pricing policy, did, however, agree to join the Council as a full-time member. All the Area Board chairmen also now sat ex officio on the Council (as did the chairman and two other representatives of the Generating Board). There were no explicit changes in the Area Board chairmanships, though in 1956 Citrine and Self had noted with alarm that Aubrey Jones three times turned down Central Authority recommendations for chairmanships of Area Boards and appointed others instead. Apart from these changes, there was considerable continuity at the top, and some chairmen (such as Norman Elliott at the South Eastern Board and Robert Brown at the Southern Board) had the warm confidence of the Ministry. None the less new men had come into some crucial positions in the centralised structure which was to take over the industry at the beginning of 1958.

In the context of the history of one of Britain's leading private sector companies, Courtaulds, Professor Coleman has stressed that changes in policy

> ... are not normally executed by committees, by long-suffering accountants, by patient intellectuals, or by unimaginative bureaucrats. The historical record suggests, instead, that they are carried out by men who combine intelligence with daring ambition which endows them with an exceptional capacity for hard work; who possess a powerful and restless urge for achievement often attended by a degree of paranoia which makes them uneasy companions; and whose decisions are marked by a certain violence of expression and action which often ensures that, in their business relations at least, they inspire respect rather than affection. Such men create successful new businesses or force radical change in existing businesses.[4]

In Hinton and Edwards, the Minister had chosen two such unusual men – a nuclear engineer and a university professor – who were both perceived by their new colleagues as restless, driven men. They often seemed worlds apart, and Edwards was a quieter, more restrained man than Hinton, but both were to be a source of valuable new ideas and to launch important changes in the industry's thinking, and indeed in the Ministry's. Both were to find some of their ambitions thwarted in a job with wider responsibilities than any they had tackled previously, and to find that their own will to change was only the first step on a difficult path. Their own role as missionaries of change was, moreover, not always to be sustained on issues on which they sometimes began to feel that the industry (and not their outside critics in the Conservative party and elsewhere) had been right.

Part IV

THE BOOM YEARS
(1958–62)

16

THE ELECTRICITY COUNCIL:
FEDERALISM AND FINANCE

We are a very difficult animal to describe. We are less than a holding company and more than a federation. . . . In the main we are dependent on persuasion.

> Professor Ronald Edwards, chairman of the Electricity Council, to the Select Committee on Nationalised Industries, 3 April 1962.

The new Electricity Council under Self, and the Central Electricity Generating Board under Hinton, each began meeting formally in September 1957, and for the first four months 'shadowed' the decisions of Citrine's CEA, as they prepared for their formal take-over on 1 January 1958. The new organisations inherited both the staff and the scattered Central London buildings of the CEA. It was not until 1963/4 that the Council and the CEGB moved to their present offices at, respectively, 30 Millbank (near Whitehall and Westminster) and in the City in Paternoster Square (next to St Paul's). The weakest part of the new structure was the Electricity Council, with a staff of just over 500 and few formal powers. Twelve of its members – a majority – were from the now independent Area Boards and three from the CEGB. These fifteen Board represent-atives could impose their policies on the five central members – Self, Eccles, Citrine (now a relatively inactive part-timer), Edwards (the newcomer), and Melling (who had left the Eastern Board chairman-ship for a new post at the centre). The new Council had no power to issue policy directives: the Ministry rather than they were the residuary legatee of the CEA in this respect. All the Boards were determined to assert their independence and limit the influence of the centre, and this was reflected in stringent controls on the Council's expansion: it was the only part of the industry to experience a decline in staffing levels over the next five years. At their first meeting Self had been conciliatory in offering to respect the spirit of autonomy implied in the 1957 Act, but his personality was quite unsuited to this new role. At last titular head of the industry, he found that much of the power had been drained from the position, and he became increasingly frustrated. Indeed he saw the Labour opposition energy spokesmen and tried to get them to agree to a quick bill to restore central powers over the Boards if (as was then generally expected) Labour were returned to power in the 1959 election, though the MPs wisely refused to commit themselves to this.

The Council only occasionally took a formal vote, members recognising that any decision which was less than unanimous would not in fact be followed by the Boards. This also made it easier for the central members, who were *de facto* a separate interest group, to express their own views rather than merely those of the Council to the Minister. Self tried to boost the Council's authority by getting ministerial backing for his policies, but, despite his considerable pliancy towards Ministry views, the civil servants and Ministers listened more to Hinton and the CEGB and to Edwards than to what they saw as the old guard. Hinton, the new CEGB chairman, was especially dominant in the early years. He was responsible for two-thirds of the industry's capital expenditure and for the vast nuclear programme which was crucial to the Ministry's new fuel policy. Unsurprisingly, then, he had direct contact with the Ministry on all important aspects of his Board's work and he used his personal standing with Mills to bolster this position. The Council's central members found him authoritarian and uncooperative, while he in turn frequently found their meetings boring and unnecessary. On a few occasions, the Council insisted that he at least pay lip service to their role. When he and Mills agreed to revise the CEGB's capital programme without consulting the Council, for example, they pointed out that this was a breach of the statutory requirement and gained an apology.

Yet after they *had* consulted, the CEGB were not obliged to take any notice at all of what the Council had said, and frequently exercised this freedom. The CEGB's truculence was seen, for example, in their withholding files on their research policy from Eccles (who wanted to fulfil the Council's duty of coordinating research), and the CEGB in fact dominated research policy in the early years of the Council, taking over the management of the

Leatherhead laboratories, including technical research done there on behalf of Area Boards. Most Area Board chairmen on the Council felt that Eccles (not Hinton) should have got the CEGB job, and they became increasingly disturbed at the independence of the CEGB, for whom they were virtually captive consumers of bulk electricity, with few practical ways of controlling what they were more and more inclined to see as its wasteful and misguided policies. One safeguard they had been given in the 1957 Act was the right to generate electricity for themselves, though it was made clear that the required ministerial approval for this would only be given in exceptional circumstances. In spite of the objections of some members of the CEGB, the South Western Board, now chaired by an electrical engineer from the aircraft industry, A. N. Irens, installed a small aircraft turbine to generate electricity in the special conditions at Princetown on Dartmoor (where these cheaply and quickly installed, quick-starting but expensive-to-run engines could increase security of supply and reduce the need for transmission lines). But there were only a few cases of this kind where small-scale self-generation could plausibly be shown to be economic. The CEGB were also unable to get their way when they wished to change the boundaries between themselves and the Area Boards: as, for example, when they wished to be allowed greater freedom to sell directly to large industrial consumers (as they already did to the railways); or when they wanted the Area Boards to take over some responsibilities for the old 132kV Grid (now increasingly used for distribution purposes rather than for the interconnection of power stations). Bickering on such issues at the top was frequently unproductive, as Area Boards, smarting at the CEGB's 'take-it-or-leave-it' attitude on general policy, hit back in the only way they could (even when the CEGB had a good case) by witholding their cooperation on these matters. At the local working level, however, relations between the engineers in distribution and those in generation and main transmission generally remained cordial and cooperative.

The introduction by the CEGB of fresh independent ideas at the top, unrestrained by past prejudices, was, moreover, in some respects a gain. Their new ideas could be half-baked, as on labour relations (see pp. 221–2 below), but, since they lacked a direct interface with the consuming public, their ideas were less restrained by the sometimes muddled and short-term thought on public relations and pricing which sometimes paralysed the Area Boards' rational faculties. The CEGB thus moved rapidly away from the compromises between Area Boards which had bedevilled the CEA discussions on the Bulk Supply Tariff, and modified it to reflect their own costs and provide a clear incentive to Boards to improve the load factor.[1] The arguments against proper cost reflection in the Bulk Supply Tariff (where metering costs are trivial) had always been the silliest. The CEGB (with Stanley Brown reflecting the view of the better headquarters engineers and presenting his ideas to Council) were no longer obliged to accept the majority Area Board view. They knew that they had the support of both the Ministry and of Edwards, the only ones who now mattered, but they also bent over backwards to conciliate the Boards by arguing the logic of their proposals. Improved thermal efficiencies of conventional generation and increased reliance on capital-intensive nuclear generation would reduce running costs and increase capital costs, so Brown tilted the tariff more towards capacity charges in their first year, and a little further in 1961.[2] A special price for large disconnectable loads (to ease demand at system peaks) was introduced in 1960, and in that year they also proposed to introduce a differential between day and night running charges. With Edwards' support, the CEGB forced this on to mainly reluctant Area Boards in 1962. The result was a Bulk Supply Tariff which, though still not perfect,[3] gave clearer and more correctly cost-based price signals than its predecessors. The clearer division of responsibilities in the new, decentralised structure thus did sometimes improve policy by clarifying issues which previously had been befogged by a spurious search for compromise between Boards.

With the Bulk Supply Tariff determining two-thirds of their costs, the Area Boards understandably became increasingly worried about the lack of control by the Council (on which they had a majority) over the CEGB, but they could be just as strident as the CEGB in insisting on their own autonomy. The early years of meetings at Council, on which all twelve Area Board chairmen sat, saw a good deal of revelling in the trappings of independence, and little serious attention to important collective issues. The process of consultation with Council central members over their annual capital budgets and tariffs was, however, more real in the case of the Area Boards than for the CEGB, and Self was able to persuade Mills that it was essential that the Ministry should deal initially with the Boards through the Council. The central members of the Council had regular meetings with the Minister and his advisers to discuss policy, while the Area Boards in practice lacked this direct connection simply because the Minister found their problems trivial and boring (a visit by Mills to the South Wales Board, supposed to be the first of a regular series to all the Boards, was in fact the last!). As a civil servant minuted, after several years' experience of the new system:

> In practice the central members have far more power than the statute provides because they have the ear of the Minister and the Area Boards do not. They can and often do, take his name in vain to put their views across to the Area Boards; and the Minister hears too little at first hand of the views of the Area Boards.

The views of central members, particularly in the later years under Edwards, were also important in determining questions such as senior promotions, for, although the statutory requirement that the Minister consult them in making appointments to the Boards had been removed in 1957, consultation continued as before and was now listened to more consistently than in the last years of the Citrine regime.

Mills was keen to prepare senior managers in the industry for promotion, though he found some reluctance among the Area Board chairmen to support his initiatives. Traditionally only the chairman and his deputy among the full-time employees had been appointed to an Area Board by the Minister, but Mills began appointing other senior officers as part-time members of their Boards in order to give them wider experience. At the lower levels of management, graduate recruitment to the industry also improved: an increased number of university scholarships was offered and the EPEA was finally persuaded to accept higher salaries for good graduate entrants. The total graduate intake rose from a low point of seven in 1955/6 to forty-one by 1959/60. The CEGB proved especially attractive to graduates, and, from 1961, Hinton insisted on the CEGB recruiting separately, arguing that they needed more first class scientific and engineering recruits than the Area Boards. Within both the generation and distribution sides, there remained a good deal of suspicion of accelerated promotion schemes for favoured candidates, but a policy of selective cross-posting in order to give engineers and managers wider experience developed on management's initiative. Edwards (who had left school at fifteen) was conscious that graduates should not be treated favourably simply because they were graduates, but he felt it important to dispel the poor image nationalised industries now had amongst potential recruits, in contrast with some of the initial enthusiasm for nationalised management in the 1940s. Both Hinton and Edwards still felt that the industry's management quality left a lot to be desired, in that they still suffered from the poor recruitment and promotion policies of the past, but by the early 1960s there was greater confidence that the right steps had been taken to improve the position.[4]

As in earlier years, the main focus of Ministry concern about Area Boards, apart from appointments, was on their annual capital investment programmes. The Council advised on cuts requested towards the end of 1957 because of external pressure on the pound, and the Ministry accepted their advice as to which Area Boards could be cut most. Towards the end of 1958, macroeconomic policy was reversed and the Boards, particularly those in the depressed regions, were asked if they could accelerate investment. They did manage to put forward small increases in expenditure, though not as much as had been wanted. As before, short-term changes in the pattern of expenditure proved difficult to enforce. By 1960, when the Boards themselves wanted more expenditure to meet rapidly growing demand, the Government's policy had again shifted and expenditure cuts were being imposed. The central members of Council had the difficult task of transmitting these changing signals to the Boards and for some years dominated the consultations. Their position was strengthened also by some instability within the Ministry, as Dennis Proctor in 1958 replaced Maud as Permanent Secretary, and, at ministerial level, Richard Wood in October 1959 replaced Mills. Wood was much liked by those in the electricity industry, who found him unusually 'non-political' and willing to listen, but he was not in the Cabinet, and government policy continued to be influenced by Mills, now Paymaster-General and still Macmillan's confidant. The responsibility for electricity lower down within the Ministry also underwent change. Murray, who was now not a well man, had progressively less influence on electricity matters than his fellow Under-Secretary Owen Francis (from the gas division and instrumental in drafting the 1957 Electricity Bill) and Philip Chantler (their economist).

The Ministry had always reserved its right to deal directly with the Area Boards. Even when *de facto* delegating ministerial oversight of capital budgets to the Council, they insisted on conveying formal Ministry approval directly to the Boards, as provided in the 1957 Act. In 1961 they further annoyed central members of Council by visiting the Area Boards individually to discuss past over-runs on capital budgets and future capital requirements. The central members were worried that this would subvert their own influence and make the Area Board chairmen as independent as Hinton and the CEGB, but they need not have worried. As one civil servant noted in 1962,

In our inevitable state of ignorance about technical matters it is very easy for individual Boards to pull the wool over our eyes. Our only defence . . . is by constant and diligent comparison of what the Boards tell us.

The Boards, for their part, lacked experience of this direct contact, and were sometimes alarmed at the political preoccupations and the areas of industrial ignorance of civil servants, though Council central members were now well used to this. The lurches in policy which had been forced on the industry – the maximum nuclear power programme, the appointments of new men – had done nothing to increase its leaders' confidence in the quality of government control, though they now accepted control as an unpleasant but necessary fact of life. That control remained basically a control by negotiation, not by directive. As before, the Boards ignored agreed budgetary limits where it was clear that failure to invest would lead to failure to connect new consumers, but they could rarely get Ministers to take responsibility by publishing a clear directive. As before, when adjustments were made to their capital programmes or tariffs at Ministerial request, this was typically done by gentleman's agreement, notwithstanding the recommendation of the Herbert Committee for more ministerial openness. Most chairmen believed it best that things should remain that way.

On most aspects of policy on which the Council might have had an innovative role, such as engineering standardisation or tariffs, little significant progress was made in the first five years of Council, but on finance, which Self initially delegated to Edwards, new initiatives were possible. Edwards had, of course, been brought in as the heir-apparent to the caretaker chairman, Self. In the early years, however, his influence was limited both by the part-time nature of his appointment, and by the clear distaste of many of the Area Board chairmen for his ideas. On tariffs, where his views were particularly disliked, Self insisted that Melling not Edwards handle matters for the Council. Like Hinton, Edwards brought a lot of new ideas to the industry and was a source of refreshing stimulus, but, unlike Hinton, he lacked the power and position to enforce their adoption. In his early years, moreover, he decided to tackle the opposition head-on and pulled no punches in his advocacy of the policies of the Herbert Committee, many of which were still vigorously opposed by the Area Board chairmen. Edwards got on best with Hinton, perhaps because both men shared the open-mindedness of newcomers and neither posed a threat to the other in the field of their respective expertises: economics and engineering. The Area Board chairmen, however, saw Edwards as an academic interloper with little real knowledge of the industry and were horrified at the thought of his eventually becoming chairman.

In 1959, when Self was due to retire from the chairmanship, he warned Mills of the Area Board chairmen's firm opposition to Edwards, but Edwards was equally insistent that the promises made to him should be honoured. He argued that Council would get used to him as an imposed chairman, and that he would be able to impose tougher policies and increase the profitability of the industry. Hinton advised the Minister to take no notice of Self's views, but some civil servants cautioned that there might be something in the view that Edwards lacked both 'presence' and experience for the job, and Mills hesitated. When he saw the chairmen collectively in July, they asked him to appoint Eccles, but this he flatly refused to do, in view of Eccles' earlier refusal to serve under Hinton. Mills now proposed, as a compromise, a new caretaker chairman, Robertson King, formerly chairman of the East Midlands Board and now Hinton's deputy. King was popular for his down-to-earth charm and commonsense rather than respected for intellectual fire, and Mills made it clear that he, too, was a caretaker and should groom Edwards for the succession. Edwards would, Mills emphasised, succeed in a few years' time, after serving a further apprenticeship, now in a full-time capacity, as King's deputy.

Edwards was not at all happy at serving under a man he did not consider his superior, with still no firm guarantee of the succession (for Mills could only express an intention, not bind a future Minister). None the less he decided to plunge wholeheartedly in, giving up his outside commitments and his major professorial duties to serve as full-time deputy chairman. His diplomatic skills and knowledge of the industry, the lack of which had earlier been criticised, developed over the following years, and he modified many of his views as his experience increased, while retaining the core of his critique of the industry's past policies. He got support from Melling and some others now, but the majority of chairmen continued to have doubts about his succession to the leadership of the industry. In 1961, the new Minister, Richard Wood, who was more willing to listen to their views than Mills had been, queried whether he should confirm Mills' proposal that Edwards should become the new chairman. King himself pressed strongly against this, asking that his own term of office be extended, and other Area Board chairmen and outside appointees were also considered. The civil servants were, however, now firmly in favour of Edwards. He had the energy, comparative youth and drive which they felt was lacking on Council, and had been given promises of the firmest conceivable kind which they felt it wise to honour, since it was clear that Edwards would otherwise leave the industry. In the summer of 1961, then, Woods confirmed that Edwards would indeed succeed to the chairmanship early the following year.

The Ministry's Permanent Secretary, Sir Dennis Proctor had felt that Edwards would grow in stature once the uncertainty in his position were resolved, and this indeed proved to be the case. As he had promised, his style of management was less committee-bound than that originally set up by Self, and his individual colleagues were given more direct personal responsibility in some areas. He did, however, reserve the central issues of finance, economics and relations with Whitehall very much to himself, and the Ministry relied more on him than they had on his predecessors for advice about the industry. In consequence, the Council's stature was gradually enhanced in subsequent years. Although Edwards had initially preached that Ministerial directives should be made public, he became a master at the Whitehall gentleman's game, and formed a closer consultative relationship with senior civil servants and politicians than had his predecessors. Thus, although he had initially suggested that they should insist on a government subsidy for uneconomic rural electrification (a proposal unanimously rejected by the chairmen who feared it would legitimise government intervention), he later came to accept that this was a burden the Boards must shoulder themselves to avoid public criticism.[5] He was, above all, to be a success at presenting the industry's viewpoint to informed public opinion, as when the House of Commons Select Committee on Nationalised Industries finally in 1962 began a serious examination of the industry.[6] Many of those in the industry felt, however, that Citrine's more arms-length relationship with Whitehall had been wiser, though they recognised that, with growing government confidence in intervention, a return to the old ways was probably impossible.

Even before he became chairman, Edwards had been effective in developing new policies in the field of finance, which Self had initially allotted to him, and on which government pressure from outside was working in the same direction as he was from within. In the first ten years of nationalisation, the industry had suffered from a shortage of economic and financial expertise. Edwards, conscious of the possibility that excessively low financial returns in nationalised industries were 'crowding out' more desirable investment projects elsewhere, was determined to implement reforms in policy. In October 1958 he had outlined his ideas to his senior colleagues at a weekend conference at Moretonhampstead. The only support he got came from Hinton, who recognised the logic of his proposals for increased financial disciplines. Most Area Board chairmen, however, advocated a continuation of historic cost pricing, and pointed to recent Ministry requests for a tariffs freeze as a clear indication that, whatever they said, the Government really preferred price stability to an increased rate of return. (In November 1957 and March 1958 the Cabinet had forced through a price freeze by gentleman's agreement against the opposition of the Chancellor who felt, as Edwards did, that prices and profits should be increased.) Edwards' colleagues were as short-sighted as the Cabinet. Self, the chairman, had a confused understanding of the role of higher rates of return in allocating resources in the more market-orientated economy of the late 1950s, and expected interest rates to fall from levels he considered high.[7] Edwards later recollected that when he urged more 'commercial' behaviour on his colleagues, they did not identify this with efficiency and profitability, as he hoped, but rather saw only its pejorative overtones of 'short-term, narrow, selfish, catch-as-catch-can'.[8]

None the less, there were pressures, both within the Government and at the Council, to increase the industry's rate of return. The interest rate charged on Treasury loans to the industry edged upwards, reaching the range $6\frac{1}{4}$–$6\frac{3}{4}$ per cent on new capital by 1960 (compared with only $4\frac{1}{4}$ per cent on their inherited borrowings). The Electricity Council also adopted rather higher target rates of self-financing for future programmes than had been planned in BEA days. This policy had been compromised for a time in 1957–8 when, despite their public calls for higher rates of return, the Government froze electricity prices. As the industry pointed out, if they bowed further to this pressure, their income would fall and their self-financing targets become unattainable. Indeed it had all along been obvious to the industry – and soon became evident to the Ministry – that the Government's three basic instructions (greatly increase expenditure on nuclear power, freeze prices, increase self-financing) were simply incompatible.

From the end of 1958, however, when they were allowed greater freedom on prices, they were able gradually to increase the rate of self-financing. As before, this meant adopting more conservative depreciation provisions nearer to replacement cost, or increasing their published surplus. Self, King and many Area Board chairmen still remained reluctant to do either, arguing that the electricity statutes merely required them to break even, but Ministry pressure and Edwards' persuasion gradually brought some Boards round. The CEGB proved most cooperative. In the later 1950s they adopted new, more conservative depreciation provisions, which were justified in the *Annual Report* as being a natural corollary of nuclear power and new large plant.[9] Within the industry, however, these new provisions were recognised as being primarily a way of concealing rising surpluses, in order not to arouse the adverse reaction from consumers or trade unions which they expected if their published surpluses appeared too high.[10] Edwards now recognised that, with economies of scale in the larger, new power stations, replacement costs were no longer above the historic book costs (by 1960 he reckoned that their replacement costs overall were in fact £20 millions below their actual depreciation provisions). He thus felt that further increases in self-financing should properly come from higher declared surpluses. In fact, in the period of reorganisation the increased internal financing came both from higher depreciation (£534 millions in the financial years 1958/9–1962/3); and from higher surpluses (£140 millions). This self-financing contributed 43 per cent of the total capital spending in this period of £1551 millions (compared with only 36 per cent in the ten previous years).

The extent to which the industry should ideally finance itself was a matter of dispute even among its critics, with Sir Roy Harrod somewhat arbitrarily advocating 100 per cent self-financing,[11] and the Herbert Committee accepting the more common view that this would be unjust to present-day consumers.[12] Edwards still agreed with his Committee (he found at Council that prices would have to be raised by a quarter in order to achieve full self-financing), but he did toy with the alternative financing strategy of raising new capital without government guarantee on the market, as was now permitted under the 1957 Act. There had also been tentative discussions with the

CEGB about raising finance for the expanded nuclear programme from the International Bank for Reconstruction and Development. However, the most elementary analysis of the nuclear programme showed that no prudent banker would touch it, and there was an understandable distaste for admitting that the Treasury were financing a self-evidently uneconomic project, so this idea was hurriedly dropped. Later, adopting a different approach, both Hinton and Edwards persuaded Richard Wood that it would be 'bracing' if the Boards could issue their own capital on the market, and other Ministers were also keen on this. However, few of the Area Board chairmen thought it desirable, and the Treasury were able to block it, arguing that any increased returns in the industry should go directly to the Exchequer and not to the investing public in what would still be virtually a risk-free investment but with spuriously higher returns than Treasury-backed stock.[13]

A Treasury committee under Sir Thomas Padmore, the second secretary, had, however, been fundamentally reappraising the position of the nationalised industries during 1959, following increasing Cabinet concern about the declining financial performance and poor management of the railways and coal industries. Ministers still placed most emphasis on regional decentralisation as their route to 'commercial' behaviour, but the Treasury were anxious to head off further initiatives such as the Herbert Committee and concentrate attention instead on what they thought were more fundamental issues. They felt that the nationalised industries were not financing enough of their own capital needs because their sponsoring Ministers were unduly reluctant to face up to price rises. Mills, who had earlier been one of the ministerial offenders in this respect, was soon behind the new policy, and after the Conservative election victory of 1959 the Cabinet seemed willing to face up to the political consequences of adopting it. A draft Treasury paper on the financial and economic obligations of the nationalised industries was shown to Edwards and the other central Council members early in 1960. Edwards was delighted at the evolution in Treasury thinking which this revealed, though he disagreed with details and he found his colleagues much less enthusiastic. All of them resented the fact that some of the general strictures on nationalised industries (for example, that they made inadequate depreciation provisions) were indiscriminately applied to them, even though they were now quite untrue. The Council were also anxious that any target imposed on them should also be imposed on their competitors in fuel markets (who were less able to stand it). Wood, the Minister, jibbed at the 13 per cent price rise the Council told him would be necessary to implement the proposal to achieve an 8 per cent net return on capital,[14] much to the annoyance of the Treasury who wanted Ministers to be firm on this. The Treasury were, however, able to get their proposals through Cabinet, though there was some opposition, both from Ministers and in the nationalised industries. The only concessions won by the Council were some drafting revisions to remove unfair aspersions cast on their past performance, and an agreement that the proposed target of 8 per cent net return should not be published. In April 1961, therefore, a White Paper on the *Financial and Economic Obligations of the Nationalised Industries*, setting out the new ground-rules for higher financial returns (but without mentioning a specific figure), was published.[15]

It was hoped that the requirement to earn a higher rate of return would be a managerial spur to greater efficiency in the nationalised industries. There were signs that the Treasury now had the upper hand over short-term political policy compromises. Where wasteful investment was clearly taking place and cutbacks were required – notably in the coal and railway industries – new appointments such as that of Dr Beeching indicated a clear determination to change policy. In the electricity industry the Government were now pressing for price increases, particularly for domestic consumers. (The Treasury consistently argued that if higher prices could not be made to stick for electricity, where demand was so buoyant, the policy could hardly be expected to stick elsewhere.) Although gas would have slightly easier targets (much to the Council's chagrin), there seemed no good reasons why the electricity industry should not fairly rapidly achieve higher rates of return as good as or better than those of the Post Office Telephones or British European Airways, and nearer to that of similar relatively safe investments in the private sector.

Edwards stage-managed all the negotiations of targets for the industry overall and for individual Boards. The target return agreed averaged only a little below the 8 per cent net return initially suggested, though it was expressed rather as a return of 12½ per cent gross, to accommodate the exaggeratedly high depreciation provisions (included in the gross figure but not in the net) which the Boards were already making. The Boards with the weakest financial performance in the past (like the South Western and South Eastern) were given the stiffest financial targets in an attempt to improve financial disciplines overall, without penalising those (like the

London Board) which were already performing well financially. The industry's surplus after depreciation and interest payments, which had traditionally been small, was under the new regime expected to rise from £33 millions in the financial year 1961/2 to £174 millions by 1964/5. Edwards thought this would enable them to raise the proportion of investment financed internally from 50 per cent to 60 per cent. The following year they were under pressure to increase self-financing even more, to 100 per cent on any *extra* capital expenditure above the levels already approved, though eventually 80 per cent self-financing of this extra expenditure was agreed. The Ministry it seemed, now really meant to use financial incentives as a tool for containing expenditure, and Edwards was hopeful that this would enable the industry to operate freer of government controls, as the Treasury had also argued was desirable.

The 1961 Treasury initiative was a remarkable piece of 'legislation' by White Paper rather than by statute,[16] and it laid low that section of opinion in the industry (basing its views on the 1947 Act) which held that they should do no more than break even, or as near to that as the Government would permit them. If many senior men in the industry did not understand the macroeconomic logic of the change, there was indeed no reason why they should do so: the decentralisation of decisions was now in principle possible because they were being given the right financial signals. In that sense, the changes of 1961 were of far greater potential significance than the organisational changes of 1957.

But how would the Boards' behaviour be affected by the requirement to earn a higher rate of return? Many of the critics from the 'crowding out' school felt that it should lead to a substantial reduction in investment by the electricity industry. There was, however, no formal requirement that all new investments should earn the higher target rate of return but merely that the average on all their capital should.[17] Yet there were changes in this respect too. The Ministry had been pressing, and now increased their pressure, for proper appraisal of new investment, and the industry was a pioneer of new techniques. Edwards had begun to appreciate that there were serious problems in applying financial appraisal techniques to the bulk of their new investment. Much of this was required by statute; moreover individual projects usually had a strong element of joint costs, making their financial returns difficult to isolate. The CEGB had been most receptive to new ideas, and in 1959 had adopted a scheme which attempted to come to terms with some of the problems. Capital expenditure statutorily required to meet demand was not consciously evaluated (its return could be arbitrarily fixed, within very wide margins, by the level of tariffs), but 'optional' expenditure (e.g. the choice of generating technique, or expenditure designed to lower costs) was in theory required to make a 10 per cent net (16 per cent gross) return. Discounted cash flow appraisals had also been introduced by the CEGB in 1959, for evaluating such proposed new investments and for analysing questions such as the economics of scrapping old plant. However, some crucial decisions on 'optional' expenditure, taken on grounds of political expediency or technical advance – notably nuclear power – were exempted from such rigorous appraisal methods. The result was that the proportion of capital expenditure subjected to the test was infinitesimal: less than 1 per cent of CEGB expenditure![18]

If higher rates of return were to influence investment levels, then, this would have to be indirectly through the impact of the higher prices necessary to achieve the high returns on the level of electricity sales. The Treasury and the Ministry did not fully appreciate this, but Edwards, by the time he became chairman, was fully aware of it. Yet there was little guidance on the likely impact.

The tradition had been to regard demand for electricity as highly inelastic with respect to price (except when competition with gas was being discussed, when the opposite assumption of high price elasticity was typically asserted). However, no systematic research had been done by the industry on the price elasticity of demand for electricity among the various consumer groups. What was very clear in the early 1960s was that sales were expanding very fast, partly in consequence of past failure to raise domestic prices; and that capacity would have to be built to meet the demand. Paradoxically, at the very moment when improved financial signals for rationally restricting investment were being devised, other factors were raising the industry's spending plans to historically unprecedented levels.

17

AREA BOARDS: INDEPENDENCE, OVER-EXPANSION AND THE NEW RATIONALITY

> We believe that each Board should be encouraged to stand on their own feet . . .
>
> *Report of* [Herbert] *Committee of Inquiry into The Electricity Supply Industry,* Cmd. 9762, 1956, p. 96

> I think the question of pricing for electricity is one to which we do not know the precise answer; I wish we did.
>
> R. F. Richardson, South Western Board Chief Commercial Officer, evidence to Select Committee on Nationalised Industries, 4 July 1962.

Both the Area Boards and Conservative back-benchers had initially been delighted that the new Electricity Council had relatively few powers of control over the decentralised distribution Boards. Their labour relations remained a central matter (see Chapter 18 below), as did some training and the arrangements for pooling bank accounts and raising capital. But the central responsibilities for policy development, economic and engineering performance, and 'commercial' behaviour now lay with the Area Boards. Their officers still met regularly (though less frequently than under the CEA) to discuss common problems, and their chairmen now all met at Council meetings every month, but they were free to go their own way on most matters if they wished. Conservative romantics viewed this as the pathway to more commercial behaviour and increased efficiency and profitability, and the Herbert Committee had itself entertained hopes in this direction; but it became increasingly clear that this particular incantation did not work.

It is in fact difficult to see any significant changes in the policies pursued by the Area Boards after the regional decentralisation of the 1957 Act. While the chairmen and their Boards appreciated the greater freedom, they did not in fact use it significantly to modify their behaviour, and Whitehall could not help but note that life went on very much as before. This could hardly be otherwise, for the pressures on them from the competitive conditions in both capital and product markets had not changed significantly either. Chairmen and their Boards had a good deal of discretion, as in the earlier regime, to set their own standards, and they continued to do so. Thus the London Board remained highly profitable and was able to finance a good deal of its expansion internally, while the South Eastern Board made no serious effort to improve its poor financial performance much above the legal minimum required. This situation could not be changed merely by decentralisation, but would only respond to clearer signals from explicit financial targets. The increasing pressures from Ministry and Council culminating in the 1961 White Paper, *not* the regional decentralisation, were thus to become the motor forces of change. The Treasury's views on improving financial performance, not the politicians' shibboleth of organisational change, got to the heart of the matter.

Until Edwards' appointment to the chairmanship in 1961, the Boards were largely left to pursue their own policies on pricing and load development. They were able to continue in the traditions established in the first decade of nationalisation. There was still little progress on national standardisation of distribution equipment, though a combination of increasing standardisation of equipment within Boards, and increasing competitive pressure on the manufacturers as the supply position eased, helped to force equipment prices downward, and to cut the Boards' unit capital costs in these years. Progress also continued towards the planning and extension of integrated local distribution systems. Area Board management was further concentrated into larger units, which were made both feasible and desirable by the increasing use of motorised transport, radio-telephones and machine accounting techniques. The latter were by the early 1960s increasingly computer-based, and computers, pioneered by the CEGB, were also used for system planning in the Area Boards. The standardisation of old networks was still proceeding rather slowly, but by 1962 most DC consumers had been converted (a rump of only 0.3 per cent of all consumers were still receiving DC supplies) and many of the 8 per cent of non-standard AC consumers still remaining were due for early conversion.

Priority, as before, had been given to rural electrification. The intention to make the Boards stand financially on their own feet in this respect had been weakened somewhat when, following Conservative back-bench and rural pressure-group activity, the Boards received cash from the break-up of the old CEA's central reserves in 1958 in proportion to their rural electrification problem, but at least in future they would have to fund the subsidy required for rural consumers from their own urban surpluses. As they brought supplies to more remote farms the costs rose, from £90 per consumer when their agreed 10-year rural electrification programme began in 1953/4 to £173 per consumer by 1960/1. By then the rural losses nationally were running at an annual level of £5.7 millions: about 14 per cent of rural revenue and equivalent to about 1 per cent on other consumers' bills. These losses were smaller than expected, because the revenue from the rural load had built up faster than predicted. British farms were typically more electricity-intensive than those in continental Europe or America, partly because they were larger and their occupants richer than Europeans, and, in contrast to America, electricity was more extensively used for heating and power purposes. On the whole the Boards were satisfied at having thus reduced the losses, and the national target of connecting 85 per cent of farms by 1965 was in fact achieved eighteen months ahead of schedule.

In the later 1950s and early 1960s electricity sales expanded more rapidly than the Boards had expected in urban as well as rural areas. They continued to win large industrial consumers such as ICI and the major steel firms away from self-generation towards taking a higher proportion of their requirements from the Grid, helped in some cases by special terms from the CEGB for large interruptible supplies. The fastest – and quite unexpected – rate of growth was, however, now in sales to domestic consumers, which between 1957 and 1962 almost doubled. The further fall in the real price of electricity (of 11 per cent in this period) helped stimulate sales growth, but consumer expenditure on appliances was rather higher than their expenditure on electricity, and reductions in the real cost of appliances contributed significantly to the growth. Incomes were also rising fast; and, as more married women went out to work, the demand for labour-saving appliances grew together with the enhanced purchasing power of such two-income families. There was also an unprecedented hire purchase boom in 1958–1960, when the total hire purchase debt for all goods doubled. The Area Boards, despite intermittent government restrictions on their borrowing for this purpose, accounted for about 5 per cent of the total h.p. credit extended to consumers for all purposes. The Boards' sales of appliances boomed and, at the peak, some two-thirds of all their appliance sales were on h.p. This business proved highly profitable as, under Ministerial pressure, they raised the terms for consumer credit nearer to the levels offered in the private sector, while their bad debts were substantially fewer than on private sector h.p. loans. Conscious that the problem of inadequate generating capacity had now been overcome, the Boards also promoted sales by increased advertising, though (by agreement with their gas competitors) they stayed out of the new medium of commercial TV advertising until 1963.

Between 1957 and 1962 the proportion of consumers owning refrigerators rose from 11 per cent to 28 per cent, of washing machines from 22 per cent to 45 per cent and of televisions from 47 per cent to 84 per cent. Labour-saving appliances were beginning to be taken for granted by the middle classes and realistically aspired to by the working classes. Electricity was promoted as clean, convenient and cheap, and consumers gradually but perceptibly were becoming less frugal. Water heaters were left on at night and householders now seemed more careless about leaving lights switched on. The latter was a noticeable change from the thirties (when electricity for lighting had been many times more expensive in real terms), and the new generation were often rebuked by their elders for their profligacy: electricity had entered the generation gap.

As in earlier years, the peak, space-heating load was the least welcome part of the increased sales to domestic users. By the mid-1950s, coal supplies had become more plentiful, and electricity sales for space heating had, as the industry had expected, slackened off; but consumer surveys revealed that in the later 1950s new factors were developing electric space heating sales. With more married women at work, all-day heating became less the norm, and electric fires were ideal for intermittent use. With improved living standards and the spread of television, the number of rooms typically heated (at a time when few British homes had central heating) increased, and electric fires often proved a convenient way of adding what was still considered the luxury of bedroom or hallway heating. Increasingly also urban areas were being designated smoke control zones, and domestic coal fires were outlawed. Householders seeing gas and smokeless-coal prices rising, and electricity prices falling, often converted to electric heating, which was also usually cheapest in initial capital cost. The proportion choosing the electric heating option reached as many as half of those affected in the independent South Scotland board, though it was generally lower in England and Wales. More than three million electric fires were being sold annually by the early 1960s – well above the totals for any other appliance – and the amount of electricity being sold to domestic consumers for space heating purposes may have tripled between 1957 and 1962.[1]

Electricity was still not the cheapest form of heating, but the growth in electric space heating was encouraged by the continued conservatism of the Boards on tariffs. As before (see pp. 90–91, above), they tended to follow the percentage rises in the Bulk Supply Tariff in increasing both the standing charge (or initial block) and the incremental kWh charge. In view of the increasing peak demands of domestic consumers, such percentage rises were quite inadequate to recoup costs. By the financial year 1961/2, the average standing charge (or initial block equivalent) in England and Wales was a little over £5, barely enough to cover the cost of servicing an account and the capital charges of connection, far less to make a contribution to power station capacity costs. Yet the average incremental kWh charge (1.22d.) was also inadequate to pay for increased peak capacity usage, which grew broadly in line with sales. (Only the Eastern Board had seen the necessity of raising the running charge to significantly higher levels to pay part of the capacity charges.)

Within Council, Eccles and Melling identified this problem at an early stage, but both Self and King were weak on this issue, and it was not until Edwards became chairman that new policies were implemented. Earlier, the Council's Retail Tariffs Committee had met once in 1958 and ended with such profound disagreement between Board chairmen that it was not convened again for five years, and the chairmen went away proclaiming they would act as they wished on tariffs. Understandably central members like Melling became profoundly disillusioned at the negative attitudes of the chairmen and it was difficult to make any progress. The one exception was in research on the domestic load which affected the Area Boards only indirectly. Schiller's research team, which had been transferred to the Council in 1958, was encouraged by Melling and Edwards, though, despite the advocacy of publication by the Herbert Committee, the Council were able to persuade the Ministry that they should not publish the results.

These remained controversial within the industry, for Schiller was quite certain that space heating now made the major contribution to the peak load, and that domestic electricity was substantially underpriced. By the early 1960s, although not everyone agreed with Schiller's estimated magnitudes, an increasing number of the senior men were coming to feel that the need to raise prices and restrict the space heating load was becoming irresistible.

The crunch came in the severe winters of 1961/2 and 1962/3 when the distribution systems of many Boards broke down under the strains of a load far heavier than they had been designed to meet. By the winter of 1959/60 it had already been evident that the load was growing faster than the power station building programme had allowed for. The CEGB had then persuaded the Council to adopt a new method of forecasting, based on Hinton's prewar experience in the chemical industry, which involved fitting an exponential curve to data for the last ten years. This produced higher load forecasts than the existing methods of the Area Boards and Council (which attempted to forecast local developments and economic conditions), and it would have proved more reliable as a guide to the conditions of the early 1960s. In the winters of these years the load was between 7 per cent and 11 per cent higher than forecast by the traditional methods five years earlier, and the CEGB had to stretch their plant to the limit. Their operators were able to achieve an availability of plant at peak times of 95 per cent (against their normal planning level of only 90 per cent), largely because the conservatively designed 30MW and 60MW sets which now formed the backbone of the system were even more reliable than expected. Planned scrapping of plant over 40 years old was also abandoned and equipment run on overload. Thus the CEGB were able to meet the unexpectedly high demand by voltage and frequency reductions rather than power cuts. The Area Boards' distribution systems were, however, unable to meet the high demand from domestic users in the severe weather over the Christmas and New Year holidays. As transformers and other pieces of distribution equipment were run on overload in the severe weather, they cut out or burnt out. Over the Christmas of 1961, this meant that some 300000 consumers (1.3 per cent of the total) were cut off, and other consumers endured under-cooked Christmas dinners because of the voltage reductions.

There was understandably a widespread public outcry and some political criticism of the Area Boards, though they themselves placed the blame firmly on the Government. There was some justification for this, for they had been complaining for some time that their budgets had been cut back too much by the Ministry. Distribution expenditure had been pruned in every year to below the level which Council and the Area Boards requested (though they had sometimes spent up to their desired levels none the less). The Council felt that the Area Boards had been less generously treated than the CEGB in capital allocation and that expenditure on distribution systems was inadequate to keep pace with load growth.[2] The Ministry had been warned repeatedly that this exposed the older distribution systems to danger in the severe winter weather which could be expected about once every dozen years. In 1962 and 1963 the Ministry implicitly recognised their earlier mistakes by urging the Boards substantially to increase their expenditure on reinforcing the system in order to make up over the next five years a backlog of distribution investment then estimated at £115 millions. The Area Boards were delighted now to find that the Ministry, which used to chide them with excessive spending, was now repeatedly urging them to spend more. The Ministry did now insist that a higher proportion of the extra spending should be financed by raising prices to increase self-financing, but the twelve Area Boards (whose capital spending had grown only from £82.3 millions in the financial year 1957/8 to £98.7 millions in 1960/1) were able to spend as much as £159.1 millions in 1963/4 as part of the programme to make up the backlog. Thereafter neither the CEGB nor the Area Boards ever had to impose power cuts because of past under-investment.

The power cuts of 1961/2 and 1962/3 were not, however, solely the fault of earlier, misguided government parsimony, but, as Edwards recognised, partly the result of the industry's own deficiencies. The Boards had not been willing to increase investment by much when the Government had asked for some reflationary spending in 1958/9, and had also diverted an excessive proportion of their resources to completing their rural electrification targets ahead of schedule, while underspending on overloaded urban systems. They had been willing to do this because they had not fully anticipated the speed of growth of the urban domestic load, which again could be traced in part to their inadequate research on load characteristics and the underpricing of domestic electricity. At the Council, Edwards set about repairing some of these deficiencies, strengthening the load and utilisation research team, recruiting economists and statisticians, and promoting some of the brighter engineers with an understanding of the commercial problems they faced and more open minds about ways of tackling them. He favoured a more robust view against further subsidised rural electrification of the remaining, most remote farms. However, most Boards wanted to continue the policy of subsidising such costly connections in the traditional way by increasing the bills of existing consumers, and Edwards reluctantly went along with this.

The significant changes came in their pricing policy for the domestic load. Schiller's research suggested that the peak demands of domestic consumers rose proportionately to domestic sales, and it seemed sensible to reflect this by increasing incremental kWh charges in domestic tariffs so that they could make a contribution to financing the new plant which the increased sales required. Both the Electrical Development Association and some of the more obscurantist Boards opposed this logic, but, with Ministry support, Edwards was able to force price rises on them, and Council acquired a new moral authority under his leadership. A working party on space heating under the new head of the Council's commercial department, Tony Lingard, examined the conflicting arguments about the cost of supplying this load, and they estimated (some thought diplomatically under-estimated) that it cost 1.65d. per kWh to supply.[3] (The working party rejected a suggestion, advanced by Hinton and the Ministry, that domestic load limiters should be installed to restrict space heating use, since they would also discourage the attractive cooking and water heating loads.)

In the following years, domestic prices were gradually raised towards a level more nearly sufficient to recover these costs. Boards still remained reluctant to move very rapidly on this, however, and effort was more enthusiastically applied to the more positive option of ensuring that new electric space-heating installations would be of an off-peak character. Despite the offer of off-peak rates by Boards, there had been little growth in the domestic storage heating load in the 1950s. This was partly because the Boards knew that purchase tax would be imposed on all night storage heaters if they were sold for domestic as well as commercial use, and partly because the models commercially available were bulky, unattractive to look at and inflexible in operation. In 1961, however, the Boards began marketing a domestic model (and, as they had expected, the Customs and Excise imposed purchase tax before relenting a few years later). In 1962 the Boards also began the highly successful 'unit-plan' storage heater marketing campaign. The night rate for electricity in the special storage heater circuits was pitched at about half the day-time level to reflect its off-peak nature, and consumers found they could gradually build up a 'central heating' system room-by-room using new, more attractive storage heaters, with a midday boost to the heating level. In subsequent years, therefore, much of the growing demand for electric space heating was diverted into off-peak hours. As a result the Boards were able to sell electricity economically for heating, while limiting the rise in the ordinary domestic tariffs to allow them to continue to sell electricity for a wide range of domestic uses with better load factors. The urge of the commercial men to expand sales, which had previously compromised the industry's position, was now sensibly disciplined and canalised into appropriate channels under the new internal commercial department slogan: 'all load is good load *at the right price*'.

The crucial decisions to start the process of raising the domestic price and increasing the promotion of off-peak space heating were made in 1962, but the changes were implemented only gradually over subsequent years and in some Boards the rise in the incremental price in domestic tariffs was arguably still insufficient to cover costs. This fundamental reappraisal of their commercial strategy under Edwards was none the less a remarkable achievement, coming only five years after he joined the industry. It may be compared, for example to the much longer struggle across the Channel of the economist Boiteux. Joining the French industry in 1950, he was unable to introduce a rational tariff for large consumers until 1958 and for small consumers until 1965. The continuing ostrich-like attitude on prices of public utility electricity rate-fixing tribunals in America today is another testimony to the extraordinary difficulty of gaining public and political acceptance of a rational price structure and to the damaging consequences of this for the efficient use of energy.

The year 1962 was, however, a good time for the British electricity supply industry to launch new initiatives on domestic prices. The industry had been severely shocked by the over-expansion of domestic sales and the distribution breakdowns, while new chairmen of some Boards were less wedded to old policies. Of course, some chairmen remained implacably opposed to Edwards' policies, but he did win the clear support of the Ministry and he exploited this to the full. In 1957–8 Lord Mills and the Ministry had been confusing and contradictory on the question of tariffs (asking for price-restraint while demanding higher levels of self-financing). After the 1959 election, however, as we have seen (pp. 204–6, above) the progress of Whitehall towards the 1961 White Paper on financial and economic obligations was accompanied by a new firmness on prices. By 1961 the Government seemed at last to be willing to back necessary price rises, even in the domestic sector, where they might lose most votes. The need to restore profitability to the nationalised industries was, it seemed, to take priority, and fortunately this coincided with the clear need to raise prices in the domestic sector for reasons internal to the industry, whose cost structure was now clearer to its leaders. The Edwards revolution in the pricing structure owes much to the man, but it would not have been achieved if he had not been able to exploit this combination of favourable internal and external circumstances to push it through.

18

INCOMES AND PRODUCTIVITY: PLANNING FOR GROWTH?

... there can be no assurance that (UK) wage increases will ... be kept in line with the growth potential of the economy.

OEEC, *The Problem of Rising Prices* (1961) p. 447.

Time and time again the gallant captains of industry have found their flank turned in the ceaseless struggle against wage inflation by the weak-kneed board of some public corporation. That the board in question might be actively in league with the trade unions in this goes without saying; that from time to time it appears to be aided and abetted by Conservative ministers of the crown provides only an ironical comment on the sad times in which we live.

M. Shanks, (ed.) *Lessons of Public Enterprise* (1963) pp. 72–3.[1]

The reorganisation of 1957 unseated Citrine, but it left his successors with all the strengths and weaknesses of the industrial relations machinery which he had created. The unions had wanted to retain this machinery at the national level (including Scotland), and the Electricity Council's role in pay bargaining and joint consultation was therefore retained. It was the only policy area in which the Council had clear executive authority over the CEGB and Area Boards. They found a wide variety of views in the Boards on the reforms which were needed to improve labour productivity in the industry. Self, like Citrine, tried to suppress discussion of pay incentive schemes, feeling that any local bonuses would lead to wage drift and increase the number of parity disputes between groups. The industry thus remained committed to what was essentially highly centralised, company-level bargaining rather than individual plant bargaining based on local performance. Hinton also opposed pay incentive schemes, though the CEGB did want to improve the status and pay of their workers generally without productivity strings. Some Area Boards, by contrast, wanted to pursue experiments with work study and individual incentives more vigorously.

Little progress was made in the first five years in either sphere. The improvement in labour productivity which occurred in those years[2] appears to have been largely a result of increased fixed capital per worker and owed little to union cooperation in work effort or the elimination of restrictive practices. Indeed some managers felt the unions had become more bloody-mindedly defensive since the Herbert Committee's strident comments on the need for redundancies, and some restrictive practices intensified. The hours of overtime (boosted by a reduction in the 'normal' working week from 44 to 42 hours in 1960) rose in the Area Boards from 4.4 hours weekly in April 1958 to 6.6 hours in April 1962. In the CEGB, the overtime hours rose by more than the 'normal' hours reduction, from 6.5 hours to 9.6 hours in the same period. The hopes expressed by the Herbert Committee, that the new structure would enable the industry to reduce its headquarters staff, were also not realised. Indeed, despite repeated assertions of a determination to control staff levels, and a statement by Hinton that he would tolerate redundancies if necessary, the CEGB registered continued increases in both headquarters and field staff over this period, so that productivity improved less than it might have done in a period of considerable expansion.

The poor productivity performance of the electricity supply industry was mirrored in the rest of the British economy, and was a matter of increasing concern to the Government. It was a simple truth, now appearing repeatedly in political speeches, that if incomes nationally grew faster than output, then prices would rise. This had indeed clearly been happening. Concern about creeping inflation had led to the establishment in 1957 of the Council on Prices, Productivity and Incomes (the 'Three Wise Men') to advise on these questions.[3] Initially they and the Government favoured monetary pressure as a means of achieving price stability, rather than the consensual approach of price and wage restraint, but the consequential high interest rates and pressures for government spending cuts provoked splits in the Cabinet. By 1958, the reflationists were again in the ascendant, and, as the economy in 1959 and 1960 moved further towards the full employment ceiling, the view gained ground that some form of voluntary cooperation on prices and incomes from employers and unions was an essential pre-requisite of price stability.

The call for restraint on incomes was one which had intermittently been issued by governments since the War and had been intermittently, but not enthusiastically, espoused by the independent bargaining groups who determined wage settlements. The problem was that the simple truth, that wage rises in excess of productivity improvements would merely produce inflation and no one would be better off, was quite untrue for any single bargaining group. The electricity supply industry, for example, was in a strong position: it had a monopoly in many of its markets, and wages were a small part of its total costs. It could, therefore, easily have afforded significantly higher levels of wage increases than those in fact conceded, and pass these on in relatively small percentage price increases. The major constraint on the electricity supply employers' side was the fear of criticism from government or from other employers if they were excessively generous. The unions well understood the position, however, and by the mid-1950s the beginning of the now clearly-established annual wage round saw them using the industry as a primary pressure point. Both the staff and manual unions found that they could get the largest rises overall by using the electricity industry settlement to force pay rates up.[4] This often established the 'going rate', which was copied in other industries, where local pressure (not possible in the highly centralised pay bargaining of the electricity industry) could be used to create further 'wage drift'. *Earnings* outside electricity supply thus rose much faster than the rise in wage *rates*. Next year this drift could be used to justify a further rise in *rates* in electricity supply, and the round would begin again. There was little doubt in the minds of supply industry managers at the time that the unions were following this strategy, and the statistical evidence on wage rounds is compatible with it.[5] Such deliberate creation of cost–push inflation as a *national* union strategy was not, of course, in the rationally conceived interests of union members, since it was self-defeating collectively, even though individual groups might gain at certain points. The explanation for the unions' adherence to it was, the management thought, that it enhanced the prestige of trade union leaders if they could periodically point to victories in wage bargaining and thus establish the confidence of their members. Much of the next decade was to be a process of learning by both union leaders and management, as they tried to work out ways of ensuring that this self-defeating spiral was replaced by large real gains in living standards for union members.

At first the initiatives in this process came from the employers' side, which in this period was strengthened by more professional management[6] replacing some of the ex-trade unionists appointed to personnel positions in Citrine's day, but their early initiatives were resisted by the unions. Most of the managerial side started out from a belief that electricity supply workers' earnings were lower than they should be. They felt that the union leaders they were negotiating with (whose membership and prestige spread over other industries as well) were sacrificing their supply industry members' earnings in order to use the industry's wage round as a means of establishing pacemaking wage rate settlements. Electricity supply workers remained well down in the earnings league, and managers remained seriously concerned at their consequent difficulty in attracting skilled labour in prosperous areas such as the Midlands.

In March 1958, the electricity supply management determined to try to break the established pattern. When the unions submitted their standard claim for an increase in rates, the management negotiators pressed instead for a 'productivity allowance' of 8s. 3d. weekly to be paid to all workers after one month's service. This allowance was misnamed: it had nothing at all to do with productivity, but was a way of increasing basic pay without setting precedents on the hourly wage rate for other sectors. Yet for this reason the unions strongly disliked it. While it was accepted in 1958, the following year the unions insisted that it be consolidated into a flat rate increase to be used in the traditional way to establish the going rate in other negotiations. Management felt obliged to give way. Later in 1959, however, they negotiated a further settlement, effective from February 1960, reducing the 'normal' working week from 44 to 42 hours. This too had the presentational advantage of not being immediately translatable into a wage rate change, at a time when they were under increasing moral pressure from both government and other employers to avoid setting the pace in that respect.

There remained, however, a strong feeling on the management side that their workers were not earning enough, and this was particularly the case on the generation side. The CEGB, indeed, wanted to break away from the Electricity Council's national pay bargaining and set its own higher rates, but the unions, the Government and the Council all agreed firmly that this should be resisted. The Council's negotiators, several times, complained that their position was being undermined by CEGB leaks to the unions and Hinton was taken to task for this by the Minister, though he persistently denied the allegations. What was true was that the CEGB pressed Council to raise earnings in the industry. They proposed a variety of schemes which would break the traditional link with the wage round by tying pay to a rather spuriously determined measure of increasing productivity. The Council opposed this, arguing that the increased output on which it was based was due to improvements in capital equipment, not to changed labour practices or increased work effort. For the CEGB, however, the bogus nature of the 'productivity' deals proposed was precisely the point: it would enable them to increase earnings (as they wished), while presenting it to government and competing employers as something unique to the supply industry and not translatable to other industries without similar improvements there. The essential strategy was to raise earnings for their own workers without creating a wage spiral elsewhere, to 'de-couple' from the wage round.

By the spring of 1960, the CEGB were seriously worried about pay problems in the light of accumulating evidence of the growing strength of the unofficial shop stewards' movement in the power stations. Citrine's policy, as we have seen (pp. 130–2, above), was to ally with the official union leaders to defeat the unofficials, but in the later 1950s that strategy was crumbling. The delays in settlements, encouraged by government, and the relatively low earnings levels in the industry, were strengthening the unofficial movement, and the official union leaders were tacitly condoning their increasing militancy in order to put further pressure on management. In the summer of 1960 this pressure led to the electricity employers' side conceding a further 3d. per hour on the basic rate (and more for skilled men) after arbitrators could not agree on a settlement. Management negotiators felt that, despite government pleas for wage restraint, they simply had to make that bargain and head off the threat of strike action by the militants. Though they recognised that some of the pay grievances among the skilled men in the CEGB (who dominated the unofficial movement) were legitimate, they were increasingly worried about the inability of the official union leaders to reflect and control that feeling. There was only patchy condemnation of the unofficial actions by the official leaders, who explained their lack of control to management in terms of their lack of the staff and resources to contact their local members in the field. (Management refused to pay the unions a subsidy to promote this work, as they requested.) Frank Foulkes, the leader of the union side on the NJIC, was, moreover, increasingly insecure in his leadership of his own union, the ETU, and he and his Communist colleagues were resorting to ballot-rigging to maintain their positions. The ETU leadership was, therefore, unusually weak in the early 1960s, as disillusioned socialists and right-wingers in the union exposed their corrupt practices, and finally expelled the Communists and Foulkes after a bitter struggle in the courts and for members' votes.[7] Management could, however, play no part in this (had they positively supported the reformers it would probably have damaged the latter's cause). The management negotiators did, in fact, respect Foulkes as a man who would honour a bargain, and it was claimed that they even bowed to pressure, probably from Foulkes, not to give a job to one of the reformers' leaders, Les Cannon,[8] though later they were to work enthusiastically with him.

In the meantime, faced with pressure from the unofficials, the management negotiators were increasingly counter-pressured by the Government not to concede significant pay increases. Formally, their position remained, as in Citrine's day, that they were free to settle as they thought best, while keeping in touch with the Government's views as one factor in the negotiations. There had, however, been some highly publicised direct government interventions in wage negotiations elsewhere in the public sector, and the unions had the impression that the management side in the electricity supply industry also were no longer free agents. This was not strictly true, but, whatever the constitutional position, the management were now engaged in far more frequent correspondence and meetings with the Ministry about wage and salary negotiations. In practice this some-times came perilously close to ceding some of their autonomy. The Cabinet had in 1957/8 tried to control inflation by suppressing nationalised industry price rises, but, with the drafting of the White Paper on financial and economic obligations, that approach was increasingly unfashionable. The Cabinet's economic policy and wages policy committees now tended to shift the emphasis to controlling nationalised industry wages. Electricity pay settlements had therefore begun to be discussed at the highest political level in some detail. The 1960 settlement, for example, though against the initially expressed wishes of the Cabinet, was made after management consultation with the Ministry had indicated that they should settle, as the Cabinet were not willing to force matters to a strike.

The Conservative Government had shied away from an explicit incomes policy for some time, but on 25 July 1961 Macmillan's Chancellor, Selwyn Lloyd, announced a 'pay pause' to take effect immediately.[9] This was a great disappointment to the electricity supply negotiators, who were ready to take a new initiative on a wage claim in hand. Following the 1960 pay talks, the management side had set up a committee under Cecil Melling to devise an acceptable long-run policy for raising their employees' earnings which they could at the same time plausibly sell to Ministers. The idea they came up with owed more to the CEGB's initially somewhat bogus productivity notions than to that minority of Area Board managers who favoured local productivity schemes. They proposed to attempt to improve the status of manual workers in the industry by paying not an hourly rate but an 'upstanding weekly wage' (based on the hourly rate for a 42-hour week), with increments for long service ranging from 5s. per week for labourers to 8s. 6d. for installation inspectors after one year's service, with further increments up to the fourth year of service. They hoped also to get a longer-running agreement by gearing future rises to average earnings. The Cabinet wages policy committee felt, however, that these proposals were too generous, and within the industry, too, there were critics of the excessively generous terms. The Cabinet asked them to talk to other nationalised industry employers (who predictably proved antagonistic, since they liked to see the blame being taken by the electricity employers and wanted to keep them in the front line). The Cabinet also suggested that they should leave the initiative entirely to the trade unions in wage negotiations rather than taking new steps, a viewpoint which was anathema to managers who saw it as an abdication of their responsibility. The unions had thus not been told of the new proposals when the pay pause was announced in the summer of 1961. Although it became clear in further discussions with Whitehall that the Government would not issue a directive to enforce the pause, it was obvious that they would be very upset if the industry broke the freeze, which was stated in October to be intended to last until April 1962.

In the following months, the Labour movement orchestrated a strong upsurge of feeling against the pay pause, and the unions in electricity supply, whose settlement was overdue, were especially determined to breach it. Discussions with management continued throughout the summer and autumn, while the unofficial movement increased its pressure by sporadic overtime bans in the power stations. In September, Melling and his negotiators told the Minister, Richard Wood, that a settlement would have to be made before April, but the Cabinet continued to press for them to delay. The

Government and the industry looked closely again at the possibility of military and naval assistance to break the threatened strike, without finding much comfort: prognostications were of widespread power failures under inexperienced operators if they put in the troops. In October, the employers, able to delay serious negotiations no further, made an opening offer in the new form of an upstanding weekly wage with service increments and began discussing dates for implementation before April. By November there were reports from the regions that unless they came to a settlement, there would be a strike; and Melling decided to concede using the occasion to package the deal as the upstanding wage favoured by management. His final offer (in response to a union claim of £2 per week all round) was of 7s. per week for all, with service increments of 5s.–8s. 6d. per week for workers of two or more years' standing. The only sticking point now was the date of implementation, and it was clear that the unions wanted above all else to defeat the Government's pay pause by bringing it well forward from the April 1962 deadline, as they had already done for some private sector settlements. Most managers in the industry agreed it would be crazy to force a disastrous strike for a few weeks on the date, recognising that for the unions this was no longer a matter of rational calculation but a political virility test, for the privilege of passing which they would accept a modest overall settlement level. They therefore eventually made a settlement from the first pay day in February.

Melling, who headed the management negotiating team, took this decision on his own initiative. Neither Edwards (the chairman-designate) nor King (the chairman) wanted to carry the can, and, though the CEGB were glad that the settlement had been made, they too kept a low profile in view of the clear risk of ministerial displeasure. Just before the settlement, Melling had in fact consulted Wood, and Edwards had consulted Mills, and neither Minister was willing to take responsibility for a break in the negotiations. On several occasions previously, Wood, who was not a member of the Cabinet, told Melling and his colleagues that he recognised that the guidance he was giving was unhelpful. The impression the negotiators had was that the Government would huff and puff and then give in on worse terms, and they were determined to avoid that. Melling and his negotiators thus had the courage to act, and they were secretly pleased at the moderation of the settlement, and the first step it represented on their new upstanding wage strategy.

Publicly, however, pressmen and politicians thereafter referred to

the electricity supply employers as the perpetrators of the first breach
in the pay pause dyke and thus the begetters of inflation. Much to the
annoyance of the industry's managers, private sector company
chairmen also weighed in with criticisms, conveniently forgetting
their own companies' complicity in wage drift which, whatever their
faults, the electricity supply industry had controlled. The Prime
Minister, Macmillan, also energetically rebuked the industry for their
capitulation.[10] The industry's managers and a few senior civil servants
saw this as a little more than bluster from a Government wanting
power without responsibility, and, when failing to get it, settling
instead for the political cosmetic of dissociating themselves from
those who exercised power. The rebuke created great resentment in
the industry, though they decided not to express this publicly,
because it would undermine the bragging of the union leadership
about the settlement, which promised to strengthen them against the
unofficials. The 'Macmillan rebuke' thus passed into the popular
annals of inflation history as the pinpoint of responsibility for a
phenomenon whose villainous perpetrators were otherwise hard to
find.[11] Somewhat more perversely it was also to be quoted in future as
an indication that the industry's negotiators were merely marionettes
manipulated by the Government.[12]

The agreement of 1961, incorporating an upstanding weekly wage
and service increments, did, however, set a new pattern of management initiative in settling the forms of the industry's pay structure.
The desire to take positive initiatives which could free them from
irresponsible government intervention on the details of wage claims
also grew after the rebuke. They increasingly thought in terms of
improving the status of the manual workers by longer-term agreements offering bonuses for increasing productivity achieved by
abandoning restrictive practices. The first agreement on this new
course was early in 1963, and it was to develop into one of the more
successful management initiatives in British industrial relations in the
decade. They succeeded in considerably increasing productivity,
reducing overtime, and increasing earnings, so that electricity supply
workers once again were near the top of the earnings league, while
labour costs were contained by reducing manning levels.[13]

Meanwhile the government was reassessing its political presentation of the pay pause, and recasting its economic policy into a form
in which the supply industry's wages policy took a back seat
compared with its potential contribution to growth through investment. The example of French indicative planning became the model

for those advocating a more positive growth strategy for output and incomes, and the nationalised industries asked to be associated with the institutional expression of the growing commitment to this approach embodied in the National Economic Development Council early in 1962. The civil servants running this recognised the central role of electrical investment in economic growth, and even called on the experience of some managers and engineers in the industry, who had been engaged in planning for longer than most of those in Whitehall. When Reginald Maudling replaced Selwyn Lloyd as Chancellor in the summer of 1962, the political presentation of a more positive growth strategy was also improved. As the aim of achieving growth rates of output and incomes of 3 per cent or 4 per cent per annum emerged from NEDC discussions, the supply industry's potential contribution to output growth became the new focus of government concern. More and more the industry's leaders found themselves urged to invest more not less, and electricity seemed at last to have become a favoured part of public sector investment. The industry understandably welcomed this change of tack, which commanded bi-partisan support, and for a time raised hopes that the British economy's growth record, and the growth in its workers' standard of living, could be raised to match those of continental European industrial rivals.

19

HINTON: THE NUCLEAR RETREAT

Select Committee Chairman: Have you ever computed what history is costing you in this context?
Sir Christopher Hinton: No, I think it is a mistake to look back and ask what history costs.
Chairman: Would it be pretty considerable?
Hinton: Yes.

> CEGB oral evidence on nuclear power, to the Select Committee on Nationalised Industries, 9 May 1962.

The early reactors will all produce plutonium as a by-product, and the whole British programme . . . is based on the assumption that it can eventually be burned later in the programme.

> The CEA's nuclear engineers, in *Proceedings of the British Electrical Power Convention 1957*, p. 546.

The industry's experience of government intervention in their planning over the years prior to the establishment of the National Economic Development Council, had been a far from happy one. They themselves recognised from experience the difficulty of forecasting the pattern and growth in demand: they had substantially under-estimated their sales growth and had fallen behind in building the generating plant and mains to meet it. Government intervention – in controlling their capital budgets, or influencing their choice of fuel for power stations – seemed in retrospect to have made matters worse in most respects save the decision to use more oil. They therefore viewed the prospect of increasing government involvement in planning with some wariness, though they were pleased that it seemed to be accompanied by a far more positive approach to investment in growth – with electric power leading that investment – than had been manifested earlier. The ambivalence of the industry's feelings about government planning was nowhere more evident than in the CEGB, which had for five years been trying to come to terms with the problems posed for the management of power generation by earlier nuclear decisions.

In January 1958, the Generating Board had taken over some 262 conventional power stations and 6000 route miles of Grid and Supergrid, assets valued in the balance sheet at nearly £1000 millions net, and operated by nearly 53 000 employees. Although they did not control electricity distribution, their planned annual capital expenditure was substantially higher in real terms than that planned by the whole supply industry on nationalisation ten years earlier. The new Board, like the BEA before them, were still the largest spender (outside Whitehall) in the British economy, though their more limited responsibilities gave them a smaller share of UK investment than the old CEA, initially 5 per cent of domestic capital formation. In their first year, the Board and their contractors were building the Supergrid and as many as 40 power stations, including three of the four initial Magnox nuclear stations ordered in 1956/7 (the remaining Magnox station was being built by the independent South Scotland Board). As we have seen (Chapters 14 and 15 above), nuclear power was now the centrepiece of the Government's energy policy; and the nuclear proportion of new power station capacity was expected to rise to two-thirds by the early 1960s, in an unprecedently high wave of capital spending. This would only be possible with a substantial diversion of skilled manpower and capital resources to the CEGB, and, to spearhead this new policy, Sir Christopher Hinton, an architect of the Atomic Energy Authority's own nuclear power programme, had been appointed as the CEGB's first chairman.[1]

Stanley Brown and the other engineers and managers who had opposed the expansion of the nuclear power programme, and who (with the important exception of the by-passed Eccles) were now Hinton's colleagues, had not, however, modified their opposition, but were merely keeping their heads down. In the last months of the CEA and the first months of CEGB, indeed, the relentlessly accumulating evidence confirmed the wisdom of their earlier opposition to the hasty and ill-considered Government decision to build 6000MW of nuclear capacity by 1965, which had been foisted on the industry in the spring of 1957. The old doubts about costs were confirmed by the tenders for the first stations, all of which were reckoned to be more expensive in overall costs per kWh than equivalent coal or oil-fired stations on the tentative forecasts of operating characteristics which were then available. While the Atomic Energy Authority were more optimistic about some aspects of performance, there was no operating experience on large-scale reactors optimised for electricity production (such as those the CEA had ordered) and, moreover, the experience would not be available for some years. Meanwhile their commitment to the large extrapolations of existing technical experience would grow. Brown was still seriously worried about both the completion dates and the prospective reliability of the nuclear stations.

In some respects, moreover, the economic outlook in 1957/8 grew significantly less favourable to nuclear power than at the time the earlier decisions were taken. Interest rates – only 4 per cent when the initial commitment was made in 1954 – were creeping up to 6 per cent and above, and few except Self and King at the Council shared the belief of the Atomic Energy Authority that this was merely temporary. The highly capital-intensive Magnox technology appeared in progressively less favourable light relative to conventional technology as interest rates rose. The larger stations they had ordered, which had in 1956 been estimated to be cheaper in capital cost than those envisaged by the Trend committee, were, little more than a year later, no longer expected to be so. The world price of uranium was falling, but it became evident that the Atomic Energy Authority, which had bought forward stocks at higher prices, intended to load a good deal of the consequent losses on to the CEGB in the high price they charged for Magnox nuclear fuel. Moreover, the prospects of selling the used fuel elements (the so-called 'plutonium credit', which had been a fundamental element in bringing down the estimated cost of nuclear power) now looked less rosy. Some plutonium from the used fuel could be used for the British atomic bomb stockpile and the Americans also agreed to take some for military purposes, but the Atomic Energy Authority (which handled this business) would not guarantee a price to the CEGB. There still remained a hope that the plutonium might also be usable as a fuel for future gas-cooled or fast-breeder reactors,[2] but recent research made it clear that this objective was now receding. The immediate consequence was that the plutonium credit (which had knocked more than a third off the estimated cost of production in 1955) was by 1958 considered likely to contribute perhaps only a fifteenth or a twelfth of production costs. (By the later 1960s, its contribution was in fact to become negative as it became evident that no economic use could be found for the waste plutonium and the reprocessing of the used fuel cans was a costly business.)

In October 1957, only a month after Hinton had taken over at the CEGB, an accident at the Atomic Energy Authority's Windscale nuclear plant raised further questions about the nuclear programme. A fire in the core of an early reactor released some radioactive materials, but no serious damage was done and the accident caused only mild public disquiet. However, enquiries showed that it stopped just short of a very serious nuclear accident, and there were clear faults in research, instrumentation and organisation at Windscale which showed that Britain's nuclear expansion was severely over-stretching staff and other resources.[3] Other awkward environmental questions such as the means of disposal of waste fission products and possible problems with the decommissioning of nuclear stations at the end of their life did not receive priority attention at this stage.[4] However, with the Windscale accident, operating safety features in the design were given more attention. This substantially increased the capital costs of Magnox reactors, as design modifications to overcome the shortcomings of the original graphite core proved necessary.

Hinton, who knew the dangers of nuclear technology better than they, was surprised and pleased at how low British insurance firms set the premiums for the new nuclear stations, and urged immediate acceptance (though in fact the Magnox reactors have proved to be safe, and the insurance companies were to find the risk a profitable one to cover). The creation of a nuclear installations inspectorate in the Ministry was another sign of increasing concern for independent safety monitoring. Hinton, as CEGB chairman, strongly supported the establishment of the inspectorate, pressing for it to be more independent of the Ministry and to have wider powers over the Atomic Energy Authority, but he was overruled by a government anxious not to place unnecessary barriers in the path of nuclear expansion. There was a strong political and public commitment to affluence which saw nuclear power as an essential ingredient in growth, and this tended to override any incipient environmental objections. Later Magnox stations were to experience more planning objections than the first ones, but in none of these cases was any serious threat posed to the programme by objectors, who usually had some local consideration rather than any blanket objection to nuclear power in mind. The focus of oppositon to nuclear bombs – the Campaign for Nuclear Disarmament established in 1958 – was not at this time opposed to nuclear power on principle. Indeed much of the moral power of the 'ban-the-bomb' case derived from the argument that man's atomic knowledge should rather be diverted to peaceful uses such as the civil nuclear power programme. On this, many of the nuclear scientists and engineers were then at one with the protest marchers.

The most worrying new development was not the growing concern about safety (which was a positive if costly development) but the fact that the very *raison d'être* of the nuclear programme, the predicted shortage of primary fuels, was rapidly evaporating. As we have seen (pp. 180-1, above) the CEA had already warned that this was a possibility, though they had tried in vain at the time to get firm estimates of coal availability from the National Coal Board. In May 1957, the Coal Board, worried that their production plan would overtake demand for coal as oil continued to win new markets, asked the CEA to increase their future coal burn by 5 million tons annually in the early 1960s, rising to 9 million tons by the mid-1960s. The CEA were not certain how much credence to attach to this (for the Coal Board had been over-optimistic about production capacity in the past), but it confirmed their fears that the electricity supply industry might come under political pressure to take more coal, as well as shouldering the burden of the nuclear programme. Within the Ministry, a Fuel Coordination Committee (chaired by R. J. Ayres and with fuel industry representation) decided that the new forecast of overall fuel surplus was insufficient, within the margins of error of the estimates, to justify major changes in policy, and the CEGB representatives agreed with this. Over the next year, however, their attempts to bury the problem in this way looked increasingly thin. By the summer of 1958 it seemed likely that, with the Coal Board even more optimistic about forward coal supplies, there would be an annual surplus as high as 16-20 million tons of coal by the mid-1960s, if existing oil contracts were honoured and the full nuclear programme were implemented.

Some engineers in the industry had welcomed the prospect of being no longer bound to one fuel but instead free to choose between coal, oil and uranium according to which proved cheaper; and certainly the emerging primary energy glut strengthened their bargaining power with their fuel suppliers. Yet, whereas smaller private companies could (and in increasing numbers did) opt for oil or coal according to which was cheaper, it became increasingly difficult for the supply industry to do so. This was partly because they themselves, as the

Coal Board's biggest consumer, recognised a responsibility for ensuring some economic health and stability in a supplier on which they would continue to depend so much. A purely arms-length commercial relationship with the Coal Board was considered both impossible and undesirable; and, even if they had not accepted this view, the Government would have forced it onto them. The ideas canvassed earlier by the Flett working party – that any coal surplus could be exported or forced on small consumers – were exposed as nonsense by the clear evidence that foreigners preferred cheaper oil and domestic consumers had political clout to preserve their free choice. The CEGB, by contrast, were fair political game for a government anxious to dispose of the emerging coal surplus. At the same time, nuclear power (partly because it could, practically speaking, only be used via the medium of electricity, and partly because of government pressure) was also an option in which the CEGB's own flexibility was limited. The burden of the adjustments of the British economy to changing patterns of supply and demand for primary fuels thus fell to a large extent on conventional electricity generation, and, as changes in forecast fuel availabilities were unusually rapid in this period, the resulting strains were considerable. The industry found that, as they had feared, the Ministry (which had initially induced them to convert to oil-firing) was now leaning on them heavily to cut back on oil. Fears of oil supplies being cut off had receded rapidly after Suez,[5] and the CEGB, like other consumers, were anxious to continue to burn oil in the power stations already converted or under construction. It would be expensive both to convert oil-fired stations back to coal-firing (as an arguably unwise economy measure the dual-firing option had been abandoned in most stations), and to get out of the long-term supply contracts with the oil companies. Oil was, moreover, now considered likely to be the cheapest fuel option in many southern locations away from the coalfields, and the Board saw no reason why they should not minimise their costs by using it.

The Government was, however, strongly wedded to the nuclear option, and had made Sir Christopher Hinton the CEGB chairman precisely in order to ensure that the old CEA caution on nuclear power should not compromise the maximum programme. Both the Ministry and his new colleagues firmly expected the nuclear knight to be fully committed to the nuclear programme. Hinton, like most nuclear engineers, had been delighted at the strong government commitment to nuclear power in 1954–6, and had accepted the doubling of that commitment, bringing in the South of Scotland Board to build the third Magnox station the CEA had resisted. He had been to Japan on sabbatical leave for six months in 1956, but had still seemed to be a nuclear enthusiast at CEA liaison meetings with the Atomic Energy Authority. In a lecture in Sweden in March 1957, though more cautious on the plutonium credit, he had made projections of future nuclear generation costs which suggested that by the mid-1960s they could be competitive with coal.[6] He had, none the less, been somewhat disquieted at the time by the over-optimism of many of his Atomic Energy Authority colleagues, although in his early discussion with Mills about the CEGB chairmanship he gave neither the Minister nor his senior civil servants any inkling of his doubts about the greatly expanded nuclear programme. Indeed, Hinton was appointed largely because the CEA men could not be trusted to share his supposed commitment to prosecute the maximum nuclear programme with vigour.

In his first months at the CEGB, however, it became clear to his new colleagues that the picture of Hinton presented to them earlier was not the correct one. He was as worried as Eccles and Brown had been about the exposure to commercial risk in such a large expanded nuclear programme with a basically untried extrapolation of a technology he had developed, and whose weaknesses he knew better than anyone. Stanley Brown was delighted to find that Hinton was soon using his authority as a nuclear expert to cast doubt on the 1957 decisions, and their views on this matter were rapidly becoming indistinguishable. Politicians, by contrast, remained optimistic about the nuclear power programme,[7] and a frontal assault on their deeply entrenched views would have been counterproductive. Hinton therefore kept his head down for a time, making small cuts where he could, but preparing for the time when more realism could be forced on government. Maud, the Permanent Secretary at the Ministry, was soon shocked to find how completely Hinton had abandoned the Atomic Energy Authority's view and adopted the supply industry's. His new colleagues, meanwhile, counted themselves fortunate that in Hinton they at last had someone who could make mandarins and Ministers listen on nuclear matters, even if he, like them, had to await an appropriate opportunity to strike.

The strongest cards Hinton had to play in getting the programme reduced were the emerging coal surplus and financial stringency. In his first month at the CEGB he was able to suggest that, to keep within the reduced capital expenditure limits imposed by the sterling crisis towards the end of 1957, the nuclear target of 6000 MW could be postponed from 1965 to 1966. This was accepted by the Government and announced publicly as a minor modification to the programme though it in fact represented a 20 per cent cut in planned nuclear investment.[8] Subsequent public admissions by Ministers of nuclear retreat proved more difficult for Hinton to obtain. The supply industry was annoyed to find that both the Government and the Atomic Energy Authority in their public statements remained optimistic about the economics of nuclear power. The CEGB engineers considered that many of these statements were inaccurate. Out-of-date nuclear cost estimates had earlier been used in the public expenditure figures presented to Parliament,[9] and the industry's leaders were worried in 1958/9 to find Ministers still publicly stating that the cost of nuclear power would be about the same as conventional power. The CEGB's own figures showed a substantial excess nuclear cost, and they did not hesitate to tell Ministers so.[10] However, when the CEGB themselves made public statements giving a more truthful (but still over-optimistic) picture, they were rebuked by both the Atomic Energy Authority and Lord Mills for casting doubt on the programme and harming its export potential.[11] Hinton did none the less increasingly express his doubts in public,[12] and it was pointed out to civil servants in private that the information being given to Parliament was in the industry's view false.

Although nothing was announced publicly, Hinton was able to exert pressure and achieved further cutbacks in the programme, in addition to the initial postponement of the target by one year to 1966. He had a particularly good relationship with Mills, who liked his crisp style and with whom he discussed CEGB policy virtually every month, bypassing the Electricity Council (except for their purely formal statutory appraisal, necessary when he changed the Board's investment programme). At an early stage it was agreed that the Atomic Energy Authority's nuclear stations (aggregating more than 300MW) should be included in the 6000MW target, and as they had not originally been included, this effectively represented a cut. The CEGB also adopted slightly lower nuclear commissioning figures for their own planning purposes where they considered this desirable. They thus delayed the fifth and sixth stations planned for Trawsfynydd (Gwynedd) and Dungeness (Kent) several times, and work on those stations did not in fact start until 1959 and 1960 respectively. The Cabinet was, however, keen to keep these changes secret for fear of losing political face, and the Prime Minister, Macmillan, insisted that Mills should not make any public announcement of the cuts.

In the summer of 1958, Hinton told Mills plainly and fully that he considered the nuclear programme was still unwisely large, but the Cabinet pressed for a firm CEGB reaffirmation of their commitment to the maximum programme. Hinton was, however, able shortly afterwards to persuade Plowden (for the Atomic Energy Authority) and Mills (for the Government) that in order to absorb the coal surplus and improve the phasing of nuclear development there ought to be a further reduction. He argued that too many low-technology, uneconomic Magnox stations were being built, and that they ought rather to be devoting resources to improving the technology so that a truly economic nuclear programme would be possible from 1966 onwards. He was, however, only able to reduce the target to 5025MW for the UK as a whole. This level enabled Ministers to continue publicly to affirm their faith in the 1957 target (which had been cautiously expressed in public as in the range 5000–6000MW) and still remain within the normal bounds of parliamentary truth.[13] With a Magnox export order for Italy in the bag and an order for Japan being discussed, both the Atomic Energy Authority and the Ministry said they were anxious to do nothing which cast doubt on nuclear economics for potential overseas purchasers. The stated objective of keeping the price of Magnox secret from purchasers who would have to pay that price must rank as a rather curious and unrealistic exercise. Perhaps more important was that the Government had no wish to lose face by admitting their earlier panic mistakes.

In 1959, however, the pressure within government for a change in policy intensified. The Treasury were worried about the forecasts of rising public expenditure in the early 1960s and were moving towards the view that public enterprises should aim to earn a higher rate of return, an objective to which manifestly the nuclear power programme did not contribute.[14] The Ministry of Power was also now even more optimistic than the CEGB about future coal availability, and politicians increasingly saw growing unemployment among coal miners as a worrying political problem. None the less in the summer of 1959 Ministers were still denying rumours that the nuclear programme had been cut.[15] Resources were then already committed to six Magnox stations under construction (five by the CEGB and one in Scotland). In March the following year, however, the Cabinet proved more pliable. Hinton then again recommended a substantial reduction, and for the first time the CEGB's views triumphed over those of the Atomic Energy Authority's in Cabinet. The Government's White Paper of June 1960 followed Hinton's draft suggestions closely, and announced, for the first time publicly, a further reduction in the programme to only 3000MW by the end of 1965, with the 5000 MW target postponed to 1968.[16] Hinton noted with satisfaction that the programme had been reduced to a level that he had initially considered desirable. He now hoped that the three-year delay in orders for the last 2000MW would enable less costly and more efficient stations, incorporating new technical advances, to be built.

The brave programme had at last given way to the wise cuts, after more than three years of lobbying from the industry. None the less, Britain still had the largest programme of nuclear power station construction in the world, though the signs were still that conventional stations would be cheaper than the nuclear stations they were building. The 1960 White Paper envisaged that in the 1960s one new nuclear station would be ordered each year. In fact after the orders for Sizewell (Suffolk, where construction began in 1961) and Oldbury (Gloucestershire, 1962) there was to be only one more further Magnox order at Wylfa (Anglesey, 1964), as the CEGB succeeded in pruning the programme further to a total of 4455MW for commissioning by 1968/9. The main result of this gradual but determined CEGB campaign to prune their nuclear orders was that a very large waste of public expenditure in the 1960s was avoided. Even so it was still estimated that in many years a third of the CEGB capital budget was going on uneconomic extra expenditure on Magnox nuclear stations.

The counterpart of the reduction in the nuclear orders was an acceleration in the building of conventional coal- and oil-fired stations, on whose advanced designs the CEGB now placed high hopes (see pp. 247–51, below). The total demand for electricity was already exceeding their expectations, but fossil fuels, far from manifesting the predicted shortages, were by 1959/60 clearly in over-supply. In the decade to 1960, particularly in the latter years as the new oil-fired stations were completed, the CEGB had increased its oil burn from 0.2 to 9.2 million tons of coal equivalent; and other users had also been switching to oil. The National Coal Board found that it had an unexpected, unsold surplus (particularly of small coals, of the kind suitable for power station boilers), and therefore instituted a programme of contraction and the closure of inefficient pits. Recognising the increasing importance of the CEGB as a customer (despite their rising oil burn, their consumption of coal had risen from 31.2

million tons to 48.9 million tons in the previous decade), the Coal Board now restrained power station coal prices, which had in any case risen less rapidly than those elsewhere, partly because of the supply industry's own policy of locating new stations on cheap coalfields.

But the price of oil was continually falling, and political pressure built up behind the Coal Board to insist on CEGB reversions to coalburning. Feeling the strength of this pressure, the Minister found the 1960 cut in the nuclear programme additionally beneficial in that it enabled a compromise to be made, with the CEGB maintaining some of their oil-burning programme, but agreeing to delay the conversion of some coal-fired stations to oil. They had been able to persuade the oil companies to release them from some of the long-term oil contracts, though they would on economic grounds have preferred to burn oil, which was now clearly cheaper in many southern coastal locations.

In 1961 a newly imposed fuel oil tax temporarily reduced the attractiveness of oil, not only to the CEGB but also to other users, yet oil prices then fell even further. The National Coal Board chairman, Alfred Robens, therefore brought extensive political pressure to bear on the industry to abandon plans for further oil-fired stations, and to convert existing oil-fired stations to coal. At the end of 1962, the CEGB offered a compromise under which they gained a two-part tariff for coal, accepting responsibilities for some of the mining industry's overheads, but reducing the marginal cost of additional supplies. This arrangement successfully induced some of the required reduction in oil consumption by improving the position of coal-fired stations in the National Grid's merit order of power station operation. The result was that in 1963 the oil burn was only 7 million tons of coal equivalent, somewhat less than in 1960. The Board none the less in principle retained the freedom to build future oil stations, which they thought might be economic for the next twenty years, though some time in that period, they hoped, nuclear power would also become attractive economically.

The unexpected primary energy glut of the early 1960s temporarily embarrassed Hinton and his CEGB colleagues, but they retained their faith that the nuclear option was one which would be required in the longer run. By 1960, the level of nuclear ordering was envisaged within the CEGB purely as a means of maintaining a nuclear capability against that time in the future. Hinton was, however, far from satisfied with the progress that had been made or with emerging options for the nuclear plant orders to be placed in the early 1960s. The original Magnox design had been substantially improved along the lines envisaged, but he was disappointed by the design capabilities of some of the consortia and by the slow pace of capital cost reduction. There were, moreover, clear limits beyond which Magnox could not be stretched. The avenues of savings in capital cost were essentially the same as in conventional power technology: indeed a Magnox station can reasonably be characterised as an ordinary power station with the reactor gas coolant circuit and heat exchangers acting as the boiler. The reactors had been increased in size to gain economies of scale and the initial cylindrical 92MW reactors of Calder Hall had given way in the supply industry's first three stations to twin spherical reactors of 137–150MW each, and in the next four stations ordered in 1957 and 1959–60 to twin reactors of 250–290MW each. The later reactors also followed the conventional paths of better engineering of space and in most cases of the adoption of unit arrangements (one turbine to one reactor). All these seven orders were placed before any working experience of reactors larger than Calder Hall had been gained. They also incorporated various new ideas about design evolved by the separate nuclear consortia. There had been some loose talk in government circles in 1956–7 about 'carbon copies' for speed, but in fact potential advantages of replication were largely foregone as the orders were shared out to different teams developing their own detailed ideas within a broadly common design concept. One of the best of the pre-1960 designs was that at Dungeness (Kent), where the move to higher temperatures and pressures (again a development path quite familiar from conventional technology) was taken furthest. The Dungeness Magnox station (on which work started early in 1960) had a gas outlet temperature of 770°F and pressure of 276psi (compared with only 635°F and 116psi at Calder Hall, and 734°F and 145 psi at Bradwell, one of the first Magnox orders). Even in Dungeness, and the similarly advanced new Magnox station ordered for Sizewell (Suffolk) early in 1961, however, the gas outlet temperatures were not sufficient to heat the steam even to the moderate levels required by the industry's obsolescent conventional 60MW turbines. The steam and electrical side of nuclear stations thus represented a regression to the prewar turbine technology, and had correspondingly low thermal efficiencies.

Some of the consortia none the less believed that the Magnox design could be pushed a good deal further, and put considerable effort into design improvements in the early 1960s. In the event, the most effective of these was the introduction of concrete pressure vessels to replace the steel vessels of earlier reactors. Steel welding technology imposed limits on both the reactor size and coolant pressures, as well as creating considerable difficulties on site, but in October 1961 the CEGB awarded the contract for the Oldbury (Gloucestershire) Magnox station to a design incorporating more pre-stressed concrete. The important innovation by the British TNPG consortium was that the whole of the gas circuit and heat exchangers was enclosed in the twin 280MW pre-stressed concrete reactor vessels. This enabled them further to increase pressures and hence efficiencies, and it also increased safety factors. The next Magnox order, placed in October 1963, for a twin 590MW reactor station at Wylfa (Anglesey) also incorporated concrete pressure vessels, but this was to be the last of the Magnox orders.

By 1960 the CEGB were already beginning to feel that the development potential of Magnox was exhausted. They were disappointed that, despite the improvements, the downward trend in capital cost had been reversed in these latest orders. In 1956–7, the talk had been of nuclear stations costing two-and-a-half or three times as much per kW to build as conventional stations, but getting cheaper later. The target proved, however, to be a moving one, as the Brown revolution reduced the capital costs of conventional stations. Meanwhile necessary engineering modifications increased the costs of Magnox stations almost as fast as economies of scale and design improvements were reducing them. The CEGB decided to treat the consortia leniently on the terms of their early contracts, and agreed to some price increases during the currency of the contracts. As a result it seemed likely that the capital cost of the early Magnox stations would be more than four times that of conventional ones, but even the later ones would be two-and-a-half or more times more expensive. The significantly lower running costs of nuclear stations would be insufficient to offset this disadvantage at the interest rates which prevailed. The CEGB were thus determined to resist pressure for further orders for uneconomic designs.

It had always been envisaged that the later orders in the first nuclear programme might be of a more advanced design than Magnox, though since the expansion of 1957 the likelihood had increased that all would be Magnox. The CEGB kept an open mind and had hoped that better designs might be available by the early 1960s.[17] The nuclear future, their engineers tellingly remarked in

1957, was 'bright but far from clear'. One of Hinton's last actions before leaving the Atomic Energy Authority had been to propose the construction of a prototype Advanced Gas-Cooled Reactor (AGR), and this was in progress at Windscale, due for completion in 1961. This was a natural development of the Magnox gas-cooled reactors, but overcame the limits of temperature set by the Magnox fuel can and permitted a smaller reactor core and increased fuel burn-up. After prolonged and unsuccessful experimentation with a beryllium fuel can, the Atomic Energy Authority successfully developed a stainless steel can which could withstand the design temperature of the Windscale prototype of 1070°F, higher than the Magnox cans could withstand, and more comparable with that being achieved in contemporary conventional power stations. Difficulties in choosing the canning material and other problems with the behaviour of graphite in the AGR delayed the completion of the prototype until the summer of 1962. These problems increased Hinton's doubts about the design, and the expense of enriched uranium (which was required for the stainless steel cans) also seemed a potential disadvantage. In 1961, therefore, Hinton decided, against Atomic Energy Authority advice, to continue to order Magnox stations rather than AGRs until operating experience of the AGR prototype became available.

There were by the early 1960s other serious contenders in nuclear power technology besides those being presented by the UK Atomic Energy Authority. A large prototype light water reactor had been operating in America since 1960. This was favoured by the Ministry's Chief Scientist and seemed cheap, but Hinton felt that it lacked development potential. He was rather more keen on the Canadian heavy-water reactor ('CANDU') which he had always envisaged as a possible alternative development path, sharing Magnox's advantages of using cheaper natural (rather than enriched) uranium.[18] On a visit to Canada in 1961 Hinton was extremely impressed by the progress they had made, and caused a stir when he returned by publishing a frank article casting doubt on the merits of the AGR and suggesting that serious attention should be paid to alternatives.[19] The electricity division at the Ministry were on his side when he argued that the CEGB should be given commercial freedom to choose reactor types without being tied to British designs, but the Atomic Energy Authority still had powerful support in the Cabinet and Whitehall. Hinton was rebuked by the Minister for his openness and told firmly that this was a matter in which the Government would definitely wish to be involved. The Atomic

Energy Authority made it clear that even if a heavy-water reactor *were* to be ordered, they would resist pressure from the CEGB to be allowed to become an independent buyer.

Hinton, once he was convinced of the rightness of his cause, as he was in this case, pursued it with relentless vigour which could sometimes be counterproductive. He resented the CEGB's position as a captive buyer not only on reactor choice, but on matters such as buying fuel elements or graphite for reactor cores; and he felt that a good deal of unnecessary Atomic Energy Authority overhead was being loaded on to the CEGB's charges. He told the Minister firmly that he saw no reason for paying the Atomic Energy Authority for Canadian heavy-water expertise, and alleged that the Authority were over-staffed and unproductive. There had indeed been a considerable expansion in the Authority's staff, from 17000 in 1954 (when the civil power programme was launched) to 41000 in 1961 (by which time there were also 5000 men directly employed by the private nuclear consortia). Hinton felt that a lot of money and manpower had been thrown at the nuclear development problem without adequate return, and he considered it vital that the Atomic Energy Authority should become more commercially aware. However, Roger Makins, the new Atomic Energy chairman, was determined to maintain his independence and avoid any back-seat driving of the Authority by their major customer, the CEGB.

The prestige the Atomic Energy Authority gained from their nuclear expertise remained considerable, and, when faced with Hinton's criticisms, they preferred to play the political game. They remained excessively optimistic about the gas-cooled path of development, and some of them personalised the issue, presenting Hinton as an unreasonable turncoat. Their arguments in favour of a substantial AGR programme were weak,[20] but they became more vociferous as Hinton flexed his muscles more successfully in Whitehall. Lord Hailsham, who, as Minister of Science, had taken over responsibility for the Atomic Energy Authority from the Prime Minister in 1959, jealously guarded its interests. He argued strongly that the sunk costs in the British research and development programme could not be ignored, as Hinton seemed to be advocating. The Government therefore decided that the collective heads of the CEGB and the Authority should be firmly knocked together, and in 1962 established a committee, on which their representatives and those of relevant ministries sat, under the chairmanship of Sir Richard Powell, Permanent Secretary of the Board of Trade. Their brief was to look at the scale of the next nuclear power programme and the type of reactor to be adopted.

The future of the nuclear industry was, then, unclear; but the completion of the CEGB's first Magnox reactors in 1962 offered some grounds for optimism. Despite their strongly expressed reservations about the size, risks, and cost of the programme, the CEGB's experience with these reactors was on the whole a good one. In an engineering sense, the designs were a success, particularly on the nuclear side. After initial teething troubles, the operators were pleased with the levels of efficiency achieved. In particular, they soon achieved the high availability, and nuclear fuel burn-up rates which the Atomic Energy Authority had predicted. In other respects, however, their early Magnox experience confirmed their determination not to be saddled with further uneconomic schemes. At a time when conventional construction projects were overrunning by only a few months, the early Magnox stations were typically two or more years late. Bradwell and Berkeley, due in 1960, were not completed until 1962. Hunterston, the South of Scotland Board's first station, took even longer (see pp. 270–2, below). The CEGB also encountered severe problems with the fourth station, at Hinkley Point (Somerset), ordered in 1957 for 1960, but not actually completed until 1965 (though on later stations they felt they had design and construction problems under tighter control). The capital cost estimates for Magnox stations were exceeded by only 10–20 per cent – a remarkable achievement by the poor standard set by later nuclear programmes in Britain and elsewhere – but the delays in construction had also substantially increased interest charges. When the Magnox stations first began operating, moreover, the anticipated credit for the plutonium in the used fuel elements had virtually disappeared: in 1963 the credit covered only between ½ per cent and 3 per cent of costs compared with the initial estimate of around a third. The higher interest rates which prevailed over the construction period also worked against nuclear economics. Even after allowing for lower nuclear running costs, the overall cost per kWh of electricity generated in the first two Magnox stations in their early years was nearly two-and-a-half times that of the best coal-fired stations which the CEGB were then commissioning. This added financial losses of £20 millions[21] (3 per cent of the industry's turnover) annually to electricity costs.

The high hopes of nuclear power were not, then, realised, and this was, indeed, no surprise to the CEGB. They had consistently argued that the strategy on nuclear power should be primarily to acquire experience in a new technology. At the time they were ordered, every one of their Magnox stations was expected by the CEGB to be uneconomic, and their expectations proved correct, though the losses in the early years were rather greater than even they had expected. The placing of these uneconomic orders could be considered a breach of their statutory duty to provide an economical supply of electricity. They had reconciled themselves to it, first on the grounds that if they did not place orders the Minister would direct them to, and later on the grounds that the nuclear industry should be kept in being against the likely eventual need to replace fossil fuels. In 1960, however, the prognostications even for new Magnox orders were still that they would be a third more expensive overall than conventional power, and the CEGB were understandably anxious not to repeat the Government's past nuclear mistakes. By early 1963 Hinton felt that economic nuclear power might be as far away as the later 1970s, but everyone recognised that such prognostications were speculative.

What was already clear was that nuclear power could not make the serious contribution to Britain's energy economy that had been expected. Instead of two-thirds of power stations in the first half of the 1960s being nuclear (as had been planned in 1957) only 2425MW in six stations were to be completed by the CEGB and South Scotland Board by the end of 1965. This was little more than the original, lower, 1954 programme, and was barely a fifth of the total power station capacity commissioned in 1960–5. This reduction in the proportion of nuclear capacity arose partly through the reductions agreed by government, but partly also from an increase in the conventional plant ordered (to meet a demand even higher than expected), and partly from unplanned slippage in nuclear construction times. The achievement of this reduction in the proportion of nuclear stations was, however, arguably the wisest action taken in the early years by the CEGB. While the logic of the CEGB's position would eventually have made itself felt, it is to Hinton above all that the credit for this achievement should go, for no one else had the nuclear prestige to make the truth stick. Without his confident leadership of the nuclear retreat, the cost of producing electricity in Britain in the 1960s would have been greatly increased. Meanwhile, he and his colleagues hoped they would not again be forced by government into unwise and uneconomic nuclear investments, but could maintain the capacity enabling them to opt for more nuclear power, if and when the cost break-through eventually came.

20

THE CEGB IN PRACTICE

Success in industry is no longer a personal achievement. Science, technology and management are now so complex that the art of management is to build up teams each of which can collaborate happily with those teams on either side as well as above and below . . .

> Sir Christopher Hinton, 'Organisation of the CEGB', *Electric Power*, February 1963, p. 27.

Natura non facit saltum.

> Motto of Alfred Marshall's *Principles of Economics* (1890).

The retreat from nuclear power had a profound impact not only on the nuclear ordering pattern but also on the traditional concerns of the CEGB's own conventional power station engineers, and on the private enterprise constructors and manufacturers of both nuclear and conventional plant. Within a few years, in the later 1950s, it became evident to those concerned with conventional plant that, far from being phased down within the decade to a minimal role, they would, as before, have to take the weight of the burden of meeting the still rapidly-growing demand for electricity.

Fortunately, many of the skills which had shown themselves at their best in the Brown revolution of the mid-1950s still survived; and when the members of the CEGB were initially being appointed, Hinton had relied considerably on the existing personnel. Both the Herbert Committee and the Ministry had envisaged a generalist Board with wide-ranging experience, but Hinton had instead persuaded Mills to appoint a Board of functional specialists. Leonard Rotherham, a former Atomic Energy Authority colleague of Hinton's, joined the Board to oversee the research and development function (where Hinton felt the old CEA were particularly weak).

Elsewhere, however, Hinton and Mills drew on the old CEA chief engineer's and secretary's departments for the senior posts. Stanley Brown, the former chief engineer, joined the Board as member for engineering, becoming deputy chairman in 1959 when Robertson King left for the Electricity Council chairmanship (p. 200 above). Brown was succeeded as Board member for engineering by his deputy in charge of power station design and construction, Eric Booth. While Hinton generally left the details of conventional power station design and ordering policy to them, he had strong ideas of his own on the general policy issues. Brown, particularly, found that he had to take a back seat, turning his attention to topics left to him by the chairman, such as relations with the Council, nuclear safety, and the bulk supply tariff.

Some of the part-time members of the Board brought a functional expertise to bear, and Hinton found Sir William Holford, the architect, and Sir Charles Geddes, the retired trade unionist, particularly helpful in the areas of their expertise. As on the CEA, the functional specialism with the weakest representation was finance and accounting, though, as we have seen (pp. 202–7, above), Edwards provided some new ideas initially from Council. Ernest Long, as the Board member for finance and administration brought some CEA financial experience, and the Board was from 1960 strengthened by the part-time membership of Peter Menzies (then ICI's finance director). At chief officer level the new secretary, E. J. ('Jack') Turner, also a CEA man, developed as a particularly effective administrative interpreter of Hinton's ideas, and the new chairman relied heavily upon him.

More generally, the relationship between engineers and administrators, which had been a weak point in the old CEA, was now significantly improved.[1] Whatever the senior engineers felt about Hinton's new policies – and they were sometimes to be in considerable disagreement – they could recognise him as one of their own kind, and indeed admired his engineering reputation and acknowledged his brilliance. He did not, then, suffer from that resentment against arguably unqualified outsiders which Self and Citrine had provoked by their interventions in the chief engineer's department; and Hinton worked hard, and more effectively than they, for the acceptance by the engineers of proper financial controls. Internal CEGB administration was also smoothed by the sweeping away of the multiplicity of CEA committees. Their work was now concentrated on the monthly CEGB meetings and the weekly meetings of chief officers with full-time members. Hinton believed that headquarters committees had been doing too much routine work, and should concentrate on policy making and review, while details of execution should be decentralised more effectively, the central policy being explained in regular meetings of headquarters staff with the regional chiefs. He replied to those who said decisions were best taken where they were right – an old chief engineer's department justification of centralisation – with a plain warning that the principles he had enunciated were right and that if the right results did not follow, it was the quality of management that would be at fault, not the principles.

Such blunt warnings were to become a not unfamiliar part of Hinton's management style. His relations with his colleagues, though cordial, never became warm. He did his best to combat hostility, but many of those who came into contact with him found him over dogmatic, authoritarian and unwilling to listen to argument. His combination of a restless urge to achieve and tremendous analytical power could be so formidable as to destroy rather than create that sense of independence and responsibility in those who worked under him which he hoped for. Many good engineers and managers found that they could stand up to him and get him to listen, but others found an inconsistency in his response which could be unnerving. People recall experiencing an almost *physical* sense of separation as he went into a decision-making reverie, and some of his colleagues never overcame the returning fear of childhood memories of the headmaster's study as they encountered his magisterial presence. Hinton felt the lack of rapport on a personal level as much as they did, fearing that his colleagues did not always pursue lines of policy formally agreed at Board meetings. This added to the inevitable problems of a new man in control of a headquarters organisation, which, for all the newness of the name, was substantially the former CEA chief engineer's department.[2]

Initially, Hinton had very little impact on the conventional generating plant programme, which for the first two years of the CEGB proceeded very much as it had in the mid-1950s years of the Brown revolution. The logic of cost minimisation remained as before, though, with both coal prices and interest rates rising, the economic pressures to improve thermal efficiencies and gain economies of scale were all the greater. Most of the sets ordered had steam conditions at the level which had emerged as the UK standard: 2300psi and 1050°F with re-heat to 1050°F. There had been tentative discussions about going to even higher steam conditions in order to improve thermal efficiencies further, and attention focussed on 'supercritical' conditions, with higher pressures of around 3500psi at which water turned to steam without change of volume. There were, however, a number of unknowns about the technology, and the risks were considerable. Hinton, conscious that they were already running many risks on the reliability in service of basically unproven nuclear designs, therefore initially ruled out this advance, which was being attempted in a number of other countries, notably in the USA. It was thus not until 1960 that the CEGB ordered two experimental supercritical prototype 375MW sets for commissioning in 1965. Hinton by then felt that they ought to acquire experience of two different designs so that in the later 1960s it might be possible to standardise on supercritical sets. The earlier doubts were, however, to prove entirely justified: supercritical sets caused considerable trouble in operation, and performed well below specification both in Britain and elsewhere. The earlier hesitation about supercritical experimentation that concurrent nuclear risks induced was perhaps the largest, if quite unforeseen, economic benefit of the first nuclear programme. However, the sets on order for nuclear stations themselves had no direct and immediate effect in furthering technical advance on the conventional side. Their steam conditions were well below those being ordered for coal-fired stations, as was the size of their turbo-alternators.

The advance in design of conventional stations was for a time perforce confined principally to the exploitation of economies of scale. In the early years, moreover, with only a limited number of conventional orders, the possible benefits of replication were ignored. CEA plans to order additional 200MW sets were abandoned, and the CEGB instead in the later 1950s ordered a wide variety of sets of 275MW, 300MW, 350MW, 375MW, and the cross-compound 550MW arrangements. Each of these was either a repeat order of a development set originally ordered by the CEA in its last year, or a new advance of size made possible by the reduced weight-for-output ratios developed with cooling systems for stators and rotors, and by the increased weight limits for the transport by road and sea of the indivisible parts of the turbo-alternators. All of these sets were ordered before the Board had adequate operating experience of sets larger than 120MW (High Marnham's 200MW sets were not completed until 1959). Only a few of each size were ordered. This was a reflection partly of the larger sizes themselves (requiring fewer sets for any given level of capacity ordering), and partly of the nuclear programme (reducing the proportion of planned conventional capacity ordering). However, Hinton became unhappy that their policy meant foregoing the advantages of replication, and urged his engineers to settle on an appropriate standard specification which could be held for a reasonable period. He recalls saying in criticism of their early policy:

> This is just damn stupid. You are not taking two bites at the cherry, you are nibbling all round the cherry. And for God's sake decide what is the right set for ... which orders can be placed over the next five years.

The year 1960 provided the opportunities to implement this policy. Early in the year, it had become clear that there was a strong prospect of the Government finally agreeing to significant reductions in the nuclear programme. The design engineers looked hard at the question of the kind of set on which they should standardise new conventional stations, and, with road transport weight limits now increased to 190 tons, they decided that 500MW sets were feasible. These straight sets were now preferred to further development of the larger cross-compound arrangements because new 36-inch turbine blade arrangements seemed likely to make them more efficient. The steam conditions would be the same as those being developed on smaller sets, and three manufacturers had expressed themselves willing and able to go up to this size or even further. The Board knew that there might be technical risks with the 500MW size, but they seemed no greater than on smaller sets with similar steam conditions, which were also untried apart from the 200MW sizes and below. In comparison with these, the additional potential economies in capital expenditure on 500MW sets seemed considerable. Some of the senior operating and planning staff (as well as some Area Board chairmen) were doubtful about the over-confident design extrapolations being made, and the problems encountered with the recently commissioned 200MW turbines at High Marnham (which had to be rebladed after only a few months) were seen as particularly worrying. Hinton and the Board asked probing questions of the designers and manufacturers, with seemingly satisfactory assurances being made. Events were none the less to show that the sets were in fact not to live up to the promises which had led to their being ordered (see p. 283, below). At the time, however, the decision appeared to be a moderate balanced one, and by the end of 1960 one station with four 500MW sets had been ordered and a second had been tentatively agreed. Some Board members and senior design staff reserved their judgement on whether they should standardise on 500MW sets for future conventional orders as Hinton wished, with some suspecting this was running too great a risk, but others were soon wanting to advance to even larger sets and more advanced supercritical conditions.

In the event the issue of standardisation versus further advance was resolved by changes in the external environment in the early 1960s, which convinced the Board that they must greatly increase plant commissioning targets and strengthened the forces of caution. Estimates of future load growth increased substantially between 1959 and 1961 as their past under-forecasting became unmistakeable. Targets were further increased between 1962 and 1964, as local power cuts reinforced Area Board impressions of under-forecasting, and the increasingly optimistic growth forecasts of the National Economic Development Council's planners began to influence expectations. Hinton warned against an excessive reaction unduly influenced by short-term experiences, but the current penalties of under-forecasting were indeed alarming. The British Grid system traditionally operated on unusually tight planning margins, exploiting to a fuller extent than was typical abroad the benefits of reducing the necessary spare capacity by interconnection. The already tight margin had recently been reduced still further. Now allowing for only 10 per cent of their capacity to be unavailable at the time of winter peak, they had only a small additional margin to cover the possibility of extremely cold weather and forecasting errors. By the early 1960s, however, the load on the system had outpaced forecasts, and peak demand could only be met because of unusually high levels of plant availabilities, which they could have no confidence in maintaining. Past under-forecasting required a speedy response in building new capacity, and this the British system was emphatically not good at achieving. In the first half of the 1960s, load forecasts were repeatedly upgraded, but nuclear orders were being cut back, and there was thus a considerable expansion in orders for coal-fired power stations. In 1960, for example, the Board had been tentatively planning 2850MW of new capacity for commissioning in 1966, but within a year higher load forecasts raised this target to 4500MW, more than twice the highest level previously achieved. Faced with this need to expand capacity rapidly on the limited number of available sites with planning clearance, the Board felt they had little alternative but to replicate large 500MW units in 2000MW stations on each site. They did in 1962 order a total of 700MW of small-scale gas turbine plant in 50MW and 70MW sets, similar to the small auxiliary 17.5MW units which were being installed in new stations as reserve back-up plant. These gas turbines, based on aircraft engines, could be constructed quickly and would be ready for 1964 and 1965. Their capital cost per MW was only half that of conventional sets, but running costs could be three times higher, so only a limited number could be ordered to meet emergency needs and to be used for peak-lopping purposes, but they helped the Board over the crisis. The bulk of the new capacity ordered came, however, in the standard size of conventional coal-fired boilers and turbo-alternators. By the summer of 1963 the Board were committed to ordering as many as thirty 500MW sets and more were to follow. Britain soon had a significantly higher proportion of sets on order in the size range of 500MW and above than any other nation.[3] As this was increasingly perceived as the only option, confident assertions by the Board's design engineers about the untried sets' likely performance and reliability increased, and the arguments in their favour multiplied. The large number of orders for 500MW sets was none the less greater than some engineers would have liked (though these were balanced by others who felt they should advance further to 600MW supercritical sets).

The concentration of orders on 2000MW stations each based on the 500MW sets, would create stations in mainly rural areas bigger than were required to supply any but a few of the largest British urban areas. They thus also required vastly increased transmission capacity to transport the energy from the power stations to the various urban load centres. The Board's planners had already concluded that, given the increasingly stringent planning controls, proximity of power stations to the load would no longer be possible. This view was confirmed in 1961 when the Minister refused consent in a test application for permission to build a station on the urban fringe of Nottingham at Holme Pierrepoint. However carefully the large 2000MW stations were designed, their physical bulk and the enormous requirements of coal (twenty fully-loaded trains a day) and of water (equivalent to all of London's supplies) were intrusive. There was also a danger that the extra Grid lines required for transmission from large, rurally-located stations would attract environmentalist objections. Hinton took a particular interest in this question, which had been underlined as potentially an area of difficulty in the debates

on the 1957 Electricity Bill, an impression reinforced by sustained
objections to planning consent applications from rural groups. The
objections were now less typically from individual landowners than in
the past, and more from groups motivated by general amenity
considerations. As Hinton argued,

> The trouble is not that a transmission tower is ugly; it is not. The
> trouble lies in the fact that nobody wants to see a transmission
> tower, or any other overpowering man-made structure, in many of
> the places where there have to be transmission lines. It is no use
> talking about knights in shining armour striding across the country-
> side. Knights in shining armour are a damned nuisance in the
> wrong place. The same is true of power stations. The trouble is that
> this is such an over-populated island that every underdeveloped
> area within daily travel distance of a conurbation is an amenity
> area, even if intrinsically it is unbeautiful, and every under-
> developed area which is more remote is a holiday area. When
> people go to these places they do so to get away from the industrial
> surroundings of their everyday life, and they do not want to be
> reminded of them by transmission towers, however beautiful, or
> generating stations, however well designed. I believe that much of
> the opposition which we get today arises, perhaps subconsciously,
> from the fact that most people are appalled by the intrusion of
> industry into the countryside.[4]

The CEGB were thus under some pressure to underground their
transmission lines, but, with this costing between eight times the
overhead line cost for low voltage circuits and up to twenty-two times
for Supergrid circuits, they understandably resisted in all but the most
favoured areas of natural beauty. They recognised, however, that
they had a unique problem in operating in a country which now had a
higher level of electrical load density than any other country in the
world. Even with the increased carrying capacity of the 275kV
Supergrid (which the BEA had planned to meet the expanded load of
1960), the proliferation of power transmission lines would clearly
soon become embarrassing. Fortunately, their research department
had now solved the problem of designing the insulators required in
British atmospheric conditions, and this would enable them to
upgrade some of the 275kV Supergrid lines to the range 380kV–
400kV, thus considerably increasing their carrying capacity. By 1960,
the Board also knew that their plans for larger stations would

considerably increase the needs for bulk transmission of energy from power stations to load centres, and they were expecting an increase from a quarter to a half of all peak demand passing over the Supergrid in the course of the next decade. They therefore decided to upgrade to 400kV those sections of the first Supergrid which could be upgraded, and to build some new 400kV lines (with additional conductors raising their carrying capacity to well above the 2000MW of a modern power station). The increase in carrying capacity from this new, higher voltage Supergrid greatly reduced the number of lines, and thus the potential amenity objections, though the new towers were larger and heavier than 275kV towers. In the early 1960s, then, when they were embarking on large investments in new power stations, planned expenditure on the Supergrid also rose markedly, and the two investments were seen as complementary.

The conceptual design of the Supergrid was more directly in the hands of the CEGB than the design of nuclear and conventional power stations, and construction of the new Supergrid was in 1960 centralised in a new CEGB transmission project group.[5] The Board's admirers later quoted this as an example of the way that central CEGB control could create engineering excellence, for despite some construction delays, the new Supergrid was, like its predecessor, an undoubted technical success.

Centralised control of transmission had had a successful and continuous history since its inception under the CEB. In contrast, the generation side had been plagued with organisational problems which they had been unable to resolve. The CEGB found answers on the operational side, but there was less confidence in the early sixties in the competence of the weaker part of the organisation inherited from the CEA, that concerned with power station construction. The reorganisation of the twelve generation divisions into five regions (originally recommended by the Central Authority's own organisation review committee in 1954) had been proceeding only slowly prior to the creation of the CEGB, with the experimental merger of the two divisions in the North West. Hinton insisted that fuller regional reorganisation should go ahead immediately, feeling that this was a pre-requisite for effective decentralisation. His colleagues persuaded him, however, that the old divisions should survive within the new regions as a transition measure, and it was not until the 1960s that they withered away. To emphasise the importance of the position of the five new Regional Controllers, their pay was higher than that of any headquarters officers except the senior engineer; and Hinton

agreed to the appointment of one of them, A. R. Cooper, to the
Board. After a little more than a year, however, Cooper (feeling that
the dual responsibility was a mistake) resigned the regional post and
became simply Board member for operations and personnel. He, and
some of his colleagues, felt that Hinton was too hasty in promoting
organisational change without regard for staff morale, and Citrine's
orthodoxy of gradualism on these matters thus survived at Board
level.

The real change came in financial control. The delegated financial
and staffing powers of the regions were not significantly different
from those of the old divisions, despite a considerable amount of
speech-making by Hinton about fostering more autonomy and a spirit
of rivalry without the dead weight of central bureaucracy. What did
happen was that Hinton and his colleagues now gave top-level
support, which Self had been unable to obtain (see pp. 96–7 above),
to attempts to introduce a proper system of budgetary controls on the
regions. This was later to form the basis of more effective decentralisation. Operationally, the regions worked well, maintaining the
record of moderately improved thermal efficiency and substantially
improved reliability in the inherited stock of power stations which the
conservative design policies of the earlier 1950s had endowed them
with. Hinton felt that more of the smaller, older stations should be
scrapped, to reduce managerial overheads, but economic analysis
confirmed the wisdom of keeping in service old plant of low thermal
efficiency which would have been scrapped in other countries. This
was largely because the peak British space-heating load required its
use for only short periods in winter, and extra expenditure on new,
efficient plant for use over such short periods of the year was in many
cases not worthwhile.[6] In the capacity crisis of the early 1960s,
moreover, even that old plant which could be shown to be uneconomic in normal conditions had to be kept in use to meet the
greater-than-expected load.

The regions were responsible for operations and for plant maintenance and reviews, but the task of power station construction (which
had been the responsibility of the old divisions) was now separated
off from them. This had been the intention neither of the Herbert
Committee nor of the Minister, who had indeed envisaged a greater
decentralisation of headquarters responsibility for power station
construction to the regions themselves (with headquarters retaining
responsibility only for advanced stations such as those in the nuclear
programme).[7] When they discussed the new organisation with

Hinton, in the months before the CEGB take-over, however, his new colleagues were surprised to find that, as on nuclear ordering, he disavowed the policy of decentralisation on which they had assumed he had been appointed. Instead, he suggested that *one* office, based at Crewe, should take over responsibility for building *all* power stations, conventional and nuclear, arguing that, with fewer, larger stations and a large proportion of nuclear orders, this was more appropriate than diffusing expertise in many different regional organisations. Very similar ideas (though for *three* separate offices) had been advanced within the Central Authority by Eccles and his engineers in charge of design and construction, Verity and Booth (see p. 120, above), though Brown at this time had shown little interest in such organisational innovations. The engineers' tentative plans for three project groups to construct all power stations were, however, now presented to Hinton as a slight modification of his own plan; and three new project groups based on Manchester, Birmingham and London were agreed by the Board. The project group directors were appointed in November 1957, and from the summer of 1958 they began gradually to take over construction work from the regions.

The new arrangements did not, however, work as well as some had hoped. Whereas it had been envisaged that decentralisation would reduce staffing requirements, there was a considerable increase in headquarters as well as project group staff; and complaints of overlapping responsibilities remained, as the headquarters engineers watered down Hinton's proposals for greater delegation of powers. The violent shifts in proposed ordering of nuclear and conventional stations were, it is true, more easily accommodated by the project groups than they would have been under the earlier regime (with nuclear plants as a separate headquarters responsibility). By 1962, however, the project groups were so overloaded with both conventional and nuclear projects that consultants were again employed for some of the new 2000MW stations. Advocates of the separation of the project groups from the regions argued that power station construction and operation were very different functions, which had in fact already been separated at divisional level. None the less, most regional directors felt that the new project groups were unresponsive in their design policy to the regions' operating needs. Whereas Hinton had initally spoken of project groups being their 'clients', the regional directors found that the groups were very much under the control of senior headquarters engineers. The operating engineers frequently complained that this meant a striving for design awards for low capital costs or high thermal efficiencies without adequate attention to operational reliability and operating economies.[8] The project groups also proved less responsive than the regions to the budgetary controls and increased research input which the Board were trying to introduce in these years.

The alleged disadvantages of the reorganisation might have been partially compensated by the achievement of one of Hinton's central aims: the reduction in average construction times. Hinton was optimistic on this, and at the end of 1959 he persuaded his colleagues to agree to a reduction in programme times from five to four years. This was not an impossible target. It left some three years and nine months for work on site, compared with the two years and nine months said to be achieved in the USA and the one year and nine months in Japan. The target of three years and nine months had moreover been beaten by Hinton's own Risley engineers on the Calder Hall nuclear station and by the old CEA divisions on some stations. To base forward programmes on the extension of this achievement was, however, gambling that a general change could be forced through by sheer willpower, and those responsible for implementing it had severe doubts about its feasibility. There was also concern about adopting more optimistic targets at a time when they were assuming high availability on new plant, despite the more difficult technologies on which they were embarking. The Board, were, moreover, heavily dependent on their site contractors and had only indirect responsibility for the efficiency and speed of sitework.

In fact the poor labour relations and site management of these contractors, together with increased problems with the design and quality of manufacture of more advanced plant, was amply to confirm earlier reservations; and Hinton's attempts to run a tighter ship did not succeed. Neither the three year construction time on a traditional station achieved at Rogerstone in 1957 nor the completion of High Marnham's 200MW development sets with only a small delay in 1959 (both achieved by the old organisation) were beaten on projects initiated by the new CEGB project groups, their best on (admittedly more complex) 500MW sets being $3\frac{3}{4}$–4 years.[9] Their cumulative backlog of behind-schedule stations actually increased,[10] but there was a continuation of the trend improvement in average time overruns, already evident under the CEA. The average overrun, on pessimistic targets, already down to 8.1 months in the last three years of the CEA, fell to 5.6 months in the first three years of the CEGB and to 3.9 months in the next three years. Subsequently the record deteriorated (though initially by only half the 1959 reduction in the planned programme time by 12 months), and the 500MW sets typically took more than five years (rather than Hinton's target of three years and nine months) to commission. Inevitably, this was to accentuate the problems of inadequate plant to meet the rapidly growing load which the Board faced in the 1960s.

The problems of construction were, as before, shared widely by other large British construction projects.[11] Investigation by CEGB engineers in America showed that the better US times were partly a result of less restrictive labour practices (which reduced the rate of throughput of site steelwork in Britain). The fatalism in management may, however, also have made things worse. The CEGB engineers and managers accepted that they were partly responsible for the poor record, and the old CEA alibi, that the manufacturers were responsible for delays, was no longer seriously tenable. Indeed Hinton noted that UK manufacturers could now supply 500MW sets to America ordered *after* the CEGB's 550MW cross-compound sets and install them *before* the sitework was ready to receive the 550MW sets here. None the less, although manufacturers' delivery times had now improved, the *quality* of manufacture by British electrical engineering firms posed an increasing problem, and at advanced stations with sets of 200MW and above the incidence of faults in the early years of operations increased to quite unacceptable levels from 1959 onwards, and became a matter of increasing concern to the CEGB.

The deterioration in manufacturers' performance was not entirely their own fault, but stemmed partly from the industry's own policies. We have seen (pp. 118–19, above) that a weakness of the Brown revolution in conventional power station planning was its failure to come to terms with changes in research and manufacture needed to implement the technical advances and increased scale of new plant on order. The massive shifts in orders towards nuclear plant further compounded these deficiencies, leading manufacturers to redirect resources and skilled manpower to what looked like the dominant source of orders in future. In 1957 this looked likely to amount to 19 stations by 1965: around two thirds of orders and perhaps 90 per cent of generation capital expenditure in the early 1960s. (The manufacturers who lobbied so strongly for an expansion in nuclear ordering in 1956–7 were, however, themselves arguably more responsible than the CEA for the over-expansion of the nuclear programme.) In addition to the four nuclear consortia organised earlier by the Atomic

Energy Authority, a fifth one was formed in 1958, and by 1959 each of the five had received one order and expected more. The turbo-alternator manufacturers, boiler-makers and other firms who had joined the consortia were, however, disappointed by the profit levels on the early orders, and by 1959 were increasingly worried by rumours of cutbacks. Hinton knew that cutbacks were necessary, and wondered whether the consortia should in any case be disbanded, and nuclear station components be ordered separately and directly from manufacturers, as on conventional stations. In the 1960s his conviction that this was right for the future was strengthened by the evidence that the consortia associated strong boilermakers with weak turbo-alternator manufacturers and vice versa, thus reducing their overall competence. Moreover, when more advanced reactors were developed he expected the steam and electrical side of nuclear stations to adopt higher steam conditions similar to those for conventional stations, and this also favoured a shift to the conventional arrangement. For the moment, however, he accepted that the CEGB were stuck with the consortia.

By 1960 it was clear to everyone that there was severe excess capacity in the nuclear industry, and, with larger individual Magnox orders and less nuclear capacity planned, there were simply not enough orders to go round. Two of the strongest consortia merged with each other early in 1960, and two of the weakest followed later in the year, reducing their number to three. Hinton still considered this too many, and felt the three remaining consortia were over-staffed, but he was cautious about forcing further changes on the industry, and some of his colleagues preferred to maintain competition between three suppliers. There were, moreover, no export orders in prospect for the consortia, for after the first two such orders it had become evident that Magnox designs were hopelessly uncompetitive with oil at the interest rates which generally prevailed abroad. Thus the CEGB were now the only buyer, and this placed them in a difficult position, since the Board's ordering policy essentially determined the consortia's fate.

This responsibility the Board accepted: indeed, as we have seen (p. 238, above) the obligation to maintain a nuclear construction capability against possible future need had become the sole justification for placing nuclear orders, which they considered uneconomic. It did, however, create problems, and the consortia themselves were nervous of their dependence on a monopoly buyer. When the weakest consortium, the United Power Company, in 1961 put in a poor tender for the Oldbury Magnox station, and failed to win it, it seemed likely they would meet serious difficulties if they did not receive further work. The CEGB therefore offered to help with the allocation of the next order. In the event, however, the company produced a technically inferior design for the Wylfa (Anglesey) Magnox station in 1963, and the CEGB turned them down again. The difficulty of the monopoly buyer was revealed when Lord Coleraine, one of the consortium's directors, resigned his post and made an uninhibited attack on Hinton under the protection of House of Lords privilege, picturing him as the dishonourable destroyer of a vigorous industry.[12] Hinton later regretted ever having offered assistance, feeling that it would have been better to have killed off the weakest consortium earlier, but the next order was in fact given to them after he retired. His judgement was to be retrospectively justified by this order, which was to be incompetently designed and executed by this weak consortium. (see p. 284, below).

Involvement in nuclear developments, and the confusions of the nuclear programme, also affected the capacity of manufacturers (who belonged to nuclear consortia) to cope with conventional plant orders. As the nuclear stations had less advanced steam conditions, the urgency of developing skills in this field was reduced. Leading manufacturers such as Parsons devoted a disproportionate amount of skilled manpower and other resources to nuclear developments, to the detriment of their design and manufacturing competence on conventional sets. The cutback on conventional orders in 1958–60, induced by the maximum nuclear power programme, and Hinton's shorter target construction times (which meant delaying orders in 1959–60), also increased the competitive pressure in the conventional field. With each conventional order for both boilers and turbo-alternators also now considerably larger, there were also not enough conventional orders to go round, and competition for them, especially among the boiler-makers, was intense.

Competitive pressure on the manufacturers was further intensified by the CEGB's extension of the CEA policy of competitive tendering. When they took over, around a half of orders were put out to competitive tender; by the early 1960s, almost all of them were. It was recognised, however, that market competition alone could not be relied upon to achieve quick adjustments in the structure of manufacturing, and the CEGB also tried to get a reduction in the number of firms by more direct pressure and agreements between firms. Like their predecessors, they eschewed using imports to pressure the manufacturers in all save a few exceptional cases. They did, however, withhold tender invitations from the most incompetent makers, and encouraged other weak manufacturers to associate with stronger ones, or become subcontractors for them, using the promise of orders as a carrot where necessary. The result of these various pressures was that, by the time the CEGB embarked on the 500MW programme, there were effectively only four boiler-making groups and four turbo-alternator manufacturers in the field. Some felt this was still too many (the American industry, with far larger markets, had only two major manufacturers), and the CEGB engineers toyed for a time with withdrawing AEI's name from the turbo-alternator tender invitations because of doubts about manufacturing quality, though in the end they decided against this.

Again, as with the nuclear consortia, the right balance for a monopoly buyer between the harsh firmness of making companies go out of business or merge, and the more passive path of apprising the manufacturers of the situation and leaving them to take their own decisions in the market, was a difficult one to strike. In retrospect, the policy of Electricité de France (who adopted a more firmly *dirigiste* role in forcing makers to associate, thus reducing the number of designs in their advanced set programmes) was considered by the CEGB to be superior, but at the time the situation they faced was difficult. With the greatly increased conventional ordering programme of the early 1960s there seemed again to be enough work for all existing works. The fact that there would be four designs of 500MW sets was even presented by Booth and Brown as a potential advantage: they would spread their risks on untried sets by having different designs. Even had they gone more firmly for the advantages of replication with only two or three designs, however (as had intially been a motive for the supposed 500MW 'standardisation'), they would have found it difficult to impose this on the manufacturers. Discussions between the manufacturers on possible mergers or the sharing of research information on projects such as the 500MW sets broke down in the early 1960s, and it was not in fact until 1967–8 that their number was further reduced by government-backed mergers. The capacity of the British civil service to assist in a *dirigiste* restructuring initiative did not match that of the French, nor even match the ambitions enshrined in the British National Economic Development Council. Indeed the civil servants in the Board of Trade (the sponsoring ministry for the electrical engineering industry), who began to interest themselves in these issues in the early

1960s, were classed by men in the industry as something between completely ignorant and benevolently willing to try.[13] Civil servants were, moreover, somewhat better informed on questions of political sensitivity than of industrial efficiency, and one thing that was very clear to them was that electrical manufacture was concentrated in areas of high unemployment. The political repercussions of any redundancy through enforced restructuring were more immediately apparent to them than any longer term safeguards to prosperity and employment through improved efficiency in the manufacturing industry.

The manufacturers themselves, moreover, were not averse to playing on government fears and prejudice in order to maintain their position. As Coleraine's attack on Hinton in the Lords had shown, ordering policy could involve the CEGB in considerable political flak. There was something in the case presented by each side in the increasingly bitter relations which emerged between the CEGB and its main suppliers of equipment in the 1960s, and paranoia on both sides tended to magnify the misunderstanding. By 1963 not only was Hinton publicly vilified in the Lords but he and some of his colleagues were attacked by manufacturing leaders privately to Ministers. Civil servants were by then referring to Hinton's 'war of attrition' against the manufacturers. Though Hinton felt they exaggerated it, the increasing pressure the CEGB had placed on manufacturers' profit margins had also weakened the firms' research and manufacturing capacity to a degree which the CEGB engineers did not at the time appreciate. The CEGB engineers were, however, increasingly worried about the quality of the 275–550MW sets ordered in the later 1950s and commissioned in the early 1960s. These revealed serious faults in design and manufacture. The CEGB's response – to intensify their intervention in design and manufacture through their progressing and inspection organisation – was condemned by manufacturers as expensive and unnecessary interference, but defended by the CEGB as justified by their bitter experience. The manufacturers had in 1960 declared themselves confident in their ability to produce the more advanced 500MW sets. By 1963, however, they more openly voiced their doubts about the risks being undertaken by placing all Britain's power station eggs in this untried 500MW basket, with which they were clearly encountering problems. The CEGB, it seemed, were forcing the pace of technical development, but it remained an open question whether they had worked out a relationship between those involved in design and manufacture which could make that pace realistically attainable.

Within their own organisation, at least, the CEGB had considerably enhanced their research capability, with generally beneficial results. One of the undoubted successes of the Atomic Energy Authority had been in promoting cooperation between scientists and engineers,[14] and Hinton's recruitment of Leonard Rotherham as the CEGB's board member for research signalled his intention of matching this achievement. In the first five years, more than 600 scientists were recruited by the CEGB, and expenditure on research more than quintupled, reaching 0.76 per cent of the industry's revenue by 1962/3. Dr John Forrest, whose proposals for extending the Leatherhead laboratories had been turned down by the CEA, found they were now accepted by Hinton, and new laboratories were also built at Berkeley (for nuclear work) and at Marchwood (for power engineering work). Old CEA hands felt that this increased research expenditure was over-lavish and unjustified, and, as with all research programmes, much of it was unproductive. Yet retrospective analysis was to show that the benefits exceeded the costs, most notably in the Leatherhead laboratories;[15] and the new image created by their research also did a good deal indirectly to improve the CEGB's recruitment of able graduates. Although it was unusual for electric utilities abroad to be involved so extensively in research (which was the province of manufacturers), the expansion of the research programme has never been reversed by the Board, some members of which considered it one of the CEGB's major successes.

Hinton did his best to ensure that the research maintained a practical orientation, and Rotherham was particularly successful in persuading regional directors to set up practical laboratories whose work programme was fully integrated with their operating needs. He had a more difficult task with the headquarters engineers and the project groups. The traditional distrust between engineers and scientists was magnified when Brown and Booth saw Rotherham's staff being expanded faster than they thought desirable. The required symbiosis between researchers and potential users simply did not emerge at first within this hostile environment. Yet, unfortunately, it was precisely in the power station design area that it was most needed, for the evidence grew that the manufacturers' own research was being skimped. Brown and Booth felt they should be able to rely on this research, as they had traditionally done. They had also been assured by the manufacturers that they had access to American research through their US associates to help with advanced set design. The manufacturers themselves distrusted the CEGB's excursions into research (though the Board offered them access to its results), but the companies could agree to sharing their own results with each other on only a limited basis. Yet, individually and collectively they spent considerably less on research than their American counterparts (though still vastly more than the CEGB), and this was increasingly recognised to be inadequate.[16] Considerable challenges to the capacity of the CEGB and the manufacturers to implement a programme of rapid technical advance did, then, remain.

In the early 1960s, it became clear to Hinton that some of his new initiatives in the CEGB were less than completely successful. The public exposure of his job, an aspect of it which he had always disliked, also increased, with growing criticism of his views and policies from both the Atomic Energy Authority and the manufacturers. Uninformed environmentalists, he felt, were also giving him inadequate credit for his efforts on amenity. His own Board colleagues, recognising that he would be leaving soon, now paid less attention to his views than they had initially. On the personal level, moreover, he had not been as happy at the CEGB as earlier in his career. He did not find London as attractive as Risley, and his life seemed to have lost much of the excitement of the earlier epic years of nuclear pioneering. In the large, bureaucratic organisation of which he was chairman, he missed his earlier direct contact with engineering problems in a team which was his own personal creation. He had several times said that he would not seek an extension of his initial five-year appointment, and he had had attractive offers from elsewhere. When in 1962 the Minister showed himself less than enthusiastic about reappointing him for a long term, Hinton regretted that pressures such as those from the Atomic Energy Authority were compromising his reputation with government, but regretted not one bit his policies, which he was convinced were right. In the event, however, he stayed on as chairman for more than two more years, to the end of 1964, before leaving voluntarily to take up a post with the World Bank.

Reflecting on his career at the CEGB, later in retirement, Lord Hinton of Bankside (as he had then become, taking the CEGB headquarters site as his title) considered himself a failure.[17] This is a harsh judgement which owes as much to high ambitions for the CEGB as it does to an objective assessment of his own performance against that which might have been attained by others. He came into the industry with the great advantage over Edwards at the Council of having clear authority, but he suffered the great disadvantage, compared with Edwards, that the Ministry were at the time of his appointment fully committed to unwise policies in central areas. It is a measure of his genius that he was able on nuclear power issues so substantially to reverse government policy as to greatly minimise the damage it might have caused. While that achievement might be seen as essentially negative – and for a nuclear engineer was not one of which he could be unduly proud – probably no one else had the prestige in the field to bring about the transformation so speedily and effectively. No similar initiatives have been open to subsequent chairmen for making such a substantial personal contribution to cost reduction in the industry. In other areas, moreover, Hinton brought new ideas to bear, and imbued policy-making discussion with a freshness which the time-consuming and unwieldy committee-bound structure of the CEA had lacked. It is difficult to read the minutes of meetings which he chaired without being profoundly impressed that the right questions were being asked, not with hindsight, but at the time of the decision. He is in that sense an intellectual's businessman.

Yet a successful industrialist needs to be more than this. He needs both to get the right answers to his questions and to make things happen accordingly. In both these areas Hinton and the CEGB to some extent failed, though, given the long lead times of their investments, it was to be the later 1960s before this became clearly apparent. Hinton and his Board might have improved their decisions if they had understood better their own organisation and its weaknesses, and understood better also the problems of their relationships with their suppliers. Additionally Hinton lacked the political instincts of Citrine, which would have made it easier to get acceptance for his policies.

Certainly Hinton's abrasive, dominating personality contributed to the deteriorating relationships of the CEGB with other organisations. He did his best to overcome the problems, but once he had made up his mind, Hinton had all Citrine's conviction that he was right, but little of Citrine's capacity for diplomacy in presenting his case. His admirers saw his distaste for diplomatic evasions as reflecting deep intellectual honesty and commitment to the public good. By 1962, however, Whitehall was more inclined to interpret it as downright foolish abrasiveness when oil needed to be poured on troubled waters. Even those who felt that he was right sometimes felt that his method of asserting his case might become counterproductive. On the Electricity Council, many Area Board chairmen felt he was exposing the industry to unnecessary risks, and running an expensive organisation which they had to pay for but could not control. Some of his former colleagues in the Atomic Energy Authority saw him as little better than a traitor to the nuclear cause, and resented his increasing influence on nuclear policy. Some in the nuclear consortia and the manufacturing firms felt that he was using the Board's power deliberately to seduce them into self-destruction and bankruptcy. The fact that such feelings could exist is, of course, no condemnation of Hinton's views, but it certainly made relations difficult. The fact that he was more often than not proved right by events and his opponents wrong, did not, moreover, make his views any easier for them to accept. Indeed, it is one of the penalties of having so much power that even when you believe events prove you right, critics can still claim that the policies you followed were self-fulfilling. Many nuclear engineers, for example, never forgave Hinton for the nuclear cutback, and argued (against a good deal of evidence of their own weak performance) that if only they had persisted with high levels of capital expenditure the nuclear programme would have turned out better.

The powers which Hinton wielded were, indeed, formidable, but they were a natural development of a tradition in thought which suggests that limited resources can best be used if a centralised agency has control of policy making and implementation. The English and Welsh electricity generating industry was more centralised than that in other Western countries. Its policies were not only Hinton's, but represented a crystallization of the BEA chief engineer's department view, upheld by Hacking and Eccles before him, that centralised technical control was the pathway to efficiency. Such a system places great demands on its leaders, and we should perhaps not be unduly surprised if its leaders sometimes fall short of their aspirations. There is, however, a different tradition of thought which suggests that organisations should be designed for ordinary mortals rather than superhuman leaders, and that no one can reasonably be expected to be so consistently right that bets need not be hedged. Within the electricity supply industry, such views were by the 1960s being voiced by critics, and it was to Scotland, which since 1955 had been organisationally independent of the industry in England and Wales, that many such critics now looked for their alternatives.

21

A SCOTTISH ALTERNATIVE?
(1955–64)

Because there are no more mugs!

> Matthew Stevenson, in evidence to the
> Mackenzie Committee on Electricity in
> Scotland, emphasising the Treasury view
> on the need for higher rates of return.

The independent North of Scotland Hydro-Electric Board had been responsible for generation and distribution in the sparsely-populated North since nationalisation (see Chapter 12 above). The new South of Scotland Electricity Board, set up in 1955, covered the central urban areas and the South (see pp. 162–3, above). Both Boards were independent of Citrine's Central Authority and later of the Electricity Council and the CEGB in England and Wales; and they reported to the Secretary of State for Scotland instead of to the Minister of Fuel and Power. The South Board was somewhat larger than the North Board (accounting for nearly three times the electricity generated by the North in the mid-1950s). Both in the terrain covered and in its mix of generating plant, the South had more in common with the English and Welsh electricity supply system than with its northern neighbour, though the two Scottish Boards were to draw closer together in the following decade. That decade was to be an eventful one for Scottish engineers and managers, and their early experiences of the new responsibilities of independence and the task of remodelling an organisation were to provide a mixed bag of lessons for onlookers from England. The CEGB, conscious of the Scots' relative inexperience on nuclear power and on generation design and construction (both of which had been largely handled from London prior to the hiving-off of the South of Scotland), saw a confirmation of their own superiority in the difficulties being encountered. The

Area Board chairmen, by contrast, tended to see in Scotland an example of fruitful cooperation between generation and distribution, which contrasted favourably with the CEGB's arrogance and independence. Being closer to the consumers in the integrated power board structure of South Scotland, the engineers and managers responsible for generation seemed to be better able to cooperate with their colleagues in distribution, who were at the sharp end of the industry's interface with the public. Both Scottish Boards were, moreover, responsible for the whole run of costs including those on the generation side. They were not the captive customers of a CEGB, which (facing little market competition and only weak direct pressure through the Electricity Council from the Area Boards) was felt to be insufficiently cost-conscious compared with the generation engineers in Scotland.

These English views owed more to frustration at the faults within the English system than they did to actual achievements and failings in Scotland, which were more complex than these superficial views suggested. The most effective part of the Scottish Boards was certainly in their distribution achievements. The North Board was, of course, using its profits from the export of hydro-electricity to subsidise the electrification of remote areas; and in the South of Scotland, too, rural electrification was a major priority. John Pickles, the South Board's first chairman, had made his name in rural electrification before nationalisation, and he continued to prosecute rural development vigorously. The South Board achieved their initial rural electrification target in 1959, several years before the English Boards. Earlier traditions of the two south Scottish Area Boards under the BEA, for example of developing off-peak loads in floor-heating installations in domestic and commercial premises, were also enthusiastically and successfully promoted when the South Scotland Board succeeded them. The labour productivity performance of both North and South Boards was also somewhat better than that of the English and Welsh boards (although they remained part of the central labour negotiating machinery). Their slightly better productivity performance was perhaps a reflection of the absence of traditional restrictive practices (especially in the North Board), and of a general tendency for worker performance to improve in areas of high unemployment (in England also, the productivity performance of the Boards tended to improve with the distance from the low-unemployment areas of London and the South East).

The South Board still obtained many of the advantages of their connections with England, particularly in National Grid operation, which remained more coherently centralised than was typically the case in cooperative regional power pools abroad. The CEGB and South Scotland Board agreed quite simply to treat the operation of power stations as a joint activity. They also consulted closely on the construction of new power stations and the new Supergrid (which was built at the same 400kV standard in Scotland as in England and Wales). The National Grid thus remained truly a national one, and the economic benefits of the interconnection of the two nominally independent systems were shared equally. The South Scotland Board was also not restricted by the size of its system in gaining economies of scale. New generating sets, which might otherwise be too large for South Scotland, could be used for a time to export power to the North Board or the CEGB; and the South Board could also rely, at intervening times, prior to the commissioning of large new sets, on imported power. Scottish representatives continued to gain access to technical research and meetings in London at both Council and CEGB on matters of common interest, and in later years began to make payments towards the value of these central services on a voluntary basis. They thus did not have to forgo the benefits of cooperation, and the earlier pessimistic forecasts of the BEA about the horrendous technical consequences of separation did not materialise.

At the same time, the Scots found that their organisation gave them some advantages over their English counterparts. Pride in independence and the responsibility of a clearly independent role promoted management morale. Being smaller, their organisation was also less bureaucratic; and it proved easier to promote the training of management talent through widening experience. (Significantly, a number of the English industry's leaders were later to be recruited from Scotland.) There were also technical advantages. Scottish engineers felt, for example, that they could plan distribution more effectively using 132kV lines than their English counterparts, who were beset for more than a decade by disputes between the CEGB and the Area Boards about who should build, own and operate them. It is difficult to say whether, overall, the result was a significantly less costly electricity supply system in Scotland, for there are many problems of different accounting systems and the age-mix of plant which vitiate comparisons; but, with some exceptions, cost comparisons show up the Scottish performance in relatively favourable light.

A major weakness of both Scottish Boards was in their financial performance and pricing policies. Like the English Boards, they were in 1956–8 subject to various kinds of government pressure to restrain tariff increases, and their performance suffered accordingly. After that, when Ministerial attitudes in England were changing, the pressures on the Scottish Boards for higher rates of return remained weaker. The Treasury were anxious to treat the English and Scottish Boards impartially, but it was generally recognised in Whitehall that the Scottish Office was more susceptible to back-bench political pressure than the Ministry of Power. Moreover, civil servants there had less specialised knowledge, and were thus more dependent on information and influences from the Scottish Boards than their English counterparts, though they did frequently consult their London colleagues. The Scottish Office was sympathetic to the Scottish Boards (except when the Boards pleaded to be allowed to burn oil rather than the costly Scottish coal for which they were also the sponsoring Ministry), and was more inclined to speak to the Treasury of 'social' obligations than the Ministry of Power. This generally resulted in somewhat lower financial targets being set for the Scottish Boards, and their actual achievement was considerably worse than target. The North Board was in deficit for most of this period, while the South Board's financial performance, initially good, began to deteriorate seriously in the early 1960s, at a time when that of the English Boards was improving. A good deal of this poor performance was due to their quite inadequate prices for domestic consumers. Although industrial consumers in Scotland paid more on average than those in England and Wales, domestic consumers paid less. Ministerial pressure to raise prices was less strong, and there was no one of Edwards' stature and opinions within the South Scotland Board either to realise the problem or do anything about it. The result was an even more drastic over-expansion of domestic sales in the later 1950s and early 1960s in Scotland than in England and Wales.

Another area of weakness which emerged in the newly-independent South Board was in generation construction. The senior management (taken over largely from the Area Boards) had little experience in this field, and did not acquire adequate expertise from the two old BEA generating divisions they took over in Scotland. The South Board continued to receive help from London on stations under construction, and from the outset used consultants on new stations. The new coal-fired plant at Kincardine (on the Firth of Forth), for example, was started a few days after the South Board was established, and employed consultants, using the standard English 120MW sets in the early stages, and later the 200MW sets of the kind Stanley Brown was promoting in England. These proved to be effective sets, and the first one was commissioned in the time which the best English teams were achieving. By the end of 1960 the South Board had commissioned nearly 700MW of new power station plant in addition to the nearly 1200MW of plant they had inherited from the BEA Scottish divisions in 1955. On later coal-fired stations, however, notably the 300MW sets planned for Cockenzie (on the Firth of Forth), they were, like the CEGB, to encounter greater difficulties.

Scottish pride in their initially creditable performance in generation planning and construction was seriously compromised by their desire to get into nuclear technology. Pickles had been annoyed that his new Board had been excluded from early discussions with the Atomic Energy Authority (feeling that they should be allowed to build one of the later Magnox stations); but he was somewhat overwhelmed when he found in 1955 that Hinton (then still at the Risley nuclear establishment) offered him one of the first Magnox stations (Eccles and the CEA having demurred when it was suggested they order more than two). He somewhat rashly agreed to postpone some of the coal-fired sets planned for Kincardine, and, instead, at the end of 1956, ordered a Magnox station for Hunterston (on the Firth of Clyde). Pickles was more optimistic about nuclear power than the experienced CEA engineers, and more inclined to believe the over-optimistic forecasts of the Atomic Energy Authority and consortia. When the South Board accepted the tender of £37.5 millions for Hunterston (for an imaginative and complex but apparently cheap design), they expected the station to be competitive with coal-fired stations. This was thus the only Magnox order placed in the expectation that it would be economic, though delays in construction and escalation in cost prevented the realisation of their hopes. Work on site started late, because of difficulties in the Scottish planning procedure, and suffered from inadequate managerial control. Responsibility was divided between the South Scotland Board, the Atomic Energy Authority, the consultants and the consortia, and this proved to be an unwieldy and inefficient management structure. Necessary design modifications soon indicated that costs would increase by half, and site labour troubles delayed the work. The delays would have produced power cuts in Scotland in the early 1960s had the Board not been able to rely on imports from the Atomic

Energy Authority's Scottish plutonium factory at Chapelcross (commissioned on time in 1959) and from England, as well as on power from the Kincardine coal-fired station, whose construction was hurriedly accelerated to make up for the nuclear shortfall. The financial worries caused by Hunterston were less tractable. The Board had not made an adequate contract with the nuclear consortium, which was the weakest of the nuclear plant constructors and now threatening to stop work if enhanced progress payments were not made. The large amount of unproductive capital tied up at Hunterston was, moreover, becoming a financial millstone; and by the end of 1961 it was evident that the station (originally planned for 1960) could not be completed until 1964.

The situation was compounded when Pickles, the South Scotland Board's Chairman, was taken ill. He was a man of broad outlook and a hard worker, much respected for his achievements, but his illness was no doubt due in part to prolonged stress and gross overwork. As a result essential decisions about the reorganisation required at Hunterston were not taken, and by the end of the year it became evident that he must retire. The Secretary of State for Scotland found himself invited to take decisions on Hunterston as Pickles advised that he and the Board would be unable to handle it. Ministers consulted Hinton, who suggested that ideally responsibility for generation in Scotland would be transferred back to the CEGB, since only they had the capacity to sort out the problems at Hunterston. This was, however, politically an unacceptable affront to Scottish pride, and the Secretary of State was determined to appoint a new chairman to handle the crisis. He chose Norman Elliott, then chairman of the South Eastern Electricity Board in England. Elliott was half-Scottish, and had for long been considered as a primary candidate for promotion, though he was reluctant to leave his rather less demanding post in England. He was, however, interested in the idea of running an integrated power board, and was persuaded in January 1962 to move immediately to Scotland to rescue the situation.

Elliott quickly and efficiently tackled the problems at Hunterston, bringing in some of the Atomic Energy Authority's best reactor engineers and managers on secondment, and giving them clear overall responsibility on site, reporting directly to him. At the same time he agreed to accelerated progress payments to the nuclear consortium to prevent a shutdown of work. The station none the less remained a financial millstone and little could be done about this.

Elliott found that it was losing the Board £4 millions a year in interest charges and higher costs of alternative electricity generation. (This was nine times their 1961 surplus after interest.) Tense financial negotiations with the consortium responsible for the design of the station and for controlling contracts for manufacture and erection dragged on for many years, but in the end the Board had to pay £66 millions for the job as well as incurring £10½ millions extra interest charges. The final bill was twice the initially estimated cost and confirmed Hunterston's position as the most incompetently executed Magnox construction project. By early in 1964, however, the new station was delivering electricity to the Scottish grid, and operationally it was to prove highly satisfactory. It achieved a higher level of availability than the CEGB's Magnox stations, and its output was initially somewhat greater than the design capacity. The financial burden of the capital cost remained, however, and was all the greater for the South of Scotland Board than their Magnox stations were for the CEGB, because it represented a higher proportion of their relatively small power station capacity. The cathartic experience of overcoming the problems at Hunterston did, however, improve morale at the South Scotland Board; and, after it, they became more skilled on the generation side. Elliott's management style did, moreover, bring out the best in his staff. Softly spoken, almost donnish, Elliott was by nature a delegator, and liked to tackle only one major problem at a time himself while stimulating others to tackle the rest and insisting they took personal responsibility for the results seriously. Some mistook this for laziness, but it was exactly what was needed in the circumstances, and his senior colleagues responded. He was thus able to correct the loss of morale and to restore the good spirit of the South of Scotland Board.

When Elliott was appointed, the Scottish Office were seriously considering a reorganisation of Scottish electricity. They had for some years envisaged that eventually the two Scottish Boards would be united under one chairman and one Board. This had been discussed at various stages in the past, but Tom Johnston, the first North Board chairman, successfully used his political influence to keep his Board independent. When Johnston eventually retired in 1959, at the advanced age of seventy-seven, the Scottish Office decided to replace him with one of their junior Ministers, a former accountant, Lord Strathclyde. He was happy to leave politics, and would, they thought, approach the problem of the planned merger with the South Board without the prejudice against it which they had experienced from Johnston and his colleagues. At this stage, the Scottish civil servants were quite convinced that a merger was required in the interests of the efficient organisation of electricity supply throughout Scotland, and the Treasury were also keen to establish more centralised financial control in Scotland. In the later 1950s, the North Board had persistently made losses, and there was a good deal of back-bench and public criticism of their alleged profligacy in capital investment in hydro-electric schemes,[1] making the Board an obvious target in the Treasury's campaign to improve public sector management and rates of return.

The Scottish Office, moreover, had had to intervene in the investment strategy of the North Board in the mid-1950s, when the Board wanted to install uneconomically small 60MW coal-fired sets at Dundee, to give them a more reliable generating base than they could get from their (partly weather-dependent) hydro-electric schemes. This was partly to meet South Scotland criticisms about the unreliability and poor load factor of hydro-electricity deliveries from the North, but did not appear as the optimal strategy to the South Board. The civil servants showed that it would be more economic to import electricity from the South Board's new Kincardine station, using the cheaper and more efficient 120MW sets there; and the North Board reluctantly accepted this, though it was a blow to their pride and sense of independence. The North Board also wished to build more hydro-electric schemes (pointing out that recently they had not been exceeding estimated construction costs); and in 1960 they proposed a new scheme at Glen Nevis. They were also discussing a possible pumped-storage scheme at Loch Awe. The latter scheme would use off-peak electricity to pump water into a large high-level reservoir, running it down again during the day to generate electricity. This was the most economic form of energy storage for evening out the load on power stations, but still involved the loss of a quarter of the energy. None the less, used in conjunction with the South Board's stations, this seemed likely to be more economic than straightforward hydro-electric schemes.[2] This increasing interdependence of the two Scottish Boards' investment plans strengthened the earlier instinct for administrative tidiness, and clinched the arguments for a merger of the Boards within the Scottish Office. This would, however, need to be presented sensitively, if they were to overcome the likely opposition in the North to what would be seen as takeover by the larger South Board, and they decided to appoint a committee to look at the problems. Early in 1961 it was announced that this would be chaired by a Scottish industrialist, Colin Mackenzie, and would include an Edinburgh University economist, Alan Peacock, and other Scottish interests, together with Sir Josiah Eccles of the Electricity Council.

By the time the Mackenzie Committee took evidence from the South Board, Norman Elliott had become chairman and knew there was a possibility of a merger with the North Board. He found that some of his officers had earlier disagreed with Pickles about the price they were paying for hydro-electric imports from the North, but that Pickles had accepted the terms as the 'price of peace'. The payments to the North Board were now significantly higher in real terms than in BEA days, and, moreover, were now the responsibility of South Scotland alone, and no longer spread over the whole National Grid system. Yet it seemed that the South Board could have generated the electricity more cheaply themselves, and that, on one set of estimates, the loss to them considerably exceeded the profit made on the sales by the North Board. This implied that the North Board's schemes were a net loss for the Scottish economy. Eccles looked at the alternative estimates for the committee and concluded that the North Board were, in effect, being subsidised by the South. Strathclyde, for the North Board, vigorously denied this, though some of his technical staff now recognised that, in future, joint calculations of the economics of hydro-electric schemes (of the kind the South Board had made) would be essential. The committee recognised the roots of the Board in the highland community and their remarkable achievements in electrifying remote areas, but they felt that the North Board were exaggerating the potential economic benefits of hydro-electric power generation. When their report was sent to the Secretary of State for Scotland in September 1962, it largely undermined the North Board's case.[3] The committee recommended that the best prospects for Scottish electricity generation lay with coal-fired stations, and that there was room for only 400MW more hydro-electric capacity. The North Board had wanted 924MW, but the Committee felt (with the Treasury) that interest rates of 6–7 per cent (rather than the 5–6 per cent favoured by the North Board), and depreciation periods of 60 years (rather than 80) were appropriate, and these made capital-intensive hydro-electric schemes look considerably less attractive. The economist on the Committee also scotched the foolish North Board argument that inflation made hydro-electricity more attractive, a view which only made sense in crude historic cost accounting terms not in any sensible real cost analysis.[4] The Committee's most controversial recommendation was that, to promote efficient joint operation and joint generation planning, the two Scottish Boards should be merged into one. However, to sweeten the merger they suggested that the Treasury should pay a subsidy to complete the uneconomic electrification of the rural and island areas of the North, as far as practicable, within a five or six year period. The new all-Scotland Board would be no larger in terms of the population served than the largest English Board, but would cover a greater area, and, like both its components, would have wider responsibilities for generation.

Ministers had anticipated that the merger proposal would be vigorously opposed in the North, and they found they were right. The Mackenzie Committee had pointed out that there was in fact very little expenditure undertaken by the North Board under its 'social' clause which other Electricity Boards would not undertake, but the North Board's mystique and image were certainly distinctive, and they were not anxious to submerge their identity in a larger all-Scotland Board. The North Board's discussions of the Mackenzie Report were highly charged with emotion, and Lord Strathclyde (whose former ministerial colleagues had expected him to be neutral) proved a powerful supporter of the Board's independence. Eventually, however, the North Board decided to accept in broad outline the technical conclusions of the Report, while vigorously opposing the proposed merger with the South. The Secretary of State at first thought that the sweetener of a rural electrification subsidy might help, but the Treasury wanted to prune this down. Moreover, it soon became evident that even the North Board's Consumer Consultative Council opposed the merger, despite this proposed sweetener. With an election in the offing, Ministers wanted to incur no risks of political unpopularity, and by 1963 the Cabinet decided to fudge the issue. It was announced that the merger proposal would not be accepted, though its objectives would, the Secretary of State promised, be pursued by cooperation between the Boards.[5] The South Board were, on the whole, happy with this solution, for they recognised they were only just overcoming their own management problems, and they did not agree with many of the more detailed proposals of the Mackenzie Committee. Although they still found the North Board difficult in some negotiations (and it was to be some years before their cooperation developed on an adequate basis), they were willing to give this new proposal for joint cooperation a try. At the North Board there remained considerable distrust about a possible takeover, fortified when the Minister appointed the two chairmen members of each others' Boards, but at working level the relationship began to develop well.

The upshot was that the South Board were able to prevent further large-scale hydro-electric development in the North, by using appropriate Treasury pressure. New hydro-electric projects proposed by the North Board were evaluated with a rate of interest as high as 8 per cent in real terms, and thus even those schemes considered economic by the Mackenzie Committee were rejected.[6] This was an early example of the Treasury insisting on individual new projects (rather than the industry overall) yielding a high return, and in this case the required yield was so high that it effectively ruled out further development of capital-intensive hydro-electric schemes.[7] Elliott's view was that Scotland should become increasingly dependent on oil, or, if that were politically impossible (as it was), on coal. He was, however, worried by the National Coal Board's new policy of relating regional prices to costs, which raised the price of coal mined in the poorer Scottish seams, from which most of their supplies came.[8] For a new station they were planning at Longannet (on the Firth of Forth), however, Elliott was able to negotiate a favourable price arrangement for low quality coal to be supplied directly from new adjacent pits in the Fife coalfield.

Cooperation between the North and South Boards proceeded more smoothly on the conventional power station side than on the question of hydro-electric generation. In the early 1960s the South Board had agreed that, to make up for construction delays at the Hunterston nuclear station, the Board should build a small steam station at Carolina Port (Dundee), which they had earlier opposed. The North Board and their consultants chose two 120MW sets (small for their time), but increased the steam pressure to 1900psi, well above the 1500psi favoured by the CEGB. Although these were relatively expensive to build, they were cheaply located near the Dundee load centre and, from first commissioning in 1965, were to be more thermally efficient than the great majority of the CEGB's sets ordered in the early 1960s. When the South Board came to design the new Longannet coal station (also using consultants), they, too, felt free to break with CEGB precedent, though some opinion within the Board favoured following the CEGB's 500MW orders. Instead, however, they developed a large new station consisting of four 600MW cross-compound sets, based on the components of the 300MW sets at Cockenzie on which they were gaining design and construction experience. The possibility of learning from experience yielded dividends in tighter project management and easier commissioning, and Longannet (which when complete generated more than a half of Scotland's electricity) was to bear favourable comparison with the CEGB's own 500MW set stations.[9]

The experiment in Scottish devolution had not been without its heavy costs in mistakes such as Hunterston, low domestic prices, and North Board overspending, mistakes which might have been avoided or alleviated under central guidance. The separation from England had, however, forced the Scottish Boards to face economic reality by themselves, with generally beneficial results. Despite initial difficulties, in the long run the Scottish experience was to show that centralising views opposing Scottish devolution, whether those of Citrine expressed in 1952–5 or of Hinton in 1961–2, did not offer the only way, or even necessarily the best way, of running an electricity supply system effectively. With National Grid planning and operation maintained intact, moreover, and a cooperative spirit in relations with their English and Welsh colleagues, they had been able to overcome the potential problems of their smaller scale.

EPILOGUE

THE SECOND FIFTEEN YEARS OF NATIONALISATION (1963–79)[1]

... The exercise of undue pressure by governments and their failure to treat public enterprises reasonably would be bound to call forth countervailing power. Governments must consider themselves lucky that the responses to what at times has been a pretty dirty game have been so reasoned and well ordered.

> John B. Heath, 'Management in the Nationalised Industries', *Nationalised Industries Chairmen's Group Occasional Paper No. 2* (1980) pp. 1–2.

In 1963 the Scottish Boards could look with a greater confidence than they had felt for some time towards their future. In England and Wales, too, the engineers and managers in the electricity supply industry could view their future optimistically, as they surveyed past achievements and recent changes on the fifteenth anniversary of nationalisation, 1 April 1963. Nor was this purely bloated pride. In February 1963, their senior men had finished a gruelling period of intermittent examination over more than a year before the Commons Select Committee on Nationalised Industries, which for the first time was showing its teeth seriously.[2] The Committee's report, published in May of that year, was generally complimentary about the industry's achievements, and gave support to the general direction of policy on which they were embarked, even supporting the industry's views against that of Ministers on some issues where the two differed.[3] The industry's presentations to the Committee had been an accomplished public relations achievement in the best sense of the word: they did not skate over difficult issues, but confronted them logically, so that their doubts and hesitations could be shared and their priorities rationally appraised.[4]

Objective grounds for optimism about the future were, then,

present. Managerially, the difficulties of the South of Scotland Board and the insecure interregnum at the Electricity Council were ended with the appointments of Elliott and Edwards. Technically, the experience with larger, more thermally efficient sets of 120MW and 200MW had lived up to most of Brown's expectations. Capital costs on stations recently completed were considerably below those of the postwar decade, and thermal efficiencies significantly higher. Average construction times were lower than at any time in the previous two decades. Moreover, their planned future standardisation on 500MW sets seemed likely to extend the benefits of replication and speed in construction. In the nuclear field, the over-optimism of the Atomic Energy Authority had been disciplined, and a good deal of expertise had been built up, which it was expected would soon be needed. The later Magnox stations, then being built to maintain this expertise, were expected to be considerably less uneconomic than their predecessors.

The pricing issue at both wholesale and retail level had been resolved in principle, and commercial policy was now being tackled in a more discriminating way, with the emphasis on positive efforts to sell the off-peak load. Financial disciplines had been established, both internally and through clearer guidelines from government in the 1961 White Paper. Although the Cabinet had then resisted Treasury pressure to commit Ministers openly to a proposed White Paper statement promising less interference, by 1962 senior civil servants were emphasising that less intervention *was* one corollary of their new policy.[5] The industry's leaders very much welcomed that prospect, even if they were rather sceptical about the political will to keep to it. For all the force of the new financial disciplines, moreover, the industry had lost none of its spirit of buoyant expansion, which, between nationalisation in 1948 and 1963, had raised their share of final energy markets in Britain from 14 per cent to 29 per cent. The auguries for the future now were good, with the Government pressing them to expand investment in both distribution and generation. Despite disagreements with government on pay policy, moreover, the managers in the industry were by 1963 more hopeful about developments in labour relations matters, which promised well for the future of productivity and the status of workers.

The confidence generated by new policies and new management arose primarily from the feeling that the Electricity Boards were now fitted to overcome the problems they had experienced in the recent past. This perspective on the future derived from the past is, of course, a necessary part of the human condition; but that is not to say that their new management and changed policies would necessarily serve as well in facing the problems of the 1960s and 1970s. Experience was in fact to reveal new problems, as well as old flaws in new light, and the optimism of 1963 was, in the event, not always justified.

In many cases, however, it was. One of the significant success stories of these years was labour relations. Productivity improved, partly as a consequence of technical progress (the operation of a typical large station with four 500MW sets required 600 men; the same capacity in 60MW sets required 2000 men). There were significant new initiatives to reduce overtime in return for adequate pay for standard hours. By October 1965 average hours of overtime were down to 1.7 hours: essentially the same work was done for the same pay but in a significantly shorter time. Work measurement was extended,[6] and the South of Scotland Board, in particular, pioneered productivity yardsticks in the industry. The union leadership, particularly the Electrical Trades Union under Les Cannon, now supported these schemes as a means of improving their members' living standards. By the early 1970s the electricity supply workers were again among the leaders in the earnings league, as before the War. On the CEGB's initiative, status differentials between manual and non-manual employees (on matters such as holidays and sick pay) were also reduced in the hope that this would increase the commitment of the workers to the industry. The tougher management policy and government incomes policies led to some labour disruption on a short-term basis, but the short-term sacrifices were a small price to pay for these significant advances.[7] These meant that for more than a decade the rate of productivity *increase* in British electricity supply matched that achieved abroad (an equality few other British industries could claim), though the absolute *level* of labour productivity in Britain remained low.

Policies on pricing and financial targets also initially developed well. The off-peak storage heater sales compaign, combined with the increase in the incremental price in domestic tariffs, enabled the industry more closely to equate prices with costs. A 'white meter' tariff – essentially the Eastern Board's time-of-day charging system – was introduced generally from 1969 in an imaginative marketing scheme. As a result of these changes the industry was able to hold the undesirable (and still probably underpriced) unrestricted space-heating load to its 1964 level or below, with all the growth in sales for space-heating purposes now coming in off-peak hours. The load factor of the supply system rose from below 50 per cent in the early 1960s to over 55 per cent in the 1970s,[8] a level nearer to that achieved overseas than had been typical in Britain in the past. Yet, despite earlier fears by the area chairmen, the new policies of more realistic domestic pricing did nothing to blunt the commercial edge of the industry, which throughout the 1960s continued to win a larger share of the domestic energy market. In appliance sales too, despite the abolition of resale price maintenance in 1964 (which the industry opposed), they were commercially successful. Their market share of appliance sales actually rose initially, in common with that of other multiples; though in the 1970s, their market share declined again, despite the vigorous promotion of their new 'Electra' brand name.

The financial policies of the 1960s White Papers, in which realistic pricing played an important role, were initially developed encouragingly. Gaps which economists pointed to in the published version of the 1961 White Paper were plugged by the industry voluntarily, before they became government policy in the subsequent White Paper of 1967.[9] The industry was also increasingly able to persuade Ministers to pay explicit financial compensation when they asked the industry to follow policies judged uneconomic. However, adherence to this ideal, promoted earlier by Edwards, was decidedly patchy.[10] The financial surpluses made by the industry were less than those targeted in 1961–3, partly because of cost increases, and, in later years especially, partly because of increasing government intervention in pricing. The political commitment to non-intervention on this issue had always been equivocal; but, in the 1970s especially, the gains of the previous decades were all but thrown away. Thus, whereas between 1960 and 1969 costs went up by 7 per cent and prices by 28 per cent (enabling a healthy increase in surplus); between 1969 and 1974, with the general rate of inflation accelerating markedly and government trying to hold it back by controlling public sector prices, costs rose in money terms by 118 per cent and prices by only 57 per cent. The result, inevitably, was that the industry went into deficit, and it is only recently that economic pricing has been generally restored to the energy sector. One recent study has found that, in the years after the supposed attempt to impose market financial disciplines on the Boards in 1961, their actual investment behaviour in fact conformed *less* closely than earlier to the models of private sector behaviour.[11] Even in their best years, moreover, the nationalised Electricity Boards had a rather lower rate of return on their capital than electric utilities in the United States, though the gap was by now small.[12]

The failure to meet financial targets was not solely the fault of government price control, but also partly arose from the Boards' (and particularly the CEGB's) inability to keep to their own cost estimates on major capital projects. The 500MW sets, in particular, proved more problematical than had been anticipated at the time they were ordered. Most were behind schedule and cost well above the estimates. Their performance also frequently fell short of specification, with both output and thermal efficiency of many of the sets remaining below the design levels. It was not until the 1970s, after a good deal of effort on the part of the operating staff, that the availability target (of 90 per cent at winter peaks) was approached and on some sets even exceeded. Technical and manufacturing problems appeared during construction and early operation in bewildering variety in the different designs of turbo-alternators and boilers. They thus had very low initial availabilities, and, if the rest of the British economy had not also performed well below planned levels in the mid and late 1960s, the problems with 500MW sets would have caused widespread power cuts in winter. In the event, however, the poor performance elsewhere (and hence slow growth in electricity demand) enabled the industry to avoid all but a few power cuts.[13]

The overall thermal efficiency of the National Grid power stations in Britain, despite this considerable investment in new plant, remained below that of the United States and, especially, of France throughout the 1960s and 1970s.[14] There are a number of factors making for this less satisfactory performance, which were not entirely within the control of the CEGB. For example, the proportion of hydro-electric plant, the availability of cooling water and national load patterns all affect the overall system thermal efficiency. The fact remains that, while Britain's performance had once been equal to or superior to these countries, this was now no longer so. Moreover, the cost of building new capacity to meet demand, which had fallen rapidly in real terms throughout the twentieth century, now ceased to do so.[15] This slackening in the pace of technical innovation and scale economies was, however, also noticeable in electric utilities overseas, and perhaps in part represents a more general, temporary exhaustion of the traditional avenues of technical advance.

In later programmes, performance expectations were reduced, and policy implementation improved. By the 1970s the CEGB did better with the development of 660MW sets, the first being commissioned at

Drax (Yorkshire) in 1973; but problems of poor sitework by contractors remained, particularly on Thameside and Merseyside. The manufacturing industry was partially restructured in a series of mergers which reduced the number of firms to two turbo-alternator manufacturers and two boiler-makers.[16] None the less, the manufacturing firms continued to experience problems, most noticeably when the worldwide stagnation of the seventies greatly reduced new orders. While it then appeared that further changes were required, political interventions and technical and market uncertainties continued to bedevil the search for an efficient structure.[17]

In the nuclear power programme, the experience of cuts in orders was even more traumatic, and the nuclear consortia were reduced by merger and bankruptcy to one. The Magnox programme itself was a qualified success.[18] The last station at Wylfa (Anglesey) was badly engineered and encountered persistent problems, which are now corrected. The operation of the others has been relatively trouble free, and the safety record of Magnox reactors has been good. Their availability for operation has been second only to the rival Canadian reactor design. In the later 1960s routine inspections discovered corrosion in many of the reactors, and in order to reduce its further progress operating temperatures in most reactors were reduced, with the result that they are currently operating at around four-fifths of designed output. It was calculated that this would extend their life to longer than originally planned, and this is considered likely to compensate for the downrating in capacity. The CEGB's own research also enabled them markedly to increase the useful energy extracted from the Magnox fuel, with an improvement of more than two-thirds in nuclear fuel efficiency by the 1970s. The result of this and rising conventional power station costs was that, in financial terms, by the middle of the 1970s the Magnox stations looked considerably more appealing. In their lifetime overall, it is possible that some of them, contrary to expectations, will have proven to be economic in resource cost terms.[19]

The big nuclear mistakes of the 1960s came with the new generation of AGR reactors. Announced as the significant cost breakthrough in 1965 (when the first, at Dungeness 'B' (Kent), was ordered), they proved to be nothing of the kind. The first AGR station, though due for completion in 1970, is still at the time of writing (1981) not commissioned. Far from being a new cost breakthrough, its cost in real terms has exceeded that of the Magnox stations. Two better-designed AGR stations – the South of Scotland

Board's Hunterston 'B' and the CEGB's Hinkley Point 'B' – began operating in 1975/6 (a few years late) and cost less than Dungeness, but there remained teething problems. The multiplicity of AGR designs greatly complicated the Boards' attempts to remedy these problems, and the on-load refuelling systems (which once seemed a major AGR advantage) are not yet operational. The other major problems have been solved with the accumulating operational experience at Hunterston and Hinkley Point, but it is still a matter of dispute whether the AGRs or rival nuclear reactor systems will be the most economic in future. What cannot reasonably be disputed is that the series of decisions of the mid-1960s to invest prematurely and heavily in several different and inadequate designs of AGR stations represented one of the major blunders of British industrial policy.[20] It was fortunate that the CEGB, though in 1965 taken in by the forecasts that the AGR stations would be cheap and effective, had been sufficiently cautious to insist that the even larger AGR programme initially advocated by the Atomic Energy Authority should be halved, and fortunate too that the Government had this time accepted their view rather than the Authority's.

The serious miscalculations of the cost of nuclear power in the late 1960s and early 1970s were a worldwide phenomenon, partly because of substantial tightening of nuclear safety standards, and partly because of problems of poor decision making and management similar to those in Britain.[21] By the 1970s (when it was generally agreed that *some* form of nuclear power would be economic), British politicians and the supply industry disagreed on the type of reactor to build after the first AGRs. By the time they had decided, load forecasts were so significantly below earlier expectations that large numbers of new power stations were no longer needed. Britain thus became the only major industrial nation in the 1970s to place no orders for nuclear power stations. Hinton's sole reason for maintaining the nuclear power programme after 1960 – to preserve the capacity to go nuclear when it was economic – proved in the 1970s to be a chimera. Britain's major European and Japanese rivals, by contrast, who had initially confined their nuclear expenditure to funding research and a few development stations, rapidly capitalised on this after 1973 when a larger nuclear programme became economic. This appears, in retrospect, to have been the more sensible policy. With a similar, smaller, initial investment in nuclear power, Britain might well have had the same nuclear expertise, yet have been economically stronger and better able to face up to the challenges of the 1980s.

The CEGB's problems with both conventional and nuclear plant intensified Area Board criticisms of their independence, and this initially evoked a sympathetic response in government. In 1964, when nationalised industry board salaries were reviewed, the Government decided to overturn the existing relativities agreed by Hinton and Mills, and Hinton's successor as Chairman of the CEGB, Stanley Brown, was paid less than Edwards as Chairman of the Electricity Council, to signal Whitehall's intention of relying more on central guidance from Council. By 1968, Edwards had also convinced many within Whitehall that a more centralised power structure should be restored to the industry. Area Board chairmen's views differed on the best solution. A few favoured the option of small, regional all-purpose power boards on the Scottish model, noting the increasingly confident and successful style of management north of the border. The majority, however, with Edwards, favoured the creation of a new statutory corporation, with the CEGB as a more effectively controlled subsidiary. Over more than a decade of political uncertainty on the issue, several governments indicated their intention of implementing the latter change. More recently, however, the Conservative Government again announced a commitment to improving voluntary cooperation between Boards within the framework of the existing 1957 Act.[22]

The industry's major problem in the 1970s derived not from such inherited concerns as this, but from the profound changes in Britain's energy economy, which followed the discovery of natural gas and oil in the North Sea and the rises in world oil prices from 1973 onwards. The rate of growth of demand for electricity had already been slower than expected in the later 1960s; but the industry seriously underestimated the challenge they faced, in the slowly-growing market environment of the 1970s, from the revitalised gas industry with its new advantages of cheap North Sea supplies. The rapid expansion of gas sales to both industrial and domestic consumers pre-empted electricity's market growth, and severely cut back the industry's rate of expansion. The electricity supply industry's share in national investment fell to less than half its former level, as capital expenditure was reduced in line with rapidly falling load forecasts.

Even so, the late completion of many power stations, ordered in more optimistic years, led to a considerable over-expansion. For the first time in its history the National Grid faced vast overcapacity. In the winter of 1975/6, for example, the CEGB met a peak demand of

41353MW but had as much as 58677MW of plant installed, a spare capacity margin of 42 per cent. This was partly due to over-optimistic forecasting (the five-year forecast made in 1970 was 24 per cent too high), but there was also a change in their views of the desirable planning margin. The probability of unexpectedly high demand in cold weather was much the same as before, but, with more advanced nuclear and conventional power stations, they were less confident of meeting construction targets or of avoiding breakdowns when running plant in, so higher allowances for these contingencies had to be built into their planning. With greater competition from other fuels, lengthening lead times in construction and more erratic growth rates in demand, the allowance for forecasting errors also increased. The forward planning margin was thus raised from 17 per cent to 28 per cent between 1968 and 1977. The actual margins of spare capacity turned out to be substantially in excess of this, for the industry was too slow to adjust to the conditions of the 1970s in its forecasting. However, the economic penalty was not as great as the over-expansion in capital investment might suggest, for the industry was able to close down a good deal of older plant whose running costs at the higher post-1973 fuel prices were considerably higher than expected, and this went a long way to compensate for the over-investment.[23]

As oil and coal prices rose, the real price of electricity (which had been falling throughout the twentieth century, to reach its lowest-ever level in 1973) began to rise again. By 1980, although still lower than in 1948, the average real price of electricity to domestic consumers in Britain was one-third above the early 1970s level. Cheaper natural gas made large inroads into energy markets in the 1970s. This unexpected newcomer thus occupied the dominant position in the growth of the energy sector which electrical men had once thought only nuclear power could fill.

Despite meeting more serious competition from the gas industry than they had experienced for many years, the industry's leaders at the end of the 1970s faced the future with some confidence. Their corporate plans suggested that internal organisational and policy changes had initiated appropriate responses to some of the problems they faced, though others, notably power station building, they recognised as remaining problematic. In the future, they envisaged, they might again be called upon to play as large a role as earlier in national investment. While natural gas will remain a formidable competitor for many years ahead, nuclear power (perhaps finally economic in an era of high competing oil and gas prices) may undergo a renaissance after its years in the doldrums.

From the beginnings of the electricity supply industry in the 1880s up to the mid-1960s, the industry's decision makers had lived in conditions of unusually stable expectations. Managers and engineers had then known that improved steam conditions, and larger scale in generation would lead to continually falling costs. Even nuclear power was seen in the 1950s as little more than the logical extrapolation of these basic rules of the industry's existence. Sales, they had felt, would continue to grow, and electricity would continue to win market share from other energy industries at a rapid pace. In the late 1960s and 1970s all these assumptions, built up over more than six decades of experience, proved false. The industry is now less sure that the future will be an extrapolation of the past. Management problems have become less tractable, as decision making depends more widely on dealing with uncertainty and geopolitical factors, and less completely on basically technical factors within a given framework of analysis. With their recent experience, the industry's managers do not need to be reminded that it may be the challenge of change and the unexpected that will stretch them most in the years to come.

STATISTICAL APPENDIX

Since the War, the quality of statistics on the energy sector in the UK has improved markedly. The annual Ministry of (Fuel and) Power, *Statistical Digest* (later Department of Energy, *Digest of United Kingdom Energy Statistics*) provides the most convenient summary of statistics for the whole of Great Britain (in most cases excluding Northern Ireland). For electricity supply, the changing divisions of the industry (with South Scotland, for example, being included with the English and Welsh figures in reports prior to 1955, but reporting independently thereafter) causes some problems, but almost all the statistical series have been separately calculated for each division. Those for England and Wales are conveniently collected in the Electricity Council's annual *Handbook of Electricity Supply Statistics*; and for the Scottish Boards in their *Annual Reports*. A well-indexed, quick reference guide to the area covered, frequency of publication, and sources of data for the industry is included in David Nuttall, 'Electricity', in W. F. Maunder (ed.), *Reviews of United Kingdom Statistical Sources*, vol. XI, (Oxford, 1980).

For the convenience of the reader, some of the more important statistical series are reproduced in Tables A.1–A.3 below. In addition, Table A.4 provides a new series for the price of electricity in real terms over the period covered by this volume. All the references to price changes over time in the text are to prices in real terms and refer to the prices in this table. I am indebted to the Electricity Council's Intelligence Section for permission to reproduce it. Unless otherwise stated, the data in all tables refer to Great Britain. Note that the figures in the text often refer to England and Wales or Scotland separately. The abbreviation n.a. indicates that data are not available.

GENERATION

The size of the electricity supply system is perhaps best measured by the total output capacity of the power stations on it (which is somewhat less than their nominal installed capacity). That capacity is available to meet the load placed on it by consumers but, especially in the postwar years, demand sometimes exceeded the capacity available to meet it. A negative spare capacity margin meant that power cuts or voltage reductions were essential; but, given the incidence of breakdowns and repairs, even a positive spare capacity margin of less than 10 per cent was sometimes insufficient to maintain supplies. Overseas systems traditionally worked on larger spare capacity margins, and since 1968 the supply industry in Britain has also increased its planned margins.

Two traditional indexes of efficiency are also shown in Table A.1. The thermal efficiency of stations measures the extent to which the useful heat in the coal or oil is converted into electricity. The load factor measures the intensity of use of capital: it is the actual electricity generated in a year as a percentage of what would have been generated if the power stations had been generating at maximum demand levels throughout the year. The thermal efficiency of power stations depends largely on the designers and operators of power station plant. The load factor, in so far as it is under the control of the industry, depends largely on commercial policy, notably the effectiveness with which sales at off-peak times are promoted. For an alternative measure of load factor, cf. p. 305, note 17 below.

ELECTRICITY SALES

Until the energy crisis of the 1970s, and with some interruption in the War, electricity sales in Britain were generally reckoned to double every seven years or so. Within this total growth, however, there were significant year-to-year variations in the major sectors of industrial and domestic sales, and in the minor ones (not shown in Table A.2) of commercial, public lighting and traction sales.

In the postwar years, the proportion of domestic sales for space heating purposes also fluctuated markedly according to the availability of alternative coal supplies, and other factors discussed in the text.

TABLE A.1   *Generation statistics, 1938–80*

	1 *Output capacity at year-end (GB)*	2 *Simultaneous maximum load at year-end or early the following year (GB)*	3	4 *National spare capacity margin (GB)*	5 *System load factor (GB)*	6 *Average thermal efficiencies of conventional steam stations (GB)*
		Load met	*Potential load*			
	MW	*MW*	*MW*	*%*	*%*	*%*
1938	n.a.	7173	n.a.	n.a.	33.3	21.7
1948	11 789	10 263	10 636	9.8	46.9	21.1
1949	12 430	11 114	12 425	0.0	42.5	21.3
1950	13 518	11 861	13 840	−2.4	42.8	21.6
1951	14 645	13 088	14 000	4.4	46.2	21.7
1952	16 079	14 047	15 347	4.6	43.6	22.6
1953	17 388	15 883	16 677	4.1	42.4	23.2
1954	18 806	17 121	17 720	5.8	44.4	23.7
1955	20 629	18 428	19 835	3.8	43.5	24.2
1956	22 597	19 357	19 357	14 3	48.3	24.8
1957	24 521	21 187	21 187	13.6	46.3	25.2
1958	25 846	23 012	23 012	11.0	46.4	25.9
1959	27 799	25 354	25 354	8.8	45.3	26.3
1960	29 582	26 918	26 918	9.0	48.4	26.7
1961	31 526	29 750	30 311	3.9	46.3	27.2
1962	34 543	32 607	35 267	−2.1	44.0	27.5
1963	36 534	33 115	33 296	8.9	50.4	27.5
1970	56 057	43 270	46 401	17.2	52.0	28.4
1980	66 541	48 284	48 284	27.4	58.0	32.1

SOURCES Col. 1 1948–63, Ministry of Power, *Statistical Digest 1963*, p. 96.
1970, 1980, Department of Energy, *Digest of UK Energy Statistics*.
Cols 2, 3, 5 1938–63, Ministry of Power, *Statistical Digest 1963*, p. 98. 1970, 1980, Department of Energy, *Digest of UK Energy Statistics*.
Col. 4 Calculated as [(col. 1 − col. 3)/col. 1] × 100.
Col. 6 1938–63, Ministry of Power, *Statistical Digest 1963*, p. 98. 1970, 1980 Department of Energy, *Digest of UK Energy Statistics*.

TABLE A.2   *Sales of electricity, 1938–80*

	1 Domestic and farms (GB) GWh	2 Share of domestic sales for space heating (England & Wales) %	3 Industrial sales (GB) GWh	4 Total sales (GB) GWh	5 Sales per head of population (GB) kWh
1938	5361	17	10 320	20 404	442
1948	13 576	40	19 121	38 821	797
1949	13 657	39	20 445	40 919	835
1950	14 911	36	22 920	45 474	924
1951	16 939	36	25 350	50 513	1033
1952	16 869	33	26 068	51 950	1059
1953	17 691	28	28 000	55 568	1129
1954	19 075	22	31 553	61 401	1243
1955	21 146	26	34 635	67 423	1361
1956	23 755	24	37 224	73 520	1477
1957	24 850	22	39 348	77 218	1543
1958	28 227	21	41 241	83 869	1669
1959	30 487	21	44 695	90 504	1790
1960	35 270	19	49 991	102 363	2009
1961	39 968	23	51 740	110 232	2145
1962	47 628	26	53 529	122 357	2360
1963	54 475	34	56 106	133 850	2569
1970	78 989	32	78 300	193 907	3598
1980	87 907	n.a.	86 453	225 053	4137

SOURCES   Cols 1, 3, 4, 5   1938–63, Ministry of Power, *Statistical Digest 1963*, pp. 97–9. 1970, 1980, Department of Energy, *Digest of UK Energy Statistics. 1981.*

Col. 2   Industry estimates, relating to domestic sales in England and Wales only. The '1938' data relates to 1939.

MISCELLANEOUS

Employment (Table A.3, Col. 1) grew less rapidly than output, and this tendency for labour productivity to increase was particularly marked in the later 1960s and 1970s. The industry was, however, pre-eminently a capital-intensive one; and the trend of investment, both in absolute terms (Col. 2) and relative to investment elsewhere (Col. 3), was markedly rising until the crises of the 1970s. Electricity's major competitor, gas, then took the bulk of growth in the market. It is possible to convert the direct use of fuels like oil, gas and electricity into the equivalent of tons of coal, expressing the electricity component of direct fuel use as a percentage of the total (Col. 4). Electricity is typically more efficient in use than fuels like coal and gas (e.g. more of the energy is converted to useful heat in an electric fire than in a gas or coal fire), and the statistics thus underestimate the *level* of electricity's role, though the *trends* correctly illustrate the winning of new markets initially in the postwar years, followed by relative stagnation in the 1970s.

REAL ELECTRICITY PRICES

While electricity might appear to be a relatively homogeneous product, its cost does in fact vary considerably according to the time at which, and quantities in which, it is supplied. This is reflected in complex tariffs, under which one industrialist or domestic consumer may pay very different prices per kWh than the next, if it is taken in bulk at high voltage or at off-peak times. For some purposes, the best measure of price may not be the average price paid, on which Table A.4 is based, but rather the price for a given quantity (e.g. 500 kWh per quarter) under given conditions (e.g. ordinary domestic supply). There is, moreover, a difference in the trends of average and incremental charges, for in recent decades a large proportion, particularly of domestic consumers' charges, has been shifted from the standing charge to the incremental running charge. The precise measure of price used will depend on the question one is asking.

Table A.4 is directed to answering two questions: how has the average price of electricity per kWh in the (changing) quantities used by domestic consumers changed relative to retail prices in general?; and how has the same changed, for industrialists, relative to wholesale prices in general? Because long-run trends in retail and wholesale prices have differed, the table cannot be used to compare the relative price of industrial and domestic electricity in any year.

Statistical Appendix

TABLE A.3 *Miscellaneous electricity statistics, 1938–80*

	1 Employment (GB) (Thousands)	2 New fixed investment (UK) (Current £Ms)	3 Electrical investment's share of UK capital formation %	4 Electricity's share of UK energy markets %
1938	109	42	7.1	8.5
1948	151	99	7.0	14.4
1949	166	122	7.7	14.9
1950	176	138	8.1	15.7
1951	181	149	7.9	16.3
1952	183	159	7.5	16.5
1953	186	180	7.6	16.7
1954	189	215	8.4	17.5
1955	195	247	8.7	18.4
1956	196	249	8.0	19.4
1957	199	266	7.9	20.6
1958	201	297	8.5	21.7
1959	204	341	9.1	23.3
1960	208	338	8.2	24.5
1961	214	364	7.9	26.1
1962	223	412	8.7	27.6
1963	231	510	10.4	28.6
1970	208	487	5.3	33.3
1980	175	1088	2.7	35.6

SOURCES Col. 1 1938–63, Ministry of Power, *Statistical Digest* 1963, p. 99.
(The 1938 figures are not strictly comparable to later figures as
additional employees were included for 1948 onwards.) 1970,
1980, industry data.

Col. 2 1938–63, C. H. Feinstein, *National Income Expenditure
and Output of the United Kingdom*, 1855–1965 (Cambridge
1972) pp. 192–3. 1970, 1980 Central Statistical Office, *National
Income and Expenditure*.

Col. 3 1938–63, calculated from data in Feinstein, loc. cit. 1970,
1980, calculated from data in CSO, loc. cit.

Col. 4 1938–63, calculated from Ministry of Power, *Statistical
Digest 1963*, p. 17. 1970, Department of Trade and Industry,
Digest of Energy Statistics 1971, pp. 12, 112. 1980, Department
of Energy, *Digest of UK Energy Statistics 1981*, pp. 16, 100.

TABLE A.4 *Electricity prices in real terms, 1938–80*

Financial year beginning April	Average revenue per kWh sold in England and Wales to	
	domestic consumers (1975 retail prices, p)	industrial consumers (1975 wholesale prices, p)
1938	4.8	2.0
1948	2.4	1.4
1949	2.4	1.3
1950	2.3	1.1
1951	2.1	1.0
1952	2.1	1.3
1953	2.1	1.5
1954	2.1	1.4
1955	2.0	1.4
1956	1.9	1.5
1957	2.0	1.6
1958	2.0	1.7
1959	1.9	1.6
1960	1.8	1.6
1961	1.8	1.7
1962	1.8	1.7
1963	1.8	1.7
1970	1.6	1.6
1980	2.1	1.4

SOURCES 1938, author's calculations, from Electricity Commissioners' data. Cf. p. 300, note 3, below.
1948–80, calculated by Electricity Council Commercial Department. The original revenue data were corrected to 1975 retail prices (for domestic consumers) and to 1975 wholesale prices (for industrial consumers).

NOTES AND REFERENCES

These notes refer to the published sources on which the text draws. Unless otherwise stated the place of publication is London.

No references are given in this volume to unpublished sources in the files of government departments, nor to documents in the possession of the various Electricity Boards or the Electricity Council. Some of the early records of government departments concerned have been destroyed in whole or in part: most of the remainder are now being transferred to the Public Record Office under the 'thirty-year rule'. (However, their reference numbers now differ from those which they carried at the time the research for this book was conducted.) The majority of the files consulted, from a later date, will not be available in the Public Record Office for some years, and will again have different reference numbers from those at present known.

The Electricity Council and the Electricity Boards are not subject to the Public Records Acts and their archives remain closed to the general public. However, they have indicated they will consider requests from bona fide scholars for access to documents after thirty years have elapsed from the events to which the documents relate.

A supplementary key to the title and reference number of documents relevant to the narrative and analysis in the industry's own files and in the government department files has been prepared, and will be made available to interested scholars from 1 January 1993.

CHAPTER 1   INTRODUCTION: ELECTRICITY BEFORE NATIONALISATION

1. This chapter is based on the author's *Electricity before Nationalisation: A Study of the Development of Electricity Supply in Britain to 1948* (London and Baltimore, 1979).
2. Assets acquired at vesting from the British Electricity Authority, *Annual Report and Accounts for the year ending 31 March 1949*, statement A16. The new investment plans are as reported to the Organising Committee in May 1947 and included £250 millions for generation (an under-estimate) and £400 millions for distribution over the next five years.
3. The transport companies nationalised under the British Transport Commission were larger in terms of acquired assets, but had less ambitious new investment plans. Large corporations in manufacturing industry were

significantly smaller – for example, at the end of 1948 the stock market value of Imperial Tobacco was £258 millions and of ICI £198 millions (calculated from data in *Stock Exchange Year Book 1948* and *Stock Exchange Daily Official Intelligence*, 30 December 1948).

4. Calculated from data from 1948–62 on electricity investment and gross domestic capital formation in the UK, in C. H. Feinstein, *National Income, Expenditure and Output of the United Kingdom, 1855–1965* (Cambridge, 1972) pp. T92–3. The exclusion of Northern Ireland (whose electricity supply system is smaller, and more closely linked electrically with that of the Republic of Ireland than with Great Britain) would make little difference to the figures.

5. The average in the 1930s was 7 per cent (Hannah, op. cit, p. 212). If allowance is made for related investment in the electrical manufacturing industry, in transport and industrial electrification, and in domestic wiring and consumer durables manufacture, the proportion of investment resources devoted to electrification is very much higher in all periods.

CHAPTER 2 CITRINE'S WAY

1. The nationalisation legislation is exhaustively treated in Sir Norman Chester, *The Nationalisation of British Industry 1945–1951* (1975).
2. E. Shinwell, *I've Lived Through it All* (1973) p. 192.
3. R. Kelf-Cohen, *Nationalisation in Britain: The End of a Dogma* (1958). These remarks perhaps owe more to their sense of awe at the size of the administrative task which had been decided on for political reasons than to a rational assessment of desirable policy options.
4. L. Hannah, *Electricity before Nationalisation: A Study of the Development of Electricity Supply in Britain to 1948* (London and Baltimore, 1979) pp. 336–47.
5. *The Structure of the Electricity Supply Industry in England and Wales: Report of the (Plowden) Committee of Enquiry*, Cmd. 6388, 1976.
6. Lord Citrine, *Two Careers* (1967) pp. 252–7.
7. One member of the Organising Committee, Johnstone Wright (chairman of the Central Electricity Board), was near retirement and did not join the Central Authority. The other five were Self, Eccles, Bussey, Hacking and Woodward.
8. Among those who left were Harry Towers and Wade Hayes of the large Edmundsons group, and a number of senior men from the London companies.
9. See Citrine's reminiscences in *Proceedings of the British Electrical Power Convention 1958*, p. 395; *H L Deb.*, vol. 150, col. 191, 8 July 1947.
10. Chester, op. cit., p. 518.
11. E.g. Randall and King among the Area Board chairmen were paid an extra £1000 p.a. to reflect their higher pre-vesting salaries; Coates (the Central Authority's accountant) and Wilkinson (their commercial manager) received respectively £2500 p.a. and £1000 p.a. extra.
12. 1946 speech (text in Electricity Council Library).

13. Citrine, *Two Careers*, p. 348.
14. Ibid., p. 257.
15. In accordance with a long-standing agreement within the Labour movement, see Hannah, op. cit., p. 332.
16. Ibid., p. 344.
17. See generally R. Messenger, *The Doors of Opportunity: A Biography of Dame Caroline Haslett* (1967).
18. Chester, op. cit., p. 421; and papers in Public Record Office, Kew, class. POWE 38/59.
19. Lord Citrine, 'Problems of Nationalised Industries', Sydney Ball Lecture, reprinted in *Public Administration*, vol. 29, 1951.
20. Speech at Torquay, June 1949, in *British Electricity Conference Report*, 1949, p. 25.
21. Chester, op. cit., pp. 407–13.
22. *H C Deb.*, vol. 432, cols 1410–11, 3 February 1947.
23. Lord Citrine's address to the Electrical Research Association, 1948, quoted approvingly in C. O. Boyse, 'Developments in Electricity Supply, *Proceedings of the Institution of Electrical Engineers*, vol. 96, part 2, 1949, p. 5.
24. See pp. 123 ff.

CHAPTER 3   MEETING THE CAPACITY CRISIS

1. For the fuel and capacity crises and their origins, see L. Hannah, *Electricity Before Nationalisation: A Study of the Development of Electricity Supply in Britain to 1948* (London and Baltimore, 1979) ch. 9.
2. Hannah, op. cit., pp. 322–3.
3. Control of Turbo-Alternators no. 1 Order, SR&O no. 2386, Ministry of Supply, 7 November 1947.
4. A less flattering picture is given by Lord Hinton in his *Heavy Current Electricity in the United Kingdom*, 1979. It should be borne in mind, however, that Hinton's atom bomb project – admittedly more rapidly and successfully executed – in practice had higher priorities in steel allocations, and was, indeed, itself one of the causes of the over-stretching of the supply capabilities of the economy, and hence of BEA difficulties. This is not to deny that more vigorous management could have raised the BEA's achievement.

CHAPTER 4   HALF-PRICE ELECTRICITY?

1. Estimate by Sir Stafford Cripps, President of the Board of Trade, in *The Times*, 5 May 1947, p. 8.
2. Early 1950s estimates in Sir Henry Self, presidential address, *Proceedings of the British Electrical Power Convention 1951*, p. 18. The price of

coal was kept well below the world price (and marginal cost) by rationing and other controls. Thus Self's estimate undoubtedly understates the true resource cost.

3. For the constancy of real incomes in 1938 and 1948 see e.g. C. H. Feinstein, *National Income, Expenditure and Output of the United Kingdom 1855–1965* (Cambridge, 1972) pp. T42–3. Average sales of electricity per domestic consumer were 617kWh in 1938 and 1247kWh in 1948. Data on domestic prices alone are not available for 1938 but can be estimated on the assumption that they bore the same relationship to 'lighting, heating and cooking' prices (which includes some commercial and industrial sales) as in 1948. On this assumption, and at constant 1975 price levels, the average domestic price fell from 4.8p to 2.4p between 1938 and 1948.

4. Some of the problems are discussed by Sir Norman Chester, *The Nationalisation of British Industry 1945–1951* (1975) chs 3 and 4, and H. Gaitskell, *H C Deb.*, vol. 447, col. 232, 10 February 1948.

5. *Incorporated Municipal Electrical Association Journal*, June 1948, p. 112.

6. *Evening Standard*, 1 April 1948.

7. See e.g. M. V. Posner, *Fuel Policy: A Study in Applied Economics* (1973). Long-run experience suggests that the trend of electricity costs is downwards, and, in the absence of general inflation or fuel price rises, it would be proper for the industry to reflect this in current pricing, an argument later used by the industry (see p. 203). However the main source of such long-run cost reductions was deliberately forgone until later in the 1950s: see pp. 104–10 on the rejection of potential economies through larger scale in favour of speed and reliability in overcoming the capacity crisis.

8. E.g. in the financial year 1938/9, 52 per cent of total book costs in electricity supply arose from capital charges (interest and depreciation); by 1947/8 only 27 per cent. But this was largely an artefact of the accounting rules which took no account of inflation: there had been no fundamental change in the ratio of capital to labour and materials in the production process.

9. For a summary of the contemporary debate, see N. Ruggles, 'Recent Developments in the theory of Marginal Cost Pricing', in *Review of Economic Studies*, vol. 17, 1949–50, reprinted in R. Turvey (ed.) *Public Enterprise* (Harmondsworth, 1968). Three economists on the government-appointed Simon Committee's expert panel had, however, given sensible advice in favour of marginal cost pricing in 1946, see L. Hannah, *Electricity Before Nationalisation: A Study of the Development of Electricity Supply in Britain to 1948* (London and Baltimore, 1979) pp. 327–8. Some senior government economic advisers also espoused the case for marginal cost pricing.

10. H. Dalton, *Principles of Public Finance*, 4th edn (1954) pp. 132–3; C. A. R. Crosland, 'Prices and Costs in Nationalised Undertakings', *Oxford Economic Papers*, new series, vol. 2, 1950.

11. Though later they were held to be consistent e.g. with the charging of replacement rather than historic cost depreciation and rates of return in excess of interest charges, cf. pp. 54–5 and pp. 204–6.

12. Electricity Act, 1947, section 36 (1).
13. *The Economist*, 1 November 1947, pp. 731–2. The article was ghosted by Paul Schiller, one of the supply industry's costing experts, whose crisp thinking was largely ignored by senior managers in the industry, cf. pp. 86–8.
14. Shortly afterwards published as *Report of the (Clow) Committee to Study the Peak Load Problem in Relation to Non-Industrial Consumers*, Cmd. 7464, July 1948.
15. This stress on the short-term efficacy of price changes was probably the committee's major error. Subsequent experience suggests considerable lags in the effect of electricity price changes, because of learning effects on consumers and the embodiment of electricity consumption decisions in related appliances, the stock of which changes relatively slowly, and in response to many other factors.
16. Partially quoted in P. Williams, *Hugh Gaitskell, A Political Biography* (1979) p. 175. A fuller version of the diary is to be published.
17. *H C Deb.*, vol. 467, col. 7, 11 July 1949.

CHAPTER 5   MINISTERS AND MANDARINS

1. *H C Deb.*, Standing Committee E, Official Report, Electricity Bill, 13 March 1947, col. 243.
2. Lord Citrine, *Two Careers* (1967) p. 348.
3. See e.g. the quotation from Jay at the head of the chapter (p. 41, above), and C. A. R. Crosland, *The Future of Socialism*, 1964 edition, pp. 316–8.
4. Citrine, op. cit., pp. 297, 354, 356.
5. Sir Norman Chester, *The Nationalisation of British Industry 1945–1951* (1975) p. 997.
6. P. Williams, *Hugh Gaitskell, A Political Biography* (1979) p. 145.
7. E.g. H. J. Farquhar (at officer level) and O. Francis (at board level). Others were invited but refused.
8. Williams, op. cit., p. 179.
9. J. Cross, 'The Lynskey Tribunal', in M. Sissons and P. French (eds) *The Age of Austerity 1945–51* (1963).
10. Chester, op. cit., pp. 949–1001.
11. Acton Society Trust, *Accountability to Parliament* (1950).
12. The 1954/5 total at 1948 prices would be £156 millions (the deflator used is the index of the purchasing power of the pound in Department of Employment, *British Labour Statistics: Historical Abstract 1886–1968*, (1971) p. 193).
13. E.g. Sir Henry Self, 'The Economics of Electricity Supply' in *Proceedings of the British Electrical Power Convention 1950*, pp. 20–1.
14. E.g. Citrine, op. cit., p. 298. Attempts to secure lower interest rates were often less successful than the example recounted there. In 1952, for example, when the clearing banks offered a borrowing rate of bank rate or 3 per cent (whichever was the higher), Self threatened to take BEA

business elsewhere. He was bluntly told to do so as they were already excessively generous terms dictated by the bankers' desire to placate the Treasury!

15. Williams, op. cit., p. 241; H. Dalton, *Principles of Public Finance*, 4th edn (1954) pp. 234–7; C. M. Kennedy, 'Monetary Policy', in G. D. N. Worswick and P. H. Ady, *The British Economy 1945–1950* (Oxford, 1952) pp. 198–205.

16. W. A. Lewis in W. A. Robson, *Problems of Nationalised Industry* (1951) p. 183; Crosland, op. cit., p. 318. See also p. 108 for distortions introduced into the choice of technique in generation. J. C. R. Dow, *The Management of the British Economy, 1945–60* (Cambridge, 1964) pp. 290–1, 314–21, 326–8, 409, plays down the misallocation due to low interest rates. His case may be valid in relation to aggregate investment (because of physical controls and other determinants of aggregate investment), but it surely understates the important distortions introduced at the level of the choice of technique.

17. E.g. Herbert Morrison in *H C Deb.*, vol. 568, col. 601, 4 April 1957.

18. See e.g. W. Eltis, 'The True Deficit of the Public Corporations', *Lloyds Bank Review*, no. 131, January 1979, for a recent restatement of the traditional 'crowding-out' argument; I. M. D. Little, *A Critique of Welfare Economics*, 2nd edn (1957) p. 215, for a contemporary statement. See also the references in n. 16 above.

19. These are summarised in *Report of the [Herbert] Committee of Inquiry into the Electricity Supply Industry*, Cmd. 9672, 1956, pp. 50–54, 87–9.

20. In their discussions in the late 1940s the Central Authority had been envisaging self-financing ratios as low as 30 per cent.

21. L. Hannah, *Electricity before Nationalisation: A Study of the Development of Electricity Supply in Britain to 1948* (London & Baltimore, 1979) p. 214 suggests a self-financing ratio of 48 per cent in the comparable interwar decades. Although there are problems of ensuring comparability, self-financing ratios in American electric utilities generally appear to be nearer 30 per cent than the level achieved in Britain. See e.g. *Electrical World*, 24 January 1955, p. 148; US Department of Commerce, Bureau of the Census, *Historical Statistics of the United States, Colonial Times to 1970* (Washington, 1975) p. 289.

22. R. C. O. Matthews, 'Full employment since the War: Reply', *Economic Journal*, vol. 80, 1970, p. 174.

23. For tabulations of overspending on a year-to-year basis see R. W. Bates, 'Stabilisation Policy and Investment 1950–60, with Special Reference to Electricity Supply', *Yorkshire Bulletin of Economic and Social Research*, vol. 18, 1966; *Report from the Select Committee on Nationalised Industries: The Electricity Supply Industry* (1963) vol. 3, pp. 182–3. For a somewhat more optimistic view of the contracyclical investment tendencies of the nationalised industries see A. Silberston, 'Nationalised Industries, Government Intervention and Industrial Efficiency', in D. Butler and A. H. Halsey (eds) *Policy and Politics: Essays in Honour of Norman Chester* (1978).

24. Calculated from C. H. Feinstein, *National Income, Expenditure and Output of the United Kingdom 1855–1965* (Cambridge, 1972) pp. T92–3.

25. The *locus classicus* is I. M. D. Little, *The Price of Fuel* (Oxford, 1953)

see e.g. p. 155.

26. E.g. J. Wright, *Britain in the Age of Economic Management* (Oxford, 1979) pp. 35, 48.
27. See e.g. *Proceedings of the British Electrical Power Convention 1951*, pp. 19–20; ibid. *1953*, pp. 111, 246. See also J. J. Carré, P. Dubois, and E. Malinvaud, *French Economic Growth* (1976) pp. 562–3.
28. Other things were not, of course, equal. Supply and demand conditions differed in each country and there is no reason in principle why a level of investment that is optimal in one country should be so in another. Yet it is as easy to think of powerful *a priori* considerations which would lead one to expect higher rather than lower levels in Britain.
29. There is, of course, a substantial literature abroad, arguing that electric utility investment there was also too high. M. Boiteux, the economist at the head of Electricité de France, believed that inherited French prices were too low, creating too high a demand for investment resources. In the USA, Averch and Johnson have argued that the method of regulation leads electric utilities to select excessively capital-intensive technologies, see e.g. W. Baumol and A. Klevorick, 'Input Choices and Rate of Return Regulation: An Overview of the Discussion', *The Bell Journal of Economics and Management Science*, vol. 1, 1970.
30. E.g. Wright, op. cit., p. 35, asserts that the greater part of the increase in sales went to heating uses, though even the most pessimistic supply industry estimates suggest this is wrong.
31. The general point on the relative importance of allocative efficiency as against technical efficiency is usefully made in this context in R. Pryke, *Public Enterprise in Practice* (1971) pp. 408–12. Another reasonable point, made at the time by the industry, was that the peak was actually met by obsolete plant (which would otherwise have been scrapped) not by new investment, which was worthwhile only for loads of longer duration.
32. See e.g. Chester, op. cit., pp. 982, 985
33. There had been a long, and somewhat exaggerated tradition in the industry prior to nationalisation of blaming all its troubles on 'politics', see Hannah, op. cit., *passim*.

CHAPTER 6   SYSTEM EXPANSION: THE AREA BOARDS

1. Electricity Act, 1947, section 1.
2. Sir Henry Self, *Problems of Decentralisation in a Large-Scale Undertaking* (British Institute of Management, 1951) p. 42; D. J. Bolton, 'Measuring Area Board Performance', *Electrical Review*, 17 August 1956.
3. For contemporary views see e.g. Acton Society Trust, *Nationalised Industry; Relations with the Public*, 1953; *Proceedings of the British Electrical Power Convention 1952*, pp. 435–8. Cf. p. 74 for an example of their impact on rural electrification.
4. L. Hannah, *Electricity Before Nationalisation: A Study of the Develop-*

ment of Electricity Supply in Britain to 1948 (London and Baltimore, 1979) pp. 234–56.

5. C. E. Knight, *An Area Board Accountant's Contribution to Management* (British Electricity Authority, 1954) pp. 54–5.

6. D. P. Sayers, 'Twenty Years of Electricity Distribution under Public Control', *Proceedings of the Institution of Electrical Engineers*, vol. 116, 1969; D. B. Irving, 'The Supply of Electricity in the London Area', ibid. vol. 102, 1955; A. G. Milne and J. H. Maltby, 'An Integrated System of Metropolitan Electricity Supply', ibid., vol. 114, 1967; J. Fisher, 'MANWEB Distribution 1950–2000', ibid. vol. 124, 1977; G. F. Peirson and J. Henderson, 'The Postwar Development of the Distribution of Electricity', *Proceedings of the British Electrical Power Convention 1967*.

7. E.g. Lord Citrine, *Two Careers* (1967) p. 296.

8. L. Needleman, 'The Demand for Electrical Applicances', *National Institute Economic Review*, no. 12, November 1960, p. 40.

9. G. D. N. Worswick, 'The British Economy 1950–1959' p. 25, in Worswick and Ady, *The British Economy in the Nineteen Fifties* (Oxford, 1962).

10. D. Bellamy, 'The Development of the Domestic Electricity Load at Home and Overseas', *Proceedings of the British Electrical Power Convention 1954*, p. 261.

11. Electricity Act, 1947, section 60.

12. J. Jewkes, *Ordeal by Planning*, 1948, p. 112, n. 3. The allegation was in any case falsely drawn because slum-dwellers, generally having a low consumption, were usually themselves subsidised.

CHAPTER 7   COMMERCIAL DEVELOPMENT: PRICING FOR GROWTH

1. E.g. N. F. Marsh, 'The Case For Simple Hire', *Electrical Times*, 9 April 1953, p. 665; C. E. Knight, *An Area Board Accountant's Contribution to Management* (British Electricity Authority, 1954) p. 91ff.

2. The agreement lasted until 1962, when the Gas Council, worried by increasingly successful electricity competition, restarted cooker hire schemes.

3. Estimate by Charles Baden-Fuller, London Business School, based on UK Census of Distribution.

4. For a survey of changing standards see e.g. E. J. Davies, 'The Economics of a Well-Wired House', *Proceedings of the British Electrical Power Convention 1959*.

5. E.g. Sir John Hacking in *Proceedings of the British Electrical Power Convention 1953*, p. 492; D. Bellamy in ibid., *1956*, p. 571.

6. C. T. Melling, 'General Factors affecting the Unification of Electricity Supply Tariffs', *Journal of the Institution of Electrical Engineers*, vol. 90, part 1, 1943; L. Hannah, *Electricity Before Nationalisation: A Study of the Development of Electricity Supply in Britain to 1948* (London and Baltimore, 1979) ch. 6.

7. There was also a contemporary concern (quite understandable in view of

acute physical shortages of coal) with simple *fuel* efficiency, rather than with overall economic efficiency (which remained the long-run problem and is given prominence in the text). For a review of the issues see e.g. P. Schiller, 'Comparison between Gas and Electricity on the Basis of Coal Economy', *Journal of the Institution of Electrical Engineers*, vol. 94 part 1, 1947.

8. *Report of the Committee on National Policy for the Use of Fuel and Power Resources* Cmd. 8647, 1952.

9. E.g. *Proceedings of the British Electrical Power Convention 1952*, pp. 21–82, 432–3. They did, however, repudiate some untruths perpetrated, to their embarrassment, in a pamphlet, *Facts about Fuel*, by the Electrical Development Association, which was then staffed by electrical enthusiasts of the more messianic persuasion.

10. Little, *The Price of Fuel*, p. 64. Although this was one of the most impressive pieces of applied economics published in the postwar period, it made significant errors both of fact and of forecasting.

11. See e.g. D. Bellamy, 'The Development of the Domestic Load at Home and Overseas', *Proceedings of the British Electrical Power Convention 1954*. An unpublished paper by P. Schiller, 'The Story of a Myth' (deposited in the Electricity Council Library) exposes the bias in this study.

12. For an account of the problems and the solutions adopted, see A. O. Johnson and N. F. Marsh, 'The Standardisation of Retail Electricity Tariffs', *Proceedings of the Institution of Electrical Engineers*, vol. 102, part A, 1955.

13. E.g. he drafted various articles in *The Economist*.

14. R. Y. Sanders, the Central Authority commercial manager in charge of retail tariffs coordination, in a lecture to the Electricity Supply Summer School, Balliol College, Oxford, 1958 (typescript in Electricity Council Library).

15. For an account of the changes see R. L. Meek, 'The Bulk Supply Tariff for Electricity', *Oxford Economic Papers*, new series, vol. 15, 1963.

16. The many studies are summarised in Department of Energy, *Report of the Working Group on Energy Elasticities*, Energy Paper no. 17, 1977.

17. The *measured* load factor remained constant around 48 per cent. The *underlying* load factor (which is corrected to average temperature conditions and for demand which was not met because of power cuts and voltage and frequency reductions) is quoted in the text as a better measure of commercial trends. For an alternative measure of load factor, cf. Statistical Appendix, Table A.1.

18. Schiller's research showed that the number of rooms was the best proxy for maximum demand. The Central Authority accepted this as the desirable norm, and six Boards standardised on it. Other Boards preferred to standardise on the dominant practice in their area (the arguments in favour of one or the other were not foolproof): six adopted floor area and two rateable value (i.e. local property tax assessment). The problem was probably in part inherited: local political pressure had already led to a small subsidy to domestic consumers in the interwar years, see Hannah, op. cit., pp. 199–203.

19. A time-of-day tariff, reflecting the costs imposed at the system peak

(rather than the consumer's own peak) would have been conceptually more appropriate. Probably 'charging what the traffic would bear' played a part in the choice: the maximum demand tariff reflected the costs to a large consumer of carrying out his own generation (more accurately than it reflected the cost to the Boards), and was thus a useful competitive weapon.

20. 'Undue discrimination' between consumers was prohibited by the 1947 Electricity Act, and lip-service was sometimes paid to this principle, but it was arguably a dead letter, given the difficulty of proving its existence and the uncertainty about its application.

21. Though proposals within the industry on an equitable solution seem fair, see e.g. A. O. Johnson and L. P. Holder, 'Electricity Supplies for Industry', *Proceedings of the British Electrical Power Convention 1953*, pp. 139–40.

22. E. R. Wilkinson, 'Electricity and Industrial Production', *Proceedings of the British Electrical Power Convention 1953*, p. 102.

CHAPTER 8   GENERATION: CENTRALISATION AND CONSERVATISM (1948–53)

1. For a fuller account of Grid procedures, see A. R. Cooper, 'Load Dispatching and the Reasons for it on the British Grid System', *Journal of the Institution of Electrical Engineers*, vol. 95, part 2, 1948.

2. See e.g. V. F. Bartlett, 'Power Station Design and Construction', *Proceedings of the Joint (Institutions of Electrical, Civil and Mechanical Engineers) Engineering Conference, 1951*; *Report on the British Electricity System by a Productivity Team from the US Electric Utility Industry*, 1953. Some BEA engineers who visited the USA and Germany were impressed by the better scheduling, extra resources devoted to design, and personal responsibility for speed and economy in the smaller electric utilities common there.

3. Calder Hall (Cumbria), the first civil nuclear power station, was built by the AEA in the mid 1950s in little more than three years; Chapelcross (Scotland), virtually a repeat design, was built by the AEA and consultants in the later 1950s in three years and four months. In the first case this was partly due to higher priorities, but the AEA engineer responsible for Calder Hall has condemned most BEA project teams as being 'beaten before they started', see Lord Hinton of Bankside, *Heavy Current Electricity in the United Kingdom* (1979) p. 76. The fastest power station construction time ever achieved by the nationalised industry was the Rogerstone (Gwent) station. The first 60MW set was commissioned in September 1957 after three years' work on the site; the second 60MW set came three months later.

4. For a review of some of the problems, see *Report of the* [Beaver] *Committee of Enquiry into Economy in the Construction of Power Stations*, 1953.

5. See e.g. *Report of the* [Wilson] *Committee of Enquiry into Delays in the*

Commissioning of CEGB Power Stations, Cmd. 3960, 1969; National Economic Development Council, *Report of the Working Party on Large Industrial Construction Sites*, 1970; for contemporary exceptions see British Institute of Management, *Construction of Esso Refinery, Fawley*, 1954; P. L. Payne, *Colvilles and the Scottish Steel Industry* (Oxford, 1979) p. 347.

6. The proportion of plant in service over 25 years old rose from 13 per cent in 1948/9 to 19 per cent ten years later. In the first ten years of nationalisation, some 86 small stations with an aggregate capacity of 828MW (the equivalent of only three new stations) were closed down.

7. L. Hannah, *Electricity before Nationalisation: A Study of the Development of Electricity Supply in Britain to 1948* (London and Baltimore, 1979) ch. 4.

8. T. G. N. Haldane, 'High Voltage Transmission in Great Britain', *Proceedings of the British Electrical Power Convention 1949*. See also his presidential address in *Proceedings of the Institution of Electrical Engineers*, vol. 96, part 1, 1949.

9. Lord Citrine, *Two Careers* (1967) p. 279. See also D. P. Sayers, J. S. Forrest and F. J. Lane, '275kV Developments on the British Grid System', *Proceedings of the Institution of Electrical Engineers*, vol. 99, part 2, 1952.

10. *The Economist*, 24 October 1953, pp. 263–5.

11. This move away from urban areas effectively ruled out any further combined electricity generation and district heating schemes such as that based on London's Battersea power station. The BEA were under some Whitehall pressure to develop such schemes, but their experience with Battersea and other appraisals suggested that, given the short domestic heating season in Britain and the high capital costs, the schemes were not economic.

12. In later years, some manufacturers, who had at the time begged the BEA not to advance too rapidly, accused them retrospectively of being excessively conservative.

13. B. Donkin and P. H. Margen, 'Economic Plant Sizes and Boiler Set Groupings on the British Grid', *Proceedings of the Institution of Electrical Engineers*, vol. 99, part 2, 1952; *Proceedings of the British Electrical Power Convention 1952*, p. 434.

14. At current prices, the costs per kW of power stations completed rose until 1952 and then declined. At constant prices the cost of power stations consistently fell. The cost per kW of stations completed in the early BEA years (at constant 1958 prices) was £83–£90; by 1956/7 it was down to £54–£63, see C. Harlow, 'Power Station Performance: Policies for Development', in Political and Economic Planning (eds) *Innovation and Productivity under Nationalisation* (1977). These figures are based on later CEGB adjustments to the data; contemporary internal BEA data suggests an even more rapid rate of real cost reduction.

15. F. P. R. Brechling and A. J. Surrey, 'An International Comparison of Production Techniques: The Coal-Fired Electricity Generating Industry', *National Institute Economic Review*, no. 36, May 1966. France's more rapid increase in average thermal efficiency was not only due to a more adventurous design policy, but partly also reflected her large (but

limited) hydro-electric base, which meant that, for any given rate of growth, a higher proportion of the total steam plant on the French system would be of more modern design than in Britain. Similarly the high American thermal efficiencies were partly due to the minimal wartime distortions there.

CHAPTER 9   GENERATION: THE BROWN REVOLUTION (1954–7)

1. For an outline of Brown's philosophy see F. H. S. Brown and E. S. Booth, 'Coal and Oil Fired Power Stations', *Proceedings of the British Electrical Power Convention 1957*.
2. As Figure 9.1 shows, these savings were subsequently reckoned to be larger, around 8 per cent.
3. C. Harlow, 'Power Station Performance: Policies for Development', in Political and Economic Planning (eds) *Innovation and Productivity under Nationalisation* (1967) p. 62. These figures (based on maximum output of power) are not directly comparable with those in Figure 9.1 (based on kW installed), but cf. n. 4 below.
4. E.g. only part of the contrast between the costs expected for 100MW, 120MW and 200MW sets shown in Table 9.1 and the actual costs in years like 1961 when they were commissioned (Harlow, op. cit., p. 62) is accounted for by cost reductions; some of it probably reflects the increased competitive pressure on manufacturers' margins.
5. For a critique of the capacity of competition in such markets to achieve efficient dynamic adjustment, see G. B. Richardson, *The Future of the Heavy Electrical Industry*, BEAMA, 1969.
6. Lord Citrine, *Two Careers* (1967) pp. 351–2.
7. Monopolies and Restrictive Practices Commission, *Report on the Supply and Exports of Electrical and Allied Machinery and Plant*, HCP 42, 1957.
8. For an account of supply industry research see e.g. J. S. Forrest, 'Research in the Electricity Supply Industry', *Proceedings of the British Electrical Power Convention 1952*; J. S. Forrest, 'Research Investigations of the CEA', *Nature*, vol. 175, 21 May 1955.

CHAPTER 10   LABOUR MANAGEMENT UNDER PUBLIC OWNERSHIP

1. For a fuller account of the consultative machinery, see R. D. V. Roberts and H. Sallis, 'Joint Consultation in the Electricity Supply Industry 1949–1959', *Public Administration*, vol. 37, 1959.
2. Speech at TUC Conference, September 1950, Brighton, reprinted in Lord Citrine, *Nationalised Industries Face the Test* (1950) p. 11.
3. M. Shanks (ed.) *Lessons of Public Enterprise* (1963) p. 117.
4. The staff differential relative to manual operatives (calculated on the

Standard Industrial Classification definition of the electricity supply industry, including Northern Ireland and some transport sector power stations), was 26 per cent in 1948, fell to 22 per cent in 1956 and rose sharply to 29 per cent in 1957 (calculated from data in Business Statistics Office, *Historical Record of the Census of Production 1907–1970* (1978) p. 241).

5. For the TUC view see Sir Norman Chester, *The Nationalisation of British Industry 1945–1951* (1975) p. 850.
6. Among those who left headquarters for more lucrative private sector jobs were Verity and Wilkinson; Area Board chairmen to leave included Steward and Randall. All of these resignations were in the mid-1950s, when the private sector salary differential for Board members and chief officers had grown particularly marked. The flow in the reverse direction was smaller, e.g. A. N. Irens came from the aircraft industry to succeed Steward as chairman of the South Western Board.
7. *Proceedings of the British Electrical Power Convention 1956*, p. 578.
8. P. Williams, *Hugh Gaitskell, A Political Biography* (1979) p. 172; Lord Citrine, *Two Careers* (1967) pp. 283–4; *The Times*, 13–17 December 1949, *passim*.
9. Presidential address, ETU policy conference, 5–9 May 1947.
10. For a comprehensive survey see H. Sallis, 'Pay and Conditions in Electricity Supply before the Status Agreement', *Electricity*, January/February 1968, on which the following paragraphs draw. Changes in earnings quoted in the text are based on Sallis's figures but adjusted to real terms by the retail price index.
11. *The Times*, 14 February 1956, p. 9.
12. The following account draws heavily on H. Sallis, 'Overtime in Electricity Supply in the Period 1954/64: its Incidence and Subsequent Control', M. Phil. thesis, London, 1971.
13. The value added (net output) per person employed in the UK electricity supply industry was £608 in 1935, or £1814 at 1957 prices (adjusted by the retail prices index). In 1957 the net output per person employed was £1709 at current prices (Business Statistics Office, op. cit., p. 79). Net output per person employed is a poor measure of productivity in a monopolistic industry which is charging depreciation according to historic cost accounting rules. The figures for 1948 would, for example, be artificially low. However, both in 1935 and 1957 there are grounds for suggesting that the aggregate electricity prices more closely approximated to long-run costs, and the broad indications given by the measure are thus more reliable for comparisons of those years. The industry and the unions usually quoted physical productivity measures (kWh sales per employee, men per MW of generating plant etc.), which showed a steady improvement over the first ten years of nationalisation. However, this basically reflects technical change, scale economies and new capital investment, and is not a sensible measure of labour productivity. The adjustments made by R. Pryke, *Public Enterprise in Practice* (1971) p. 112, which show a favourable rate of total factor productivity increase in the first ten years of nationalisation, are in the right direction, but fail to take into account the early underpricing problem which undervalues initial outputs and thus may exaggerate the rate of productivity gain,

which may, indeed, have been negative.
14. Pryke, op. cit., pp. 134–9. The difficulties of international comparison arise from factors such as the higher level of labour-intensive activities like retailing and contracting undertaken by the British Electricity Boards.
15. Lord Citrine, *Two Careers* (1967) p. 281.

CHAPTER 11   RETROSPECT: CITRINE, SELF AND THE
                        MANAGEMENT OF CHANGE

1. Lord Citrine, *Two Careers* (1967) p. 281.
2. See e.g. the views of the Herbert Committee on pp. 163–7.
3. L. Hannah, *The Rise of the Corporate Economy* (1979) ch. 4. On the weak profit performance of private sector mergers (which posed fewer managerial strains due to less rapid core growth) see G. Meeks, *Disappointing Marriage: A Study of the Gains from Merger* (Cambridge, 1977).
4. The British Transport Commission was divided into smaller units by the Conservatives in the early 1950s; the National Coal Board was criticised for inadequately positive central control of a decentralised structure by the Fleck Committee in 1955.
5. W. J. Reader, *Imperial Chemical Industries: A History*, vol. 2, *The First Quarter Century 1920–1952* (Oxford, 1975).
6. R. Kelf-Cohen, *Nationalisation in Britain: The End of a Dogma* (1958) p. 263; R. Pryke, *Public Enterprise in Practice* (1971) ch. 2 and 3.
7. On this theme, generally, see R. Currie, *Industrial Politics* (Oxford, 1979).
8. This was partly because of the greater level of aggregation in accounts than in the days of a large number of undertakings, but also because of the BEA's determination to manage information, e.g. by suppressing Schiller's work.
9. W. J. Reader, op. cit. McKinseys in the 1960s played a significant part in reforming the structure of both ICI and many other British industrial companies.
10. D. F. Channon, *The Strategy and Structure of British Enterprise* (1973); L. Hannah (ed.) *Management Strategy and Business Development: An Historical and Comparative Study* (1976). *A fortiori*, criticisms of local government and the civil service for similar lack of clear delegation of authority and strategic planning were made in the 1960s, see Ministry of Housing and Local Government, *Report of the* [Maud] *Committee on the Management of Local Government*, vol. 1, 1967; *The Civil Service. Report of the* [Fulton] *Committee*, Cmd. 3638, vol. 1, 1968.

CHAPTER 12   THE NORTH OF SCOTLAND HYDRO-
ELECTRIC BOARD (1943–60)

1. Scottish Office, *Report of the* [Cooper] *Committee on Hydro-Electric Development in Scotland*, Cmd. 6406, 1942.
2. Sir Norman Chester, *The Nationalisation of British Industry 1945–1951* (1975) pp. 431–3; see also correspondence and minutes in PRO POWE 38/27.
5. For their views see e.g. A. E. MacColl, 'Hydro-Electric Development in Scotland', *Transactions of the Institution of Engineers and Shipbuilders in Scotland*, 1946; A. A. Fulton, 'Civil Engineering Aspects of Hydro-Electric Development in Scotland', *Proceedings of the Institution of Civil Engineers* (1952): T. Lawrie, 'Highland Water Power: The Development of the North of Scotland Hydro-Electric Board', *Proceedings of the Institution of Electrical Engineers*, vol. 103, part A, 1956; C. L. C. Allan, 'Hydro-Electric Power Stations for Peak Loads', *Electrical Review*, 28 December 1956, pp. 1169–74.
4. *Select Committee on Nationalised Industries (Reports and Accounts) Minutes of Evidence, Appendices* (1957) p. 197.
5. Scottish Development Department, *Hydro-Electric Schemes* (1963) p. 20.
6. The proportion of electricity from hydro-electric sources in Scotland alone was, of course, higher, accounting for around a quarter by the mid-1950s.
7. See, generally, G. McCrone, *Scotland's Economic Progress 1951–60*, 1965.
8. Hydro-Electric Development (Scotland) Act, 1943, section 1 (3).
9. E.g. they insisted on the letter of the law, even when it was obvious that the legal prescription failed to take proper account of incremental costs of new competing steam generating stations.
10. In one sense the price was clearly too low, since, being based on historic costs, the bulk supply tariff was well below the incremental cost of new steam stations in the early 1950s, though, by the mid-1950s, it had risen to nearer that level. On the other hand longer delays in construction and the unpredictability of rainfall made hydro-electric supplies less reliable than supplies from steam stations. There were also difficult problems connected with the apportionment of the costs of transmission and bulk supply points. It is striking that at the time few of the right economic questions about the correct comparisons of alternative real resource costs were being asked, and indeed, economic appraisal remained a fundamental weakness of the North Board.

CHAPTER 13   DEVOLVING POWER

1. *H C Deb.*, vol. 520, col. 23, 3 November 1953.
2. Though in fact some BEA engineers had wanted to amalgamate the South West Scotland division with the South East division, which was recognised

as being too small, and this was part of the Scottish reorganisation proposal.
3. Electricity Reorganisation (Scotland) Act, 1954.
4. *H C Deb.*, vol. 523, cols 369–490, 3 February 1954.
5. *H C Deb.*, vol. 529, col. 2510, 9 July 1954.
6. Sir Norman Chester, *The Nationalisation of British Industry 1945–1951*, p. 973.
7. It was published the following month as *Report of the Committee of Inquiry into the Electricity Supply Industry*, Cmd. 9672, 1956.
8. Central Electricity Authority, *Comments on the Recommendations and Conclusions of the Committee of Inquiry into the Electricity Supply Industry*, 1956. The comments were printed but, at Ministerial request, not published. Copies were, however, deposited in the House of Commons library.

CHAPTER 14   COAL, OIL AND NUCLEAR ESCALATION

1. *Report of the* [Ridley] *Committee on National Policy for the Use of Fuel and Power Resources*, Cmd. 8647, 1952, pp. 9–12.
2. See e.g. Lord Citrine, *Two Careers* (1967) p. 302.
3. M. Gowing, *Independence and Deterrence: Britain and Atomic Energy 1945–1952*, 2 vols (1974).
4. E.g. Lord Citrine in *Proceedings of the British Electrical Power Convention 1949*, p. 20; Sir John Hacking, lecture at the Institute of Fuel, 24 April 1952.
5. *A Programme for Nuclear Power*, Cmd. 9389, 1955.
6. Text of Minister's speech for press conference, 15 February 1955.
7. For a defence of this choice see Gowing, op. cit., vol. 2, pp. 56–7, 161–2.
8. For a later, but characteristically enthusiastic response see e.g. Sir Claude Gibb, 'The Development of Nuclear Energy for Electricity Supply Overseas', *Proceedings of the British Electrical Power Convention 1958*.
9. G. D. N. Worswick, 'The British Economy 1950–1959' in Worswick and Ady (eds) *The British Economy in the Nineteen Fifties* (Oxford, 1962) pp. 39–41, 60.
10. H. Thomas, *The Suez Affair* (1970) p. 32.
11. *H C Deb.*, vol. 562, col. 1055, 17 December 1956.
12. H. Macmillan, *Tides of Fortune 1945–1955* (1969) pp. 395–7, 399; H. Macmillan, *Riding the Storm 1956–9* (1971) pp. 9, 188; A. Sampson, *Macmillan* (Harmondsworth, 1968) pp. 98, 129, 173.
13. *H L Deb.*, vol. 203, cols 184–6, 5 March 1957; *H C Deb.*, vol. 605, cols 184–6, 5 March 1957.
14. All at mid-1950s prices, as were the contemporary calculations. The *actual* expenditure over these ten years was even higher in money terms than envisaged by the Flett working party but this was due partly to inflation and partly to a higher level of *conventional* capacity ordering than envisaged at this time, *not* principally to the nuclear programme.

(On the subsequent cut-backs in actual investment to less than half the 1957 target for 1965 nuclear commissioning, see pp. 234–7.) The highest proportion of national investment ever achieved in these years by the UK electricity supply industry was 10–10.5 per cent in 1963–5. (C. H. Feinstein, *National Income, Expenditure and Output of the United Kingdom 1855–1965* (Cambridge, 1972) p. T93.)

CHAPTER 15 THE NEW MEN

1. Written in later life, see Lord Hinton of Bankside, *Heavy Current Electricity in the United Kingdom* (Oxford, 1979) p. 76.
2. These were later published as R. S. Edwards and H. Townsend (eds) *Business Enterprise* (1958) chs 19–22.
3. A Minister cannot bind his successor, but the hints given to Edwards were in the strongest form. The Minister's intention and the fact that the old CEA guard had been temporarily 'kicked upstairs' to the Council were an open secret, see e.g. *H L Deb.*, vol. 203, col. 920, 20 May 1957: *The Economist*, 10 August 1957, p. 486.
4. D. C. Coleman, *Courtaulds: An Economic and Social History*, vol. 3, *Crisis and Change 1940–65* (Oxford, 1980) p. 317.

CHAPTER 16 THE ELECTRICITY COUNCIL: FEDERALISM AND FINANCE

1. See e.g. C. Hinton, *Proceedings of the British Electrical Power Convention 1958*, p. 363.
2. For a fuller account of changes in the Bulk Supply Tariff, see R. L. Meek, 'The Bulk Supply Tariff for Electricity', *Oxford Economic Papers*, new series vol. 15, 1963 (which, however, speculates inaccurately on the Area Boards being the motivating force in changes).
3. E.g. some fixed overhead expenses were irrelevantly included in the (variable) capacity charges; arguably there should have been more variation in the seasonal and time-of-day charges.
4. *Report from the Select Committee on Nationalised Industries: The Electricity Supply Industry*, vol. 2, *Minutes of Evidence*, 1963, pp. 64–5, 181–6, 457–69.
5. R. S. Edwards, 'The Influence of the Nationalised Industries' *Public Administration*, vol. 39, 1961, p. 54. The industry did, however, use this as an argument for reducing the Boards' target rates of return in subsequent years, an economically similar, but politically less noticeable, solution.
6. See e.g. his evidence to the Commons Select Committee in *Report from the Select Committee on Nationalised Industries: The Electricity Supply Industry*, vol. 2, *Minutes of Evidence* (1963) pp. 52–88, 361–421, 437–77. Some of his colleagues felt he devoted too much time to this activity, and

was drawing the Council too close to Westminster and Whitehall.

7. Radcliffe Committee on the Working of the Monetary System, *Minutes of Evidence*, vol. 2, 1958, pp. 753–7.

8. R. S. Edwards, 'Objectives and Control in Nationalised Industries', *Journal of the Institution of Electrical Engineers*, vol. 9, 1963, p. 153. See also G. Turner, *Business in Britain* (1969) p. 177: R. S. Edwards, 'The Finance of Electricity Supply', *Lloyds Bank Review*, October 1960.

9. Central Electricity Generating Board, *Annual Report and Accounts 1958/9*, p. 79. The changes then and in the following year included reducing the book lives of assets and depreciating power stations from the start of construction rather than of operation.

10. E.g. the shorter lives were not used internally for economic appraisals.

11. Sir Roy Harrod, *Policy against Inflation* (1958) p. 238.

12. *Report of the* [Herbert] *Committee of Inquiry into the Electricity Supply Industry*, Cmd. 9672, 1956, p. 90.

13. For one contemporary view on the issue, see e.g. (Radcliffe) Committee on the Working of the Monetary System, *Report*, Cmd. 827, 1959, pp. 219–21.

14. Defined as the gross return, less depreciation, as a percentage of net assets. A net return of 8 per cent was equivalent to around 13 per cent gross return for electricity supply.

15. Cmd. 1336, 1961.

16. This is not to say that it was not economically woolly (as many economists pointed out), but as a political statement of a new direction in economic policy it was a considerable advance.

17. In 1963 the Select Committee on Nationalised Industries recommended that the target rate should be applied to each investment project. When the Electricity Council pointed out that this conflicted with their approval of continuing rural electrification (which was uneconomic), they were advised by the Minister to ignore the point. A test rate of discount for new projects was not explicitly prescribed until 1967.

18. CEGB evidence to the Committee in *Report from the Select Committee on Nationalised Industries: The Electricity Supply Industry*, vol. 3, *Appendices and Index*, 1963, p. 8. See also P. A. Lingard and G. England, 'The Electricity Supply System and Economic Growth', *Proceedings of the British Electrical Power Convention 1964*.

CHAPTER 17   AREA BOARDS: INDEPENDENCE, OVER-
                EXPANSION AND THE NEW RATIONALITY

1. The internal estimates of the increase in the space heating load had varied considerably, but there was agreement that it lay somewhere between a doubling and quadrupling. The mean of these is taken in the text. Cf. P. Schiller, 'The Select Committee and the Domestic Load', *Electrical Times*, vol. 144, 8 August 1963, p. 200.

2. R. S. Edwards and D. Clark, 'Planning for Expansion in Electricity

Supply', *Proceedings of the British Electrical Power Convention 1962*, pp. 161–3, 189.
3. The conclusions of the working party were outlined in P. A. Lingard, 'The Economics of the Domestic Space Heating Load', in E. M. Ackery (ed.) *Electricity and Space Heating* (1965).

CHAPTER 18   INCOMES AND PRODUCTIVITY: PLANNING FOR GROWTH?

1. This anonymous article was written by J. D. M. Bell, who was then employed at the National Coal Board, and subsequently moved to the Electricity Council. The tone is, of course, ironical.
2. In the UK electricity supply industry the net output per person employed rose from £1913 in 1958 (or £2116 in 1963 prices) to £2864 in 1963, a rise of 35 per cent in real terms (calculated from data in Business Statistics Office, *Historical Record of the Census of Production 1907–1970* (HMSO, 1970) p. 79). However, cf. ch. 10, n. 13 of this book. Some of the increase in measured productivity in 1958–62 was due to the higher rate of return being earned in the latter year, and not to a physical increase in total factor productivity.
3. For general accounts of the changing fashions and initiatives in economic management see S. Brittan, *The Treasury under the Tories, 1951–1964* (1964); J. C. R. Dow, *The Management of the British Economy 1945–60* (Cambridge, 1964).
4. E.g. A. Spoor, *White Collar Union. Sixty Years of NALGO* (1967) pp. 325–42.
5. K. G. J. C. Knowles and E. M. F. Thorne, 'Wage Rounds 1948–59', *Bulletin of the Oxford University Institute of Statistics*, vol. 23, 1961.
6. Three men at Council played an increasing role: C. T. Melling, D. G. Dodds and R. D. V. Roberts, the latter a Fabian appointee from Citrine's day who became a highly professional personnel manager. The CEGB's personnel management was increasingly influenced by Lord Geddes (the ex-trade unionist who was a part-time Board member) and was strengthened by the appointment of H. C. Spear from BOAC. The initiatives for the Scottish Boards were increasingly taken by A. Christianson.
7. See, generally C. H. Rolph, *All Those in Favour? The ETU Trial* (1962); O. Cannon and J. R. L. Anderson, *The Road from Wigan Pier* (1973).
8. Cannon and Anderson, op. cit., pp. 221-2.
9. *H C Deb.*, vol. 645, cols 222–3, 25 July 1961. The Electricity Council were informed of the freeze a week earlier.
10. *H C Deb.*, vol. 649, col 1146, 21 November 1961. A statement by the industry the day before that they had not breached the pay pause was understandably treated with some scepticism.
11. S. Brittan, *Steering the Economy* (1969) p. 164. A curious feature of the press and political criticism was that it pinned the responsibility on King, who had actually had little to do with the negotiations and tried to wash

his hands of them. Even *The Times*, which praised the industry's resistance to government pressure, incongruously directed its praise at King!

12. E.g. H. A. Clegg, *The System of Industrial Relations in Great Britain* (Oxford, 1972) p. 389.

13. For a fuller account, see R. S. Edwards and R. D. V. Roberts, *Status Productivity and Pay: A Major Experiment: A Study of the Electricity Supply Industry's Agreements and their Outcome 1961–1971*, 1971.

CHAPTER 19   HINTON: THE NUCLEAR RETREAT

1. The nuclear power programme has attracted a disproportionate amount of attention for an energy source which played a tiny part in Britain's overall energy economy, a reflection perhaps of the lurid attractions of failure, for few projects can display such a large gap between aspirations and achievements over the timescale of the 1950s and 1960s. Among the best published accounts, written respectively from economic, technical, and political viewpoints, are D. Burn, *Nuclear Power and the Energy Crisis* (1978); R. F. Pocock, *Nuclear Power* (Old Woking, 1977); R. Williams, *The Nuclear Power Decisions: British Policies, 1953–78* (1980).

2. E.g. F. H. S. Brown and J. Henderson, 'Progress on the First Nuclear Power Stations: Bradwell, Berkeley, Hinkley Point and Hunterston', *Proceedings of the British Electrical Power Convention 1959*.

3. The inquiries, which (unthinkably for today) were dominated by Atomic Energy Authority personnel, successfully underplayed the seriousness of the incident, while clearly expressing the underlying problems, see *Report of the Committee appointed by the Prime Minister to Examine the Organisation of Certain Parts of the UKAEA*, Cmd. 338, 1957; *Report of the Committee appointed by the Prime Minister to examine the Organisation for the Control of Health and Safety in the UKAEA*, Cmd. 342, 1958; *Final Report of the Committee appointed by the Prime Minister to make a technical evaluation of information relating to the design and operation of the Windscale piles and to review the factors involved in the controlled release of Wigner energy*, Cmd. 471, 1958.

4. The waste disposal problem was considered to be alleviated by the saleability of plutonium, but see e.g. Goodlet, in *Proceedings of the British Electrical Power Convention 1958*, pp. 65–6, for signs of concern. In May 1958 Hinton told the Minister that de-commissioned reactors would be left on site and new stations built round them to mask the original reactor. Cf. the views of Duckworth and Pilling in *Proceedings of the British Electrical Power Convention 1957*, p. 478.

5. E.g. H. Macmillan, *Riding the Storm 1956–9* (1971) pp. 535–6.

6. Sir Christopher Hinton, *The Future For Nuclear Power*, The Axel Ax:son Johnson Lecture, Royal Swedish Academy of Engineering Sciences, Stockholm, 15 March 1957.

7. See e.g. R. Maudling, *Memoirs*, 1978, p. 66 for a telling indication of

how weakly the grave messages about nuclear overcommitment pene-
trated Cabinet minds, though at the time Maudling on several occasions
appeared to be on the brink of understanding the Government's
mistakes.

8. *H C Deb.*, vol. 575, col. 53, 29 October 1957.
9. E.g. in *Capital Investment in the Coal Gas and Electricity Industries*,
Cmd. 13, 1957. The following year's statistics were based on more
reliable data.
10. E.g. R. Maudling in *H C Deb.*, vol. 598, col. 47, 27 January 1959.
11. E.g. C. Hinton, 'The Development of Nuclear Energy for Electricity
Supply in Great Britain', *Proceedings of the British Electrical Power
Convention 1958*.
12. E.g. *Fifth Report of the Select Committee on Estimates, United Kingdom
Atomic Energy Authority: Production Group and Development and
Engineering Group* (1959) pp. 384ff. for Hinton's evidence of 22 April
1959. This suggested that nuclear power would be 40 per cent more
expensive than coal in cheap coal areas, and 25–20 per cent more
elsewhere. The press were also now less optimistic, see e.g. 'Can Nuclear
Power Compete?', *The Economist*, 9 May 1959.
13. *H C Deb.*, vol. 595, cols 31–2, 10 November 1958. The agreed target was
in fact 4475MW for the CEGB and 275–320MW for the South Scotland
Board, with the rest coming from the AEA (which had not been included
in the 1957 programme totals). Hinton had pressed for the CEGB total
to be reduced to 4075MW.
14. Though as we have seen (p. 207) the nuclear programme was politically
determined and exempted from CEGB rate of return tests. Without that
exemption no nuclear power stations would have been ordered between
1958 and 1964.
15. *H C Deb.*, vol. 607, cols 848–9, 22 June 1959; *H L Deb.*, vol. 218, col.
65, 15 July 1959.
16. *The Nuclear Power Programme*, Cmd. 1083, 1960.
17. E.g. J. C. Duckworth and W. H. C. Pilling, 'Nuclear Energy in Great
Britain', *Proceedings of the British Electrical Power Convention 1957*, p.
456.
18. M. Gowing, *Independence and Deterrence: Britain and Atomic Energy
1945–1952* (1974) vol. 2, p. 298.
19. 'Nuclear Power', *Three Banks' Review*, no. 52, December 1961.
20. E.g. the AEA introduced a number of red herrings into the debate
(which for a time were accepted in Whitehall). Notable among these was
that inflation helped nuclear economics (an assertion true only in crude
accounting terms and not on any sensible analysis of resource costs). Cf.
pp. 274–5 for the same fallacious argument advanced in favour of
similarly capital-intensive hydro-electric power generation.
21. This estimate includes only CEGB costs, and excludes development
costs incurred by the Atomic Energy Authority but not recovered.

CHAPTER 20   THE CEGB IN PRACTICE

1. See e.g. Hinton's philosophy on the cooperation of administrators and engineers in *Proceedings of the British Electrical Power Convention 1958*, p. 370.
2. For an excellent, balanced but admiring character sketch of Hinton see M. Gowing, *Independence and Deterrence: Britain and Atomic Energy 1945–1952* (1974) pp. 7–21. Hinton's faults, described there, were arguably more of a handicap in the situation of taking on an existing team, rather than, as in his earlier Risley career, building one up from scratch.
3. R. Pryke, *Public Enterprise in Practice* (1971) p. 384.
4. Hinton, *Proceedings of the British Electrical Power Convention 1959*, p. 412.
5. For a general account see F. J. Lane and A. Chorlton, 'The 400kV System in England and Wales', *Proceedings of the American Power Conference*, vol. 28, 1966, pp. 897–914.
6. F. H. S. Brown and R. S. Edwards, 'The Replacement of Obsolescent Plant', *Economica*, vol. 28, 1961.
7. *H C Deb.*, vol. 562, col. 942, 17 December 1956.
8. E.g. among the complaints were that small coal bunkers were designed for low capital costs rather than for optimising power station labour costs, and that operating spaces were too constrained because of similar biases.
9. Definitions of construction times vary, and comparisons between times claimed in different organisations in different periods should be approached sceptically. The project group performance looks better on the now generally accepted technical definition of construction time as lasting from the placing of the main contracts to the synchronising of the set to the Grid frequency. Figures in the previous paragraph and this one up to this note rather refer to the time elapsed between the start of work on site and the synchronising of the first unit: a concept also used at the time for targets and comparisons.
10. *Report of the* [Wilson] *Committee of Enquiry into Delays in the Commissioning of CEGB Power Stations*, Cmd. 3960, 1969, p. 12.
11. See the references in ch. 8, n. 5, p. 307 above.
12. *H L Deb.*, vol. 251, cols 1380–1457, 10 July 1963.
13. This was not true throughout Whitehall. For example, the Ministry of Defence (which had a closer and more consistent interest in the prosperity of the defence industries) had taken more appropriate restructuring initiatives in the aircraft industry.
14. See e.g. Gowing, *Independence and Deterrence*, vol. 2, pp. 355–7.
15. A somewhat happier experience than some private enterprise research laboratories, cf. D. C. Coleman, *Courtaulds: An Economic and Social History* (Oxford, 1980) vol. 3, pp. 295, 316.
16. N. A. H. Stacey with R. D. Haynes and A. W. P. Stephens, 'Domestic Electrical Appliances – A Look into the Future: Research, Styling and Design', *Proceedings of the British Electrical Power Convention 1963*; cf. H. M. Matthew, 'Research and Design in British Electrical Manufacturing' in ibid.

17. Christopher Hinton, 'Memoirs', typescript, Churchill College Archive Collection, Cambridge, class 143. (These memoirs are closed until the end of 1990. I am indebted to Lord Hinton for permitting me to see them in advance of this date, and to draw on them here.)

CHAPTER 21   A SCOTTISH ALTERNATIVE? (1955–64)

1. E.g. D. L. Munby, 'Electricity in the North of Scotland', *Scottish Journal of Political Economy*, vol. 3, 1956; *H C Deb.*, vol. 581, cols 103–6, 27 January 1958.
2. Scottish Home Department, *North of Scotland Hydro-Electric Board Constructional Scheme no. 28, Awe Project, Exploratory Memorandum*, Cmd. 681, 1958.
3. It was published in November, see Scottish Development Department, *Electricity in Scotland: Report of the* [Mackenzie] *Committee on the generation and distribution of Electricity in Scotland*, Cmd. 1859, 1962.
4. The same argument was advanced by the Atomic Energy Authority in spurious justification of their own capital-intensive technology, cf. ch. 19, n. 20, p. 317 above. Both might more reasonably have argued that the real rates of return being demanded were unreasonably high.
5. *H C Deb.*, vol. 680, cols 1243–5, 10 July 1963.
6. Scottish Development Department, *Report on Hydro-Electric Schemes* (1964); see also *H C Deb.*, vol. 721, cols 1002–3, 1004–7, 29 November 1965.
7. 8 per cent *real* return is a very high level, even by private enterprise standards, though in view of the tendency of capital projects to escalate in cost during the 1960s, it may have been a realistic *ex ante* if not *ex post* test. Subsequently, hydro-electric proposals in Scotland, other than pumped-storage schemes, have failed to pass a more modest 5 per cent real return test. Cf. R. Turvey, 'On Investment Choices in Electricity Generation', *Oxford Economic Papers* new series, vol. 15, 1963.
8. A. Robens, *Ten Year Stint* (1972) pp. 144–5.
9. F. L. Tombs, 'Longannet Power Station', *Coal and Energy Quarterly*, no. 8, Spring 1976.

EPILOGUE: THE SECOND FIFTEEN YEARS OF NATIONALISATION (1963–79)

1. This is not in any sense a history of these fifteen years, but rather an attempt to show how some major issues covered in earlier pages evolved in this period. In an industry in which investment decisions have an unusually long lead-time, and operating lives of plant are also unusually long, this seemed essential to provide a perspective on the longer run results of the events described. For the most part, however, this chapter

is based on published materials only.

2. *Report from the Select Committee on Nationalised Industries. The Electricity Supply Industry*, vols 2 and 3, *Minutes of Evidence, Appendices and Index*, HC paper 236, 1963.

3. *Report from the Select Committee on Nationalised Industries. The Electricity Supply Industry*. vol. 1, *Report and Proceedings*, HC paper 236, 1963.

4. The same could not be said for some civil service evidence, which was on several points a masterpiece of misleading diplomacy.

5. *Report from the Select Committee on Nationalised Industries. The Electricity Supply Industry*, vol. 2, p. 492.

6. National Board for Prices and Incomes, *Pay of Electricity Supply Workers: Report no 42*, Cmd. 3405, 1967.

7. For a general account, see R. S. Edwards and R. D. V. Roberts, *Status, Productivity and Pay: A Major Experiment: A Study of the Electricity Supply Industry's Agreements and their Outcome 1961–1971, 1971*.

8. These are adjusted load factors for the National Grid Control Area (with an allowance for weather conditions and potential load not supplied). They differ from the unadjusted, Britain-wide figures in Table A.1. Cf. ch. 7, n. 17.

9. *Financial and Economic Obligations of Nationalised Industries*, Cmd. 3437, 1967. In particular the industry adopted test discount rates in discounted cash flow analyses for new investment projects, and the (somewhat confusingly named) long-run marginal cost pricing rule. The confusion in nomenclature in the latter was dropped in a later White Paper (*The Nationalised Industries*, Cmd. 7131, 1978); but the whole formulation of pricing and investment policy then became fuzzier, in recognition of the many ambiguities in the nationalised industries' position.

10. Among the items for which they were compensated were price restraint, holding excessive coal stocks, burning coal (rather than cheaper oil), and accelerating plant orders to help the plant manufacturing industry.

11. D. Targett, 'Testing whether the annual capital investment of nationalised industries can be explained by private sector investment models: a working paper', *Applied Economics*, vol. 10, 1978.

12. R. Pryke, *Public Enterprise in Practice* (1971) pp. 194–6, 197–9. It is, of course, arguable that the rate of return in the US was too high.

13. *First Report from the Select Committee on Science and Technology: Generating Plant Breakdowns: Winter 1969–70*, HC paper 223, 1970.

14. E.g. *Revue de L'Energie*, Avril 1978, no. 703, p. 185.

15. Notably, if overall investment (including complementary transmission capacity), rather than only the cost of power stations themselves, is taken into account.

16. R. Jones and O. Marriott, *Anatomy of a Merger: A History of GEC, AEI and English Electric* (1970).

17. See e.g. Central Policy Review Staff, *The Future of the United Kingdom Power Plant Manufacturing Industry*, 1976; 'Generating a Turbine Nightmare', *The Economist*, 9 December 1978, p. 82.

18. K. P. Gibbs and D. R. R. Fair, 'The Magnox Stations: A Success Story', *Nucleonics*, September 1966.

19. In the period to March 1980, the expenditure (at current prices) on the CEGB's eight Magnox stations aggregated £1930 millions (including all capital and operating costs, interest during construction and decommissioning provisions, but excluding Atomic Energy Authority costs not recovered and the plutonium credits). The building and operating of equivalent coal-fired stations (assuming they would have cost the same as those actually built) would have cost £2040 millions over the same period. The comparison is misleading in that a higher proportion of the Magnox expenditure was incurred in (high-valued) 1950s and 1960s pounds, while the bulk of the coal costs were in (low-valued) 1970s pounds. In inflation-adjusted resource cost terms, Magnox would still appear to be uneconomic, as the CEGB had expected, though after a further decade or so of (relatively cheap) Magnox operation, *some* of the stations may turn out to have been economic, even in resource cost terms.

20. P. D. Henderson, 'Two British Errors: Their Probable Size and Some Possible Lessons', *Oxford Economic Papers*, new series, vol. 29, 1977.

21. E.g. W. D. Montgomery and J. P. Quirk, *Cost Escalation in Nuclear Power*, Environmental Quality Laboratory Memorandum no. 21, Pasadena, California, 1978.

22. E.g. *Reorganisation of the Electricity Supply Industry in England and Wales*, Cmd. 7134, 1978. The issues had been thoroughly aired in *The Structure of the Electricity Supply Industry in England and Wales. Report of the* [Plowden] *Committee of Inquiry*, 1975. For the decision not to proceed with reorganisation, see *H C Deb.*, vol. 988, no. 213, col. 446, 14 July 1980.

23. The general phenomenon is known to economists as the 'envelope' theorem. In the early 1960s, this had been expressed concretely as follows: for 900MW of excess capacity, the real capital cost was only £5 per kW rather than the £40 per kW direct cost, the difference being made up in operating savings. For larger quantities of excess capacity, the real capital cost was somewhat higher. However, by the 1970s, internal CEGB studies suggest, the capital cost in historic cost accounting terms may have been negative, i.e. the operating savings probably exceeded the capital charges. This was not only because of the 'envelope effect' but also because of fuel price increases in excess of those expected at the time the capacity decisions were made.

INDEX